The
Home
Extension
Manual

Acknowledgements

SPECIAL THANKS TO
Basil Parylo, G. D. Rawlings, Bill Carless

PHOTOGRAPHY
The Author, Basil Parylo, David Davies, Richard Woodroofe MRICS

Thanks also to
Alan West (Trombé Ltd), Kristian Kolby Hansen (Clear Living Ltd), James Fraser-Harris (Oak Apple Frames Ltd), Aylesbury Vale District Council, David Snell, UK Timber Frame Association, Mark Harding @ Birmingham City Council, Duncan & family builders, Ian MacMillan FRICS, Buildstore.co.uk, Jeremy March MRICS and Mrs Linton.

And
HeritageBathrooms.com, InStyle Products Ltd, Solalighting.com, Capitalfireplaces.co.uk, Caple Kitchens, Roycebathrooms.co.uk, Celcon, Milbank Floors Ltd, PolarLight UK, Capel, Bristan.com, Potton Ltd, Raindance, Hepstore.com, Designer-radiators.com, Shower-guide.com, Acantha Lifestyle Ltd, DCLG & HMSO, Savrow Stilts, Visionhouse-software, GA fixings, Sadolin.

Published in March 2007
Reprinted 2007, 2008 and 2010
Second edition published July 2011
Reprinted in 2012, 2013, 2014 (twice), 2015 and 2016
Third edition published May 2018

British Library Cataloguing in Publication Data: A catalogue record for this book is available from the British Library

ISBN 978 1 78521 170 6

Published by Haynes Publishing,
Sparkford, Yeovil, Somerset BA22 7JJ, UK
Tel: 01963 440635
Int. tel: +44 1963 440635
Website: www.haynes.com

Haynes North America Inc.
859 Lawrence Drive, Newbury Park, California 91320, USA

Printed in Malaysia.

LABC
Local Authority Building Control
www.labc.uk.com

By the same author

The
Home
Extension
Manual

Third Edition

Ian Rock MRICS

Technical consultants
Colin K. Dale FRICS, **Michael Haslam** MSc FRICS

CONTENTS

Home Extension Manual
INTRODUCTION

Sooner or later, most homes can start to feel a little crowded. So if you find yourself hemmed in and running out of space, there will be two possible alternatives to consider: moving, or improving.

The problem with moving house is that it's officially one of life's all-time most stressful events, ranking somewhere alongside the joys of personal bankruptcy, death, divorce, and redundancy.

So if you're happy with the location of your present home, and your neighbours are simply the best, the ideal solution may be to make it bigger and build on. By making the most of your existing house you can avoid all the dreaded pitfalls of moving – broken chains, inexplicable delays, damning surveys and gazumping, not to mention the pleasures of dealing with estate agents and solicitors – all of which can conspire to send your blood pressure rocketing. Extending your home makes even better sense when you consider the small fortune you will save by not having to pay sales fees and stamp duty.

On the other hand, there are plenty of folk who can reel off spine-chilling stories of cowboy builders and breathtakingly incompetent DIY disasters. So 'getting the builders in' is unlikely to prove much of a rest-cure. There are many good reasons to extend, but the desire for a peaceful life probably isn't one of them.

It's important to be realistic about what can be achieved. TV property programmes make compulsive viewing, but

they can also be highly misleading. Going from zero to 'property hero' in the space of a 45-minute programme doesn't really tell the full story. TV cameras make saints of us all. The reality is that construction projects can go horribly wrong. Even the smartest people can come unstuck, marooned in half-finished buildings nursing ruinous bills.

But do the job right and you will find the experience of getting your new home extension designed and built highly rewarding. Apart from significantly upping the value of your main asset and saving shed-loads of money, you should emerge from the project with many useful new skills (and a few good stories), well equipped to carry out future grand designs.

So whether you intend to take the conventional route by employing an architect and main contractor, or to save money by directly employing your own sub-contractors and doing some of the work yourself, this comprehensive *Home Extension Manual* explains all the tips and traps at every stage, from design through to successful completion.

WEBSITE
Further detailed information, plus free downloads of sample plans, letters and documents can be found at our website **www.home-extension.co.uk**.

Photo: H+H Celcon Ltd

EXTENSION TIMELINE

This is a rough checklist of what needs to be done, and when to do it, in a typical home extension project. Where you appoint an architect and a main contractor they will be responsible for most items.

Before work starts
- Agree design and produce planning drawings
- Get planning permission (if required)
- Check locations of underground drainage and services
- Produce detailed drawings for Building Regs including engineer's calculations
- Submit application to Building Control
- Find builders and/ or trades
- Specify required works and get quotes
- Plan your finances & draft budget
- Confirm builder's appointment and agree works, price, timescales, retention, payment stages etc
- Confirm with written contract or detailed letters; advise of any DIY input
- Check lead-in times for materials and place orders to avoid delays (eg windows, blocks etc)
- Check contractor's insurance and notify your home insurers / or take out new policy
- Inform neighbours
- Plan for site safety

WEEK 1

Preparation
- Advise Building Control of start date
- Ensure clear access to site and consider where to place skips and deliveries
- Arrange water and electric supplies on site
- Hire site portaloo toilet for trades
- Set up trade accounts with suppliers / builders merchants etc
- Set up detailed rolling weekly programme and co-ordinate deliveries of materials
- Have bricks and blocks etc delivered and stacked
- Hire any necessary plant, eg cement mixer and digger

WEEK 2

Groundworks
- Builders arrive
- Set out and dig foundations
- Building Control visit to approve foundations
- Pipework, drainage etc laid
- Foundation concrete poured and levelled
- Building Control visit to approve concreting

WEEK 3 – 4

Superstructure
- Bricklayers build up to DPC
- Trenches dug for rainwater and foul drains.
- Construct ground floor, eg beam & block or solid concrete slab
- Building Control inspection for DPC and ground floor
- Book scaffolders in advance

WEEK 5 - 6

Main walls built
- Main wall construction / joined to existing house
- Wall ties built-in and cavity insulation fitted as walls built up
- Lintels fitted to openings
- Fit any steels / beams to walls on padstones
- Window and door frames (or templates) fitted as walls go up
- Scaffolding erected for upper walls - first lift
- Construct upper walls

WEEK 7

Internal walls

- Internal masonry walls constructed
- Upstairs floor structure built
- Building Control visit to approve structural works
- Order roofing materials

WEEK 8

Roof structure

- Scaffolding erected for roof - second/third lift
- Carpenter starts building roof structure
- Any roof windows fitted and/or dormers constructed
- Building Control visit to approve

WEEK 9 -10

Roof coverings

- Breather membrane laid over rafters
- Battens cut and fitted over membrane
- Soakers fitted and valleys lined or tiled
- Tiles or slates laid
- Ridge and any hip tiles laid and bedded
- Flashings fitted
- Facias, soffits and any gable bargeboards fitted and verges finished

WEEK 11

Building now weathertight

- Windows and exterior doors fitted
- External rendering or claddings fitted (where required)
- Guttering and downpipes fitted
- Paint upper walls (rendered) and external joinery while scaffolding is still in place
- Strike down scaffolding

WEEK 12

Breaking though

- Protect existing house from dust with temporary sheeting / sealing off
- Form opening from house into extension with steel or lintel over new opening
- Draw plans showing locations of electric sockets, switches, rads etc

WEEK 13 -14

First fix

- Advise trades of any DIY input so as not to clash
- 1st fix plumbing & electrics
- 1st fix CH and/or UFH
- 1st fix carpentry: stud walls, upper floorboards & skirting, door linings and pipes boxed in
- Rafters lined with insulation (where upstairs ceilings sloped with roof)

WEEK 15 -16

Plastering

- Main walls dry-lined with plasterboard, interior walls tacked and lined
- Ceilings plasterboarded & taped
- Skim plaster to plasterboarded walls and ceilings
- Ground floor DPM and insulation laid
- Ground floor screeded

WEEK 17 -18

Second fix

- Fit kitchen
- Insulate loft
- 2nd fix electrics: sockets, switches, light fittings, smoke alarms, extractors etc
- 2nd fix joinery: hang interior doors, fit architraves etc
- 2nd fix plumbing, CH /rads, bathroom fittings, showers, taps etc
- Test and commission electrics, heating and plumbing and obtain certificates
- Building Control final inspection

WEEK 19

Decoration

- Paint exterior walls (where rendered) and external joinery
- Paint interior walls, ceilings once plaster dry
- Interior wall tiling
- Paint interior joinery
- Lay flooring to ground floor when screed fully dried (sometimes before kitchen)
- Fit skirting to ground floor

WEEK 20

Snagging and landscaping

- Fix any leaks, heating issues, sticking windows etc and report to relevant trades/contractor
- Exterior paving and landscaping
- Obtain completion certificate from Building Control
- Make final payment to contractor, including half of (eg 5% total) retention sum
- Keep remaining half (eg 2.5%) of retention as agreed for 'Defects Liability Period' (usually 6 months)

1 BEFORE YOU START

There's no point going to all the expense and trouble of extending your house if it's not ultimately going to make your home-life considerably more enjoyable. By improving the practicality for everyone living there and adding to your property's value, it should be a win/win situation. But a successful outcome will only happen by thinking ahead very carefully and planning for all eventualities. So before getting up from the sofa to set off on this costly expedition into the unknown, it is well worth taking a few moments to mull over the following issues.

What's the point?

Let's face it, building work can very easily end up being a massive intrusion.

No matter how well things are planned and managed, you won't get thanked for the inevitable dust, mud, noise and disruption. And if the builders manage to cut through your mains services (which happens surprisingly often) you will instantly be promoted to the status of household Public Enemy Number One. So it's well worth making sure at the outset that your partner and the rest of the family are as keen on the idea of extending as you are.

A quick internet search for books about 'how to build a home extension' comes up with this helpful piece of advice: 'Customers who bought this also bought: "How To Get Divorced In Ireland".' You have been warned.

Is it practical?

Before involving anyone else, it's important to first consider what you really want from the project. Reasons for wanting to extend typically revolve around the need for:

- **More space** – At the end of each year, as the 'Battle of Cooking Christmas Dinner' draws to its weary close, there is an inevitable realisation in many households that 'the kitchen is just too small'. The resulting New Year's resolution may be to build a dream kitchen in a new extension. But of course, the need for more space can occur at any time as our lifestyles continuously change – babies arriving, oldies needing a 'granny' annexe, or somewhere to farm out teenagers.
- **Greater comfort** – There was a time when clashing interests meant that the male of the species would spend half his life exiled to a cold, dank garden shed. But with the addition of a warm, well insulated, extension your home will be transformed into a haven of sexual equality.
- **Improved saleability** – This is perhaps the hardest reason to justify extending, because it's not that easy to stand back and look at your home through the impartial eyes of a property developer.

The most common reasons for extending are to create larger kitchens or add bathrooms. But before embarking on a major project, check that you've made the most of the space you've already got. That means utilising all available storage space and underused rooms. For example, it may be possible to add a small en suite bathroom without extending, just by partitioning off a corner of a bedroom. A space measuring only 1 x 2.6m is the minimum required.

If you do decide to extend, it pays to be critical about your ideas at the outset. Be harsh with yourself now, rather than discovering after all the hard work and expense that everyone in the house detests the new layout. Ask yourself if your Grand Design will significantly improve the desirability of the property for all who live there? Or will it take up too much of the garden, drastically reducing the amount of useful 'amenity space'?

Physically your options may be quite limited, if, for example, the house already occupies most of its plot, or has already been extended. If you live in a terraced house with a small garden there may be very limited scope for expansion. Converting the loft space is often the cheapest option, but is not always possible, especially on some more modern properties with shallow roofs. In terms of cost, two-storey extensions are about 20% cheaper to build per sq m than single stories, because

Loft conversions are often the most economical way to add space.

the cost of the foundations and roof is effectively halved, being spread between two floors.

Later we'll consider the minefield of technical issues arising from the site itself. The presence of nearby drain runs, tree roots and buried pipes and cables all need to be checked. Also there may be legal nasties waiting to jump out and bite you, in the form of party walls, old rights of way, and vaguely defined boundaries.

Your freedom to design will also be restricted by things like the location of existing services, which can dictate the position of new kitchen and bathroom fittings. Of course, anything's possible if you throw enough money at it, but to keep within any realistic budget sensible planning at the outset is crucial.

Will you get your money back?

Don't automatically assume that you will make loads of money by building on to your house. Having a poorly designed and badly built monstrosity stuck on the side of your home could seriously damage its resale value.

For the majority of home-extenders the motivation behind extending is to improve lifestyle rather than to reap any immediate profit. Nonetheless, making such a massive financial investment means that it's essential to be aware of all the monetary implications before reaching for your debit card.

It's always possible that your initial assumptions could

be way out. For example, the proud owner of a small ex-Council semi who enthusiastically transforms his back garden into a giant swimming pool complex may be convinced that the value of his house has sky-rocketed. But the sad truth is that for most buyers this kind of 'improvement' is a real disincentive. On the other hand, the same sort of improvement could be perfectly appropriate for a more expensive house with larger grounds.

Of course, for each type of house there are limits as to how much value can realistically be added. There will be a maximum price anyone will be prepared to pay for a property in a particular location regardless of how superb it looks and how many aircraft carriers you can fit in the living room. To get an idea of what your house is likely to be worth once extended, seek the opinion of an experienced local estate agent.

So what adds the most value? Basically, if your plans help overcome a seriously negative aspect of the original house then you should be onto a winner, for example enlarging a tiny original kitchen. As a rule of thumb, things like well-planned extra bedrooms and en suite bathrooms normally add at least as much value as they cost to build. But be careful not to let your enthusiasm for gaining extra space actually detract from the layout of your existing house. It is not unusual for new rear extensions to blot out light to the old dining room, which then becomes a sort of murky no-man's-land that nobody uses; or for a loft conversion to require a new staircase that results in the loss of one of the original bedrooms – ie gaining one room, but in the process losing another.

Link detached house (right) would become an end terrace, if extended above garage, potentially detracting from value.

Kitchens are best located so that you don't have to traipse through them to get somewhere else, so adding a new bathroom that's accessed via your kitchen could detract from the existing layout. And increasing the size of an already large room by a metre or two won't normally pay back the cost of the work.

As a nation, it seems we are becoming ever more hygienic. Current tastes demand one 'family bathroom' for every three bedrooms, plus en suites for the master bedroom and guest rooms.

But of course house prices are influenced by more than just the extent of the accommodation. 'Kerb appeal' can determine whether prospective buyers fall in love with a property or run off screaming. Considering the way a property looks, and how the new extension will affect first impressions, is particularly important with older 'classic' houses – Georgian, Victorian, Edwardian, and even inter-war properties. Happily, the planners will generally welcome designs that enhance the original architecture. For listed buildings or those in conservation areas, architects may have no choice but to come up with something 'sensible', rather than being tempted to spin off into orbit with anything too outrageous.

Is it neighbourly?

It's a strange fact, but neighbours can live together in perfect harmony for decades – until relations suddenly turn sour as soon as the builders arrive. Fortunately, nine times out of ten the solution is down to simple communication. Just taking time out to talk, well in advance of the work starting, should help ease any potential conflict. A few soothing words now will be far cheaper than conducting warfare via solicitors at a later date.

So at this stage it pays to consider what effect your proposed building work is likely to have on your neighbours. Even if the extension itself is not a problem for them, the inevitable noise, mess and large trucks delivering building materials at all hours of the day, surely will be. Builders have an endearing tendency to commence work on site at the crack of dawn accompanied by much

whistling, singing, swearing, thudding and crashing. This can strain even the best of relationships.

Involving the neighbours in your plans at this early stage not only helps prepare them for inconveniences to come, but may also help sweeten things a little before the Council planners thoughtfully invite them to submit objections to your scheme.

So it's a good idea to refine your plans before they get cut to ribbons by the planners, by considering how you would feel if your neighbours were proposing to build a similar design.

How much should you do yourself?

Building work
Don't bite off more than you can chew. Speaking from bitter experience, it is sometimes easy to underestimate the amount of work involved whilst overestimating one's own abilities. Unless you have good experience at plumbing, bricklaying, joinery etc and there's no great urgency getting it built, it's probably a good idea to make it easy on yourself and get the professionals in.

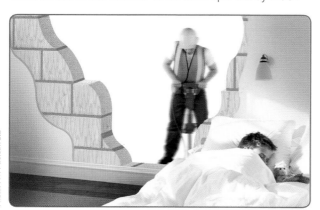

If you're determined to tackle some of the work personally, one golden rule is to never be in a position where you're under pressure to rush a job. Give yourself a break by doubling the amount of time that you first estimated that particular task would take. It's always a good idea to select jobs that aren't too time-critical. Getting to the stage where the roof is on and the building is weathertight can often be a race against time. After that you may find there is less urgency. But bear in mind that different trades need space to work without tripping over each other or you. To save money, you may find it easier to have a bash at doing some of the decoration and finishing works, such as landscaping, at the end of the project, once the contractors have completed the main works.

Design

You may find it easier to make a serious contribution by doing some of the design and planning work rather than attempting hod-carrying. This could make a significant saving on costs without crippling your back.

However, whilst there is no legal requirement to use an architect or surveyor, it usually pays to tackle things yourself that you're good at and employ others with special skills to do the rest. So it's normally a good idea to discuss your plans with an experienced professional designer at the outset – which may even avoid the need to extend at all – perhaps they'll know some ingenious way to make space-saving improvements at a fraction of the cost (e.g. by converting your garage or outbuildings).

Project management

Part of the fun of TV property programmes is watching in horrified disbelief as people who haven't got the first clue about construction suddenly decide they are perfectly qualified to take on the role of 'Project Manager'. In fact, the Project Management role is a highly skilled one, the objective being to successfully steer your project to achieve a quality product, completed on time and within budget. This is not at all an easy task, as national newspaper headlines routinely remind us – massive delays, unfinished works and staggeringly huge cost overruns are only too familiar, even on projects managed by major award-winning firms of architects. Think of Wembley Stadium, the Channel Tunnel, and the British Library, to name but a few.

The good news is that yours is not a complex mega-build, and that any decent firm of contractors will be aiming to achieve a successful completion within the agreed timescale, with or without someone standing over them. In which case you may think 'If they're so good at managing themselves, why not just let them get on with it?' One reason is that, with the best will in the world, the builder's objectives will be different from yours, and handing over total control of your home and your wallet to them is a somewhat risky strategy – see Chapter 5.

But to be a successful Project Manager you don't need to be a genius. Clear planning ahead, and applying common sense to problems as they arise, will do much to ensure a successful outcome.

Will it blend in?

To get some idea of what kind of extension is likely to be permitted, take a wander round the local area and make a note of the size and style of extensions that other people have built. In most cases you are restricted to four basic variations: a single-storey or two-storey building which can have either a pitched roof or a flat roof. Having decided which combination works best for you, the design details can then be considered.

Your proposals will need to broadly comply with the Local Development Plan, which can be viewed at the planning department of your local Council, or online.

Taking a look around could also provide you with useful ammunition if the planners decide to resist your proposals. Identifying similar recently completed developments in the neighbourhood to the one you want to build can present a very powerful argument in your favour (assuming they weren't built illegally). Or you may be lucky and find that the size

Photo: trombe.co.uk

and style of extension you want falls within 'permitted development' rules, so you don't need to worry about getting planning consent at all. See Chapter 3.

Can you afford it?

There seems to be an unwritten rule that building projects must inevitably overshoot their budgets, usually by a substantial margin. Fortunately, newbuild projects such as constructing a typical home extension are considerably easier to cost than the equivalent refurbishment of an old building.

With a little careful planning at this stage, the total payments you'll have to make should be fairly predictable. If you want to get a rough idea of the likely costs now, run your plans past a friendly architect or surveyor, or check construction prices per square metre (m^2) published in self-build magazines. In reality, builders' prices sometimes bear little relationship to the actual cost of materials and labour. Like other businesses they'll be riding the waves of supply and demand, perhaps with a bit added to reflect the builder's view of 'what your area will take'. Some boast shamelessly about adding an extra 25 per cent as soon as they enter a 'posh postcode area'! On the other hand, smaller jobs can often turn out to be more difficult than large projects, generating relatively small sums in profit. So a significant mark-up is needed to make it worthwhile. Fees for a designer, not including managing the project, will probably add another five to ten per cent (typically costing £3,000 to £5,000 for the design work and all the drawings plus another £1,000 for structural engineer's calculations and site visit). Not forgetting Local Authority charges for Planning and Building Regulations which can add upwards of £1,000.

That just leaves the small matter of coming up with the ready cash. It is essential to arrange funding early on, as nothing sours relationships with builders more than delayed payment.

A few money matters worth pondering at this stage are:

■ Don't finance building work on your credit card – the interest rates can be ruinous. Mortgage funding is normally the cheapest option, and because banks know that building an extension means the value of your property should increase proportionately it shouldn't be too difficult to arrange. Unsecured loans are dearer, but still better than credit cards.
■ Keep a contingency sum in reserve as there will

Over-large rear extensions can give rise to an oppressive environment.

Drawing: Aylesbury Vale District Council

inevitably be some unforeseen extra expenses. The biggest budget breaker is not actually overspending, but producing an unrealistic budget in the first place. Probably the biggest source of unexpected expense is the need for unforeseen drainage or foundation work.
■ Grants for disabled facilities are available for registered disabled owner/occupiers, such as funding towards the cost of an extension for a suitably equipped shower room. The Local Authority may even assist with the design.

VAT

Whilst on the subject of finance, one of the great iniquities of life in this country is the way VAT is charged on building works. Essential maintenance, improvements and extensions to existing homes are charged at the full rate, whilst property developers building new houses pay nothing. The cost of paying VAT will add a significant amount to the price of your extension. Builders' quotes are often rather vague on this subject, so make sure it is clarified early on. There are, however, some possible small consolations. Your contractors may agree to you deferring payment of VAT to them until completion.

Renovations including necessary extension work to dwellings empty for two years or more can be eligible for the reduced rate of VAT of 5% via a VAT-registered contractor. Extending a bathroom for disabled use should be zero rated.

Of course, it is always possible to save on VAT by directly employing individual tradespeople who aren't VAT registered because their annual earnings are less than the annual threshold (currently around £85,000). But main contractors are highly unlikely to have a low enough turnover to fall into this category. See Chapter 5 and www.hmrc.gov.uk.

Is your health up to it?

Those of a nervous disposition would be well advised to consider spending their money on a relaxing holiday rather than getting the builders in. Alternatively, it would be prudent to arrange for the whole project to be professionally managed at arm's length by an experienced firm of architects or chartered surveyors. Watching your home become transformed into a building site for months on end can be somewhat disheartening, even for the hardiest of souls.

Is it legal?

As a general rule, the less you have to do with lawyers in life the better, so it's worth considering some basic legal issues on day one. Here are some of the more common 'legalities' to ponder:

■ Houses and bungalows are almost always freehold, but if your property is leasehold (normally flats and maisonettes) you'll not usually be permitted to extend or make structural alterations without the prior written consent of the freeholder.

■ Extending your home may be legally prohibited by a 'restrictive covenant'. These are conditions sometimes written into the deeds of the property by the original developer at the time of construction. Their intention is to prevent residents 'lowering the tone of the area' by such activities as parking a fleet of kebab vans in driveways, running brothels, or erecting inappropriate structures in their gardens. Even if you have planning permission to build, you can still fall foul of the law by breaching such a condition. Fortunately, it is usually possible for solicitors to have them overturned or to arrange an indemnity insurance policy that covers you

in the highly unlikely event that someone should try to enforce it.

■ Mortgage lenders like to know in advance of any proposed significant alterations to their security (*ie* your home).

■ Check that your buildings insurance cover remains fully valid during the works. If not, will the builder's insurance cover the cost of any damage, theft or injury? You may also need to take out insurance for the works themselves.

■ Nothing cheeses neighbours off more than discovering that their boundary walls have been totally redeveloped. So check the Title Deeds and land registry documents in advance to see who owns which boundaries and if there are any rights of way over the land. If you infringe someone else's land, their lawyers will be licking their lips at the thought of embarking on costly litigation, at your expense. It doesn't help that official drawings of plots on the deeds are usually such an incredibly small scale that it may be virtually impossible to pinpoint the exact dividing line on the ground, so you may need to formally agree the precise boundary line on site with the neighbour, with a land surveyor present. This is particularly important if you need to build right up to the boundary line. See party walls in Chapter 5. Bear in mind also that any excavation alongside existing walls, particularly those with shallow foundations, must be done in small stages under professional supervision to avoid the risk of collapse, death and serious injury.

Personal safety

You are about to experience some of the most hazardous weeks of your entire life. Building sites are dangerous places, so it's essential to take all sensible safety precautions. There's no point building yourself a brilliant new home extension but only being able to appreciate it squinting from inside a mobile life-support system.

However, you could be forgiven for assuming that many builders welcome a spot of self-harming, since the sad reality on many sites is that health and safety is routinely ignored. Most safety advice is just common sense, like not mincing around building sites in sandals, or operating power tools with long hair, anorak toggles or jewellery dangling down. You don't have to be Oliver Stone to work out how a cinematically gruesome death can result from a combination of heavy loads, hidden trenches, slippery mud, and working at height.

A guide to body-care on building sites would have to include:

■ **Brain:** A 'Bob the Builder' safety helmet is essential anywhere you might cut your head open or where stuff could drop on you.

■ **Hands:** Gloves must be worn for all work shifting

life – like an ageing heavy metal guitarist, but without the fun. Wear ear protectors.

■ **Lungs:** A dust mask is a cheap and easy way to stop you inhaling dangerous particles and developing irritable lung syndrome.

■ **Back:** Back injuries are surprisingly common – from trying to lift too much or in the wrong way, or from falls. Take special care with bags of cement, plaster, and heavy beams etc. Keeping the site tidy will help avoid tripping hazards.

On large professionally managed housing developments, the signs are unambiguous: '*No hard hat, No safety boots, No job*'. They will also insist on site staff wearing lurid, luminous, lime-coloured safety jackets (on some sites different trades wear different colours). You might need to enforce similar safety standards on your site to comply with the 'CDM' rules.

And finally…

If all the above hasn't completely turned you off the idea of extending your home, now is a good time to take a look in some detail at what lies beneath your feet – the ground that will need to support the new wing of your residence.

materials around – especially bricks, blocks and chemicals. Even cement and concrete can burn your skin.

■ **Toes and feet:** Always wear steel-capped boots.

■ **Eyes:** Wear goggles/eye protectors, especially when operating power tools. It just takes one tiny shard to fly into your face to blind you for life.

■ **Ears:** Operating noisy machinery, especially in a confined space, means risking partial deafness in later

Virgin plot awaits new side extension.
Unknown to the contractors a live electric cable
is buried less than 300mm beneath the grass!

Home Extension Manual

2 INVESTIGATING YOUR SITE

If you thought you knew everything there was to know about your own backyard, prepare to be surprised. Even the most tranquil of suburban gardens can conceal all manner of underground nasties awaiting the unwary builder.

Although there's a fairly good chance that your plot will turn out to be perfectly sound for development, it's just too expensive a risk to simply assume all is fine down below.

The official figures make alarming reading. 440,000 UK homes are on ground that's liable to subsidence, and another 100,000 on sites at risk from landslip. That's not counting the ones potentially at risk from flooding, radon gas, and wind damage.

It may seem obvious to check what you're likely to hit before letting the mini-diggers rip into your lawn, but the reality on many projects is that the first major disaster occurs on day one. It's not unusual for over-enthusiastic excavators to slice through your gas, water or drainage pipes, or sever your neighbour's electricity and phone cables. Not only does this result in massive inconvenience and unnecessary expense but it is also potentially lethal.

Planning condition required excavation of trial pit for archaeologists .

And that's before the unwelcome discovery of hidden treats like unstable subsoil, old plague pits or subsiding mineshafts lying in wait. The good news is that your garden is probably virgin territory, so you shouldn't have to worry about ground contamination from old factories and petrol stations. But some modern town houses are built on old 'brownfield' sites formerly occupied by buildings with basements, which have not always been properly demolished or filled.

Things to check before designing

It's simply not possible to design a successful building without first doing a little detective work to find out what you're building on top of. Some concerns are fairly obvious – things like springy ground (suggestive of a high water table), slopes greater than 1:25 or nearby trees. Site investigations typically begin with some initial desk research and a 'walkabout' around the site, followed by the physical digging of trial pits and taking of soil samples. Before spending a lot of time sketching out your design in any great detail, the following factors must first be considered, since they can all have a crucial impact on the design, and cost, of your extension.

Existing foundations

You may be shocked to discover how shallow the existing foundations of your home are. Start by digging a small trial hole with a spade next to the outside wall, at the point where the new extension will join the existing building. Taking great care to avoid any hidden pipes or cables, dig sufficiently deep to expose the old foundations and reveal their type and depth. This is not wasted effort since the hole can later be incorporated into the new foundation trenches.

What you find will depend to a large extent on the age of your home. As a general rule, the older properties are, the shallower their foundations. Footings on Victorian houses were commonly less than half a metre deep, gradually increasing throughout the next century. Make a note of the depth of your existing

Newly excavated trench exposes shallow Victorian footings.

foundations, as both Building Control and your designer may want to take a look. In the unlikely event that old body-parts start appearing in the excavated soil from under your patio, fill it in quick!

Drainage

There are two very good reasons for taking a close interest in the precise whereabouts of your underground drains. First, so that you don't go smashing into them when the foundations are excavated, and second so that you can design an effective new connection into the existing drain run (assuming your extension includes a new kitchen, bathroom or WC).

But pinpointing the position of underground drain runs isn't always that simple. Traditionally, it was done by consulting old plans from the Council or water authority, but these weren't renowned for their accuracy. Even 'the official map of public sewers' available from your Local Authority won't include private sewers or drains running under your land or underground pipes and soakaways dispersing rainwater. With luck, these may be recorded in your property's deeds, or if it's a more modern building the developers or Building Control may have copies. Although a set of plans is always a good starting point, to trace them accurately, a 'drain survey' may be required.

A useful course of action might be:

- Start by lifting up covers of inspection chambers (manholes), beginning with the ones nearest the house. Ideally there should be an inspection chamber at each bend in the pipe run, but in reality this is rarely the case.
- Make a note at each chamber of the depth from the cover to the bottom of the channel (known as the 'invert depth'). Measure the precise positions of the chambers in relation to the house, noting any branch pipes, and mark these on a scale site plan.
- To check the route that waste water takes from bathrooms and kitchens, you can mix coloured dyes in each WC, bath, sink and shower and see where it appears in the chambers.
- Metal detectors may be useful in helping pinpoint any Victorian cast iron drainage pipes, although most old pipes were made of salt-glazed clay.

It isn't unusual to discover that there is a drain run just where you want to build, and once again, the age of your house should provide some useful clues as to what to look for. For example, in Victorian houses a shared sewer often runs across the back gardens. The foul drains may run straight back from the house, connecting to this sewer at a 'T' junction.

Typical 1930s semis, on the other hand, were built with upstairs loos discharging via a soil and vent pipe on the side or rear wall, which connects underground to a

Existing surface water pipe runs exposed.

drain run parallel to the side wall, leading out to the street. By the 1960s and 70s houses were increasingly being designed with the kitchens and bathrooms to the front, so the drains could run straight out to the sewer in the road.

The most popular reason for extending is to enlarge the kitchen. For many of us this means building a simple addition onto the back wall of the old kitchen. Unfortunately, this also happens to be the most common spot for kitchen waste drainage to discharge underground, often via a gulley. And rather inconveniently, the rainwater downpipes may also have chosen this location to disappear into the ground.

If this is the case, you can't just cover up old gullies and carry on regardless, pretending they don't exist. The waste water system in this area will need to be extended or diverted with new connections made to the existing underground drains. See Chapter 8.

Even if there are no downpipes directly where you plan to build, underground rainwater pipes may be crossing the proposed site, en route to soakaways further out in the garden (soakaways are underground rubble-filled chambers used to disperse rainwater).

The most popular reason for extending is to enlarge kitchens.

Sewers and pipes – who's responsible?

When it comes to the subject of foul drainage, ignorance may be bliss – until you need to build an extension. 'Foul waste' is the name for waste water from kitchen sinks, bathrooms and toilets etc, and there are three main parts of the underground drainage system that carry foul waste away from your home.

Private drains

A drain is the name for a pipe that carries waste water from just one property. This is your responsibility as the householder until it goes beyond your boundary, or until it connects with a waste pipe from another property, becoming shared.

Lateral drains

Where a drain serving just one property runs through another person's land, it's known as a lateral drain – for example where your pipework runs under next door's garden (or in some cases under the pavement before it joins the main sewer). Any such pipework that's situated outside the boundaries of the house it serves becomes the responsibility of the water company.

Public sewers

Public sewers carry foul waste away to be treated. Public ownership commences at the point where a drain serves more than one property (ie becomes a sewer) or where it passes across the boundary from private land and under the public highway. These 'branch pipes' then connect to main sewers that normally run below the road. The word 'public' means the sewer system (including associated manholes etc) has been 'adopted' and is the responsibility of the water company who should pay for repairs. Water companies are similarly responsible for repairs to any surface water systems (for discharging rainwater) connected to the public network.

 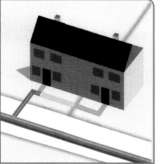

— Public sewer/drain - responsibility of the water and sewerage company
— Privately owned - responsibility of property owner
— Property boundary
— Lateral drain

Implications

Since 2011, homeowners have only been responsible for foul waste pipes located within their boundaries serving their own home - plus of course any surface water drains leading to soakaways etc. Obviously if your house isn't connected to mains drainage and you instead have a private system such as a septic tank, then the whole caboodle remains your responsibility.

Whilst it's good news that water companies are responsible for looking after sewers and lateral drains, there are some important implications when it comes to building on or near sewers. In some cases building work could be restricted or even prevented. If allowed, it will require a formal 'building over agreement', a survey and maybe a legal agreement for access. Water companies have a right of access to any sewers or lateral drains located on private property, so their consent will be required to build an extension on top of them. There is also the possibility that the water authority could have put in place a condition on the planning consent for your house restricting future development - see page 42.

Services

Make a note of the position of your gas, electricity, and water meters. Then try to calculate the route of the incoming supplies to those meters, normally from the street. Water main supply pipes commonly make their first above-ground appearance below the kitchen sink or in the cloakroom, and may have to be diverted if the kitchen is being extended or relocated.

However, it is not unknown, especially on pre-war houses, for water or electricity supplies to enter not from the street at the front but underground from the side or rear. Some electricity supply cables will enter at roof level.

Your energy, water, and phone suppliers should be able to provide plans showing the locations of their pipes and ducts, or offer a free site survey using special detection equipment. But location plans used alone without a site survey can often be inaccurate; for one thing the depths of pipes and cables are often shallower than officially indicated, so take extra care when digging.

Below: High level power supply

Wells, cesspits and soakaways

Old wells, soakaways and cesspits are a surprisingly common feature of the hidden underground landscape. Build over one of these without taking suitable precautions and you risk witnessing your freshly completed extension subside into oblivion.

If you do happen to come across one, the first thing to check is that it isn't still being actively used. Septic tanks and cesspits are private drainage systems that treat foul waste where no mains sewers are connected and require periodic emptying. There are various ways of spotting a 'live' tank. One big clue is if your water bills exclude sewerage charges; in which case the existence of any private drainage should have been made clear by your solicitor and surveyor when you bought the house. Alternatively, if the mother of all foul stenches overcomes you when the cover is lifted (often a concrete slab) it would suggest that it's 'live'.

Matters become immensely more complicated when the tank is shared, with someone else's loos discharging into it. So check with the neighbours, since relocating the tank away from your building plot will not be cheap, although you may be able to share some of the cost.

If septic tanks or cesspits need to be relocated they'll need to be replaced with a modern system set at a suitable distance from buildings. Because potentially explosive methane ('sewer gas') may still be lingering, they need to be decommissioned by being emptied, doused with lime, then filled with hardcore and capped under reinforced concrete.

At least such private drainage systems should be fairly easily located (since there will be some kind of cover for emptying access, probably overgrown). By contrast, the precise location of soakaways serving your rainwater system may be a complete mystery. The first you may know of them will be the distinct 'crunch' when you dig into one, since soakaways are basically holes filled with a load of old stones, bricks and gravel.

To prepare the ground for construction, any deep holes should first be filled with hardcore. However, because this will settle over time the concrete for your foundations must be reinforced with steel mesh so that it can bridge over the hole and reach good load-bearing ground on either side. If the old hole is dry and shallow it can simply be filled with concrete before being bridged over. Unfortunately, the soil surrounding old pits may have become damp and soggy where foul water has seeped out over many years. Great care must therefore be taken locating adjacent firm ground. In all such cases, the foundation design must be checked by a structural engineer. Even if old pits and wells are not within the immediate footprint of the extension, they may still need to be filled, so as not to destabilise nearby foundation trenches or pose a danger to occupants. Aim for a safety zone of firm ground extending about 8 metres beyond the building.

Ancient history

Do you know who or what once occupied the site of your house? A good way of researching your plot is by perusing old Ordnance Survey maps, which are widely available from Victorian times onwards (1:2500 and 1:1250 scale).

These can reveal the existence of previously unknown buildings on the site. It's possible that remnants of foundations of long-demolished buildings may still exist underground. Who knows, right now you and your sofa may be perched directly over an ancient archaeological gem.

OS maps may also reveal the position of old ponds and pits, long since filled in but still a concern for the construction of sound foundations. Aerial photos of your area can also help locate any obscure ancient burial mounds or prehistoric settlements. As part of the planning application process local archaeologists may be consulted and it is not unknown for them to require shallow trial pits to be excavated (at your expense) prior to construction work starting. On the plus side, unearthing a Jacobean treasure trove might go some way towards financing the project…

Where your house was built as part of a development on former 'brownfield' land, the site history can be more of a worry. The danger tends to be where heavy industries once existed, so this is more of an issue on modern housing estates where old factory sites were redeveloped. Previous uses such as gasworks, refineries, heavy manufacturing and blast furnaces mean there's a risk that toxic heavy metals, slag waste, or unstable backfill could be present in the ground. In such cases serious detective work will need to be done to clarify what remedial work, if any, was undertaken by the developers. Such work may have included removal and replacement of all topsoil down to a specified depth with a suitable membrane installed to seal potentially polluted subsoil below. So the fact that your lawn doesn't physically glow in the dark needn't necessarily mean that everything's fine and dandy down below. First stop would be the archives at the Council planning department, then a trip to Building Control to check how deep you can excavate new foundations without risk. Building Control Officers often have excellent local knowledge about ground conditions.

Photo: Wessex Archaeology

The strange case of the disappearing back garden, Redruth, Cornwall, 2000.

Mines and sink holes

There's rarely any warning other than a brief rumbling noise: then there's a gaping abyss where your garden used to be. Disasters of this type have occurred for many years. In 1992 a 75ft deep crater suddenly appeared in the garden of a house in Woodland Way in the Cornish town of Gunnislake. In less than 30 seconds it had not only swallowed the entire back garden but also two telegraph poles and the garden shed. In another case the corner of a house disappeared down an old 1,000ft deep mineshaft.

So if your region was at some point in the past known for mining – and much of the UK was – you'll need to consider the possible existence of underground tunnels and mineshafts, even where local collieries have long been closed and their pits capped off. Land searches are supposed to flag these up when you buy a property, but they have sometimes missed them, causing whole estates to become blighted. Since it did not become a legal requirement to maintain accurate plans of underground workings until 1872, many ancient shallow mines have never been recorded.

In the 1960s it was not unknown for new housing estates to be built on top of overgrown, derelict sites which later turned out to be former mining land. If you live in an area known for mining, it is therefore essential to thoroughly check local records before digging.

Subsoil

The design (and therefore the cost) of your foundations will depend on what type of subsoil you're building on. To be certain what secrets the ground below your feet may hold, you really need to dig a trial 'borehole'. This should be excavated to a depth of at least a metre, and be about 5m away from the house and any other buildings. Using a

mini-digger will prove a lot easier than a hand-held auger for this purpose. The objective is to reveal whether the ground is predominantly chalky, sandy, or composed of clay, gravel or peat. Of course it would be a lot simpler to find this out from a geological map of your area (see downloadable maps via our website), but these are drawn to such a small scale that they only provide a very rough guide to what you're actually likely to discover.

Much of southern and south-east England is notoriously comprised of shrinkable clay, which in dry spells has been known to cause structural movement to some older properties with shallow foundations. One obvious clue to the presence of clay is where the soil dries out quickly in summer, with evident shrinking and cracking. Also keep an eye open for sudden changes in vegetation that may also be indicative of unusual ground conditions, for example streaks of brown grass across an otherwise green lawn may indicate the path of pipes running close to the surface.

If, when digging your trial pit, you start unearthing bits of old china and fragments of tiles, bricks or bottles, this is a strong indication that you're into 'backfilled' ground. This is where previously excavated ground has been filled in with old earth and rubble. The problem is that backfilled ground tends to be softer than the firm surrounding earth if it wasn't properly compacted (compressed). In such cases you need to discover the depth of the backfill by digging down until you reach virgin ground underneath. Small areas

Sloping sites mean extra expense with foundations .

can be bridged over, but larger amounts of backfill can be a problem and a structural engineer will need to advise. The worst case scenario is extensive backfill across the entire site to an indeterminable depth, in which case the cost of specialist foundations could make the project uneconomic.

So if you take a chance and skip any site checks, or your architect simply makes an assumption that the foundations will need to be only, say, 750mm deep, the builder will price up the work accordingly. This can cause trouble later in the project when work on site is in full flow, if the Building Control Officer instructs the builder to change the foundation depth or type (at your expense) or holds up work awaiting engineer's calculations. It's obviously a lot less risky to dig a trial hole before designing the foundations, or at least seek the early opinion of Building Control.

It's not unknown for geological fault lines to run through sites. Cracks called 'fissures' exist where one type of subsoil collides with another, so you might have more than one type to contend with. Thankfully Britain is free of major intercontinental tectonic plates, so such geological curiosities should pose little problem. However, if your plot is on a steeply sloping site the foundations will need to be specially designed to prevent any risk of the excavation work destabilising the hilly ground.

Trees and hedges

Make a note of all nearby trees since the foundation design will need to take account of them. Species such as oaks, poplars and willows are notorious for affecting nearby ground conditions, especially during long dry spells. Clay subsoils and sloping sites are most at risk from trees. Fast-growing species such as leylandii and eucalyptus can

also cause clay to shrink and swell, which is bad news for houses with shallow foundations. See Chapter 9.

But before rushing out to do battle, clutching your favourite chainsaw, remember that there are severe penalties for removing trees and hedges protected by Preservation Orders. In conservation areas all trees are effectively protected. And it's not just their felling or removal that's forbidden – even minor lopping can get you into trouble. So if the proposed route of your extension happens to clash with any substantial foliage, you'd be well advised to check it out with the Council before finalising the design.

Whilst on the subject of protected species, note that animals and their habitats can also enjoy legal rights. So if you encounter bats, great crested newts or other rare wildlife be sure to consult Natural England (or the equivalent Scottish, Welsh or Northern Irish bodies) for their considered opinion before setting about annihilating any protected habitats.

Flooding, ditches and streams

Do you live near the coast? Are there any rivers or streams in the vicinity of your home? If you can answer 'yes' to either question there may be some potential risk of flooding to your property. If you find evidence of a high water table, such as freshly excavated trenches filling with water, it should ring alarm bells. Today more than ever, this must be taken into account in the design of the foundations. With global warming high on the agenda, the risk of flood damage is increasingly real, potentially affecting more and more people. So constructing the ground floor of the extension a little higher than the one in your existing property may prove to be a sound decision. The marginal cost is minimal compared to the potential benefits should flooding occur.

Take time to research this subject. If you're fairly new to an area consult your neighbours, since they may be able to recall any history of local flooding. Maps are now available from the Environment Agency showing the location of flood plains and risks of flooding by postcode (see website). If your planning application needs to include a Flood Risk

Photo: eddystoneselfbuild.co.uk

Radon-proof floor membrane.

Assessment (FRA), rather than cough up several hundred
pounds for a consultant, there are online DIY guides that
show you how to put together your own report.

If you have a ditch or stream running through your
garden you'll be legally responsible for maintenance of the
banks as well as the 'river bed', which might mean having
to clear out debris now and again. The law also stipulates
that if there are any pipes or drains that run under your
land (known as 'culverts') it is down to you to keep them
clear. If your land happens to border a ditch or a stream,
the responsibility for maintenance is normally shared with
the owner on the other side.

Whilst on the subject of ditches, it is an offence to
obstruct a watercourse, so wise men are never seen
chucking loads of old garden rubbish into them.

Radon gas

Sounding a little like something from *Doctor Who*, radon is
a naturally occurring radioactive gas concentrated in parts
of the country rich in granite most notably in Cornwall and
Devon (see map on website). It is estimated that more than
half a million UK homes are potentially exposed to radon
which is linked to an estimated 1,100 deaths from lung
cancer every year.

However, it is very difficult
to detect since it is invisible and
odourless, but if exposed to large
enough doses over time it can be
harmful. Fortunately, new buildings
in high-risk areas can be fairly easily
radon-proofed and the occupants
sealed from exposure by the use of
a radon-resistant floor membrane
that prevents the gas from entering
the building. Some additional minor
precautions are also needed, such
as ensuring seals around service
openings are fully airtight. Modern
'beam and block' concrete ground
floors must be fully ventilated to
allow effective dispersal.

Rights of way

Having to worry about invasions of backpackers exercising
their 'right to roam' across your land may seem like
something only rich celebrities and royalty need worry
about. However, it's fairly common – in Victorian terraces,
for example – to find a shared right of way running across
all the back gardens, close to the rear walls just where you
want to build. And such rights of way are not always visually
obvious on site. Keen ramblers can become quite upset to
discover their favourite route has just been obliterated by a
massive new extension. So to stay on the right side of the
law, it's important to check for the existence of any public
footpaths or private rights of way across your plot.

These matters are normally investigated by your
solicitors carrying out a local land search when you
purchase a property. If you do find such rights across your
land they may by now be defunct so it may be possible for
them to be legally overturned. Sometimes a right of way
can be legally re-routed by the Council making an order to
close or divert it. The order must be advertised and anyone
can object, which makes it a fairly lengthy procedure.
More commonly found are legal rights for service supply
cables and pipes known as 'wayleaves'.

It's important to note that even if planning permission
has already been granted it doesn't mean you can then start
building and interfere with a path. In fact, if you carry on
regardless and obstruct a right of way the Local Authority can
force you to demolish the extension or pay a crippling fine.

On that happy note, assuming you're now fully
confident that the piece of land you want to build on isn't
about to disappear down a mineshaft, and that death
from radon poisoning, explosion or flooding pose no
threat, the next step is the big 64,000 dollar question of all
property development: will you get planning consent?

Terraced houses sometimes have rear access but may only
accommodate smaller delivery lorries.

3 PLANNING PERMISSION AND BUILDING REGS

The extent to which you can enlarge your home isn't simply down to the size of your budget. The planning rules dictate what you're legally allowed to build. And the Building Regulations determine whether it's physically possible to construct it to an acceptable standard.

Extending in contrasting materials can often enhance 'kerb appeal'.

You now have to overcome what is probably the single biggest hurdle of the entire project: getting planning permission. Without it, you may not be allowed to build much more than a glorified dog kennel unless your extension counts as Permitted Development. And when the planning's all sorted, you then need to satisfy the folk at Building Control. Without their approval you would find it virtually impossible to sell your house, since prospective buyers and mortgage lenders would assume it was structurally unsafe. So the purpose of getting drawings produced is very specific – first to gain planning consent, and then to show that your ideas will comply with the Building Regulations (which need a lot more technical detail). These will also form the basis for working drawings to guide the builders on site.

It's important to realise that Planning and Building Regulations are two totally separate things. What the two normally have in common is that they're both implemented by the Local Authority, respectively the Development Control Department and the Building Control Department at the Council offices.

The chief concern of the planning department is essentially to balance one person's right to build against the rights of other interested parties, such as the neighbours. They'll also aim to protect the character of an area from being wrecked by hideous, overbearing new buildings, or from potentially disturbing changes of use. Which is why you can't suddenly convert your living room into a 24-hour lap-dancing establishment (the killjoys). Basically, the planners will want you to achieve a decent-looking home extension that doesn't unduly detract from other local residents' enjoyment of their homes. They will also take into account any road safety implications resulting from new driveways. The objective of Building Control, on the other hand, is to ensure compliance with basic safety standards and prevent the erection of jerry-built death traps. But both departments have draconian enforcement powers should anyone choose to carry out an illegal development.

Planning Permission

Until 1 July 1948 it was every British citizen's God-given right to build pretty much whatever they wanted on their land with the bare minimum of interference from government. Which was fine, until your neighbours decided to erect a giant monolith in their back garden, blotting out the sun and casting a permanent shadow over your home.

So today, before you can even think about laying one brick on top of another, in many cases you'll need to apply for planning permission (a.k.a. 'consent' or 'approval'

This will either be granted or refused in accordance with the plans you submit. The process is designed to ensure fairness by requiring compliance with the Council's policies as shown in their 'local development plan', although the principles are to a large extent dictated by central government.

Each year there are over half a million UK planning applications, yet the system is not particularly user-friendly. However, when you consider all the areas where the planners can potentially fault your ideas, and that most applications are not submitted by architects, it may come as something of a surprise to learn that approximately 80

Below left and below: Planners are more likely to want extensions to period properties to be 'in keeping' with the original.

per cent of all applications are successful. It's always worth talking your plans through with a planning officer before officially submitting them. This gives you the chance to take on board any suggested changes at the design stage, thereby improving the likelihood of success. The process of submitting your planning application is explained later in this chapter. But first, there are some circumstances where you may not need to bother with all the hassle of applying for planning…

Will my new extension need planning permission?

When modern planning legislation was originally introduced in 1948 (in The Town & Country Planning Act), a certain amount of minor building work known as 'general development' was still permitted without the need for formal consent. So today, things like inconspicuous front porches, lean-tos, small to medium sized extensions and conservatories can often be constructed quite freely as long as they don't go beyond specific limits.

Rather cunningly, however, Councils can choose to remove such rights where they feel the character of an area is particularly vulnerable, by slapping on an 'Article 4 Direction'. Or there might be a condition attached to the original planning consent for your property that removed Permitted Development (P.D.) rights in a bid to restrict future development. So to avoid any confusion, it's always best to run your proposals past the planners in the first instance. If it turns out that your project doesn't need consent, and you want a formal ruling to prove it, for a small fee they'll issue a Lawful Development Certificate (or give you a confirmatory letter for free!).

Permitted development rights

At present, you're normally allowed to build without planning consent in cases where the 'permitted development' rules listed below apply. Of course, in reality every case is different and your local planners may need to advise on individual schemes. Specifically, your 'free allowance' for building without planning permission applies as follows:

FRONT EXTENSIONS

No extensions are allowed without planning consent to the front of your 'principal elevation', which is normally the main front wall of your property (or whichever wall faces the road). The exception to this is small porches which are usually permitted - see opposite page.

SIDE EXTENSIONS

In some cases your side wall may count as the 'principal elevation', e.g. where it faces a highway. Otherwise side extensions are normally permitted if they're:
- Single storey
- Maximum height: 4 metres
- Maximum width: up to half the width of the original house*
(*the 'original house' means as it was first built or as it stood on 1 July 1948)

REAR EXTENSIONS

Both single and multi-storey extensions are normally permitted subject to limits on how far they extend back from the house:

Single storey
- Maximum depth: 4 metres (detached houses)
                3 metres (semi-detached or terraced houses)

  N.B. For single-storey rear extensions these depths can be doubled under the 'neighbourhood consultation scheme'. This involves you first notifying your local authority planning department who will then write to adjoining neighbours. But if any objections are received the planners will decide whether it can go ahead. You can download an application form at Planningportal.co.uk
- Maximum height: 4 metres)

2 storey or higher
- Maximum depth: 3 metres (including the ground floor)

ALL EXTENSIONS

Height
- No extension to be higher than the highest part of your property's existing roof.
- The extension's eaves and ridge height must be no higher than those on the existing house.
- Extensions within 2 metres of a boundary are limited to maximum eaves height of 3 metres.

Garden plot
- No more than half the area of land around the original house* must be covered by your extension and any existing outbuildings.
- 2 storey or higher rear extensions must be no closer than 7 metres to your garden's rear boundary.

Design
- The roof pitch on 2 storey or higher extensions must match the existing house.
- Materials must be similar in appearance to the existing house.
- No balconies or verandas.
- Side-facing windows to upper floors to be obscure-glazed and non-opening, unless the parts that can be opened are more than 1.7m above the floor of the room.

Just in case you were thinking this is all surprisingly generous, there are inevitably some 'buts'. The main problem is that your 'free allowance' may have long since been eaten up by a lot of stuff added on since 1948 – such as old lean-tos, outbuildings and even dormer roof windows. These only count if they're

Listed thatched cottage extended with contrasting but traditional stone walls and clay roof tiles.

bigger than 10m3 and within 5m of your planned new extension, but even so, you may have no free allowance left. However, this isn't necessarily bad news – it may be possible to demolish an old garage and build an extension in its place without the need for a planning application. But remember that all these nice permitted development allowances are cruelly snatched away if you live in a listed building, and are severely restricted in some other locations (see below). Also, the height of a building is measured from the ground level next to it – so constructing a basement or semi-basement can be one way of getting more 'bang for your bucks', subject to the technical feasibility of actually building it within the available plot. And that's an important point to bear in mind at the design stage – a great design that the planners think is the cat's whiskers may not actually be financially viable or technically practical.

Listed buildings and conservation areas
Special rules apply for listed buildings and for properties in conservation areas, where your freedom to build is more tightly controlled. So an extension that might be permitted elsewhere could in such cases be unacceptable.

If your property is listed in any form, ie Grade I, II star or II (or Grades A, B or C in Scotland and N. Ireland), it means it has been deemed of 'special architectural or historic interest' and particular importance will be placed on retaining its character, identity and appearance. So you'll need special Listed Building Consent for any alterations, including internal changes that normally wouldn't interest the planners.

On the plus side, building work on listed buildings should be zero rated for VAT purposes, so you should be able to claim back VAT paid on materials. In fact, the contractors should not charge VAT at all on their labour (so you need to notify them in writing asap that it's a listed building).

Conservation areas are 'areas of special architectural or historic interest' and there are currently around 10,000 of them. It's crucial to check whether you're located within one, since your Permitted Development allowances are severely restricted; for example you can only build single-storey rear extensions, plus you're not allowed to make roof alterations or apply wall cladding (the same limits apply in Areas of Outstanding Natural Beauty, Areas of Special Control, National Parks, and the Norfolk and Suffolk Broads).

Here the planners have a duty to ensure that any external alterations 'preserve or enhance' the character and appearance of the area. Essentially this is intended to prevent incompetent DIYers from blighting the neighbourhood with artificial stone cladding and clumsy uPVC porches. In effect, it gives the planners carte blanche to get closely involved with the style of your design, even down to your precise choice of external materials. They may, for example, stipulate that your extension's modern cavity walls are built to look like traditional Victorian 'Flemish bond' solid walls using dearer second-hand stock bricks, 'snapped headers' and traditional lime mortar pointing. Or they may insist on more expensive clay tiles or natural slate for the roof. Paying for such historic detailing may well cost you more than you'd like, but it should ultimately add to the 'kerb appeal' of your property and hence boost its value. Basically, if you live in a conservation area it's safest to assume that you'll need special consent for any visible external changes, even down to fences, railings and trees.

Other stuff
Here's a rough guide to all those other awkward 'bits and pieces' planning questions:

Porches and conservatories
Small porches are exempt from needing planning if the floor area is no more than 3m^2 (measured externally) and where the porch is less than 3m high and not within 2m of a public highway. Conservatories are classed as single-storey extensions and will often fall within your permitted development allowance, but it's always best to check first.

Loft conversions
Loft conversions that add less than 50m3 volume to the house in addition to the existing loft space (40m3 for terraces) should also be exempt as are roof extensions such as dormer windows which do not face a highway and do not raise the overall height of the roof.

However, the front of the property is always going to be

Right: What a pair of front dormers! – unlikely to be approved today.

Below: Porches of similar form and materials to the house are generally acceptable.

a sensitive area, so you could consider fitting skylights instead, which are more discreet and do not normally require planning consent. See Haynes *Loft Conversion Manual*.

Demolition

Should the fancy take you, it may well be permissible to knock down outbuildings or even part of your own house without the tedious business of having to first tell the planners, provided that the external volume of the building in question is less than 50 cubic metres. The trouble is, it doesn't automatically follow that you'd be granted planning permission to build a suitable replacement, which could prove a trifle embarrassing. So it's always advisable to include any demolition as part of your overall application. Building Control, on the other hand, must always be notified in advance of any proposed demolition. And unless your house is detached, adjoining houses will have a mutual legal right of support.

Outbuildings

If all else fails, an alternative way to add space is to build a separate new structure in the garden. A new home-office, playroom or gym is always an attractive proposition, particularly in the light of the benevolent Permitted Development rules.

You're normally allowed to erect new outbuildings (garages, garden offices, summerhouses and sheds etc) without planning consent where:

- The outbuilding is not built forward of the front (or principal) elevation, and is not visible from the road.
- It is single storey with a maximum roof height of 4m (3m for flat roofs) and max eaves height of 2.5m.
- Where it's located within 2m of a boundary, the max height is 2.5m.
- It mustn't cover more than 50% of the original garden area.
- It must be 'for the use and enjoyment' of your property, ie used in association with the house and not a separate dwelling.

But before dancing in delight at your good fortune, it's always best to double check with the planners as tougher rules apply in Conservation Areas and for Listed buildings etc.

There's more good news when it comes to designing and building your new garden accommodation because some attractive ready-made kits are available for a range of insulated, hi-tech, log cabins.

Storage tanks for heating oil

These need consent if they're nearer to the road/footpath than the original house (unless they're more than 20m away from the road) or if they're taller than 3m above the ground or contain more than 3,500 litres. If the tank contains any liquid fuel other than oil (such as LPG) there are no exemptions – you'll need consent in all cases. You will also need to fully comply with Building Regs.

Fences, walls and gates

These normally don't need consent up to 1m high next to a road, or 2m high elsewhere. You're also normally allowed to demolish or alter existing fences, walls and gates to your heart's content no matter how high, without getting consent (except, of course, to listed buildings and in conservation areas or where Councils have imposed boundary restrictions).

Hedges

Planting hedges doesn't normally need planning consent, unless they could block a driver's view or are restricted by some old planning condition. But don't forget that hedges may be protected under a preservation order, or there may be a legal restriction preventing them from being cleared and uprooted. Conversely, some housing estates with 'open plan' front gardens (typically c.1970s) have restrictive covenants on the deeds that restrict new planting and fencing.

Patios, paths and driveways

It is heartening to note that British citizens are still free to do entirely as they please with hard surfaces in their back gardens without anyone from the Council having the right to stick their oar in. Although the neighbours may find your creative ideas slightly alarming, so long as the hard surfaces in question are at ground level (or near ground level) you have complete freedom to cover your private fiefdom as you see fit – with layers of tarmac, crazy-paving, decking, concrete or gravel, perhaps garnished with a tasteful sprinkling of luminous, banana-coloured stone chippings. Your call.

The exception to this liberal regime is where you want to construct parking areas between the front of your house (or its 'principal elevation') and the road. Where the area of hard standing exceeds 5 sq. metres, hard surfaces must be made of porous materials. Alternatively, rainwater must be directed to a lawn or border so it runs off and can drain naturally. Where you want to construct new car access from the road over a pavement or kerb, clearly there are safety issues involved, so consent will be required. Even widening your existing driveway can require permission, depending on how busy the road is.

Ex-Local Authority properties

Although not strictly a planning issue, ex-Council homes can have a sting in the tail – there's often a

Front extension transforms ex-Local Authority semi.

restrictive covenant on the deeds requiring you to get additional legal approval from the Council's Housing Department before extending. However, judging by the large number of ex-Local Authority properties that have been successfully extended this is unlikely to prove too draconian a restriction.

Basements and cellars

If you're going to build an extension, why not go the whole hog and build yourself an underground 'den' in

the process? After all, you're officially the owner of all the ground down to the centre of the earth as well as the house that stands on it. So if the planners aren't keen on building upwards, surely they can't object to you going underground where no one can see?

The downside of this cunning wheeze may lie with the technical challenge of excavating in close proximity to adjoining houses. Digging giant holes next to old buildings with shallow foundations can cause the opposite of underpinning – undermining. So new basements need to be very carefully and professionally designed from the word 'go'. See Chapter 7.

Alternatively, you may want to extend your existing house downwards into the ground. Converting an existing

Below: Spot the local councillor's house!

basement (a potentially habitable room) or cellar (used only for storage) in most cases won't require planning consent, though you're likely to confront some serious technical challenges. Most cellars have low ceilings, so to get some decent headroom the floors need to be excavated. Unfortunately, this will also involve expensive underpinning of shallow foundations – at least doubling the total cost compared to converting an existing full-height basement. Old cellars are almost inevitably damp, requiring expensive remedial wall lining, and the provision of light and ventilation can prove troublesome. Consequently, the cost and complexity of such a task compared to the resulting increase in property value can often render such a project unrealistic.

Planning principles

If your design doesn't meet the Permitted Development (PD) rules, you can of course apply for planning permission. Some Councils offer a special fast-track application service for extensions that comply with 'LDO' conditions (Local Development Order) with approval granted within 2 weeks. This doesn't apply to extensions on terraced houses and the design criteria are similar to those for Permitted Development, but it's worth checking your Council's website to see if your plans qualify for fast-tracking.

At the end of the day, despite the fairly generous Permitted Development rules, most decent-sized home extensions still require a formal planning application. To win consent it helps if you talk the same language as the planners. There are a number of key criteria used to judge all proposals, in order to be fair and objective, although local interpretation will inevitably play an important role. Getting planning consent has nothing to do with funny handshakes and buying generous rounds of drinks for local councillors (or so we're told!).

Should your neighbours decide to object, they will also need to couch their arguments in planning terms rather than, say, moaning about possible noise from builders etc.

These are the kind of planning considerations your design must take into account:

Overlooking

If the planners consider that your design could seriously compromise your neighbours' privacy, it may well be sent back to the drawing board. It is for this reason that 'exotic' features like balconies, roof gardens, upstairs conservatories and windows in side walls are often resisted.

The trouble is, for most urban or suburban houses it can be difficult to come up with a design where the windows don't in some way overlook a neighbour's house or garden. One solution is to design the extension with the upstairs bedrooms built largely within the roof space so, in effect, they're 'loft rooms' with sloping ceilings and skylight windows that gaze harmlessly out into space. Or windows can be designed at high level with sills at least 1700mm above the bedroom floor (or obscured and not opening below 1700mm), which should allow sufficient sunlight in whilst preventing the occupants from easily seeing out. For bathrooms, windows can be fitted with obscured glass.

Overdevelopment

In built-up urban areas, plot sizes may be fairly small, so extending the house could seriously eat into the available garden space. The planners will therefore want to be satisfied that your plans provide sufficient remaining amenity space, otherwise the project may be construed as 'overdevelopment'. If this looks like it could be a problem, providing evidence of similar local extensions that have previously been approved should help your case.

Overshadowing and 'right to light'

Especially relevant to rear extensions, excessive overshadowing of adjoining houses can be a good enough reason alone for refusal. Obviously this is going to be more of an issue for multi-storey designs or where the back of the property happens to be south-facing. (See 'The 45-degree guideline' opposite.)

Although not specifically a planning issue, there is an ancient piece of land law dating from 1832 that still protects homeowners' 'right to light'. Basically, if you build or plant something that substantially blots out light from a neighbour's window, then the neighbour can take legal action against you for infringing their 'right to light' – as long as their window has been in existence for 20 years or more. There are exceptions to the right, such as where developers of some estates took the trouble to remove the legal 'right to light' of future occupiers of their properties.

Conversely, there is no such thing as a 'right to a view' in law, so if you happen to live at 'Ocean View' and

Sunlight should be considered even where extensions comply with the 45° guideline.

someone decides to construct a tower block smack in your line of vision, thereby massively reducing the value of your house – tough.

Parking and highways

Some planning authorities set a lot of store by how many off-street parking spaces your new design will provide. They know that properties with increased numbers of bedrooms can ultimately mean more car-owning occupants, all requiring extra parking spaces. So if you want to convert your existing garage for use as living space, or you want to build over part of the driveway to the side of your house, you'll normally be asked to compensate.

If your house occupies a corner plot, or is near a busy road, and you want to build a front or side extension, the planners will refer your plans to the Highways Department for their considered opinion.

Landscaping

Attractive landscaping is more than just 'the icing on the cake'. It's a secret weapon that can be used to help swing a decision in your favour. Omitting landscaping details from the application is therefore a lost opportunity. Where landscaping isn't shown on the plans, consent is normally issued with a condition that details of planting and landscaping must be submitted before commencing any work on site. This can, of course, lead to delays further down the line.

Because building an extension inevitably means losing some of your former garden space there'll be less remaining land for 'amenity use'. So the environmental impact of your plans will be a serious consideration. Things like planting, surface treatments, screening and retention of existing hedgerows and trees can all influence the ultimate decision.

Where trees are protected by tree preservation orders (TPOs) you'll need the Council's consent to prune or fell them. As noted earlier, all trees in conservation areas are effectively protected.

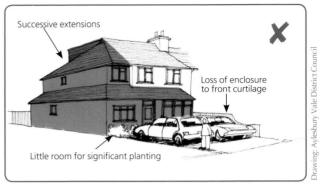

Successive extensions

Loss of enclosure to front curtilage

Little room for significant planting

Drawing: Aylesbury Vale District Council

Gradually increasing the size of a house inevitably leads to greater demands for off-street parking, often to the detriment of visual amenity.

Drawing: Aylesbury Vale District Council

The 45-degree guideline and other rules

When you make a planning application, the planners sometimes apply 'the 45-degree guideline' to predict the likely impact of your design, preventing undue loss of daylight to neighbouring properties or excessive overshadowing of their gardens.

Rear extensions

The distance you are allowed to build back from the main house will be more restricted for two-storey or higher extensions, even if your back garden is huge. Typically you may be limited to no more than about 3.5m.

You can calculate the effect of your proposed extension by taking a plan (ie looking from above) and drawing a line at 45° from each corner of the furthest new wall back towards the main house.

If you imagine the line casting a shadow over next door's property, then it must not engulf the window closest to your house. This only applies to windows of 'habitable rooms' ie not to utility rooms and cloakrooms etc. If the line does hit anywhere beyond the nearest part of their window, you'll have to amend the design. Or only build a single storey.

Side extensions

Although building out to the side is a popular improvement, some Councils may want to resist the

infilling of gaps between dwellings, for two-storey or higher extensions, in order to preserve the open character of an area. They may also prefer you not to build within 1m of a shared boundary. However, many side extensions are designed to replace existing structures such as old garages, and are therefore less contentious.

Front extensions

The front elevation of a house is the most vulnerable to unsympathetic alterations. Large front extensions are rarely acceptable particularly where you need to have regard to the original 'building line' of the street. For a typical semi or terraced house, a porch may be about the most you could hope for, since the 45-degree principle means you'll be very restricted in what you can build without it 'overshadowing' the nearest part of next door's house. But the more set back the property is from the street the more freedom you're likely to enjoy with your design. And a well designed front extension can transform the kerb appeal of even the blandest properties.

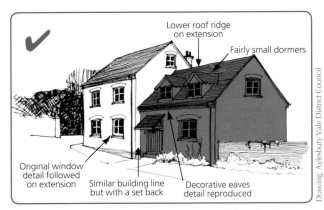

Drawing: Aylesbury Vale District Council

Extensions which are smaller, lower and which follow the design of the original houses are normally acceptable.

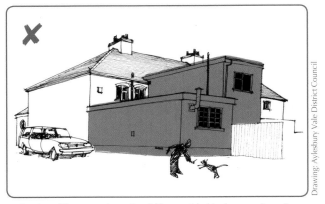

Drawing: Aylesbury Vale District Council

Bulky, box-like extensions should be avoided in favour of smaller additions which respect the form of the original building.

Design and the planners

How do you define 'good design'? One person's fabulous home improvement is another's ghastly eyesore. The trouble is, the planners may not agree with your opinion of 'good design', and it's the overall appearance of the extension and how it will change the look of your property that's probably *the* most important consideration of all. Nonetheless, there are some good common sense general rules which, if followed, should lead to a happy outcome.

Shape and scale

It's a matter of respect. Extensions should not overwhelm the existing building. Once they get anywhere near the size of the original house, the old architecture could be swamped and lost, harming its appearance. Flashy, eye-catching 'look-at-me' designs are often rejected. Basically, your new extension should complement the existing building rather than dominate it. To get a large extension through planning is not impossible, but requires real ingenuity, imagination and design flair to reduce its apparent bulk. You're more likely to get a big one through if its shape is traditional and blends in with the old place.

Planners claim that they don't rule out contemporary designs that contrast with the original building as long as

the design also enhances it. For example, a substantially glazed or oak-framed extension to a period house can appear striking and new, and yet at the same time can be somehow 'in keeping'. Or perhaps a neat timber-clad barn design bolted on to a traditional brick house. Different and distinctive, yet complementary. This is where a good architect can make a real difference.

Set-backs

In order to provide a visual break between old and new, side extensions usually need to be set back a little from the existing building. 'Set-backs' can make the extension seem more visually pleasing by reducing apparent bulk, like a smaller 'echo' of the main house. Technically this is also a good trick to help disguise tricky joints between different sized ancient and modern bricks and varying course heights. It also helps separate the old and new eaves details, which otherwise may be hard to match, and minimises damage to the old brickwork on visually important front-facing walls.

Materials

You can do everything else right, but choose the wrong materials and your extension will stick out like a Day-

Left: Despite bulk, large rear & side extension is in harmony with the existing house (see completed project p257).
Below: Side extensions should be set back from the main building line.

Drawing: Aylesbury Vale District Council

Glo Scottish Parliament on acid. Perhaps it was because the choice of materials didn't show up too well on old monochrome plans that some shockingly awkward designs seem to have got through the planning net in years gone by. This is a slightly contentious subject, since getting involved with the precise specification of materials is starting to go beyond the limits of planners' powers on a normal application, unless you're listed or live in a conservation area.

Happily, the chances are that you, the planners and everyone else in the street will be singing from the same hymn sheet on this one. Employing matching materials should help achieve a design that discreetly blends in with the original house, in terms of size, shape and style.

Tracking down suitable matching historic bricks and tiles etc may involve some detective work, but reintroducing original, natural materials should add to the quality and character of an older property.

Roofs

Extensions that are higher than single storey will often need roofs of a pitched design, simulating the style of the existing roof, perhaps with the new roofline a little lower than the main house. You'd normally want to match the existing roof tiles or slates, or even use better quality roof coverings than the originals. Where the original coverings have been replaced years ago with inappropriate modern ones, such as large concrete interlocking tiles on Victorian roofs, this may be a good opportunity to strip the whole lot and reinstate original natural slate or plain clay tiles throughout.

Pitched roofs are normally also preferred for single-storey extensions because they last far longer than flat roofs, and look a lot nicer. But there may be technical obstacles, such as on many terraced houses where there simply isn't space for anything other than a flat-roofed extension.

In some circumstances a special architectural argument could be made in favour of flat roofs, for example with 1930s art deco properties when they were very much in vogue.

Roof extensions

Alterations to the height and shape of roofs will normally need planning consent. Dormer windows need to be designed quite discreetly as they are inherently rather prominent, sticking out from roof slopes. Small pitched roof dormers that match the main roof slopes can look rather cute and are often a welcome addition. But dormers are not cheap and, at around a third of the cost, skylights can be a better alternative, although planners tend to prefer discreet 'conservation' roof windows.

The rules are more relaxed for rear roof slopes safely away from the public gaze. Where you sometimes see monstrous front box dormers it's because they were classified as 'Permitted Development' prior to 1988.

Rear extensions are rarely permitted higher than the main house.

Small, vertically proportioned dormers designed to respect the character of the house are normally acceptable.

Drawing: Aylesbury Vale District Council

Extending a terraced house

More than a quarter of UK houses are terraced – that's nearly seven million properties. Although many have minimal space in which to extend, there's normally some scope for enlargement. But designing a successful extension with such limited options means the likely effects on adjoining properties must be very carefully considered.

Although terraces can be the most challenging of all properties for which to design a good quality extension, getting planning consent needn't be a major obstacle. For example, it may be perfectly possible to build a single-storey rear extension, as well as a separate attic conversion for an extra bedroom, all quite legally under Permitted Development Rights.

Probably the most popular extension to the standard Victorian or Edwardian terraced house is to 'fill in' the small side return alley space alongside the kitchen, to the rear of the dining room. This is likely to involve chopping out part of the main side wall to the kitchen, a major structural alteration.

A side return extension usually adds only a couple of metres to the kitchen width, but this should be sufficient to transform formerly 'dead space' into an attractive family room with breakfast bars and a dining area.

One challenge with this kind of project, as indeed with most home extensions, is that the new structure will inevitably reduce the amount of sunlight entering your property, often drastically darkening the dining room. This calls for the architect to utilise their complete armoury of ingenious glazing solutions to let maximum light flow in. You may also be able to compensate by moving windows and doors around, but to look right, new windows should line up with those on the original house. Single-storey extensions are easier to make bright and airy as they can employ roof lights or glazed roofs.

In some circumstances you may be allowed to build right up to the neighbour's boundary or party wall, although planners sometimes like to see a gap of at least 900mm for future maintenance access.

End terrace houses offer more scope for extending, although where a large multi-storey side addition brings you within range of a highway you may only be permitted to build up to 1m from the road. However, for a single-storey extension you may be allowed to build right up to the boundary with the pavement.

In many areas there's a maximum permitted distance that a rear extension can be built back from a terraced property, typically 3 metres on north-facing elevations where there will be no loss of sunlight. Also, if there are other houses at the bottom of your garden, in order to preserve privacy some Councils insist that the space between their windows and the rear windows on your extension must typically be no less than 18 metres (14 metres for a ground-floor extension).

One of the toughest dilemmas when extending terraces is where to put the new windows. There are minimum guideline distances you need to maintain between the side windows on your new extension and next door's

Photo: Architect-your-home.com

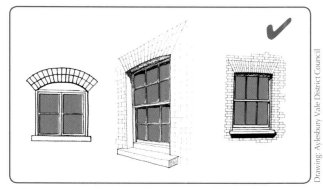

Drawing: Aylesbury Vale District Council

Following original designs and proportions will help relate extensions to the main building.`

Detailing

The devil, as they say, is in the detail. Window and door openings are especially important details to get right, as they strongly influence the look of your extension. These are a crucial architectural feature particularly on period properties so you'll earn extra brownie points with the planners if the new windows are compatible with the original house (even if those in the main house have long since been replaced). As well as getting their shape and size right, your design should carefully consider the alignment of all the door and window openings, and try to respect the original window pattern. Old sash windows and period doors can be duplicated with modern equivalents, custom-made to old designs. Features such as original deep stone windowsills can also be copied.

Extensions to older properties usually look best with a matching pattern of brick bonding and traditional eaves details (such as projecting decorative 'corbelled' bricks). Authentic arches above doors and windows (available as pre-cut sets) are often more suitable than simple flat soldier courses.

Although builders who are familiar with traditional skills, such as working with lime mortar, can be hard to find, it will be worth the trouble if you're extending a historic building. But don't let the builders talk you out of doing period detailing – it is perfectly possible to echo traditional details and to still comply with current Building Regulations.

Design details can have serious practical implications. For example, your neighbour's permission will be required if your extension roof overhangs their property or is attached to it. They will also need to be consulted if your foundations encroach on their land, or if your builders need access through their garden. This may involve having a legal agreement drawn up, so if you're not on speaking terms right now, it's probably best to 'design-out' any such potential obstacles at this stage. Certain features can also make your house potentially more vulnerable to crime. Even a new porch or downpipe can give access to an unlocked upstairs window, and features like balconies and flat roofs need to be carefully considered from this perspective at the design stage.

windows – ie where the sides of the two properties face each other. To respect the privacy of adjoining neighbours, no new windows should normally be placed within 2.4m of a boundary which they face. If this isn't possible, an acceptable compromise can be to install a wide horizontal 'clerestory' window high up the wall, above your eye level, with an internal sill height of at least 1.7m. For two-storey extensions, so as not to overlook a neighbouring property, any side-facing window needs to be obscure glazed and fixed shut or have any opening fanlights positioned no lower than 1.7m above the floor level. But the reality for most urban properties is that space is always going to be limited, and the planners may agree to relax the guidelines, especially if there's a substantial boundary fence or garden wall between the buildings.

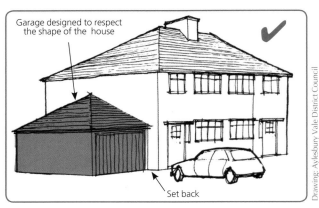

Garage designed to respect the shape of the house

Set back

Drawing: Aylesbury Vale District Council

Garage design which appears to belong to the existing home.

Drawing: Aylesbury Vale District Council

The use of parapets is not encouraged. A preferred arrangement is for pitched roofs of similar form to the main roof.

Garages and parking

As noted earlier, planners may take a dim view of schemes that cause a major loss of off-street parking space. New extensions tend to encourage more demand for parking at the same time as eradicating former car spaces by building over them. This can be a difficult issue to resolve, since so much UK housing was built before car ownership was commonplace. Even as late as the 1950s it was not really expected that house buyers would be able to afford to run a car as well as a mortgage.

Obviously it's important that your new extension does not impair the 'line of sight' for drivers at road junctions. Equally, any proposed new 'ingress' from the road into new parking areas (as well as 'egress' coming out of them) must satisfy the Highways people in terms of adequate visibility for drivers.

Clearly, highways issues will depend to a large extent on how busy the road is, so if your home faces straight onto the A40 don't be too surprised if concerns about parking and manoeuvring get flagged up. Many otherwise

Pleasing 2 storey side extension with integral 'coach style' garage and dormer echoing original Edwardian design.

acceptable proposals have fallen at this hurdle. Loss of turning space for cars in front gardens can also be a worry. You may be able to make amends by offering to convert some of the front garden into car space, but it may then be viewed negatively as a 'loss of amenity space'.

If it looks like your application is headed for rejection on these grounds, you could try a proactive approach and contact the Council Highways people direct to see if they can suggest a viable solution.

New garages don't generally belong in prominent locations, like urban front gardens. So designs that dramatically stick out, forward of the established building line are likely to be rejected. However, in villages and semi-rural areas permission is sometimes granted for detached free-standing garages in front gardens. This depends on local circumstances and the available space. It also helps if they're designed with a suitably traditional appearance, perhaps 'barn style' with steeply pitched roofs and black timber cladding, or maybe 'cottagey' white render or brick and flint, reflecting local styles.

Planning conditions

When you finally receive the formal planning permission document that (hopefully) approves your plans, there will normally be a number of conditions attached. Read these carefully as, legally, the approval is conditional upon them being actioned. Don't allow the conditions to get overlooked amidst the general excitement of winning consent. Some of these may significantly affect the final appearance and cost of the building. Others may relate to fairly minor standard details. Perhaps the most common condition is the stipulation that work must be started on site within three years of the date of the consent or the permission will lapse. Ignore this, and it could prove to be an expensive mistake. Note, however, that it refers to *starting* work, not finishing it, so getting some foundation work under way in time may be sufficient to secure the consent.

If you're really unlucky, your humble garden may suddenly be deemed to be of 'archaeological interest', with a condition imposed requiring you to give 6 weeks' notice prior to construction. The dimensions and locations of the required trial pit(s) will be specified (usually overlapping with a section of the proposed foundation trenches). So to save time and money you could agree to hire a mini-digger and excavate them yourself whilst liaising with the archaeologists painstakingly sifting through the ground with teaspoons. On the plus side, you may become the lucky owner of some interesting fossils or shards of ancient pottery!

Penalties

If, after due consideration, you've concluded that you prefer the pre-1948 planning rules better (*ie* no rules), and if the temptation to build without the inconvenience of getting official consent is overwhelming, then it's worth noting that the planners have *extreme* enforcement powers. They can force you to demolish and remove any unauthorised building work at your own expense, or do it on your behalf and fine you. Or even, as a last resort, impose a jail term.

If a structure has been built illegally, it is possible to apply retrospectively for consent, but if it's then refused you'll be watching it come down at demolition time. So it's generally better to co-operate.

There is such a thing, however, as the 'four-year rule', which basically means that if an unapproved building has managed to stay hidden from the disapproving gaze of the planners for four whole years after completion, and you can indisputably prove the date that construction was completed, any enforcement action may be void. A harsher ten-year rule applies where planning conditions are ignored. But attempting anything like this is a mad gamble – it just takes one phone call from a disgruntled neighbour…

The Building Regs are predominantly concerned with safety, structural stability & thermal efficiency.

Building regulations

Your extension will need Building Regulation approval regardless of whether you've got planning permission. Your designer will normally submit an application to Building Control, either 'full plans' or a 'building notice' - see page 77. This is a legal requirement but it's very much in your own interest to comply with the Building Regs so that the resulting structure can be shown as being safe, and will therefore be mortgageable and sellable. Only if the work has been carried out to the satisfaction of the Building Control Officer (formerly known as the 'Building Inspector' or 'District Surveyor') will you receive official Building Regs approval, in the form of a 'final certificate' upon completion of the build.

Primary responsibility for making sure your design complies with the regulations rests with the designer. But the person doing the building work is responsible for constructing the extension in compliance with the regulations, so if you're employing a firm of builders it's important to remind them of this at the outset. Be clear about whose job it is to liaise with Building Control.

The 'approved documents'

Practical guidance showing how to comply with the Building Regulations is contained in 'approved documents' issued by the Government. As far as your build is concerned, these are the bible, and are legally enforceable. The full documents can be accessed on the website.

Approved documents

A Structure
B Fire safety
C Site preparation and resistance to contaminants and moisture
D Toxic substances
E Resistance to the passage of sound
F Ventilation and condensation
G Hygiene, hot water safety and water efficiency
H Drainage and waste disposal
J Heat-producing appliances and fuel storage systems
K Stairs, ramps and guards (protection from falling, collision and impact)
L Conservation of fuel and power
M Access to and use of buildings
N Glazing – materials & safety (now included in Part K)
P Electrical safety
Q Security
R Electronic communications

In addition, 'Approved Document 7' provides guidance on materials and workmanship.

Left and right: Building Control need to inspect all major structural work before it's covered over.

The Scottish Building Standards comprise seven documents ('Section 0 to Section 6') and Northern Ireland has Parts A to V. However, the nitty-gritty areas of concern are largely the same as those for England and Wales. The main difference is that in Scotland you'll require permission in the form of a 'building warrant' before work can start.

The Building Regs are primarily concerned with health and safety – stuff you'd want to get right anyway, like sanitary fittings that don't leak and wiring that doesn't kill. Their objective is to enforce minimum standards for such things as fire protection, safe access and drainage, as well as to make sure buildings are structurally sound and weathertight. Increasingly, however, the emphasis is on meeting insulation standards in order to conserve fuel and power and reduce carbon emissions. Their aim is also to ensure that building work on site is undertaken safely.

Site inspections

Inspections are carried out by the Building Control Officer at several important stages. They carry out spot checks to enforce minimum standards but do not supervise the works on your behalf. For that you'd need to privately appoint your own surveyor or architect.

The builder is required to notify Building Control in advance at key stages, and leave the work exposed for inspection before covering it up and continuing. Should

It is possible to echo traditional details and comply with current building regulations.

Drawing: Aylesbury Vale District Council

they fail to do this, they may later be required to break open and expose parts of the structure for inspection, which in the case of concrete floors and foundations can prove a trifle messy. So if the Officer doesn't arrive within the time limit don't be tempted to cover up and press on regardless – make contact!

Stages for inspection	Notice required
1 Start on site	2 days
2 Excavation of foundations	1 day
3 Concreting of foundations	1 day
4 Oversite concrete	1 day
5 Damp Proof Course (DPC)	1 day
6 Drainage commencement	1 day
7 Drainage completion – ready for testing	1 day
8 Completion of the whole job	5 days

This list is the bare minimum, the stages where you must legally provide notice. Check the precise stages with your local authority as they are subject to local interpretation, for example Stage 1 is often combined with Stage 2. More than one inspection may be carried out for each stage, and additional inspections are often required. For example, the following works would also normally need to be checked:

- The roof structure.
- All major structural work – before covering any beams and lintels etc.
- At damp-proof membrane stage to ground floors.
- Construction of upper floors.
- At wall plate level (when the walls are finished and the roof about to start).
- New connections or alterations to drains, soil pipes etc.
- New boilers, flue liners, heating appliances, hot water cylinders.
- New water supply and waste pipes.
- Fire and sound insulation, fire escapes, fire doors, stairs etc.
- Thermal insulation and ventilation.

Notice is usually required to be submitted in writing by your builders, using a 'commencement notice' form for stage 1. Subsequent stages can normally be notified by phone or by email.

Building Control Officers are busy people, so site inspections often tend to be fairly brief affairs. This is normally the case where they judge that the extension is not too challenging technically, and where they know the builder to be competent, an opinion possibly formed from working on previous projects with the same contractor. Don't be horribly offended personally if Officers choose to discuss construction issues directly with the builders. It's just quicker that way, but they'll gladly involve clients in the debate if desired.

Only when the final inspection has been carried out will the completion certificate be issued, but you will need to specifically request it. This is a valuable certificate, so keep it safe along with the planning consent documents, since it will be required when you come to sell or remortgage.

Policing and penalties

If you contravene the Building Regulations or obstruct Building Control Officers from doing their job then you could be fined, or even sent for a short holiday care of HM Prisons. Officers have the right to enter sites at all reasonable hours to check if the rules have been contravened. Action is normally taken against the main building contractor, but the Local Authority can alternatively serve an enforcement notice against owners, demanding the taking down and removal (or rebuilding) of anything that contravenes a regulation, or they may force you to finish the works so that they fully comply. If you refuse, they can employ other builders to take down non-conforming parts of your extension, for which they will send you the bill.

There are only a few areas of building work where you don't need to apply for consent. Things like small porches (up to 3m²) may be exempt, and even most conservatories, car ports, outbuildings and detached garages (up to 30m² floor area), but it depends on the specific design, since details like the electrics will always have to comply. It's therefore best to assume that all structures require consent unless officially notified otherwise.

Local Authorities do have the legal right to relax any part of the Building Regulations (known as 'varying the provisions') if they believe that the requirement is unreasonable in a particular situation. Just don't bank on them being too keen to do this!

Conservatories & glazing

Conservatories are defined as having at least 50% of the walls and 75% of the roof area glazed (or made of translucent material). Whereas the planning rules are essentially the same as for single-storey extensions, most conservatories are exempt from the Building Regs because, like porches, they are not considered to be part of the permanent habitable zone of a house. To qualify as exempt conservatories need to comply with the following rules:-

- Floor area less than 30m2 (most are no bigger than about 12m2).

Photo: trombe.co.uk

- Built at ground level, not on upper floors.
- 'Thermally separated' from the rest of the house with external quality doors, walls or windows.
- At least half the wall area and three quarters of the roof made of translucent materials and the combined roof and wall areas made from these 'see through' materials should total more than 150% of the floor area.
- Any fixed heating must have independent temperature and on/off controls isolated from the central heating system in the house.
- Safety glazing to Part K in critical zones of doors, side door lights and low level window glazing.

However, unless yours is going to be used exclusively for growing marrows it's probably best to assume it will need to comply at the very least in terms of glazing and electrics. It's also very much in your interest to ensure compliance in other important aspects of construction, such as foundation depths.

To make the most of a small conservatory it might be tempting to integrate it into the main house with no dividing wall or doors, to create an open-plan 'substantially glazed extension'. But if they're not fully separated, they count as normal extensions and the large amount of glazing could scupper your plans for windows elsewhere by eating up your extension's 'door and window allowance' - see Chapter 4. The reason this is such an issue is because of heat loss; the rate at which heat escapes through conservatory windows it is typically 2 or 3 times that of the walls; and polycarbonate roofs leak heat at least 8 times the rate of proper insulated roofs! Cheap lightweight conservatory roofs can also be prone to leakage from badly weathered joints and cracking from ground movement; some south-facing conservatories have even physically buckled due to extreme heat! This may explain the recent trend for replacing glazed roofs with insulated lightweight moulded resin roofs that give the appearance of tiles or slates, thereby converting old conservatories into sunrooms or 'orangeries'. However this is defined as 'material alteration work' so it normally requires a Building Regs application. Because uPVC windows have very limited strength, installing a heavier new roof with extra weight from ceilings etc will often require the construction of a new supporting framework of lintels and corner posts to transfer the new loads down to the walls and foundations. Even then, because the extent of the windows will be more than the 25% floor area limit (see page 55) this won't by itself create a habitable extension that can be made open-plan, so the new 'orangery' will still need to be thermally separate from main house. All-in-all it's probably better where possible to fork out a bit more for a pukka new home extension.

Structural calculations

Building Control will normally require structural calculations for your proposed extension from a qualified structural engineer. These will prove that all the structural elements such as beams, lintels, floor joists, roof timbers and foundations are up to the job, and that the structural stability of the extension as a whole is adequate. Any structural alterations you plan to make to the existing house, such as knocking through new openings into the extension, are also likely to need accompanying calculations. In Scotland you have to submit a special 'Structural Design Certificate' that confirms the stability of the proposed new structure.

Choosing materials

The materials used to build your extension obviously need to be safe and fit for purpose, as well as looking good. Your designer and builders should be familiar with the materials available, and the specification for the works will normally state the quality required (eg 'plywood shall be in accordance with BS 1455').

Products should normally carry a recognised quality branding such as the BSI (British Standard Institute) kitemark or BBA (British Board of Agrément) approval. Products with 'CE' marks are also acceptable as it means they comply with European standards. If in doubt, ask Building Control what they'll accept.

The biggest problems with materials usually relate to the way they've been installed. If a dispute arises with the builders, the manufacturers normally have product advisers available who should be able to clarify matters.

Building over (or near) drains

Most extensions are built to the side or rear of the house, which, rather inconveniently, is often just where the drains are located. Having previously identified your underground drain runs, it may now be possible to revise the design to avoid building over them (thereby saving a lot of expense and hassle). Maybe you can shift the extension over a bit, or make it slightly smaller. If not, then the first thing to check is whether the drains are private or public.

A quick rewind back to the previous chapter tells us that private drains are the ones nearest the house that only serve your property and are therefore entirely your responsibility. Further out these often join up with other people's drain runs to become shared drains – which are classed as sewers. These will then connect to a public sewer, usually found under the road. Some older sewers run across a whole series of back gardens very close to the houses. Drains may even run underneath some Victorian or period houses.

Building over a public sewer or lateral drain (both the responsibility of the Water authority – see page 21) can be a major undertaking. If you choose to ignore the rules, the water company has the legal right to stop your building works. They can take down any buildings erected without prior agreement. Even building within 3m of a sewer normally requires official consent (the precise distance will depend on local water

Where a section of pipework is serving more than just the house being extended, the water company must first be notified.

company requirements). This is because constructing new buildings near sewers increases the pressure on underground pipes, potentially causing the sewer to collapse. Not only will this block everyone's drainage but it can in turn cause structural damage to your new extension. To prevent this nightmare situation arising, there are three options:

- ■ *Avoid the sewer*: as noted earlier, the easiest and cheapest solution is to modify your plans so the extension will be at least 3m away from the sewer.
- ■ *Divert the sewer*: where practical you could divert the sewer away from where you want to build (with the agreement of the water company). Most pipes should be less than 160mm diameter, which means the water company may allow your builder to do this work (subject to written consent).
- ■ *Go ahead and build over it* (or within 3m). But before work starts you must enter into a legal 'building-over agreement' with the water company. There will naturally be additional charges to budget for, and until the sewer agreement is completed Building Control cannot formally approve your plans, which could potentially hold things up. A 'building-over agreement' often requires a preliminary CCTV scan inside the sewer by the water authority to check its condition. Any defects should then be repaired prior to building work, and in most cases you should not be charged for this work. Once your extension is completed, a follow-up CCTV scan is carried out to tell if your construction works have damaged the pipes. Any repairs at this stage will be charged to you. The agreement will also go into some detail about the water company's rights of access for future maintenance and will record exactly what building works you're proposing to undertake and the methods you'll employ to protect their pipes.

First-floor extensions/ building over a garage

Extending the house by building over an existing single-storey extension or over an attached garage is a good use of space, but it involves adding large loadings to foundations that may already be barely adequate for their purpose.

The first consideration must be to dig trial holes to expose the foundations to see if they're up to the job. If they need underpinning the cost could well blow the entire project out of the water. Invite your Building Control Officer to take a peak down the trial hole. If it looks promising then they'll probably request engineer's calculations. These will clearly need to take into account the extra loadings to be imposed (which can be as much as three tonnes per metre run of foundation for a first-floor extension). The quality, depth and thickness of the existing foundations must be considered together with the type of subsoil and any risks from nearby trees. Any existing hidden weaknesses in the structure will be amplified by such works, so lintels and beams subject to increased loads should also be checked.

One option may be to construct a lightweight first-floor structure, perhaps of timber frame and cladding, although you'll still need to provide structural calculations. Fortunately, most single-storey extensions built in the last 30 years or so should have been constructed with sufficiently deep foundations to take account of the possible need for extending upwards at a later date. This can be checked with Building Control.

If you've got a garage next to your house then building over it can also raise a number of tricky issues. Garages are usually built to a very basic standard. The walls may only be the width of a single brick, strengthened every couple of metres with brick piers. And that's the posh end of the market. Plenty of garages are little more than asbestos-ridden shacks made of old breeze blocks and rotten timber. Even if your garage has any foundations at all (many are built straight onto a dodgy concrete floor slab) they probably won't be sufficient to take much additional loading. So to extend over the garage you may actually be better off demolishing and starting again.

But there is another way. It may be possible to strengthen the old structure, or bypass it entirely, using steel posts bedded in concrete pad footings to support the new loadings above. The downside is that you'll need to excavate small foundation points in a confined space, possibly through an old concrete slab.

If you want to convert an integral or attached garage to living space, even without structural changes you'll still need Building Regs consent, to ensure things like ventilation and thermal insulation are suitably upgraded. Any new structural openings to create windows etc, as well as glazing, electrics, drainage etc, will need consent, and they'll want proper foundations (or a suitable lintel) to support the new infill walls where the garage door used to be.

So what now?

Before going to the expense of getting detailed plans drawn up and formally submitting your applications to the Council, the next step is to select the optimum method of construction...

4 CONSTRUCTION METHODS AND GREEN TARGETS

To comply with current Building Regulations there are some pretty stiff energy-efficiency targets that your new design will need to meet – even if you're bolting it on to the back of the world's draughtiest hovel.

Photo: Oakwrights.co.uk

Photo: Velfac.co.uk

Photo: Oakwrights.co.uk

Photo: Trombe.co.uk

Above and left: Highly glazed designs may need SAP calculations to offset heat loss.

Above right: Oak frame skeleton.

Right: Building with SIPs panels.

Photo: ClaysLLP.co.uk

When you're building from scratch there are some basic common-sense things you can do to make your extension super-snug and slash your fuel bills. But before coming over all eco-friendly, you first need to make what is probably the most fundamental decision of all – selecting the optimum method of construction.

After all, there's no law that says you have to use precisely the same building techniques and materials as your existing house.

Construction methods

Extension-builders are increasingly being lured away from conventional designs by exotic alternatives. For example, the clean lines of a futuristic pure glass box might be just the thing to spice up an otherwise architecturally uninspiring house. Or in stark contrast, you might fall for the siren charms of a traditional Olde Worlde timber post and beam extension that oozes period character; with centuries of inspiration to draw upon, the beauty of hand-crafted exposed beams can transform even the plainest property. It's even possible to combine these two apparently conflicting styles (see below), merging the best of the past and future.

Of course, these aren't the only options. But without wishing to dampen anyone's creative ardour, it's worth

noting that, as a rule, costs tend to fall as materials increase in popularity. Bear in mind also that picking a non-conventional method of construction means that Building Control will probably require more extensive technical information to demonstrate compliance. And the more extreme your design, the fewer trades and contractors you're likely to encounter who are familiar with the construction techniques. So if your heart is set on building in eco-friendly straw, hempcrete blocks or compacted cob and earth, now might be a good time to switch to 'Plan B'.

At this point it's probably worth reminding ourselves that unless you're planning to build in conventional masonry, custom-made components will probably need to be ordered weeks or even months in advance, based on the precise dimensions shown in your approved drawings.

Below: Traditional oak frame is hard to beat but expensive. Oak can be combined with glass for the best of ancient & modern (right).

Photo: Oakwrights.co.uk

Photo: trombe.co.uk

This obviously means having to plan some way ahead in considerable detail – which is no bad thing. It also means having to cough up a fair old wedge of the cost earlier than you might otherwise need to.

Traditional masonry

Masonry cavity walling is the most popular method of construction in Britain both for new houses and extensions. It's one of the most widely understood and least expensive options. Crucially for extension builders it also lends itself to flexibility, which is ideal for those tricky shapes and sizes you sometimes encounter when trying to meld a new

addition with an existing building. Another big plus is that the materials are readily available. You don't have to place advance orders for exotic prefabricated components with interminable waiting periods.

As everyone knows, masonry walls comprise an outer wall of brick, stone or blockwork tied to a separate inner leaf normally built from aerated 'thermal' blocks, with a gap or cavity in between. External blockwork can be finished with render or clad with timber, tiles, slates or even UPVC. The outer leaf is not predominantly load bearing, but plays an essential role in stabilising the wall by being tied to the inner leaf with stainless steel wall ties.

Because the inner leaf does most of the hard work supporting loadings from roofs and floors, it's essential to select the correct type of blocks. Heavier, dense concrete blocks have a high load-bearing capacity (compressive

strength) but don't score highly for their insulation qualities and are prone to heat loss due to their thermal conductivity. Lightweight aerated 'thermalite'-type blocks, on the other hand, have much better thermal efficiency but are not as strong.

Your designer and engineer will specify the type of block with the necessary strength to support the loadings and simultaneously resist the cold with a decent thermal rating. Their compressive strength is expressed in Newtons per square

millimetre ('N'). A typical minimum strength for inner leaf blockwork walls would be 3.6N, whereas for a three-storey structure – depending on the loadings being supported – the blockwork to the lower storey is likely to be stronger 7.3N (sometimes rounded down to '7N').

To improve the property's thermal efficiency, walls are usually dry-lined with plasterboard internally and the cavities insulated.

A masonry structure gives a house a feeling of solidity, while the density of the blocks provides an element of 'thermal mass', acting as a background heat store at night, and also contributes a higher level of acoustic mass, helping to deaden noise from outside.

From an eco viewpoint, natural clay bricks or blocks are preferable to materials made from concrete, and reclaimed bricks set in lime mortar are even better.

Photo: Oakwrights.co.uk

Timber frame

You don't have to follow the herd and build your extension in bog-standard brick and block. If, instead, you plump for prefabricated timber frame construction, you should end up with a super-cosy building that can be erected quicker on site.

There are two basic types of timber frame: traditional 'primary frame' and modern 'platform frame'. Despite sharing the same generic name, these could hardly be more different. The one that Shakespeare would most readily recognise today is primary frame, with its beefy post-and-beam framework that supports all the loadings. Traditional green oak framing is currently enjoying something of a comeback, and a home extension of this type can provide a massive injection of character to even the blandest properties. But it's modern platform 'stud frame' construction that's now widely used by major house-building firms. Here factory-made stud frame panels arrive on site on the back of a lorry in kit form ready to assemble with considerable savings in labour costs. One thing both methods have in common is the need to pre-order the custom-made components.

STUD FRAME PANELS

There's one thing that's very striking about the way modern timber frame houses look: contrary to what you might expect, they look just the same as any other house. The outer leaf of the cavity wall is normally constructed with the same brick, stone or rendered blockwork as conventional masonry-built properties, so you can immediately banish thoughts of draughty wooden scout huts. The description 'timber frame' refers to the panels that form the inner leaf of the cavity and support the building's main structural loadings. Inside the completed rooms all you will see is a plasterboard lining, just like any other modern dry-lined

conventional wall. Both make the same hollow sound when tapped.

This may be one reason why modern prefabricated timber frame buildings are today very much part of the mainstream, and are by far the most popular method of new house construction in Scandinavia and Scotland. In a cold climate, any system that can offer high performance thermal insulation qualities whilst substantially reducing time spent standing in the freezing rain on site is obviously very welcome. For a typical

Masonry versus modern timber frame

Timber frame walls tend to be a little slimmer than the masonry variety. This is because the cavities can be much narrower and yet still achieve impressive U-values, since the insulation is placed within the timber frame inner leaf rather than the cavity.

Wall comparison

	Typical timber frame wall	*Typical masonry wall*
Outer leaf	100mm brickwork	100mm brickwork
Cavity	50mm cavity	100mm cavity (part insulated)
Inner leaf	140mm insulated studwork +10 mm OSB sheathing and breather membrane	100mm blockwork
Lining	15mm skimmed plasterboard with vapour barrier	25mm dry lining (skimmed plasterboard + air gap)
Total thickness	315mm	325mm

home extension it should be possible for the basic timber frame structure to be erected in a single day, and a fully weather-resistant shell ready in less than a week. Some timber frame suppliers can also supply roof trusses (or special SIPS roof panels).

If this sounds like your cup of tea, you'll need to carefully select a specialist firm to manufacture your home extension kit. Bear in mind that lead-in times can be as long as 6 to 12 weeks, so you need to start comparing quotes and delivery times for the specification you want as early as possible. Your chosen firm will need a copy of the drawings you submitted to Building Control. These plans will then be redrawn by the timber frame supplier, who'll also work out the structural engineer's calculations, which can be passed to Building Control prior to approval.

Open panel

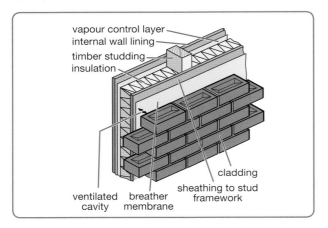

vapour control layer
internal wall lining
timber studding
insulation
cladding
ventilated cavity
breather membrane
sheathing to stud framework

With a standard 'open' system, wall panels are manufactured from a framework of typically 38 x 145mm (or 140mm) vertical softwood studs nailed to top and bottom timber plates. To provide stability and prevent the panels from deforming under wind-load (known as 'racking'), the outer face is lined with large sheets of timber sheathing, typically 18mm OSB (Oriented Strand Board) or 8mm plywood.

The panels are manufactured with the inner face left open, hence the name 'open panel'. The timber is pressure pre-treated with preservative and has a moisture content no higher than 20%. Studs are normally at 600mm centres (sometimes 400mm) and doubled up where loads are supported. The width of individual panels varies up to a maximum of 3.6m – any wider and they become difficult to handle.

To protect the sheathing from moisture, its outer face is clad with a waterproof breather membrane, either factory-fitted or stapled in place later on site. This vapour-permeable layer shields the timber from any rain that may find its way across the cavity, whilst allowing any moisture vapour in the panels to escape.

With some cheaper kits the panels are not pre-insulated, so once the walls and roof are in place the insulation will need to be installed on site by squashing thick chunks of mineral wool between the open studs. From a quality perspective it's better to specify factory-insulated panels.

Once your foundations and sub-walls below DPC level and ground-floor structure are complete, timber sole plates ('baseplates') need to be fixed in position before the big wall panels can be erected. The sole plates are laid over a mortar bed and a DPC, using special anchors or brackets. This is a key stage. It's essential they're fitted accurately, since any faults will be magnified as each storey is erected. The wall panels can then be positioned with their sheathing side facing outwards, and the panels joined together.

Modern timber frame systems are 'platform frames' built one floor at a time. Once complete, each storey forms a 'box' that acts as a platform for the next storey (as opposed to traditional 'balloon framing', where full-height walls of two or more storeys are constructed as complete units,

continuous from the sole plate up to the eaves). So the wall panels for upper storeys are normally only erected once the upper floor deck has been installed.

With the roof on, the building should be weathertight, and you can crack on with some of the internal works such as plumbing and electrics while the outer walls are being built, saving precious time. Window and door frames are fitted on site to factory-prepared openings. The masonry outer skin is then tied to the timber panel inner leaf using special wall ties, leaving a cavity of at least 50mm incorporating special cavity barriers to prevent fire spread. Unlike conventional masonry walls, the cavities must be kept completely clear to allow a through-flow of ventilation.

For obvious reasons, with this type of construction there's a strong emphasis on keeping out any moisture. But the threat of damp doesn't just come from outdoors. Should airborne water vapour from within the atmosphere of the home succeed in penetrating the timber structure, the resulting damp could have devastating effects over time. To tackle this potential problem, large polythene-sheet vapour barriers are stapled to the inner face of the insulated wall frame before it's plasterboarded. This acts as a deterrent to the old enemy - condensation. See Chapter 14.

Photo: Oakwrights.co.uk

Closed panel

In Scandinavia, sophisticated 'closed panel' systems are favoured, with the wall panels delivered already 'fully furnished'. This doesn't mean having your telly and couch already nailed to the floor, but it's not far off – entire wall panels are delivered in virtually finished form with the windows and doors pre-fixed, the insulation already in place, and ducting for services pre-installed. Because considerably more pre-fabrication is carried out in the factory you can save more time and money on site, and the whole thing can be put together in a few hours. With advanced timber frame 'cassette' systems, whole rooms can be craned into position and stacked on top of each other. The advantage is an airtight structure that doesn't leak heat, with site work reduced to a minimum. The main disadvantages are the extra cost and having to commit to detailed decisions about fittings and services at a very early stage of the design.

OAK FRAME

Oak frame extensions suit a wide range of properties, looking just as good on a 1970s house as a period property. The most popular type is the classic 'garden room', a single-storey, highly glazed extension projecting to the rear or side of the property, with a conventional tile or slate roof incorporating a couple of skylights. Oak is a premium building material so construction costs will be significantly

more expensive than for standard brick and block (from around £ 2500/m2). Perhaps the easiest way to picture traditional oak post and beam construction is to think of Stonehenge. A pair of upright posts supporting a horizontal beam laid across the top is one of the simplest yet most durable forms of construction ever devised. Alternatively, for an authentic medieval look you could instead opt for traditional 'A'-shaped cruck frames with their full-height curved timbers.

Oak frame can easily include architectural features like vaulted ceilings, and works well with glass, even incorporating metal tie rods for a hint of modernism. Unlike conventional masonry or timber panel walls the spaces between the load-bearing posts can be left free to accommodate large expanses of windows or wide glazed door openings. But what most homeowners are after when they specify this type of construction is good old-fashioned quality and craftsmanship with plenty of exposed floor joists and rafters.

Green oak

Oak is hard to beat for quality and character. One of its great strengths is its natural resistance to weathering and insect attack so it doesn't need treating with preservatives. Once seasoned it's incredibly hard so to make the frames easier to work they're normally constructed from green oak – fresh, recently felled timber with a high moisture content (around

Photo: Oakwrights.co.uk

Photo: Oakwrights.co.uk

Photo: Oakwrights.co.uk

Photo: Oakwrights.co.uk

20–25%). The wood normally has to be worked within a couple of years of felling, before it gets too hard. But as green oak dries out over time it starts to shrink across the grain, causing the joints in the structure to tighten up. This makes the frame even stronger, but in the process creates minor splits along the frame, known as 'shakes'. Although signs of cracking and movement may look slightly scary, it's simply part of the natural drying process and isn't a structural weakness, just a feature. Harder air-dried oak contains less moisture (and is more expensive) but even this will shrink to some degree. The drying process can also open gaps between the frame and infill panels so they need to be designed to accommodate movement. Given the fact that green oak shrinks there is also the question of how you tie the extension to the house. In practice the extension is treated as a structurally independent stand-alone element sitting next to the host building. This requires an expansion joint to accommodate movement with weather-stripping details in between the two structures to form a seal. Internally, where the frame abuts plasterwork, stop beads should be used to cover the gaps that over time will open up.

Design and planning

Planners are generally pretty keen on oak frame extensions. Even in areas where they insist on traditional facings like local stone, oak can still be an option where it's clad externally. Problems are more likely to arise with Building Control when it comes to meeting heat loss targets particularly if you want large areas of glazing (see page 52). At the design stage one of the key factors to consider is how you want the completed framework to be in-filled. Traditionally the spaces within the framework would be filled with wattle and daub or clay brick and lime. Being relatively flexible, such materials could accept a certain amount of shrinkage movement without cracking. Today however, to achieve greater thermal efficiency and avoid 'cold bridging' to solid walls, Building Control will normally require some form of external cladding. Some might say that leaving the oak timbers exposed only on their inner face rather defeats the point of paying for a beautiful handcrafted hardwood structure which ideally should be left exposed outside and as well as indoors for all to admire. But to meet demanding thermal targets the structural frame normally needs to be encased (or 'encapsulated') within some form of cladding. High-performance SIPS panels *(see opposite page)* are the most commonly used material because of their super-low U-values and ease of achieving airtightness. However oak frames can be encapsulated with almost anything, including brick, stone, render or insulated timber boarding, although

heavier claddings need to be built off their own foundation.

One possible solution may be to exceed insulation targets elsewhere in the home and persuade Building Control to accept a compromise with high-performance rigid insulation boards fitted between the framework. These panels can be given a traditional lime render finish on the outer face, applied over mesh, leaving the timbers exposed both inside and out Elizabethan-style. But modern infill materials still need to be able to accommodate a certain amount of movement, for example by incorporating sliding joints.

Fortunately the frame supplier should be able to assist with the detailed design work as well as providing a structural engineer's certificate for the structure which Building Control will require.

One potential downside is the limited length of span before you need a post – the maximum span is about 6.5 metres unsupported. So if you want a completely open plan interior this may not be the best option. Also, traditional construction methods of this type are less able to be adapted to awkward plots or designs where the planners have dictated unusual window positions – which can make this method of construction unsuitable for some tightly defined home extensions. This is why the design process should always start with the frame, rather than working backwards and trying to make the frame fit your design. For example, the positioning of doors and windows needs to relate to the location of posts, beams and braces. Once you've established the position of all the structural elements, the rest of the design will follow naturally. Where extra-wide spans or complex curved structures are required, modern composite timbers such as Masonite I-beams or Glulam (glue-laminated) beams are sometimes used, but may not be aesthetically compatible.

One thing that's sometimes overlooked with single-storey extensions is that oak frame doesn't suit flat or very

Photo: Oakwrights.co.uk

Photo: Oakappleframes.co.uk

low-pitched roofs and a steeper roof can make it difficult to accommodate existing first-floor windows.

Key stages of construction
Although kits are available for smaller projects like sunrooms, for larger extensions a bespoke design and construction service works best. The main difference with conventional masonry buildings is that most of the work on the frame is done in advance. Being manufactured off-site means the extension can be made watertight on site with a much quicker build time, one of the key benefits of oak frame. The encapsulation system is also prefabricated under factory conditions. This means first employing a builder to do the groundwork and construct the base walls that the frame will sit on. The oak-frame supplier will then build the frame with each component crafted in a workshop in advance. Huge green oak timbers are cut, planed, and shaped to form the building's skeleton. Once complete the supplier will deliver and erect it on site. The frame is usually supported on dwarf sub-walls of conventional brick or stone (historically, plinths of rubble stone were known as 'grumplings'). The load-bearing posts can then be built off a thick timber sole plate over a DPC. Foundations are normally the same as for mainstream construction methods, ie strip or trenchfill, although self-builders sometimes construct pad foundations that support individual posts.

A crane is commonly used to erect both the frame and the encapsulation panels. Traditional mortise-and-tenon joints are secured in the time-honoured way using tightly cleft oak pegs or wooden dowels and hammered wedges. Once erected the visible frame structure is then sand-blasted to remove the marks resulting from the construction process.

Finally, the builders will need to finish the roof work and a specialist glazing company can install the double glazed units.

Clearly this all requires a high degree of co-ordination between the builders on site and the frame constructors. Good communication is essential to ensure there are no lengthy delays between the groundworks being finished and delivery of the oak frame. However to avoid the nightmare scenario where handcrafted frames don't match up with the newly built sub-walls on site, frame constructors generally prefer to delay taking final measurements until the foundations and base walls have been started. But this cautious approach is likely to mean a time lag once the base walls are complete.

Hybrids and durable softwood
The downside to building in oak is, of course, the relatively high price tag – at least a third more than a similar design made from softwood. One way to keep costs within the Earth's orbit is to have the framework hewn from sweet chestnut, a less expensive English hardwood. Kits made from larch or Douglas fir, highly durable softwoods, are a cheaper alternative for those on a slender budget, capturing the traditional charm of exposed timber beams throughout the house without the daunting expense of oak. To save on skilled labour costs, joints are formed using bolted metal plates that are largely hidden.

If you want the best of both worlds, hybrid designs can provide a sensible solution that still retains the charm of oak. Costs are reduced by restricting the oak framing to the more visible parts of the house, using less expensive softwood for concealed stud walls and hidden rafters, and employing sympathetic period-style brick or stone construction elsewhere.

SIPs
There is another form of timber construction that comes from a different planet altogether. Looking a bit like a large wafer ice-cream sandwich 'Structurally Insulated Panels' (SIPs) are formed by bonding a thick core of foam insulation (typically expanded polystyrene or polyurethane) between two rigid sheets of plywood or OSB. This makes them exceptionally strong yet lightweight. Load-bearing main walls can be swiftly constructed simply by slotting a series of panels together. Alternatively, SIPs can be applied as cladding to conventional structures, such as oak frame.

Below: Oak frame 'sun room' extensions are popular.

Photo: Oakappleframes.co.uk

Below: SIPs panel extension clad in brick to appear 'Olde Worlde'.

Photo: ClaysLLP.co.uk

Photo: ClaysLLP.co.uk

SIPs are extremely versatile and can even be used for roof construction. They don't require support from roof trusses and, being relatively light, can be swung into place fairly easily and rapidly secured. The boards can be cut with a saw, so it's easy to carve out window and door openings.

From a structural perspective, SIPs are very efficient, and are increasingly being used as the main load-bearing wall element of self-build kit houses and 'ready-made' extensions. The entire structure can be factory-produced and delivered to site for assembly. A wide variety of external wall claddings can then be fixed to the structural panels.

SIPs also score very highly on thermal insulation values,

Photo: trombe.co.uk

Photo: trombe.co.uk

Photo: ClaysLLP.co.uk

Photo: trombe.co.uk

which means that Building Control may allow you a 'trade-off' with lower insulation or additional glazing elsewhere. They have the added advantage of very swift speed of construction, with

Photo: ClaysLLP.co.uk

consequent savings on site labour, and can usually be delivered reasonably quickly once ordered. The downsides are their fairly high cost and their relative unfamiliarity to many trades on site.

Highly glazed extensions

Exotic designs featuring enormous expanses of glass have long been the exclusive domain of the architectural elite – a dazzling wonder material confined to gleaming hi-tech office blocks, glitzy sheet-glass shop fronts and bespoke house designs. But in recent years the benefits of high-performance glazing technology have trickled down to aspiring home extenders. Today, massive walls of floor-to-ceiling glass are a realistic option for anyone considering adding more space. Even glazed staircases, balconies and internal walls can now realistically be part of the home extender's repertoire. Let the light shine in.

Of course, living in a highly-glazed environment doesn't suit everyone. It probably helps if you have a bit of an exhibitionist streak and can lay your hands on copious supplies of Windowlene.

But what exactly is a 'highly glazed' extension? The simple answer in Building Regs terms is any design where the total area of glazing exceeds about a quarter of its floor area. Depending on how exotic your tastes are, you could go the whole hog and opt for a frameless 'box'. These are constructed entirely of glass supported by a framework of glass beams or 'fins'. Alternatively, they can be held together with clear structural silicon, an extremely strong glue that acts as a glass frame, creating a totally transparent effect. If that sounds a bit too 'goldfish bowl', you could always temper the effect by incorporating materials such as wood, stone, or stainless steel. Or you could compromise by building a conventional masonry extension with some highly glazed walls and super-wide bi-fold doors (see page 56).

Cynics might mutter about glorified conservatories that bake in summer and freeze in winter, but today's contemporary glazed extensions have nothing in common with cheap polycarbonate sheeting that rattles with each gust of wind. Twenty-first century hi-tech glass is incredibly tough and has advanced thermal qualities, which means it can be used in ways that previous generations could only dream of.

Photo: clear-living.co.uk

But this magic material doesn't come cheap. Sophisticated glazing is always going to be more expensive than bricks and mortar (at least £1,300 per square metre

Photo: trombe.co.uk

Photo: trombe.co.uk

Control. But whoever installs your glass masterpiece, it's essential to ensure the materials are covered by an insurance-backed warranty for at least ten years.

PLANNING

You may love the idea of a big glass box adorning the back of your charming period home, but surely the planners will go bananas at the mere suggestion of an uncompromisingly modernist design juxtaposed unsympathetically against a graceful old house? After all, how appropriate can it be to slap huge expanses of ultra-modern glass on to, say, a Georgian townhouse?

Strange as it may sound, Conservation Officers are increasingly warming to pure glass extensions to listed buildings. There's a strong argument that they actually preserve the integrity of the original because you can still see the old building behind the glass. So in many cases this may provide a more appropriate solution than trying to build a half-baked 'pastiche' that clumsily mimics the original masterpiece. It's claimed that pure glass boxes are neutral and anonymous without any character of their own, and even 'disappear' in certain lights. Their transparent nature makes them 'almost invisible' so there's no clash with the existing building.

Whether you buy this line or not, they're certainly less intrusive than the average conservatory. But that doesn't mean planning applications will be a cakewalk. One key technical problem is how to join a glass extension to an existing period building without damaging the original walls. Also, planning applications sometimes encounter resistance on the grounds of 'light pollution'. And there's a pretty good chance that when the neighbours catch sight of your plans they'll choke on their Hobnobs in the headlong rush to lodge objections. But increasingly people are coming round to the

of glazing). Fortunately, such an investment can reap rewards by boosting your home's value. According to estate agents, if two otherwise identical properties are for sale side by side, the one with lots of glass making it look lighter and more spacious will always outsell the other.

You normally need to employ a specialist firm to handle the design, supply and installation of custom-made glazing. They should also provide all the drawings and engineering calculations to ensure a smooth passage through Building

Steel frame extension under construction with extensive high performance glazing. Modern design complements traditional period cottage

Photos: trombe.co.uk

idea of melding the old with the new, so you may not have to endure such a bumpy ride from the planners after all.

Loadings

Glass boxes may look lighter than air, but glazed units can actually weigh over 50kg per square metre – as much as two large bags of cement. So a key design issue with structural glazing is how to support the weight of the glass without making it too obvious with clumsy beams that ruin the clean lines and the light, airy effect. With most pure glazed structures the loadings are taken by glass beams ('fins'). The substantial weight of all the glazing and the supporting beams is transferred to point loadings and down to individual pad or pile foundations. Other designs use a steel frame structure behind the glass units. Alternatively, three-quarter-height glazing can be supported on dwarf cavity brick or stone walls built on conventional strip or trenchfill foundations.

Planners permitted hi-performance 'glass box' extension to Georgian townhouse. But complying with heat-loss targets could be challenging.

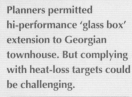

Amazing glazing

One of the main things that people are generally looking for when they opt for a 'pure glass' extension is to maximise the amount of light and space by effectively merging the garden with new accommodation. But the most fundamental question for anyone contemplating a highly-glazed lifestyle is quite simply whether the new building will be practical for day-to-day living. The fact is, introducing acres of glass into a design can raise a number of potential technical problems.

As anyone who's familiar with conservatories can testify, glass doesn't traditionally offer a great deal of protection against hot or cold weather. Conventional double-glazed windows can leak up to six times more heat than walls or roofs. So you obviously can't just install any old glass over such a large area. As well as being highly energy efficient, it needs to have passed UV absorption tests and also to have satisfied a wind deflection test so that it doesn't shatter at the first strong gust. And some more practically-minded homeowners might be put off by the thought of stupendous window-cleaning bills, although it's claimed that 'self-cleaning' glass can nail that particular problem.

A more obvious concern is privacy. If this is an issue blinds can be set within the glazing, which also help deflect sunlight. But there is an intriguing hi-tech alternative. Technology has moved on to such an extent that with the flick of a switch, a minute electric current pulsing through the glass can turn it opaque, providing instant privacy as well as keeping out the sun. 'SmartGlass' panels are manufactured using a lamination process incorporating a virtually invisible liquid crystal 'privacy film' sandwiched between two or more glass sheets. Predictably, such features come with an equally impressive price tag.

Perhaps the biggest challenge

when building a big transparent box is to ensure that the room feels comfortable. To prevent sweltering in the summer, there is solar control glass, and window film that can reflect up to 90% of the sun's heat.

But although its performance has come a long way in recent years, glass is still not as efficient in terms of insulation as the equivalent area of wall. So to make the new space comfortable, a critical part of the design process is to specify systems that heat the space effectively during the cold winter months whilst extracting moist stale air, and provide sufficient cool air in summer. This often means installing a suitable mechanical extraction system.

Photo: timberdevelopments.com

Photo: trombe.co.uk

Can a highly glazed extension comply with Building Regs?

Achieving Building Regs approval for extensions with large amounts of glass can be a bit of a challenge. This is because Document L1B (conservation of fuel and power) limits the amount of glazing to a total of 25% of the floor area plus an extra amount to compensate for any window or door openings that are covered over by your new extension. If you choose to stick within this limitation, your design should sail through the system like a dream. This is because the regulations merely require that your new glazing meets an easily achievable U-value of 1.6W/mK (see 'U-values', below) – and modern glazing can achieve around 1.4W/m2K without even breaking a sweat.

Thermal efficiency can be substantially improved by specifying argon or krypton-filled cavities, where the void within each sealed unit is filled with inert gas which has better thermal properties than air, slowing the transfer of

heat across the cavity. Performance can be further boosted by fitting special 'low E' (low emission) glass, which has a microscopically thin metal oxide coating applied to the inside of the inner pane that allows the sun's rays to pass through but reflects infrared back into the room, thereby retaining warmth. It's also worth specifying silicone-edge seals that protect the edges against damage from sunlight and moisture that, over time, can cause misting, drastically reducing performance.

So with a little appliance of science, U-values can now reach 0.7W/m2K or better (triple glazing). Which is all very impressive, and light years ahead of a standard conservatory. However, the fact is that even high-performance glazing comes nowhere near the efficiency target of 0.28W/m2K that walls now need to meet. So with designs that feature large amounts of glazing, thermal performance is the biggest problem to overcome.

One possible way round the problem is to have your glazed extension reclassified as a 'conservatory' by separating it from the main house with an exterior-quality door between the two. But this obviously rules out the creation of spacious kitchen/diners and suchlike. Also, it can seriously cramp your style in other ways since to qualify as a conservatory there are additional restrictions on heating and you're limited to just a single storey.

Fortunately there's another possible solution that, in most cases, should keep everybody happy. This involves standing back and looking at your home as a whole. By

Photo: trombe.co.uk

Photo: trombe.co.uk

improving thermal performance elsewhere in your house you should be able to justify greater amounts of glass in your new extension. In other words, to be allowed large extra areas of glazing you need to prove that your newly extended house will be no less energy-efficient than the old house is now, prior to being extended. See 'SAP ratings'.

Incidentally, technology may be about to revolutionise this part of the design process – the next big thing is photovoltaic double-glazed units that generate their own electricity. Watch this space.

Walking on glass

Not only do the Building Regs limit the *amount* of glazing you can use, they also determine what type is acceptable. Recognising that glass can be a lethal weapon in the wrong hands, it lays down strict rules for materials and safety.

Most people don't realise just how strong a material glass can be. Modern double-glazed units for glazed extensions can be made from one 12mm and another 6mm sheet of toughened glass, which is many times stronger than regular glass. So strong, in fact, that the panels can be walked on with impunity, which the makers claim makes cleaning them 'very easy'. It's also claimed that a brick thrown at one will bounce off (just don't tell the kids).

Both panes of each double-glazed unit employ toughened safety glass (*ie* meet BS6206 Class A). This is based on ordinary float glass that's heated to about 650°C and then quenched with air jets so that the surfaces are cooled quickly and the inside core more slowly. This means that should a panel get broken, the core releases tensile energy and the glass shatters into small harmless glass particles, just like a car windscreen.

Bi-folding sliding doors

If you want the best of both worlds – conventional construction that won't break the bank, but with some added 'wow factor' – bi-folding doors can be just the thing. Incorporating super-wide folding glass doors can transform even the plainest extension, opening up your garden and 'bringing the outside in'. Rarely a TV property makeover show goes by without someone excitedly ranting

Photo: Best4doors.co.uk

on about 'blending living spaces' and 'removing barriers between inside and outdoor environments'. Cynics might point to the miserable British weather that can sometimes make you glad of a thick wall separating you from the driving wind and rain. Even so, an unobstructed opening that offers a serene vista directly on to your garden can create a feeling of space and light even in our climate.

Whereas conventional patio doors are now considered the height of naffness, and traditional French doors (*ie* 'French windows') are restricted by their narrow openings and thick frames, a set of smooth-gliding, super-wide bi-fold doors can add a feel of contemporary character and 'glass wall ambience' to an otherwise ordinary room, seemingly disappearing when open. Even when closed, the huge expanse of glass allows natural light to flood in and brighten up your morning bowl of Rice Krispies.

Just to make life more confusing, folding doors come disguised in a number of aliases, being variously termed *sliding folding doors*, *bi-fold*, *accordion doors*, *folding windows* or *concertina doors*. Whatever you decide to call them they're perfectly suited to new extensions, because knocking enormously wide openings in existing load-bearing walls isn't usually a good idea. But incorporating them within a new design means they can be installed in

Photo: trombe.co.uk

Photo: timberdevelopments.com

otherwise impossible locations, for example opening up the corner of a room.

Configurations

Unlike old sliding patio doors where half the opening width always remained blocked by one of the doors, bi-folding doors can be configured with up to ten separate panels that can open inward or outward.

Available in heights up to about 2.5 metres (standard heights are 2090mm or 2100mm) and widths typically up to 4.8 metres with up to 6 doors. Or you can have them made-to-measure for custom sizes. Many designs include a single 'traffic door' (or swing door) for normal day-to day access so that you don't have to fully open the whole caboodle every time you want to pop out to the garden. So that the panels can stack tightly up against each other when fully open, special fold-flat handles are fitted. Folding doors are available in a range of materials, namely softwood, hardwood, UPVC or aluminium. Timber doors come factory-finished with stain or paint coatings.

Photo: Foldingdoors_2u.co.uk

Interestingly, their use is not exclusively external – they're sometimes installed as internal room dividers, and are well suited for separating conservatories from the main house, because the Building Regs stipulate that such doors must be of external quality. In fact, as well as meeting the Part L (thermal insulation) requirements they're also ideal for Part M compliance, providing easy access for wheelchair users.

Flush thresholds

The perception of 'bringing the outside in' is largely down to a cunning trick. To make the outdoors feel like it's part of your new room, 'flush thresholds' are commonly specified, at a stroke ditching the rules of sensible design. Conventional wisdom has it that ground levels outdoors should normally be at least 200mm lower than the internal floor (and a minimum of 150mm below the DPC). This provides a barrier to rainwater and damp. But to maintain the illusion of the great outdoors being part of your home, the ground level outside needs to be a continuation of

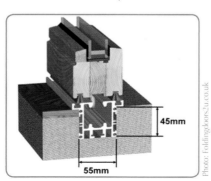

Photo: Foldingdoors2u.co.uk

the internal floor. With a concealed aluminium track system buried in the floor, internal and external floor levels are merged, eliminating the need for a step-over threshold. Hard flooring materials such as slate, concrete and limestone can complete the deception if laid internally and extended out to the patio area.

But excursions from centuries of wise building practice tend to give surveyors panic attacks. Flush thresholds may look great, but they're a potential weak point that might allow damp to seep under the doors. So your design needs to minimise the risk of an unplanned water feature troubling your tootsies as driving rain beats against the giant panes and gushes down, collecting in torrents at the base. For this reason track systems need severe weather-rated seals. The worry is that over a period of years seals of all kinds have a nasty habit of developing tiny cracks that allow ingress of moisture. So in order for surface water to disperse away from the house the outside slab should be set to a slight fall, and, ideally, a discreet drainage channel should be incorporated at the base of the doors, so that storm water can't accumulate at the critical point. Or fit the threshold slightly raised as with conventional doors.

Insulation

As we saw earlier, with any large expanse of glass, thermal performance is crucial. Argon-filled, low-E coated 24mm double-glazing is claimed to achieve U-values as low as 1.1 and to reflect 57% of direct heat from the sun. It should also reduce glare by 35% so that the room doesn't bake on hot summer days, and yet retain warmth during the colder months.

Security

Even unskilled trainee burglars know how easy it is to force open old-style patio doors. Modern bi-folds may look uber-sexy, but they share the same potential weakness – they run on a track. Security risks can be designed out by specifying hardened steel hook bolts. Intermediate panels and traffic doors need to be fitted with internally-operated shoot bolts to both top and bottom. And handles to traffic doors should be fitted with key locks protected by a cylinder guard to prevent tampering from outside.

To further fox potential intruders, the hinges between door panels must be super-tough, and designed so that they're concealed when the doors are closed. Individual door panels should feature an interlocking facility so they can't be forced apart. And as with all modern (non-puttied) windows, glazing beads should be fitted from the inside so that the sealed units can't be removed from the outside.

Photo: Foldingdoors2u.co.uk

Green targets

Phenolic foam cavity insulation 50mm thick combined with thermal blocks comfortably beats U-value heat loss targets.

Energy efficient design is no longer an optional extra. New extensions need to meet increasingly stringent targets – something that has become one of the major hurdles in achieving Building Regs compliance. Part L1B sets thermal performance standards for each element of the building, as well as dictating efficiency criteria for boilers and heating controls etc. So from the outset your design will need to take account of how these green targets are going to be met.

By designing-in the latest energy-saving materials, you can boost the 'miles per gallon' factor of your extension by achieving minimal heat loss and slashing your fuel bills. If you want a building that's warm in winter and pleasantly cool in summer, then adding a touch of 'eco' to your design will pay dividends.

The first step is always to make the most of passive design factors. To prevent heat leaking away, it's important to specify high-performance insulation and glazing as well as ensuring that any air gaps in the structure are sealed. Then, having minimised the building's consumption of energy, you could boost your eco credentials by generating some of your own 'clean' power from renewable sources.

U-values

The main elements of a building's fabric – its walls, roof, windows, doors and floors – have to conform to minimum heat loss figures, known as U-values. These describe the amount of heat leakage (measured in Watts) transmitted through one square metre of a wall or roof etc (taking into account air temperature differences between the inside and outside). The lower the U-value figure the better, as it means less heat can escape and that the material is more energy efficient. So, for example, if the walls have a stated U-value of 0.28W/m2K it means 0.28W is the maximum amount of heat permitted to pass through each square metre of wall. This is one reason why Victorian-type solid brick walls are no longer

How do you work out a U-value?

U-values measure how easy it is for heat to pass through a wall or roof etc (stated in W/m2K). The lower the figure the smaller amount of heat is escaping. But you can't buy a ready-made wall in Wickes so how do you work out its U-value? An exterior wall is basically a giant sandwich made up of blocks, bricks, insulation and plasterboard etc. Similarly roofs and floors comprise layers of different materials that separate you in your home from the weather outdoors. So to figure out how good a wall or roof etc is at stopping heat leaking through it you need to look at the performance of each individual component and add them all together.

K-values

When you buy materials like concrete blocks, to see how 'thermally efficient' they are you need to look at their stated 'thermal value' (known as 'K-value' or Lambda). It might say something like 0.24W/mK. That tells you how well the material conducts heat (thermal conductivity), in other words how easily heat passes through it. Of course you don't want much heat to pass through your walls so the lower this figure is the better (just like U-values). If all the layers in your wall have super low K-values then the total (U-value) for the whole wall will also be nice and low.

R-values

Just to make life more confusing there's another way of judging the performance of materials for heat loss. Each element of a wall also has an R- value (stated in W/m2K). The 'R' stands for 'Resistance' because it's a measure of the 'thermal resistance' of a material to the transfer of heat across it. In this case the higher the figure the more resistant it is to heat loss, so the higher the better.

In sum, to arrive at a U-value you need to consider all the components, and calculate the values of the plasterboard, skim plaster, inner leaf blockwork, cavity insulation, external leaf brick or block, plus any cladding or render etc. The good news is there are online calculations that can do this for you. See website.

Photo: Penycoed-Warmcell

Photo: Velfac.co.uk

Far left: Cellulose fibre insulation is ideal for timber frame

Left: Triple glazing can achieve U-values as low as 0.7Wm2/k

Right: Insulated inner leaf on modern timber frame wall

Typical U-values of British homes

U-values measure the amount of energy in Watts transmitted through one square metre of the element for every degree Kelvin/Centigrade difference between the internal and external air temperature.

Example: If a wall has a U-value of $1.6W/m^2K$ (typical 1930s cavity wall), the heat loss through the wall (surface area say $100m^2$) on a cold winter's day ($20°C$ difference between inside and outside temperature) could be $100 \times 1.6 \times 20 = 3,200W$. If the wall is well insulated, with a U-value of only 0.30, the heat loss will be a lot less at 600W.

Typical U-values for walls

Victorian solid brick wall (229mm thick)
$2.1W/m^2K$

1930s cavity wall, both leaves 100mm brick + 50mm cavity
$1.6W/m^2K$

1970s cavity wall, brick and lightweight block, both 100mm + 70mm cavity
$1.0W/m^2K$

1990s cavity wall, 100mm brick outer leaf, 50mm cavity batts, 100mm aerated block inner leaf
$0.45W/m^2K$

2018 cavity wall, 330mm thick comprising 100mm brick outer leaf, 100mm part insulated cavity and 100mm aerated block inner leaf, plus dry-lined; insulated plasterboard will achieve lower U-values
$0.25W/m^2K$

acceptable. Whereas modern cavity walls should be able to achieve a respectably low figure of around 0.25 without too much trouble, traditional solid walls may be hard pushed to go below 1.25 even when fully lined with insulation.

U-value requirements for extensions (*W/m2K*)
(Building Regs Part L1B)

Element	England	Wales	Scotland
Walls	0.28	0.21	0.17
Pitched roof			
standard ceilings	0.16	0.15	0.11
sloping rafter ceilings	0.18	0.15	0.13
Flat roof	0.18	0.15	0.13
Floors	0.22	0.11	0.15
Doors	1.8	1.8	1.6
Windows and roof lights	1.6 or WER band C		

SAP ratings

A SAP (Standard Assessment Procedure) estimates the energy efficiency of a whole building, rather than just elements like the walls or roof, as with U-values. SAP calculates a property's running costs (for space heating and hot water) per square metre of floor area. It also provides an easy way to compare the environmental impact (carbon footprint) of buildings, a bit like fuel consumption figures for cars. The score is expressed on a scale of 1 to 100 – the higher the number, the lower your energy consumption, with 100 representing the holy grail of zero energy cost. If you want to qualify as an environmental yob your house needs only achieve a disappointing rating of 50 or less (apparently the average British home scores a lowly 51).

SAPs and highly glazed extensions

Unlike building a new house, there's no obligation for home extensions to have a SAP assessment, either at the design stage or upon completion of the build. But the reason SAP ratings can be of interest for some more challenging designs is that they can provide a handy 'way around the rules', allowing a fair amount of freedom with individual elements of your design. Rather than sticking religiously to meeting U-values for every element of the building, a SAP may allow you to 'trade off' heat loss in one element like windows with another like floors or roofs. Or you may be able to use less insulation in one part of the building in exchange for fitting a more fuel-efficient boiler. So if your architect

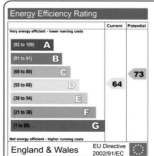

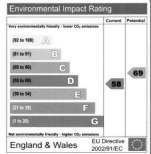

is determined to install giant, snazzy glass panels the size of a runway, it may be OK as long as everywhere else is super thermally-efficient, and meets the overall target for the whole building.

Photo: Velfac.co.uk

There are 3 ways to demonstrate compliance for extensions:

1 *Meeting U-values*

If all the main elements of your extension meet their individual target U-values, congratulations, your design has already complied. This means, for example, that the U-value of your windows should not exceed 1.6W/m2K (or meet WER energy rating band C), doors 1.8W/m2K, and the U-value for walls should be no higher than 0.28W/m2K. However, there is one caveat – this only works if your extension is relatively parsimonious when it comes to glazing.

As we saw earlier, there's a cap on the amount of glazing you're normally allowed, equivalent to no more than 25% of the floor area of the proposed extension plus a bit more to compensate for the area of any windows or doors which, as a result of the extension works, no longer exist or are now covered over. The majority of extensions should easily fall well within this limit. If, however, your total glazing requirements (ie windows, roof lights and glazed doors) exceeds this, then you'll need to try a more sophisticated approach.

2 *Area weighted U-value calculation*

If the amount of glazing in your extension exceeds the '25% floor area plus a bit more' rule, but not by very much, there's another way you can demonstrate compliance. With this method, by upping the insulation in one part of your extension, such as the walls, you can 'trade it' to justify weaker performance in another component, such as the roof or windows. This involves calculating the average or 'area weighted' U-values of all of the elements in the extension.

Start by working out what the average U-value would be for your extension assuming it actually complied

Photo: Buildstore.co.uk

Ten tips for greening your design

- Fully insulate your whole house and build thicker extension walls.
- Put more windows on the south-facing side than north-facing, to get free heat from the sun.
- Elsewhere, don't use too much glass, putting it mainly where it will reduce the need for electric light.
- Use materials made from recycled waste, such as eco-concrete, eco-blocks, and softwood 'I-beams'.
- Use renewable materials, such as softwood rather than hardwood.
- Replace your boiler with an 'A'-rated energy-efficient model.
- Fit low-energy lighting throughout.
- Fit intelligent controls for heating, lighting, and appliances.
- Consider rainwater harvesting and grey water recycling.
- Generate your own energy with solar panels, PV cells, heat pump systems or wind turbines.

Photo: Helifix.com

with the 25% glazing rule, as in option 1 above (with all the individual U-value targets met). You then simply need to show that the average U-value figure for your actual extension, with the additional glazing, is no worse than the first figure. As long as each individual element meets a (much less demanding) *minimum* U-value figure, this can be a very handy 'get out of jail free' card for smaller extensions with a glazed area no more than about 30% of their floor area.

3 *Whole house 'full SAP' calculation*

If your extension shamelessly boasts acres of glazing, the only way to make it comply is to take into account the performance of the whole house, *including* the new extension. The general idea is that by upgrading the main house and making it super energy-efficient, you should be able to offset these improvements against a less efficient extension.

This will require two separate 'whole house' SAP calculations, typically setting you back around £300. The first one calculates the performance of your newly extended house on the assumption that the new extension actually complied with the 25% glazing rule, meeting all the various U-value targets, as described above. The second calculation looks at the house assuming it's been upgraded with lots of additional insulation etc and extended in the way you're actually proposing. To pass, you have to show that the CO2 emission rate figure for the extension you want to build, combined

Photo: Charnwood Stoves

with the sweetener of improvements to your existing house, is no greater than if you built a compliant 'goody two shoes' extension but didn't bother to upgrade the main house.

Obviously this all has to be calculated at the design stage before you've actually built anything, and therefore needs to be based on a full set of plans for the existing house and extension, plus information you've provided on heating systems, insulation, glazing, ventilation etc. But this method offers considerable flexibility when it comes to complying with Part L.

Only authorised Energy Assessors can carry out SAP calculations (see Rightsurvey.co.uk). Probably the simplest course of action is to first approach your Local Authority Building Control Department. A SAP assessor can advise how your existing house could be modified to make the figures add up and pass. For example, you could upgrade your loft insulation, install cavity wall insulation, fit high performance double glazing or change an old boiler to an efficient 'A'-rated modern condensing type. A more efficient heating system with new radiators and controls (timer, programmer and thermostatic valves) can make a big difference. Or you might be able to boost your score by adding a secondary heating source such as a wood-burning stove. All of which should have the additional benefit of making your home a more comfortable environment.

However, there is a catch. By definition, this solution provides more impressive results in older dwellings with lower standards of insulation and decrepit heating systems. Newer properties are harder to upgrade for the simple reason that they're already pretty efficient, so you may have

Solar PV is more widely installed than solar hot water.

Photo: SolarCentury.co.uk

Photo: SolarCentury.co.uk

Solar PV roof tiles.

to go the extra mile and consider adding renewable energy sources such as solar panels.

Green energy

When you're about to embark on a major home improvement project, it might be worth investing a little extra to generate your own renewable energy and achieve super-low running costs. The intelligent way to approach this is to design your extension to exploit free energy wherever possible. This means (if possible) putting more windows on the south-facing side (ie SE to SW) to get free heat from the sun or 'passive solar gain'. Of course, with home extensions your options may be fairly limited because the position of the windows is largely dictated by the orientation of the existing house and planning considerations. But even a few strategically placed roof windows or light tubes can make a difference.

It also makes sense to minimise heat leakage throughout your home by upgrading the insulation in your existing house (see Haynes Home Insulation Manual). Only then will it be worth considering the option of generating your own energy with a view to slashing future power bills and securing a degree of energy independence. You may even be able to generate an income and make profit selling some power back to the grid.

Renewables

The best known 'micro-generation systems' are solar panels, heat pumps, biomass boilers and wind turbines. Each method has its pros and cons but since you've already forked out for roofing work and scaffold hire etc part of the installation cost for some of these will already have been paid for.

However, the deciding factor usually comes down to hard cash. Government subsidies in the form of 'Feed In Tariffs' (FiTs) and 'Renewable Heat Incentives' (RHI) have made generating your own electricity considerably more attractive by paying homeowners a guaranteed tax-free income on top of savings on energy bills. This means payback periods have been significantly reduced. Bear in mind, though, that to qualify for any available grant assistance the system you've selected has to be within a recognised scheme and must be fitted by an approved installer who is registered with that scheme.

Solar PV electricity

Photovoltaic (PV) panels make electricity from light, as opposed to solar water-heating panels that absorb heat from the sun (see below). PV panels incorporating silicon cells are basically the same technology that's used to power pocket calculators and remote traffic signs. Silicon mono-crystalline cells are the most efficient (and expensive) type of mass-produced cells. Each panel is made up of several modules of tiny cells, and several panels grouped together are known as an array.

Solar PV roof tiles.

Solar hot water vacuum tubes,

PV panels silently convert sunlight to DC electricity, which then needs to be converted to 240V AC. This requires a small 'inverter' box, which is the only item that takes up any internal space. A cable connects the panels to the inverter and the system is connected to the mains. PV panels don't require direct sunlight and are still effective even on cloudy days, but overshadowing from chimneys or trees etc can significantly reduce power output. Panels are normally mounted on south-facing roofs, although any roof facing south-east to south-west should perform satisfactorily, ideally at a slope between 30° and 40°. The support rails should be of aluminium rather than cheaper galvanised steel which can be prone to rust. Also, panels shouldn't be positioned too close to the eaves at the bottom of the roof slopes or rainwater will overshoot, soaking passers-by! Alternatively they can be mounted on flat roofs angled on brackets.

Solar PV is the most common form of renewable energy, thanks largely to generous Feed in Tariffs (FiTs). Although these subsidies are now much reduced, installation costs are also considerably lower. A system of around 4kW generation typically comprising between 12 to 20 panels costs around £7k for on-roof panels. PV cells are also available in the form of roof tiles or slates that can be laid flush and fully integrated into the roof coverings. Although dearer they look more pleasing, but the variety of solar tiles currently available is fairly limited. Payback periods are typically around 10 to 12 years after which you should benefit from another decade or so of free energy. You should get small savings on your electricity bills and from any unused energy sold back to the National Grid. Because there are no working parts these are low-maintenance installations that should last 20 to 30 years, requiring periodic checking of the cleanliness of panels. However inverters may need replacing after a decade or so, costing around £800 to replace.

Output from PV panels varies significantly over the course of the day, peaking at around 1:00pm if the sun is out. Output is measured in kWp – kilowatts produced at peak. A 1kWp system can produce at least 750kWh of electricity per year, about 20% of average (non-heating) consumption for a typical household.

The obvious drawback with PV panels is that they generate most electricity during the day, when demand is low, the opposite of what's required. They will not give you all the energy you need in your home without the use of expensive banks of heavy-duty batteries. So PV systems need to be connected to the grid so power can be supplied when the panels aren't working, and surplus electricity can be sold back to the supplier. This requires two-way metering, which adds to the cost.

Solar water-heating (SWH)

Solar water-heating systems collect heat from the sun to generate hot water. They are sometimes referred to as 'Solar Thermal' (ST) or 'Solar Hot Water' (SHW). These systems basically comprise a 'solar collector' (usually on the roof) connected to a special hot water cylinder incorporating an extra coil (a 'high recovery solar coil') which acts as a 'transfer unit'. There is also a pump and controller that manages the flow through the panel and accommodates heat expansion. The heat generated in the roof panel and transferred to the hot water cylinder by means of a mix of water and antifreeze pumped through the panel in a closed loop with the coil in the bottom of the hot water cylinder where it is stored.

There are two main types of collector – flat plates or glass vacuum tubes. Tubes are slightly more efficient than flat panels and although dearer can be installed by one fitter with savings in labour. Some can be mounted on flat roofs or can even work well at low level against a wall or in the garden.

The best-performing flat plates have double-glazed plate collectors with a microscopic film applied to the collector plate to increase the amount of solar radiation absorbed. In terms of size, panels or tubes typically comprise an area of around 2 sq metres each and for an average family house will need to total at least 4 sq metres.

Even in overcast Britain, solar water heaters work remarkably well. Even on cloudy days they can collect sufficient radiation to generate a useful amount of heat. A shadow falling on a solar hot-water panel is much less critical to performance than it is on an array of PV cells (see below). On warm days enough energy is collected to heat water to normal bath temperatures, while on dull days they can still heat the water to lukewarm temperature (heating water from cold to lukewarm uses considerably more energy than from lukewarm to hot). They therefore need to be used in conjunction with a boiler or some other heat source as a backup.

Solar hot-water systems need frost protection, which can either be in the form of a direct system with a frost-resistant

Photo: Solarwall.co.uk

Air source heat pump.

collector and plastic pipework, or, more usually, an indirect system with a separate water circuit from the collector to the hot-water cylinder, which has antifreeze in it.

To work effectively the collectors can face anywhere between south-east and south-west, at a tilt of between 10° and 60°. This should still achieve 90% of optimum performance (the optimum tilt is 32°, facing slightly west of due south).

Solar panels can typically supply up to half your hot-water requirements, but most aren't compatible with conventional radiator central heating. They're better suited to underfloor heating systems, since these run at lower temperatures. Total cost of installation is likely to be upwards of £5,000 including a new twin coil hot water cylinder.

Alternatively, if you already have solar PV installed it's worth considering fitting a 'solar diverter'. These are much cheaper (costing around £500 fitted) and work by re-directing the excess electricity your panels generate direct to your existing immersion heater heating up your hot water.

Heat pumps

Heat pumps are the second most popular renewable energy product after PV solar and subsidies have recently been raised for both types - Air Source and Ground Source. Operating like a fridge in reverse they use electricity to move heat from the air or ground and transfer it into useable heat in your home. These units physically replace the boiler, but as they deliver lower temperatures than boilers they only make sense in well insulated airtight homes and are better suited to underfloor heating systems (UFH) than conventional radiator systems.

Ground source heat pumps (GSHP) extract heat from the ground by circulating fluid through pipes buried in trenches in the garden (or vertical boreholes). Heat from the ground is absorbed into fluid in the pipes which passes through a heat exchanger into the heat pump. The ground stays at a fairly constant temperature under the surface, so the heat pump can be used throughout the year. But you need a sizeable garden. For example a 14kW heat pump needs around 700m^2 of unshaded land and the pipes need to be kept 5 metres away from boundaries which can limit their practicality in most urban extensions. Also some soil types hold more heat than others – e.g. clay is better than sand. Installation can be relatively expensive, typically around £10,000 to £18,000.

Air source heat pumps (ASHP) are easier to install as they don't need any trenches or drilling, but they are often less efficient than GSHP. They work by absorbing heat from the outside air to heat UFH (or smaller numbers of radiators) and can absorb warmth from the outdoor air even when the temperature is as low as -15° C. They take the form of a large

'condenser unit' similar to an air conditioning box, usually installed externally on side or back walls with plenty of space around them to get a good flow of air. The downside is they can look a little bulky and some units can be a bit noisy. Installation costs are around £7,000 to £11,000.

Biomass

Conventional woodburning stoves (see chapter 12) heat the room they're in, whereas wood-fuelled biomass stoves with back boilers additionally provide hot water (for up to 9 radiators) and sometimes for bathrooms too (typically 5kW to 20kW of water heating plus space heating). Biomass stoves normally burn either wood pellets or logs although RHI subsidies only apply to pellet boilers. Most biomass pellet stoves feed themselves semi-automatically loaded from the top with an augur and integral hopper system capable of storing 2 days worth of fuel, cutting out much of the hard labour involved in stoking old-fashioned boilers.

Photo: Charnwood Stoves

Biomass boiler stoves can be used for room heating and hot water.

Pellet stoves with back boilers are larger than ordinary woodburning stoves and being quite tall (around 1600mm) are often located in garages or outside stores. A HETAS registered installer can advise on the best way to plumb a boiler stove into your existing heating system and hot water cylinder. Note that emissions are controlled in many urban areas where units must be certified as being clean burning. It's also best to specify models with a direct air intake from outside or Building Control may require you to cut ventilation holes in the walls. Installation costs can be fairly high (typically £6k to £12k) although some of the cost for flue or fireplace construction may already be included in your budget.

Wind turbines

These are the least suitable renewable for most home extensions, due to their high cost, complexity, need for maintenance and recent reductions in subsidies. Even sites with sufficient wind can suffer from obstructions like trees and buildings. On top of that there are limitations on where they can be physically sited, and they tend to attract planning objections due to visual prominence, noise and 'flicker' (caused by blades passing in front of the sun making sunlight).

5 DESIGNING IT AND SUBMITTING YOUR APPLICATIONS

By now you probably already have a pretty good idea of how you'd like your new home extension to look. So the next step, designing it in detail, should be one of the most enjoyable parts of the process. This is where you begin to see your ideas 'come alive'. However this is the stage where you'll need to make a real commitment to the project, in terms of both time and money. Getting plans professionally drawn up is not cheap, but careful design at this point in time can save a lot of unnecessary expense later.

NORTH - EAST ELEVATION

SOUTH -WEST ELEVATION

Drawing: Colin K. Dale FRICS

The Design

Design details

So far, we've decided on most of the big stuff – the size, shape and overall style of the new building. But there are some key details that must first be considered before finally signing off the design. One of the most important considerations at this stage is precisely how the new extension will join onto the existing house.

Roof detailing

The biggest weak point on extension roofs is where they join up with the main house. Single-storey extensions often have simple flat roofs, but they rarely look good and the coverings tend to have a short life. So for a single-storey addition, a simple lean-to (monopitched) roof may be a better option, where space permits. Visually prominent two storey or higher extensions normally need a pitched roof, which means a number of design features can be explored, such as whether to opt for triangular gable ends or a sloping hipped roof.

Let there be light

Many otherwise brilliant designs have never left the drawing board because the extension would have made an existing room too dark. So it's important to consider which windows and doors will be covered up by the extension. The Building Regs are more concerned with ventilation than light, so the risk of inadvertently making your existing rooms unbearably gloomy may actually not be noticed until after the build is complete.

As noted in the previous chapter, adding a new window or skylight in the roof can sometimes compensate for any resulting darkness, but this is not always practical. One solution may be to fit a discreet 'light tube'. As the name suggests, these are metal tubes through which daylight from the roof surface is channelled. These are typically positioned within the loft space connected to the ceiling of the room or landing below, utilising a prism and reflector arrangement

Left: Bright new extension makes existing dining room dark (also lower step doesn't meet Building Regs!).

Right: Light tubes - simple but effective

to bring daylight into areas where it would otherwise be difficult to admit natural light. Best of all, they still work on cloudy days and have no maintenance requirements.

A more exciting solution for getting plenty of light into the existing rooms as well as the extended space is to incorporate a 'glazed link' between the original house and the extension. Even where the planners insist on materials matching an existing period property they may accept a contemporary twist because the glass connection makes the new extension appear separate, despite being physically attached, thereby maintaining the profile of the old building.

Downpipes

Wouldn't you know it – there's a rainwater downpipe exactly in the place you want to build. The reality for most extensions is that you're probably going to have to rearrange the guttering to the main house anyway, so this shouldn't be a major obstacle. But it will probably mean having to install at least one new downpipe, and its position will need careful consideration.

New downpipes should disperse into an underground rainwater system rather than into an overflowing water butt or illegally connected to the foul drains (waste water from WCs, kitchens, bathrooms etc must be discharged separately from rainwater).

This will normally mean budgeting for excavation and laying new pipework out to a soakaway in the garden via a new gulley. Downpipes obviously need to be located away from window and door openings and not too close to boiler flues (a 100mm gap is usually sufficient).

Glass roof solves light problem

Corridors

Adding more rooms means considering how each room should be accessed internally. This is not always as easy as it sounds and can be more of a challenge when extending bungalows. If you're not careful this can result in long, dark corridors and passageways.

Windows

One of the chief design issues that will determine whether the final product looks right is the position of the windows. Visually it's important to align window openings at their tops, not at the sills. It just looks better that way! Also, it's easy to overlook the impact that windows can have internally – for example, the height of the sills above floor level can clash with fittings in kitchens and bathrooms. Secure burglar-proof lockable windows are fine, but make sure you're still able to escape quickly in the event of a fire. This applies to windows in all habitable rooms upstairs. Fire escape 'egress windows' should be positioned no higher than 1100mm above floor level and have a clear opening width of at least 450mm. To achieve this most standard windows can be adapted simply by replacing scissor hinges that don't open wide enough with 'egress hinges'. But for 3 storey or higher (ie floors more than 4.5m above outside ground) you also need a protected stairway leading down to an external door. On the ground floor be wary of inadvertently creating inner rooms – a room off a room when extending. If you can't get out to the hall, stairs or external door without walking through another room then it needs an escape window (but some inner rooms are acceptable such as kitchens, utilities and bathrooms).

Dimensions

It's good practice to design the lengths of your main walls spanning between corners and openings for windows and doors so they correspond to the dimensions of whole bricks and blocks. This avoids having to cut bricks which can look unsightly in finished walls, smoothing the path to a quicker build. The same thinking can be applied to wall heights; the most common ceiling height in modern housing is 2400mm which happens to be exactly 32 brick courses at 75mm (65mm + mortar joint). Higher ceilings can be designed in jumps of 75mm. Standard window and door frames are designed to exactly match the standard brick bond. The normal height of a door opening is 2100mm (28 courses) and the width of an entrance door frame is 910mm (4 bricks wide + 1 joint). Rather like building in Lego!

Neighbours

Your work may fully comply with the Building Regs, but if your extension obstructs next door's extractor fans, air vents or boiler flue, causing them to malfunction, the neighbours won't be too amused. Also, if you can avoid covering any existing external gas and electric meter boxes it could save a small fortune having them relocated (although indoor meters are common in older properties and new 'smart meters' can be read remotely).

The Building Regs are very much concerned with preventing fire jumping from one building to another. So when you're extending close to a boundary (within 6 metres) they restrict the use of materials that aren't fire-resistant. To prevent the spread of external fire, you need to avoid combustible stuff like plastic windows and gutters, timber cladding, or external wall insulation. Wall finishes and materials within 1 metre of the boundary must be 'Class 0' rated (of 'limited combustibility'), so materials like concrete, slate, fibre-cement boards, and clay hanging tiles are commonly used in boundary situations. Timber can be treated to achieve Class 0. Roofs and rooflights don't need any special fire resistance.

DIY (Drawing It Yourself)

If you're prepared to devote the time, and you're not too bad at drawing, this is one area where significant savings can be made. Even if you came bottom of the class at school for artistic merit don't despair. You may be blessed with IT skills, in which case the CAD software available for drawing simple plans may be of interest. See website for downloads.

Don't be intimidated by the thought that all professional designers' drawings are masterpieces – they aren't. So it may well be worth having a go at producing the planning application drawings yourself. Naturally there are limits to how far you can go first time around and there is a large chasm of knowledge between doing your own planning sketches and getting all the construction details right for your Building Regulations application. Most DIY designers employ an experienced pro at some stage, at least to make sure they satisfy the more complex specification details for Building Control.

But whether you choose to pay a professional designer or go the DIY route, there are some key quality points to check in the finished plans. A badly drawn set of plans will not only be confusing and misleading for the builders on site, but it won't present your proposals in the best possible light, crucially failing to 'sell' your ideas to the planners.

What to look for in a decent set of drawings

The right scale: Unlike a sketch, scale drawings don't use perspective, although submitting an additional sketch or photo-mock-up of the finished building can help demonstrate to cynical planners just how attractive it will look. (See 'Submitting your applications' on page 71.)

Clarity: Accompanying text and notes should be easy to read, so avoid the use of fancy handwriting or bizarre fonts. The design details should be clear and the ground levels should look realistic.

Separate drawings are needed for each of the required elevations, floor plans, cross-sections etc. The use of some artistic flair on the 'proposed elevation' drawings,

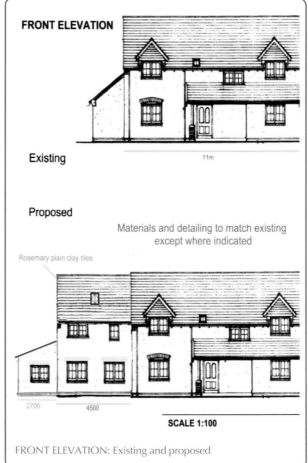

FRONT ELEVATION: Existing and proposed

Drawing: Colin K. Dale FRICS

showing how it will look when built, can help promote the design.

Plenty of measurements, usually in millimetres, marking the dimensions of external walls and the positions of doors and window openings.

Sufficient detail: In particular, the drawings for Building Regs need a considerable amount of text explaining how the design will comply with the regulations in key areas. This may be explained in detail on the drawings, perhaps in addition to a separate 'specification' document. If you just write something lazy like 'work to comply with Building Regulations' it may well get sent back for clarification. Fortunately you can now download detailed wording and ready made construction diagrams to incorporate in your drawings for Building Control - see website.

Finally, there's the question of the physical size of the plans. Traditionally they've been produced on whopping great folded A1 or A0-sized sheets. But in practical terms, A2 may be more convenient and easier to refer to. On site, smaller A3 copies can be pinned up on walls and are more easily photocopied and distributed to different trades.

Photo: Oakwrights.co.uk

Finding a designer

Choosing a designer to draw up your plans doesn't necessarily mean having to appoint an architect. Anyone with a good reputation for designing residential extensions could be considered. That said, most people tend to select architects (qualification RIBA) or chartered surveyors (MRICS or FRICS) who specialise in architectural services. It's always a good idea to talk through your ideas with a professional right at the very start.

What matters most is finding someone with the right experience and knowledge to do a good job. So a warmly recommended local person with plenty of experience of similar projects but with no formal qualifications would normally be a better choice than an eminent firm of architects renowned for their groundbreaking retail mega-complexes in Abu Dhabi. A list of local architects and designers may be available from the Council (but they're not allowed to make recommendations).

Ideally choose someone who is already familiar with your Council's planning policies and how to overcome technical queries. A 'free consultation' visit should normally be offered to discuss your ideas. Note that designers have a legal responsibility for their designs to minimise safety risks on site associated with building work (See CDM regulations p 96). Some may also be able to fulfil the Project Manager role, if required. Although local recommendations are a good start, you'll also want to see examples of previous work, drawings and completed buildings, and check they have the necessary indemnity insurance. It's surprising how much the style of drawings can vary between different designers, so compare several before confirming the appointment.

Architects traditionally work on a fee basis, charging around 3% of the contract value to prepare plans and another 3% or so for working drawings and tendering. If you want project management and an 'architect's certificate' upon completion, you'll need to budget at least another 3%. But these days many are happy to submit quotations instead.

What does the price include?

It's important to be clear about the terms of engagement and to be sure exactly what you're getting for your money. Agree a fixed fee with your designer only once the following points have been clarified:

■ Does the price include all drawings needed to apply for planning permission and separate detailed construction drawings for Building Regulations plans approval?
■ Are all fees included? Legally it's the homeowner who's responsible for paying the fees for the Planning and Building Regs applications, so they may not be included in the price. The designer should be able to confirm how much the fees will be (alternatively check on your Local Council website). Don't forget any additional fees that may arise, such as structural engineer's calculations or for building over a sewer.

■ Are minor amendments included? The price should always include the need for small revisions to the plans required by the Council. If amendments are due to the designer omitting information on the original drawings, the cost of revisions shouldn't be down to you. Small amendments shouldn't be too difficult as plans are normally drawn on a computer. If a total 're-draw' is required because the plans were fundamentally unacceptable to the Council, an experienced local designer should have detected the warning signs early on and pointed out the likely risk to the client. If you accepted this risk, they may now be justified in charging extra.

Always be sure to get fresh copies of any amended plans. To avoid later confusion, the first drawings are usually numbered version 'A' and each revised version 'B', then 'C', etc. To be on the safe side it's best to mark all old plans very clearly as 'superseded'.

■ Fees for structural engineers' calculations should normally be included for Building Regs drawings. If not, the designer should at least be able to provide a rough idea of the likely cost.

It is with the structural engineers that the buck finally stops, since everyone else is relying on their calculations

Is the fee for structural engineers calculations included?

to prove that the finished building is going to stand up soberly and not wobble or collapse. Architects may love giant expanses of glass, and doors in weird places, but engineers tend to regard window and door openings as annoying interruptions that weaken the walls.

At the design stage it may help to bear in mind some structural facts of life. Your main walls will not only need to support vertical loadings, such as those from the rest of the building (the roof and upstairs floors etc) as well as from the occupants, but they also have to be strong enough to withstand extreme sideways forces and powerful suction from storms or freak winds. The designer has to assume the worst possible combination of such circumstances – a Sumo wrestlers' convention upstairs whilst a Force Ten gale rages outside.

Walls can only be safely built to a certain length between main supports (such as the corners of a house). Lots of openings for windows and doors can only reduce the strength of the structure, and must normally be designed no closer than 665mm from the outside corner of the wall to the inside edge of the opening.

■ Is project management included? Project management is a major task involving frequent site inspections, approving stage payments, and ultimately signing any necessary certificate upon completion. If you intend to employ your designer to oversee the whole project on site through to completion, how much will it cost and what will it include? If you drew your own plans, you may wish to project manage it yourself or appoint a professional (although architects may not be too keen on implementing someone else's design).

Design and Build

An alternative but fairly unusual option is to go down the 'Design and Build' route. This is an all-in-one package deal where specialist building contractors can prepare the drawings in-house to your requirements, obtain all the necessary Local Authority consents, and then build the extension. The problem is, you need to be extremely sure that the contractor has the appropriate experience and isn't just being over-confident. Builders sometimes regard the 'deskwork' part of the job as a bit of a doddle, perhaps not fully appreciating the sometimes confusing array of formalities and rigorous regulations you need to satisfy before getting anywhere near starting on site. You'll also need to trust the builders implicitly since the designer won't be 'on your side' if things go wrong. In such cases good communication about exactly what you want is paramount from the outset, as is a watertight legal contract.

Builders' drawings

For the more complex parts of the work (such as where the new extension meets the main house, and for any new service connections, structural alterations or stairs) the builders should be provided with additional large-scale

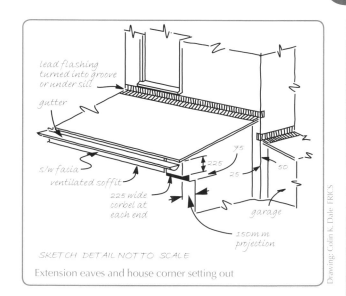

lead flashing turned into groove or under sill

gutter

s/w facia ventilated soffit

225 wide corbel at each end

75
225
25
50

garage

150mm projection

SKETCH DETAIL NOT TO SCALE

Extension eaves and house corner setting out

Drawing: Colin K. Dale FRICS

drawings that clearly explain the details. This will help ensure it all gets built right first time. If you don't, the builders will always 'know better' and will do it their way – which may be fine with an experienced contractor, but could be a disaster if they're unaware of some important element at a later stage that depends on getting this part exactly right. Without guidance, they may get hacked off and be tempted to do it cheaply and badly.

As you will see, the drawings will later form part of your legal contract with the builders, so they need to be 100 per cent accurate.

At this stage the contractors don't need to know the precise location of every switch, power point and radiator in order to quote for the job. But don't neglect this information for too long. Soon after work starts on site you'll need to provide modified drawings showing exactly where the various pipes and sockets are to be placed. Otherwise things will inevitably get positioned in the wrong place (and you may be charged handsomely for the trouble of repositioning them later). Finally, because drawings tend to get rather mashed up on site it may be worth laminating a couple of copies of the approved plans in an attempt to make them builder-proof.

DESIGNING IT AND SUBMITTING YOUR APPLICATIONS

The Party Wall Act can apply when excavating within 3m of an adjoining property

A load of party walls

The Party Wall Act 1996 may sound like a lot of unnecessary hassle, but its objective is to prevent serious disputes arising between neighbours. It's nothing to do with Planning or Building Regs, but is a totally separate piece of legislation based on the old London Building Acts, which proved so effective that they were extended to the rest of England and Wales. For home-extension builders, the Party Wall Act is important because it can affect the way your foundations have to be excavated.

You can understand neighbours not being overjoyed at the prospect of having their home's foundations undermined by reckless builders in mini-diggers excavating alongside them. They may need some reassurance that their property isn't about to keel over, crack, or subside from under them. On the other hand, you want to get on with your building work without being hindered by unreasonable neighbours. The Act is designed to assist both sides.

What boundary?

The official boundary line between terraced and semi-detached properties will run through the middle of the party wall. Strange as it may sound, both owners legally have rights to the whole wall. This is because both properties rely on it structurally as well as for protection from fire and from noise intrusion. So each side needs to know in advance if the other is planning to muck about with it.

But the legislation also applies to your overall plot, including the boundary lines between gardens, which may correspond to the position of the new side wall that you want to build. Most garden boundaries are defined on the ground with well-established fences or walls separating neighbours. But the mere thought that your extension could cause the loss of a single square inch of garden can outrage some homeowners. Pinpointing the precise legal division between adjoining gardens isn't always easy. Land registry plans are not much bigger than a postage stamp and may have thick red pencil lines daubed over them. Not exactly satellite precision.

When does the Act apply?

■ Where work is proposed to an existing shared wall.
■ If you build a new wall across the legal boundary line, such as a garden wall or fence.
■ When excavating foundations within 3m of an adjoining property, if your trenches are deeper than next door's foundations – which they normally will be. It can also apply within 6m of next door if your new

New extension built within 3m of adjoining property.

foundations are deeper than a line drawn at 45° from the bottom of next door's foundations for example where you want to excavate a basement.

What needs to be done?

Before any work starts, you'll need to serve a formal notice on the owners of the adjoining property. If the property next door happens to be a block of flats – bad luck! You will have to entreat with each occupier individually. But in any case, it's normally best to appoint a party wall surveyor to manage the whole process from the outset.

■ You have to give at least two months' notice before the work commences.
■ A written notice must be served explaining what building work is proposed, giving the owners 14 days to respond.
■ Notice needn't be on an official form, but must include drawings and details of the work (see website for sample notice).

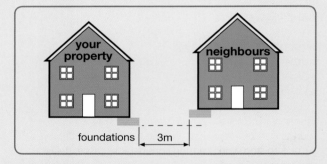

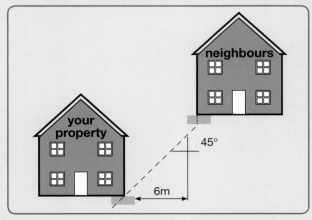

The catch is that unless the neighbours write back within 14 days the law will assume that they do *not* consent, and that a dispute has arisen. This means you then have to jointly appoint an independent 'agreed surveyor' (at your expense) to draw up a legal agreement known as an 'award'. Alternatively, each neighbour can appoint their own surveyor, in which case the award will be drawn up jointly by both surveyors. The 'award' is a document that describes your proposed works and confirms that you will pay for any damage that's caused by your digging and building activities. Specifically:

- ■ It sets out how and when the work will be carried out (*eg* not at weekends).
- ■ It records the condition of the next-door property before the work begins (so that any damage can later be attributed and made good).
- ■ It allows access for the surveyor(s) to inspect the building works.

If you want to build your extension right on the boundary itself, your underground foundations are normally allowed to cross underneath the boundary line, subject to the neighbour's consent and agreeing to compensate them for any damage caused to their property as a consequence.

But what if your neighbours have already built an extension up to, or on, the boundary? In such cases you'll probably need to build right up to their extension, so that it becomes your new party wall. But, again, you must give them notice and hope they agree to you going ahead. You could try 'selling' the idea by explaining how it would make their extension warmer (by their external wall becoming an internal wall), but if they object you cannot proceed, and you have no rights to construct a new party wall. All you can do then is change the design so that it is set back a bit onto your land. See also Chapter 7.

Ultimately, if you start on site without having served a Party Wall notice then the adjoining owner can go to court to obtain a Party Wall injunction forcing you and your builders to stop work, causing considerable hassle, delay and expense. Even if your neighbour isn't aware of the law, claims firms are increasingly trawling through planning registers and writing to adjoining owners in a bid to drum up business. So it makes sense to play by the rules.

Foundation trench excavated to avoid boundary fence, so new wall will be set back about 200mm.

Submitting your applications

Right now, you'd probably like to crack on with physically building your extension, rather than having to spend time getting your ideas approved by a bunch of 'meddling bureaucrats'. But unfortunately you have no option other than to make sure your application is well enough organised to sail swiftly through the system. There is, however, one possible shortcut you could take. Because planning applications normally have a timeframe of eight weeks, and a 'full plans' application for Building Regs can take five weeks, you can save time by applying for both simultaneously rather than wait until planning is granted.

The downside is that if you steam ahead on both fronts, should things go pear-shaped with the planners there will then be a lot more expense and delay getting rehashed Building Regs drawings submitted.

So a good compromise is to wait a couple of weeks until the case officer's site visit and if they seem reasonably happy then start the ball rolling with your detailed Building Regs drawings.

Submitting a planning application

You want to apply for 'detailed' planning consent (as opposed to 'outline' which is consent for the general principle for complex or controversial developments). Having discussed your initial ideas with the Council planners, and assuming they're generally happy and don't foresee any major difficulties, you should now be in a position to finalise the drawings with any necessary amendments included.

What drawings to submit

You need to submit a full set of scale drawings in metric measurements, clearly showing the work you propose to carry out. Some Councils prefer the proposed extensions and alterations to be shown in colour so that the new works are immediately distinct from the existing building. Drawings must clearly show all openings such as windows and doors. Elevation plans should also show architectural details like timber cladding. Each drawing needs to be clearly labelled with its title (*eg* 'Existing Front Elevation'), the number (001 A etc), the scale, and the address of the property, not forgetting to include contact details. You will need to run off at least six sets of drawings, plus a few spares for yourself. See website for sample drawings. The exact requirements vary from council to council, but the drawings normally required are shown on the following pages.

NORTH-WEST ELEVATION

Drawing: Colin K. Dale FRICS

■ **Existing elevations** 1:50 or 1:100 scale, showing
the relevant front, side and rear elevations *before* any
work is carried out.

NORTH-WEST ELEVATION

Drawing: Colin K. Dale FRICS

■ **Proposed elevations** 1:50 or 1:100 scale, front,
side and rear elevations showing what the property will
look like *after* the work is completed.

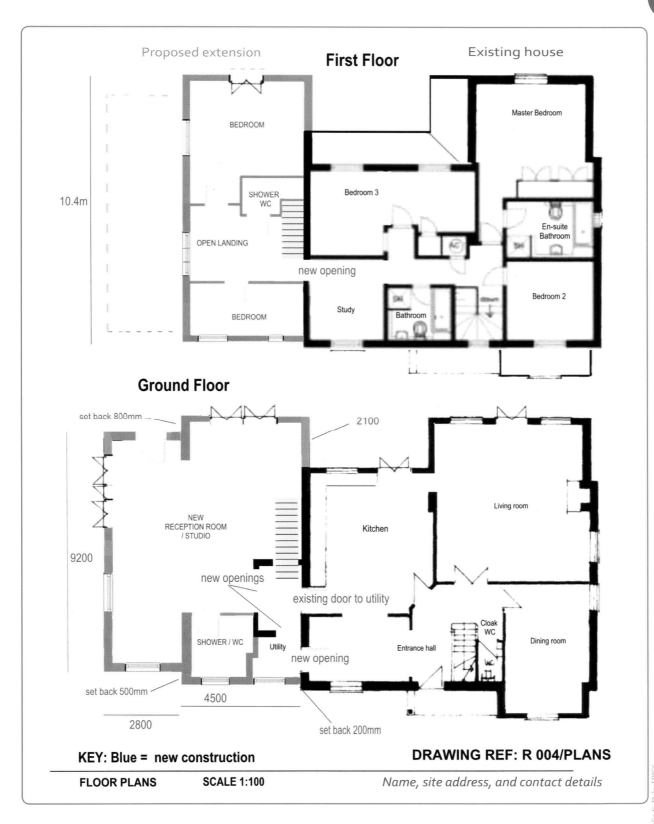

Proposed extension **First Floor** Existing house

10.4m

BEDROOM

SHOWER
WC

OPEN LANDING

Master Bedroom

Bedroom 3

En-suite
Bathroom

new opening

BEDROOM

Study

Bathroom

Bedroom 2

Ground Floor

set back 800mm

2100

NEW
RECEPTION ROOM
/ STUDIO

9200

new openings

Kitchen

Living room

existing door to utility

SHOWER / WC

Utility

new opening

Entrance hall

Cloak
WC

Dining room

set back 500mm

4500

2800

set back 200mm

KEY: Blue = new construction

DRAWING REF: R 004/PLANS

FLOOR PLANS **SCALE 1:100** *Name, site address, and contact details*

■ **Existing / proposed layout plan** 1:50 or 1:100 scale
showing the floor layouts of each level (e.g. ground floor and
first floor, shown from above) with the name of each room
clearly marked

Drawing: Colin K. Dale FRICS

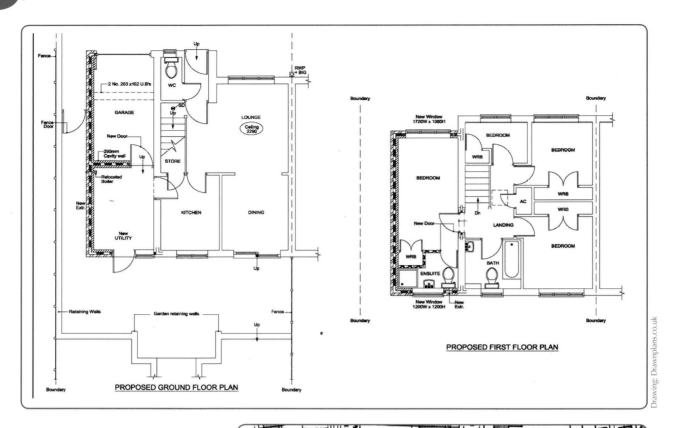

PROPOSED GROUND FLOOR PLAN

PROPOSED FIRST FLOOR PLAN

Drawing: Drawnplans.co.uk

■ **Layout plans** Either submitted as separate plan drawings showing existing and proposed layouts or combined as shown above and on previous page

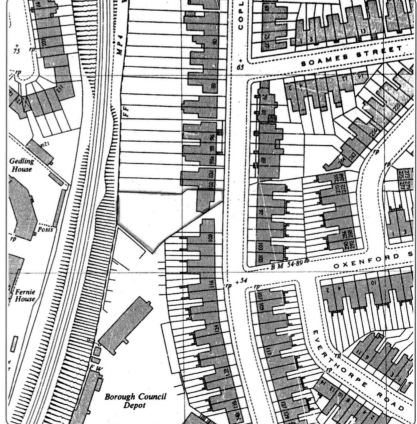

■ **Location plan** 1:1250 scale (not less than), a copy of the Ordnance Survey plan of your street, available from the Council for a smallish fee. Your site must be outlined in red.

■ **Site or 'Block' plan** 1:500 or 1:200 scale. Often combined with the location plan, this is a 'close-up' plan of your plot showing where the extension is going to be built. The site boundaries should be outlined in red, and the positions of drives, roads, drains, trees, garages and outbuildings clearly marked. It shows how the proposed extension will fit into the plot and how it relates to your immediate neighbours and the boundaries. Mark the orientation compass points.

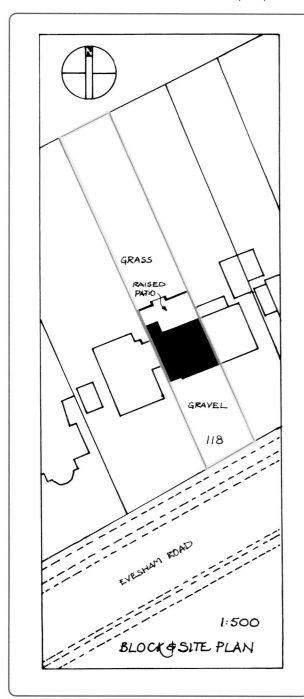

GRASS

RAISED PATIO

GRAVEL

118

EVESHAM ROAD

1:500
BLOCK & SITE PLAN

The 'Section' plan is the only drawing not included in this list. This is the key additional one you'll need for the Building Regs application. It shows a cross-section through the new building and is normally the most technically detailed of all the plans. See 'Submitting a Building Regulations application' on page 76.

Registering new applications

With all the drawings now prepared, you should be in a position to formally apply for planning permission. The only remaining task is to complete the Council application form, which can be done on paper or online. If some of the questions seem a bit odd, it's best to phone the Council planners for assistance rather than guess, otherwise it will only get sent back. You can then submit your completed application form to the planning department, together with the various sets of drawings and site plans, not forgetting to include the appropriate fee. You can apply to every local authority in England & Wales through the Planning Portal website planningportal.co.uk.

Within a few days, the Council should acknowledge receipt of your application in writing, confirming the name of your case officer. Having checked all the right documents are enclosed they'll then place your application on the 'planning register', which means that anyone can download it from their website. Small laminated notices (often coloured yellow) may be physically posted on or near your home and the application may also be advertised in the local press as well as being listed on the Council website. For larger projects the Council may write to the neighbours alerting them to your intentions by giving them three or four weeks to lodge any objections, which is why it's always advisable to consult them personally at an earlier stage, in order to soften the blow. Other interested parties may also be consulted, notably the Highways Authority, the Archaeology Service, Environmental Health department, and the Parish Council. The case officer will normally visit the site within 3 weeks of the registration.

The Council should decide your application within eight weeks but they may write to you requesting more time. You can either agree to this or you can appeal to the Secretary of State, but since such appeals can take several months this doesn't usually get you very far!

Your case officer has to decide whether there are any good planning reasons for refusing permission, always remembering that there's a positive presumption in favour of development (not that you'd ever guess this by talking to some planners). The Council cannot reject a proposal just because lots of people oppose it. It will look at whether it's consistent with the local development plan, consider any design issues such as overlooking and overshadowing neighbouring properties and assess its impact on the surrounding area, including any associated loss of amenity or possible traffic problems. It's worth phoning periodically to find out what's happening to your application. If the feedback is totally negative, it may be wise to withdraw the application and start again. If minor

changes are needed to resolve a difficulty, they may ask you to amend the design and resubmit it so that a decision can still be made within eight weeks.

Eventually, after considering the various consultations and objections, and having completed their site visit, the case officer will prepare a report with a recommendation either for approval or refusal. This will then be submitted to the planning committee (made up of elected councillors) and in about 80% of cases, the official recommendation wins the day. However most home extension applications are relatively straightforward and senior officers can usually make the decision under 'delegated authority' without involving the committee.

Planning approval is normally granted with conditions, some of which are standard clauses, such as the condition that work on site must commence within three years. But for more sensitive developments (conservation areas etc), approval is sometimes subject to more onerous restrictions, such as a requirement that samples of your choice of materials (typically bricks and roof tiles) be submitted for the planners to have a good look at and, hopefully, approve prior to commencement of any building works.

Refusals and appeals

A refusal will be accompanied by specific reasons for the decision. Frustrating though refusal is, it may leave the door open for the resubmission of modified plans which the planners would be prepared to accept. The reasons tend to be expressed in planning jargon with references to policy numbers, so it's best to have a chat with the case officer to understand in plain English how you can best revise your design to get it approved. You're normally allowed to submit another application free of charge within 12 months of a refusal. This should take on board the reasons given for refusal and, to this end, background papers can be downloaded from the Council website such as comments from Highways, objectors and supporters that may have influenced the final decision.

If you feel the reasons for refusal aren't valid you can appeal within six months of the decision, to the planning inspectorate. They are an independent body, but your chances of success are fairly slim – less than one third of appeals are successful. Although there's no great expense

in submitting a written appeal if you put it together yourself, it can be very time consuming. Employing a planning consultant to handle your appeal means having to pay fees, but it could be money well spent if they know the ropes. Appeals can also be made against individual planning conditions if they're unreasonable.

The basic procedure is to submit evidence that proves the Council's refusal was inconsistent with its relevant policies and with Government planning guidance. What can help clinch a result is being able to demonstrate that similar local developments have recently been permitted. Above all, it's essential to stick to the facts and avoid emotional arguments. The inspector's site visits take place once both sides have made their written submissions, normally after four or five months, and it then takes another couple of months for a decision.

Another reason for thinking very hard before appealing is that it can actually make matters worse. For example, a design that would have been accepted if modified to a smaller scale with windows not overlooking the neighbours, could now be totally rejected by the inspector as unacceptable.

Submitting a Building Regulations application

Before submitting your application to the Local Authority Building Control Department you may wish to consider an alternative method that bypasses them, in the interests of consumer 'choice'. If you wish, you're allowed to submit your application via an independent 'approved inspector' instead. Approved inspectors are private firms approved by the Council to do basically the same job as in-house Building Control staff. If you take this route they will notify the local authority (sending them an 'initial notice'), and then process your plans, carry out spot checks on site as the building work progresses, and ultimately arrange for the final certificate once the works are completed to their satisfaction. In other words, it's all pretty much the same, but may suit those who prefer a bit of private-sector involvement. Both are referred to as 'BCBs' (Building Control Bodies').

For simplicity we will here assume that you're going to

apply in the time-honoured manner, direct to your Local Authority. You now have to make an important choice, whether to submit your application by the 'full plans' method or as a 'building notice'.

Building notice

For most home extensions, a full plans application is advisable (see below). But there's a useful short-cut. For smaller, straightforward extensions where you have unshakeable faith in the skill and knowledge of your designer and builders, you may wish to save time by skipping the full plans application. Instead you can submit a simple Building Notice. Here you're basically making a promise that you'll comply with the Building Regs later on site, rather than submitting detailed drawings to prove it in advance.

You'll still need to complete a form giving details of the extension and this should be submitted together with a 'block plan' (showing the position of the extended building in relation to boundaries, and the provision for drainage), and you may still be asked to provide drawings and additional information, such as design calculations. The fee is usually a little dearer than a full plans application and is paid in advance when you submit the notice. Only one fee is payable no matter how many site visits are later needed.

Once the building notice has been checked and accepted, the next stage is simply to give the Building Control Officer a minimum of two working days' notice of your intention to start work on site. The officer will then inspect the work at key stages, just as with a full plans application.

The big risk with this method is that because your plans haven't been fully approved in advance, a site inspection could uncover something that contravenes the regulations while it's being built (such as excessive areas of glazing). Obviously this could prove highly disruptive not to say expensive.

A building notice is valid for three years, after which it will automatically lapse. Strictly speaking a Local Authority is not required to issue a final completion certificate under the building notice procedure, but they'll normally do so upon request.

Full plans application

Here, the applicant demonstrates by way of detailed drawings that the construction will comply with the regulations. This way, your design is checked in advance so any issues can be sorted before building work starts. If you're proposing to build some or all of your extension yourself, it's best to go this route so that you'll have an approved set of plans to work to. Also, if you're proposing to build over, or close to, a public sewer this is the only kind of application allowed.

Making your application

If you wish, you can do things the traditional way and physically deliver or post hard copies of your drawings direct to your Local Authority (or the 'BCB' of your choice), not forgetting to include the application form and fee, plus any supporting documents like engineer's calcs. Inevitably, however, most applications are now submitted online. Your Council website will explain how best to do this but you

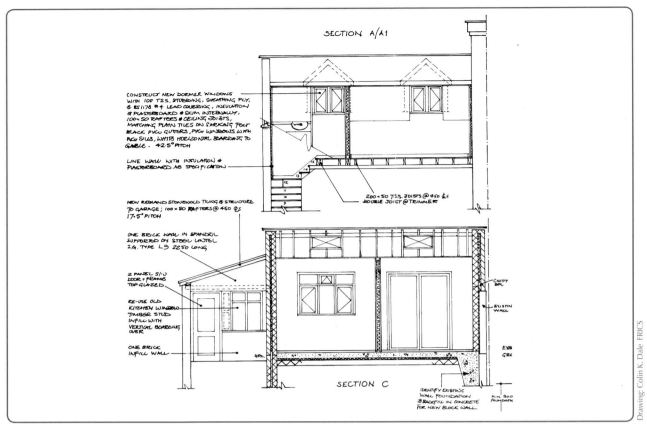

SECTION A/A1

CONSTRUCT NEW DORMER WINDOWS WITH 100 T.S.S. STUDDING, SHEATHING PLY, & BS1178 #4 LEAD COVERING, INSULATION & PLASTERBOARD & SKIM INTERNALLY, 100×50 RAFTERS & CEILING JOISTS, MATCHING PLAIN TILES ON SARKING FELT BLACK PVCU GUTTERS, PVCU WINDOWS WITH PVCU SILLS, WHITE HORIZONTAL BOARDING TO GABLE. 42.5° PITCH

LINE WALL WITH INSULATION & PLASTERBOARD AS SPECIFICATION

200×50 T.S.S. JOISTS @ 450 ¢s DOUBLE JOIST @ TRIMMER

NEW REDLAND STONEWOLD TILING & STRUCTURE TO GARAGE; 100×50 RAFTERS @ 450 ¢s 17.5° PITCH

ONE BRICK WALL IN SPANDRIL SUPPORTED ON STEEL LINTEL I.G. TYPE L9 2250 LONG

2 PANEL S/O DOOR + FRAME TOP GLAZED

RE-USE OLD KITCHEN WINDOW TIMBER STUD INFILL WITH VERTICAL BOARDING OVER

ONE BRICK INFILL WALL

SECTION C

IDENTIFY EXISTING WALL FOUNDATION & BACKFILL IN CONCRETE FOR NEW BLOCK WALL

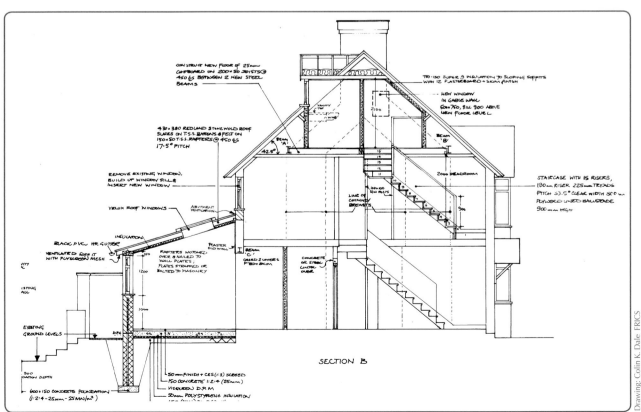

SECTION B

Drawing: Colin K. Dale FRICS

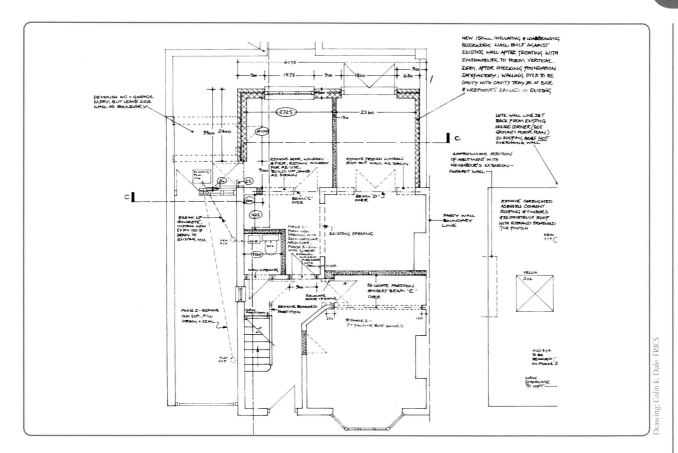

Within the drawing (handwritten notes):

6075
900 — 1575 — 900 — 1800 — 680 — 900

NEW 150mm INSULATING & LOADBEARING BLOCKWORK WALL BUILT AGAINST EXISTING WALL AFTER TREATING WITH SYNTHAPRUFE TO FORM VERTICAL DPM. AFTER CHECKING FOUNDATION SATISFACTORY; WALLING OVER TO BE CAVITY WITH CAVITY TRAY &c AT BASE & WEEPHOLES DRILLED IN EXISTING

DEMOLISH WC + GARAGE ENTRY, BUT LEAVE SIDE WALL AS BOUNDARY.

3300 2400 — 2100

2725

2560

130

NOTE: WALL LINE SET BACK FROM EXISTING HOUSE CORNER (SEE GROUND FLOOR PLAN) SO ROOFING DOES NOT OVERHANG WALL.

REMOVE DOOR, WINDOW & PIER, RETAIN WINDOW FOR RE-USE, BUILD UP JAMB AS SHOWN
900

REMOVE FRENCH WINDOW & CUT OUT WALL AS SHOWN

APPROXIMATE POSITION OF ABUTMENT WITH NEIGHBOUR'S EXTENSION — PARAPET WALL

C

BEAM 'C' OVER   BEAM 'D' OVER

PARTY WALL BOUNDARY LINE

REMOVE CORRUGATED ASBESTOS CEMENT ROOFING & TIMBERS & RECONSTRUCT ROOF WITH REDLAND STONEWOLD TILE FINISH

NEW S.V.P.

BREAK UP CONCRETE, INSTALL NEW S.V.P. 100 Ø DRAIN TO EXISTING M.H.

NEW S.V.P.

PHASE 1 — FORM NEW OPENING WITH SEMI-CIRCULAR ARCH OVER. PHASE 3 — FILL WITH ½ HOUR 2 PANEL GLAZED FIREDOOR WITH FANLIGHT OVER

EXISTING OPENING

VELUX 506

1125

WC

1200

NEW OPENING

RELOCATE PARTITION & INSERT BEAM 'E' OVER

PHASE 2 — REMOVE OLD S.V.P., FILL DRAIN + SEAL

NEW PARTITION

500

RELOCATE DOOR + FRAME

REMOVE BOWED/BONDED PARTITION

250   150

*PHASE 3 — FIT FALLING BUTT HINGES

OLD S.V.P.

OLD S.V.P. TO BE REMOVED IN PHASE 2

NEW STAIRCASE TO LOFT

Drawing: Colin K.Dale FRICS

can make applications to any Local Authority (in England & Wales) via Planningportal.co.uk or Submitaplan.com.

What drawings to submit

You'll need to submit heavily revised versions of the planning drawings with additional detailed information written on them, along with a completed application form and fee. The drawings must clearly show the proposed building works and explain the details of construction. Specifically:

■ **A location plan** showing the new building relative to neighbouring streets, houses and boundaries.

■ **A section plan** drawing showing a cross-section 'sliced through' the middle of the proposed new extension, paying particular attention to details of wall construction, insulation, joist depths, floor levels, room heights, and any stairs (typically drawn to 1:20 or 1:25 scale, and preferably no smaller than 1:50). These are the most informative of building plans since they expose the details of the new building's construction, showing materials and thicknesses as well as heights and dimensions. This is often the plan that has most of the specification written on it.

■ **Plan and elevation drawings** together with technical notes that fully describe the proposed works including information about the materials you want to use for the walls, roofs, floors, and types of insulation etc.

■ **Structural calculations** for new or altered load-bearing elements, and details of any proposals to build over or near sewers.

If it's not already shown on the drawings you'll need to provide additional information to explain how your design meets the various U-value targets and complies with limits on total areas of glazing (see '25% rule' page 55).

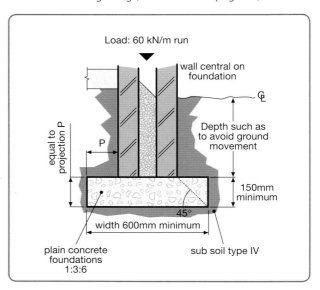

Load: 60 kN/m run

wall central on foundation

GL

equal to projection P

P

Depth such as to avoid ground movement

150mm minimum

45°

width 600mm minimum

plain concrete foundations 1:3:6

sub soil type IV

Non-habitable outbuildings and garages up to 30m² floor area are normally exempt from Building Regs.

You'll normally need to print about four copies of your drawings, plus a few more at a later stage for builders to quote from and some to keep spare. There are two payments you'll need to make: a 'plans fee' paid up front and an 'inspection fee' paid at start-on-site.

Having submitted your full plans application, Building Control should write confirming who'll be dealing with your case. Your application should normally be passed or rejected within five weeks, although this can be extended with your consent for up to two months.

Ultimately you should receive a 'plans approved' notice to confirm that the plans comply with Building Regulations (ie the 'Approved Documents'). The Building Control

Officer will then inspect the work on site at key stages as it progresses. A 'plans approved' notice is valid for three years, and will then expire unless building work has commenced. It's not the same as a final certificate (a.k.a. completion certificate), which should be issued once all the work is satisfactorily completed.

Approval or rejection
There are basically three possible outcomes to your Building Regs application:

Approval
If you receive a 'plans approval notice', congratulations! But even drawings submitted by professional designers are rarely perfect first time, so it's unlikely that you'll get everything 100 per cent right if you submit your own plans. Unless you're

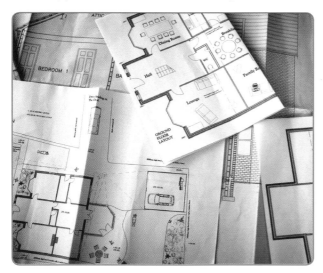

already familiar with current Building Regulations don't be shy of asking for a little professional input.

Conditional approval and amendments
It's more likely that Building Control will write back to you with an 'amendments letter' asking for clarification on various points or requiring additional information, such as updated engineer's calculations.

Being bombarded with highly detailed questions about your design at this stage can seem rather irritating. But remember it's a whole lot easier sorting out problems on paper than it would be trying to rebuild walls on site. And you can be sure that if Building Control aren't entirely clear about what you mean, the builders certainly won't be. If you haven't got a clue what they're on about just phone or visit your Building Control Officer, who'll normally be pleased to explain matters in plain English.

Alternatively, they may issue approval on a conditional basis. In both cases it means that the design requires some amendment. Conditional approvals normally have the conditions listed as an attached document (*eg* stating required modifications) or they may simply request further plans to be submitted for approval. Sometimes they will add their own notes to your plans before they are 'approved with endorsements'. It's important that your designer resolves these conditions in good time before the start-on-site date.

Rejection
A rejection notice needn't be as bad as it sounds. It can usually be overcome by resubmitting amended plans, for which no additional fee should be charged. Fees should also not apply for giving advice and for work that benefits people with disabilities, *eg* where extensions are being built specifically for this purpose.

What information to write on the plans

On simple projects, the construction details can all be fitted onto the plans on 2 sheets of A1 (840 x 592mm). These are fine for getting approval but their large size makes them awkward to use on site where smaller A2 or A3 are more practical. On the section drawing and the elevation plans you need to show:

Levels

■ Ground levels: Outside ground levels are rarely perfectly level, so show them true-to-life on the drawings.
■ The levels of new drains: Show the 'invert levels' (depths) where new drainage is to be connected, at inspection chambers. You can take your own levels from the existing drains by measuring the depth between the manhole cover and the bottom of the channel.
■ Floor levels: The finished floor levels (FFL) of the extension can be shown in relation to the existing floor level of the main house.

The specification

The specification describes the types and thicknesses of materials – see page 87. This should clearly state:

■ The dimensions of all the main components of the building (foundations, floors, joist layouts, walls, windows, doors, roof structure etc), also explaining their type and their position in the building.
■ The type and size of insulation to be used (to floors, walls and roofs etc) and their K or R-values (see page 58).
■ The drains: their routes (layouts), falls (angle of slope), invert levels (depth), the position of junctions and inspection chambers, and access points for rodding, should all be described or shown, and details of how pipes are protected, eg where they pass under the building.

See website for samples.

6 MEET THE BUILDERS

If there's one decision that can really make or break your project it's selecting the right builder. You may have the finest drawings and the most eloquent specifications in the world, all beautifully tied up with watertight legal contracts. But a dodgy builder can, at a stroke, turn your dream extension into a traumatic nightmare. This chapter should help you avoid vexed relationships with builders.

Even the best builders need a tea break (4 sugars!).

There are three main ways you can run your project:

- **Employ a main contractor** to carry out and co-ordinate all the building works.
- **Directly employ your own specialist trades** for each stage of the works and project manage it yourself, with the option of some DIY input.
- **Self-build the whole thing**, with a bit of extra help here and there.

For the vast majority of home extensions, the favoured route is the simplest one – method 1. This still leaves room for you to help project manage and to cherry-pick a few jobs where your skills are strongest, though the extent of your involvement should be agreed with the contractor at the outset. Methods 2 and 3 are only suitable for more experienced home-extenders.

Finding the right builder

Anyone with zero qualifications, lacking even the most rudimentary experience, is perfectly entitled to set up in business calling themselves 'building contractors'. This may explain why TV schedules are packed with grim tales of builders from hell preying mercilessly on vulnerable homeowners. If it's roof work, plumbing, or a new driveway that you need, it seems there's no shortage of dodgy tradesmen out there to choose from.

Perhaps because of all the negative media coverage, the general public's perception of the building trade is somewhat negative. Admittedly there's no smoke without fire – over 100,000 complaints about cowboy builders are registered with trading standards officers each year – but the plain fact is, cowboy builders are a tiny minority. Most builders will try to do a difficult job well. Remember that the builder is only one part of the equation. Architects are fond of using the expression 'a good client', because it greatly helps when clients are clear about what they require from the outset. Builders, too, have to deal with their fair share of 'cowboy clients' who constantly change their minds, demand extra work free of charge, play tricks and make excuses for delayed payment, and then turn out not to have any money. Good clients tend to get good building work done for them.

Like anything, there's a right way and a wrong way to approach a job, and the golden rules for running a successful building project are explained later.

But first, how do you choose a decent builder? What you *don't* do is pick the first nice-looking advertisement you come across. A glossy, professional looking ad doesn't mean the firm advertising is professional. Neither is it true that 'the posher the van, the better the builder' – it simply means he's good at spending money on vans.

The best place to start is with a personal recommendation, or by speaking to previous customers.

From a shortlist of four or five firms you should be able to find one that fits the bill in terms of price, quality, and availability to start the job within a reasonable timescale.

The criteria for selecting a builder

Recommendations
Ask people you know locally if they can recommend someone. Architects and surveyors are particularly well placed to make recommendations. Best placed of all to provide sensible advice are Building Control Officers, but regrettably they may not be at liberty to make recommendations. Citizens Advice Bureaux often keep lists of local contractors, such as those with a good track record working for senior citizens.

Trade association membership
Builders sometimes belong to trade federations, but these exist primarily to represent the interests of their members, not the customers, and the requirements for joining are not always terribly demanding. It's not unknown for unscrupulous builders to 'borrow' logos to make their ads look nicer, or even to make up their own 'guilds', 'leagues' and 'federations', of which they're the only member! So proceed with caution and check that your chosen firm's membership is still current.

Membership of 'proper' trade associations with their own codes of practice can, however, be a useful way to identify good firms. And there may be additional benefits, such as dispute resolution services and complaints

  procedures, or even insurance-backed warranties. But don't automatically reject a builder because of their lack of 'badges' – many excellent individual tradesmen may work entirely from local references and feel that they don't need to belong to an organisation.

Membership of trade bodies is no guarantee of site quality, but federations that offer additional insurance if you employ one of their members are a definite bonus. To be of any real value, insurance-backed warranties need to cover you for a period of up to ten years after completion, for defects caused by poor workmanship or materials, or if the builder goes bust during the job.

Perhaps the best-known trade association is the Federation of Master Builders, but each trade has its own professional body. All the leading logos are listed on the website.

There are also Government-funded schemes such as 'TrustMark' which claim to be able to provide consumers with a list of reliable firms. Thousands of tradespeople, including many sole traders and small specialist firms, are registered with websites with customer feedback reviews like checkatrade.com and ratedpeople.com

Quality Assurance
ISO 9001/2 and BS 5750 may sound familiar. These are widely held Quality Assurance accreditations, but although they might appear to be some kind of guarantee of quality for site work, they are not. They simply prove that a firm is able to reproduce the same standard of work time and time again. And some builders have absolutely no problem faithfully reproducing poor work! Nonetheless, they do indicate a general intention by a firm to deliver a good-quality job.

Previous work
This is where a little detective work can really pay off. Although you should always obtain written references, bear in mind that they may sometimes be of limited value. A builder who's a crook will have written them himself, and the referee will turn out to be his mum or one of his mates! All decent contractors should be able to easily

Above: Space is limited on many sites.
Below: Did they get round to finishing the last job?

provide a list of recently completed jobs, and a list of customers (such as Housing Associations) to whom you can write.

Go and take a look at the work, and ideally speak to the homeowners – most people will be happy to help. Asking some fairly detailed questions will help ensure they're genuine, for example:

- Did the builders turn up when agreed?
- Did they clear away their rubbish and use dust sheets to protect furniture?
- What was the quality of work like?
- How was their attention to detail?
- Did they price extra work reasonably?
- Did the job start and finish on time?
- Were they considerate?
- Would you employ them again?

If all the referees sound the same and can't give much detail except to say the firm is 'really great', forget it.

Also, visit one of the builders' current sites to see work in progress. Note how tidy the site is, and whether materials are protected and stored neatly, or just chaotically littered about. Is it a rushed or badly planned job? Running the name of your chosen firms past Trading Standards isn't a bad idea either.

Bankers' references
Ask for a banker's reference. A firm with insufficient funds to finance the work without demanding a cash deposit for materials up front will be trouble.

Insurance

Suppose someone accidentally drops some tiles off the scaffolding, injuring a passer-by. Or the delivery driver falls down an unprotected hole in the ground. If it turns out your builder isn't fully insured you could be held jointly liable to pay compensation as owner of the property. More likely some irritating minor damage will occur, like next door's fence getting dented or their phone cable being cut through. So it's important to cover yourself by asking the building contractor to produce his current certificate of public liability insurance, which must provide cover to a minimum of £1 million. This is a reasonable request, and any bona fide builder will have no trouble co-operating.

However, if you employ individual trades directly, you are deemed to be an employer at least from an insurance angle. This means you will need two policies – public liability, covering risk to the public, and employer's liability which covers you should someone working for you have an accident and promptly sue you. Most employers' policies now cover you up to £10 million, and public liability for £2 million.

It also would be advisable to get 'all risks insurance' which covers theft of plant and materials from the site, as well as fire and structural damage to the buildings you're working on. In total, you might have to cough up about 0.5% of the contract sum to get a project comprehensively insured.

VAT registered?

Unfortunately, VAT is chargeable on home extensions. Even if your builder only undertakes a few small extensions in a year, his turnover will almost certainly place him above the VAT registration threshold, so he'll need to be VAT registered. It's wise to assume that tax has to be added to the quotation, unless it is clearly shown. You should obtain proper VAT receipts for all payments, so check the builder has a valid VAT number and isn't just pocketing it. Cash deals are generally best avoided other than where individual tradespeople are working for just a day or so.

Guarantees

Defects in major components such as foundations, floors and double glazing can take several years to appear. For extensions there is no direct equivalent to the NHBC warranty for new houses, but fortunately with most standard contracts like the JCT Minor Works (see below) six-year warranties are included. In any case, guarantees are only as good as the firms offering them, so to have any meaning they need to be insurance-backed.

Small builders

Smaller firms of builders will have less labour available to share between competing jobs, so you should have more chance of getting their undivided attention for the full project. If you're very lucky they may even finish one job at a time rather than juggling resources between different jobs, as larger firms

Scaffolding must be installed by licensed specialist firms with plenty of insurance in accordance with BS EN12811

invariably do. But avoid small firms that don't have enough funding to pay for materials up front. That said, the builder is in a vulnerable position, effectively extending you credit, and will be as wary of potential clients as they are of him.

Contingency sums

The chances are that as you watch your extension take shape there'll be something that will occur to you (or your partner) that 'would look nice'. Something you wish you'd included in the specification. You're not alone. It's not unknown for architects and surveyors to omit things from specifications, or it may turn out that you need beefier and more expensive foundations than anticipated. It's therefore always wise to budget five to ten per cent more than the quoted cost, to allow for the inevitable 'human error'.

The contract

A building contract is simply an agreement between you and your builders, for them to undertake a list of specified tasks to a certain standard, for an agreed sum of money.

Although, strictly speaking, accepting a verbal offer could form a contract in law, to run the job properly it's advisable to use a written contract, signed by both parties.

Dodgy builders have been known to quote for a job but never actually start on site, and then try to claim compensation when your patience is finally exhausted

What's in a building contract?

These are the key points you need to fill in:

- **The parties** – You and your builder (be sure to write their full name, so that there's no wriggling out later).
- **The works** – A brief description of the project.
- **The contract documents** – List all the specific drawings by number and the tender documents specifying the agreed work.
- **The professionals** – The names of any architect or surveyor who'll be managing the contract for you.
- **The tender sum** – This is the contractor's agreed price, unless any post-tender changes have been made.
- **Project duration** – Clearly state the agreed start and finish dates (many disputes relate to time overruns).
- **Liquidated damages** – If a project significantly overruns, any 'unwarranted delays' will give you the right to make deductions from the money due to the builder. Normally a weekly sum known as 'liquidated damages' is filled in.
- **Payment terms** – Contractors are normally paid every four weeks or every fortnight or at agreed stages in the construction work. A small 'snagging' retention (typically 5%) is normally held back until completion, half of which is retained for a period of three or six months after the completion date.
- **Insurance** – The contractor must confirm that they have adequate insurance throughout the build period.
- **Solving disputes** – A description of what action the parties can take if there is a dispute.

and you tell them to sling their hook. They may claim that you entered into a verbal contract. So if you do accept a builder's offer to do a job without a formal contract, always make your acceptance conditional upon confirming in writing their agreement to a specific start date and completion date.

By providing a quotation based on your drawings or where a contract can be proved to exist, there are two key implied legal conditions – that 'the work shall be performed within a reasonable time' and 'with reasonable care and skill'.

Using a written contract is always advisable because it shows that both sides are serious, and gives you both certain rights and duties which are enforceable in court. Without something written down it's your word against theirs. If things all go horribly wrong later, your case will be a lot stronger if you can produce a contract, signed by the builder, saying that he agreed to finish by the end of September, when in actual fact your roof's still not on in October. Rather than sitting there feeling a complete berk, it allows you (the innocent party) to seek compensation ('damages') for any losses incurred, or to withhold payment, or even to terminate the contract and employ someone else.

But which contract to use? There's nothing to stop you writing your own if you want, but it's a lot easier to use a ready-made 'off the shelf' variety, such as a

suitable JCT (Joint Contracts Tribunal) contract. The JCT 'Building Contract for a Home Owner/Occupier' can be used for most home extensions where homeowners are dealing directly with a contractor. Or for more complex or expensive projects there's the JCT 'Minor Works' contract. Alternatively, the Federation of Master Builders have a free one you can download from our website.

Don't be too gobsmacked when you first read the contract. It's basically a collection of all the things that could ever go wrong with a property development, based on other people's bad experiences over many years. It clarifies who's responsible for what, thereby reducing the risk of a major dispute messing up the job. All the important stuff is there, including how frequently you pay the builders, and who's responsible if the extension is only half finished by the completion date.

There's nothing to stop you adding your own specific conditions if you wish. For example, you might want the builder not to start work until after 7.45 am, not to work at weekends, and not to entertain the neighbours by blasting out Def Leppard's greatest hits all day long. You might also want to stipulate that they take all reasonable measures to protect your newly paved drive from damage.

Before you sign the contract, remember it's your last chance to ensure you'll be getting exactly what you want: any changes from now are likely to cost you more money.

Specifications

Most disputes with builders are (surprise, surprise) about money. This is often down to misunderstandings about what work was meant to be done for the quoted price. This may be because the client or architect didn't clearly specify the required work at the outset. Builders aren't psychic. The key to a smoothly run scheme is, above all,

to specify clearly what you want, so you know exactly what you'll be paying for. This, of course, is easier said than done.

An architect or surveyor can write a specification of the work, often referred to as 'the spec' (pronounced 'spess'). This is basically a long shopping list stating each separate piece of work required which is sent to the contractor to work out how much the job will cost. If anything, having a professionally drawn up specification is of more value than a formal contract, because it should prevent a lot of misunderstandings arising in the first place. More upmarket jobs tend to have the spec written separately from the drawings. Together, the spec and drawings should make it clear exactly how many square metres of plastering, roof slates, tiling etc are needed, so the contractor can simply write a price next to each separate component of the job. The whole lot is then totted up to produce a grand total.

This is especially useful later on when it comes to paying the builders, since you can pay them the price they've quoted for each completed piece of work. It also helps in avoiding overpaying for any 'extras', as you can base the price for any additional work on the figures quoted here for similar work.

Much of this information will already have been written down on your Building Control drawings, which, if adequately detailed, may be sufficient for the builder to price from. Even so, it's always a good idea to write down your own detailed list of requirements because it helps focus on exactly what you want, reducing the risk of misunderstandings later. See website for examples.

Briefs

If it's your first time attempting to write a specification, it would be a good idea to first run it past someone with good construction knowledge, because if you miss stuff out that later needs to be done on site it will count as an 'extra', which could prove expensive. So if you're going to do a DIY spec it may be better to refer to it as a 'detailed brief' when you submit it to the contractor. Whereas a spec is regarded as a definitive list, a brief is simply 'your best attempt' to convey your requirements. A brief doesn't exempt the contractor from his responsibility to use his expertise to interpret your desires, and to employ suitable methods and materials. In the event of a later dispute, a brief can be a little more forgiving.

Start by writing down a general outline of the work and then list specific requirements, explaining what you want and the standards you expect. You need to research the available sizes and quality of materials such as bricks, tiles and lintels (available on manufacturers' websites).

Using the phrase 'allow for all necessary work in connection with…' covers a multitude of sins and will reduce the risk of the contractor trying to charge extra for something which is obviously needed but which you might have forgotten to include in the brief.

Design detail – choosing materials

Never assume that the builder will automatically do everything just the way you like it. This may sound obvious but many disputes grow out of misunderstandings over tiny details. For example, you might have visualised classic Victorian-style moulded architraves and bespoke 170mm high skirting boards to beautifully complement your new bathroom fittings, but unless instructed otherwise the builder may just stick on the cheapest bit of MDF he can find. And unless you clearly specify that roll-top, claw-foot cast iron bath you've always dreamed of, the contractor will be perfectly entitled to plonk in a cheapo plastic jobby. So think carefully about the details – the precise kind of light switches, sockets, taps and basins that you want – or you'll inevitably find they've fitted ones left over from the last job.

On the other hand, your builders may well come up with helpful ideas as the job progresses, which can sometimes reduce the cost. Most builders know their stuff and have seen it all before, so don't be too proud or suspicious and reject all their ideas out of hand. Just be aware that some suggestions come with a price tag. If your builder suggests that something 'might as well be done', don't assume he'll do it out of the kindness of his heart.

Now is the time to do your homework. There'll be less room for mistakes if you quote details and catalogue numbers. If you intend to supply some fittings or materials yourself make sure that your specification or brief states that the contractor is to 'allow for fitting only'. This means that you're solely responsible for ensuring these items are available on site exactly when the fitter needs them. If they're delivered too soon there'll be more risk of theft or damage – too late, and the plumber or chippie may not be on site again for another month.

The responsibility for supplying materials and fittings must be made very clear at the start, or it can very easily

flare up into a major issue later. Rather than supplying things yourself, it's usually simpler to specify exactly what materials you want by writing 'allow price of £X to supply 1 no. pair *Pegler* bath taps ref: ABC123' (*ie* quote the reference number). This will save a whole lot of your time fetching and delivering things.

Prime Cost sums (PC sums)

Most of us like to take our time mulling over the precise choice of visually important things like taps, worktops and tiles. After all, rushing such key design decisions could result in catastrophic style errors that haunt us for the rest of our days. On the other hand, you don't want to hold up the entire project whilst umming and ahhing over samples and colour swatches for months on end. And you certainly don't want to keep changing your mind as work progresses on site.

Thankfully there's a convenient solution. Using 'PC sums' in your specification allows you to have your cake

Photo: Royce Bathrooms

and eat it, so the builders can get on with the job whilst you buy some time, postponing such tough decisions. PC sums allow clients the freedom to select the precise product at a later date. So you might write in your specification '*allow the PC sum of £1500 for supply only of bathroom suite*' as an estimate of what you think it's likely to end up costing. The contractor will have to include this amount in his quotation, but the actual figure you pay will be down to which suite you actually choose. The builder then quotes only for the labour to fit it and adopts your stated 'guide price' for the materials. Similarly, *provisional sums* are 'an allowance for unknown items of work or goods, including labour costs, overheads and profit'. They are useful where there is some doubt about the likely extent of work to be carried out, such as for underground drainage works.

These are only estimates, not firm prices, so the actual costs (which could be higher or lower than estimated) will need to be sorted out later. Adjustments will normally be made in the final bill. The downside is they can introduce an element of uncertainty and should only be used sparingly, or avoided where possible.

Workmanship

So much for accurately describing the job and defining the required materials. But there's one thing that's a lot harder to nail down, and that's the standard of workmanship. Under the terms of the contract, the builder will normally be required to 'use reasonable care and skill', which is

obviously open to some interpretation. One solution is to specify 'British Standard BS8000' on the plans, and to make sure the plans are included as contract documents so that, if push comes to shove, they are legally enforceable (so staple a set of plans to the contract and have each party jointly sign all pages and drawings). Then if the workmanship becomes unsatisfactory at any stage, your builder will be in breach of contract and you'll be able to terminate the contract or to give notice to correct defective work.

Preliminaries

The 'prelims' are your way of explaining to the contractor the arrangements for all those important little things that make a job run smoothly – such as provision of toilets for the lads on site, rubbish collection, site security, scaffolding, temporary power supplies, and arrangements for storage of materials. If you skip this, it may only be when you notice rubble-filled wheelbarrows being carted through your expensively wallpapered entrance hall that you realise you should have agreed site access arrangements in advance.

Another crucial prelim is to arrange for a convenient water supply, such as from an outdoor tap, or perhaps from a large water butt, since running a hose from your kitchen all day long will drive you bananas. Not unreasonably the builder will expect free access to the site for the duration of the contract, so if you suddenly jet off on holiday halfway through the project leaving the house locked up, the builders may well disappear off to another job and may never be seen again. Indeed, if the client causes delays to the work the builder can submit a claim for losses and expenses incurred as a result, which would make it rather an expensive holiday.

Prelims are also important because there are a lot of potential costs involved – things like hiring toilets, security fencing, and storage containers. If things are not spelled out clearly, family mealtimes may be enlivened by builders trekking through the house to use the loo. Or you may

wake up one day trapped in your home by mountains of concrete blocks deposited outside the front door.

Tendering

The best way to get a major building job priced is to tender it. A competitive quote is the next best thing – see 'Pricing the job' on page 93. A tender is a sort of super-detailed competitive quotation. There are two good reasons for tendering a job. First, it immediately weeds out dodgy builders, who won't want to go to all the trouble of completing and replying to tenders. And second, it lets you easily compare rival firms' prices for the same job.

Start by phoning or emailing your shortlisted building firms to ask whether they'd like to tender for your extension. This saves wasting time sending out documents to firms who are either too busy or just not interested. Next, send out your tender documents and wait for the reply. It's best to select four or five firms as this should allow for 'drop outs' and overpricing (e.g. where a firm doesn't really need the work but submits a high price on the off-chance).

The tender documents together amount to a written list explaining exactly what you want built, against which the builder can offer a price:

- The latest version of the drawings used for Building Control, plus any additional builders' drawings illustrating key construction details.
- A detailed brief or specification.
- Preliminaries (or you could list these in your covering letter instead).
- A completed form of tender (see samples on website).
- A photocopy of any contract you propose to use, left blank.
- A covering letter clearly stating the precise deadline by which completed tenders should be submitted. If you allow any less than three weeks they may not have time to obtain prices from subcontractors and suppliers, and will 'guesstimate' with inflated prices to allow for risk.
- An addressed envelope or email address for the return tender.

It's worth asking the contractors to quote their rates per square metre for works such as plastering and pointing, or per metre run for jobs like laying pipes. This may come in useful if you later need to ask for additions to the quoted job.

Comparing offers

Come the stated deadline you should have at least three completed tenders to choose from, but no matter how many weeks' notice you've given you can be fairly sure one will arrive at the last minute in the hands of a motorcycle messenger or you'll get an urgent phone call asking for more time. When you're ready, take a deep breath, open all the envelopes, and check the bottom lines.

If it transpires that all the prices submitted significantly exceed your budget, don't despair. There may be ways to reduce the costs by agreeing to omit some parts of the design that weren't essential.

Unfortunately, selecting the best tender is not as simple as just choosing the lowest bid. Naturally, the cheapest price will always appear very attractive – who can resist a bargain? But take a minute to consider why it's that cheap. Is it because they're desperate for the work? This is where you need to get smart and read between the lines. One builder may have undercut the others because he's inexperienced or inept at pricing. Another may have underpriced part of the job, and may need to recover that loss by cutting corners as the work proceeds. But sometimes, wide variations in quoted prices for the same job may simply be down to each builder assessing the risk of the job differently, and loading prices accordingly.

Just to get you really paranoid, it's not unknown for a builder to deliberately submit a super-cheap price as a strategy to secure the job, and then pile on lots of expensive 'extras' later. An unscrupulous firm may be quite skilled in spotting loopholes in your specification, knowing they can later charge you premium prices. So it's worth spending some time comparing all your tenders, section by section, since this may reveal surprising differences in quoted prices for the same works.

Suppose you have four tenders and you're looking at all the prices for the same roof job. One may be significantly cheaper perhaps because roofing work is that firm's area of expertise. Fair enough, but if it's absurdly cheap compared to the others it may be that they've forgotten to include some materials or labour. This means you'll either end up with a badly done job or paying for lots of hugely profitable extras. Unless the firm has been highly recommended, it may be cheaper in the long run to select another, rather than risk them scrimping on materials and labour to recoup losses. High standards don't tend to go with low prices.

Then there's the important matter of the start-on-site date. It's unlikely that a good small firm would be so in need of work that it could start tomorrow. But on the other hand, a firm that can't begin for another year may not be ideal either.

Finally, use a little intuition about the people themselves. Are they people you can do business with? Or is there something about their attitude that makes you feel uneasy? If in doubt, go for the good communicator, or the one you get on with best, as they'll be more likely to understand your requirements.

13 Subsidence Street *new rear extension*	
PROGRAMME OF WORKS	**Date**
1 Start on site	3 March
2 Demolish old garage/patio	7 March
3 Groundwork: excavate foundations & pour concrete	14 March
4 Excavate and lay drainage	
5 Ground floor slab	
6 Construct main walls up to DPC	
7 Build main walls to first lift	
8 Complete main walls	
9 Roof structure	
10 Roof coverings	
11 Windows & doors	
12 Knocking through	
13 Plumbing, heating & electrics 1st fix	
14 Floor screed and plastering	
15 Internal joinery	
16 Kitchen and sanitary fittings, connect drainage	
17 Plumbing, heating & electrics 2nd fix	
18 Decorations	
19 Practical completion	
Bodgit & Scarper Building Contractors, Old Nick Lane, Dartmoor DN1	00/00/00

And the winner is...

Having made your choice, you'll then need to set up a meeting to go through your drawings and specification in some detail prior to signing the contract. If you're employing an architect, they should also be present so that any complex parts of the design can be discussed.

Run through key things like the depth of foundations, the type of bricks (stone, render, cladding etc), the sizes of roof timbers, types of windows and doors, and the number of coats of paint on external timbers.

If the builder's face turns a peculiar shade of ghostly white at any stage it means he's just realised something's been seriously underpriced. If his pricing is very low for one particular part of the job compared to the others, mention this by saying 'Your price for the [whatever] seems to be a lot less than the average for this work. Would you like to check your price before signing the contract?' It's always better to agree a revised price at this stage than to have a dispute later on site, but it must be agreed in writing since it changes the tendered sum. Legally you could hold them to their tendered price, but this would only encourage a cheap job to save money.

This is the honeymoon stage, and everything is sweetness and light as the contractor basks in the warm afterglow of winning the tender. It's therefore as well to bring things sharply down to earth and remind them about all the important issues – the agreed start date and completion date, arrangements for storage of materials on site, the welfare facilities (loos etc), health and safety matters, frequency of site meetings, and the agreed method for dealing with any changes you might later require to the work (*ie* written instructions).

Although as a rule they don't like doing this, ask the contractor to provide a detailed week-by-week programme, so that you can monitor progress. Even a simple 'milestone programme' would be useful, as shown left.

Having satisfied yourself that the builders are fully aware of what's required of them and are happy to deliver it, the next step is to fill in all the important parts of the contract. These will include the start and completion dates, any damages (penalties) for overrunning, the dates you'll make payments, and the amount of retention you plan to keep (see 'Payments and retentions', page 101).

As far as the agreed timescales are concerned, it's not unknown for contractors to be prone to bouts of over-optimism at this stage, which will only cause problems later if you have to apply for damages for their non-completion. So it may be worth asking them to think twice about the projected time to finish the job. If necessary they might want to agree an extra couple of weeks, just in case. They are, of course, perfectly at liberty to finish the job earlier if they wish (but they won't). All contract documents, including the drawings and the form of tender, now need to be signed by both parties and stapled together with the contract itself. Hang on to the originals, and provide photocopies to the contractor.

Photo: Wavin Hepworth

If you're not using a ready-printed legal contract, you can complete the deal by emailing or writing to the contractor to formally accept his offer. Your 'letter of acceptance' is a legally binding contract document and should include a list of the drawings and documents on which he based his quote, together with confirmation of the agreed price (the 'contract sum'), the agreed timescales, and the stages of payment etc. You must also request that the builder formally replies and acknowledges receipt of your letter.

Directly employing your own trades

If you've always wanted to manage your own team, now's your chance. Of course you can't expect to instantly become the Sir Alex Ferguson of the home extension

world without a little prior experience, so only take this role on if you know your headers from your stretchers. Otherwise, there is always going to be the risk that if some less scrupulous subcontractors figure they're working for a novice, they could be tempted to cut corners.

Strictly speaking, subcontractors are tradesmen employed by a main contractor. If they work directly for you then they aren't actually subbies at all, just plain old tradespeople. They tend to operate either as one-man bands or as small firms – but everyone still calls them subbies.

This arrangement often suits people who plan to do some of the building work themselves. But there are some important differences between employing a main contractor and running your own show. Subbies expect to be paid weekly or for shorter jobs daily (preferably in cash) rather than in stages like main contractors. Their true loyalty tends to be to larger firms of contractors who can provide them with regular employment as part of a

building team (although some dislike working for builders who are sometimes slow to pay them). They can't afford to let down a good main contractor who consistently provides them with work, but they can afford to lose a one-off client.

This means that potentially there's a greater chance of them not turning up on an appointed day, or even leaving a job only part-complete.

As a client who has chosen to employ some trades direct, perhaps doing some of the building work yourself, you'll need to take on many of the time-consuming responsibilities that you'd otherwise pay a main contractor

to do. This means budgeting for increased overheads, especially phone bills, mileage and time spent ordering or collecting materials. This project management role is virtually a full-time job, and the buck stops with you.

As client and employer rolled into one, your managerial responsibilities should not include policing your subbies' tax affairs. A one-off building project should not be construed by the Taxman as being connected to running a business or trade. Only if they deemed you to be a 'professional developer' would you get lumbered with all the main contractor tax liabilities.

Your mission is to achieve nothing less than the smooth running of the project, which means having to co-ordinate all the various materials and trades on site at each stage of the build. Easy to say, harder to deliver.

Finding trades

Good tradespeople can afford to be picky. For the same reasons that clients often play safe and only appoint builders by recommendation, many subbies will be reluctant to accept a job unless it comes via a trusted contact.

The fact is, even major house-builders sometimes struggle to find reliable trades when the economy's booming. At worst you may have to take a calculated risk and employ someone and be prepared to sack them if you're not happy.

As always, the best way to find good tradespeople is through other satisfied customers. But it's also worth asking around at builders' merchants and tool-hire shops – they're unlikely to recommend people who don't return tools or fail to pay bills. Strangely, it's rarely worth asking tradesmen to recommend someone from within their own trade, as they tend to be critical of competitors' work. However, they're usually happy to recommend trades that go before or alongside them, as they don't like following a bad one.

When someone's dead keen to win a job, they may act like your new best mate. But what will they be like when things go wrong, or at the fag-end of the job? The only people who really know this are clients for whom they've

---

Quirks of the trade

Each trade has its own quirks and particular ways of working:

- **Brickies** – Often work in gangs of two, plus a labourer. They don't usually supply materials but often own or arrange hire of cement mixers. When calculating a quote, they may simplify things by 'measuring through openings' on the walls, not deducting anything for the air spaces that comprise the window and door openings (perhaps 25% of the surface area). This compensates for all the 'fiddly bits' at reveals, and window templates etc.
- **Carpenters and joiners** – Usually work as individuals and don't supply materials.

Trades that supply materials as well as labour ('supply and fix') typically include roofers, plumbers, electricians, plasterers, and some kitchen fitters. They make a mark-up on the materials they buy on your behalf.

- **Roofers** – May be hired individually or in gangs, sometimes also organising scaffolding.
- **Plumbers and electricians** – Usually one-man bands or small firms.
- **Plasterers** – Often work in pairs or small gangs.

---

worked before. This means plucking up the courage to ask complete strangers questions about someone who carried out a job for them in the past. If possible, take a look at the finished building to judge the quality for yourself.

When employing individual trades, a written contract of the type you'd use with a main contractor is not realistic. Many will run a mile at the thought, and in any case contracts can sometimes be difficult to enforce against an individual. The best arrangement is to get written quotes and confirm acceptance in writing, making reference to the relevant drawings (by plan number and date issued).

An exchange of letters and plans approved by Building Control is often sufficient.

It can sometimes be tempting to cut costs by arranging for 'a friend of a friend' to undertake jobs such as electrics or plastering. But with these kind of informal arrangements it's not unusual to find yourself left in the lurch because something else has come up at the weekend when they promised to finish your job. And if an important piece of work hasn't been done, the following trades will be held up, making this a false economy. According to urban folklore, the legendary 'Polish builder' will do a good job for a very fair price. But employing non-English-speaking trades means that, with the best will in the world, communication problems can arise (not unlike some Premier League football teams). For example, a roofer who's just arrived from, say, Bulgaria may have a totally different way of working that doesn't take account of UK Building Regulations. Plus there's a tendency for illegal migrant workers to grab their tools and leg it out the back door as soon as the Building Control Officer makes an appearance! So for the more complex parts of the job, it's normally safer to stick with experienced, home-grown trades folk.

Pricing the job

To get each individual job priced, you need to obtain quotes from each trade in turn. But first, it's worth doing a little homework online to get a feel for the 'going rate', so it's easier to judge whether a quoted price is reasonable. But should you get quotations or estimates? A *quotation* is a firm price that is legally binding. It's a fixed sum for a fixed amount of work. If you're presented with a larger final bill, you're only obliged to pay the agreed quoted price, unless you've requested 'extras' or you've agreed to 'changes'. An *estimate*, on the other hand, is the builder's best guess as to what the cost might eventually be. It's not legally binding, and allows the builder to present a higher (or lower) final bill, and is consequently far too risky for major works.

If you're clear about what you want and provide sufficient information, you should in return receive accurate quotes. This means there's less chance of misunderstandings arising later on site and being charged expensive extras for things you forgot to include. But whilst a surveyor or architect might reasonably be expected to nail down every last detail, there's always a

Tips for appointing and working with trades

- Go by personal recommendation where possible.
- Get more than one quote for each job.
- Take up references and talk to previous clients.
- Check that membership of any trade bodies is up to date, and especially that electricians and gas fitters are suitably qualified and registered (*eg* Gas Safe registered).
- Be careful about beating them down on price – if they feel 'robbed' they may claw it back later.
- Make sure you have sufficient insurance in place.
- Be very clear about what you want, and try not to change your mind.
- Remember, if you leave finding a trade to the last minute you'll be charged more.
- Agree a price rate in advance for any extras.
- Guard against poor quality work by confirming everything in writing, with reference to drawings.

risk that you could forget something. So it's best to keep the wording fairly general, for example writing *'to include all necessary roofing work'* and *'all first and second fix work'*. This should prevent them claiming that a particular task wasn't included and charging it as an extra.

If possible, get at least two quotes for the same job. These should be submitted in writing as a firm price for the completed job. If you can't get a fixed price for the job, individual tasks may be quoted in terms of a 'metreage rate', known as 'pricework'. This is where you're given a price expressed as a 'measured rate', either *per square metre* (tiling, brickwork, plasterwork etc) or *per metre run* (for laying pipes etc).

If someone claims there are too many uncertainties to know in advance what the job entails, it usually means they're too lazy to read the plans. Such a claim may be true for some refurbishment jobs, but not for new build. So unless you trust someone implicitly, it's normally best to avoid quotes based on time taken, such as 'day rate' (a price per day), because of the obvious temptation to sit around and string the job out indefinitely. Daywork may be acceptable for small parts of the job, at agreed rates, but not for the whole job.

If any prices come in a bit on the high side compared to the competition, be prepared to negotiate. But knocking the price down too far can backfire. By reluctantly accepting a lower price, a tradesman may be tempted to skimp on the job or go out of their way to charge for extras. So it's important to be clear about what exactly is included in each individual's price.

Like any team, yours will only be as strong as its weakest link. So you need to ensure that each person knows exactly what's expected of them. Otherwise the job will get done the way that's easiest for them rather than the way you want it.

Home Extension Manual

7 PROJECT MANAGEMENT

'Project management' is one of the most misunderstood terms in the English language. There's considerably more to successful project management than many aspiring TV property developers might imagine.

One thing is certain about any building site – at some point things will go wrong. No matter how well you've planned and organised your project, you can never cover *every* eventuality. So you need to be ready to take effective action to prevent any problems that arise from getting out of hand.

Most of the advice in this chapter is equally relevant whether you've chosen to appoint a main contractor or to directly employ individual tradespeople and 'cut out the middleman'. However, some of the issues discussed later in the chapter ('Extras and changes', 'Penalties', 'Disputes' etc) are applicable for projects where a main contractor is primarily responsible for all the day-to-day hiring and firing of subbies as well as coordinating materials and trades on site. Here, the project manager's role should essentially be limited to overseeing the main contractor.

In contrast, where you directly employ your own workforce, the management role will be considerably more demanding and time-consuming. As we saw in the last chapter, this will mean taking personal responsibility for the smooth running of the entire project on a daily basis.

Overseeing the works

The objective of the project manager is nothing less than successfully achieving the holy grail – a *quality* building, delivered *on time* and *within budget*. On a day-to-day level, the job is about ensuring that everything is proceeding according to plan and that when problems do arise, they're dealt with swiftly. Project managers are often the unsung heroes who prevent problems arising in the first place.

If you decide to personally take on this responsibility, think of yourself as the hub of a large wheel. It's your job to ensure clear communications between all the various parties – which includes you (wearing your client hat), the contractors, the designer, Building Control, and your suppliers. One secret to a successful outcome is to 'build the house in your head' first, identifying who is going to do what, when and with

what. Every hour spent planning the job can save three or more hours sorting out problems later on site.

ATTITUDE

It's generally agreed that the appropriate attitude to adopt when managing a building project is one of 'friendly formality', but it

can be a difficult balance to get right. If you get too matey it may become hard to maintain authority, but if you strut around treating builders as an inferior sub-species they may be tempted to seek payback (weeing down your cavity walls is one well-known method, but there are others…)

JUST CHECKING

It's surprisingly easy to unnerve builders on the job. Despite their hard reputation, all a client needs to do to psychologically antagonise the workforce is to continually walk about wearing a gravely worried expression, peering over shoulders whilst waving around sets of drawings. Checking everything very obviously with a spirit level and tape measure every couple of hours is also guaranteed to disturb the peace. Since it doesn't pay to irritate the hell out of your workforce, it's best to wait until work has finished for the day before doing some of the more obvious and invasive checks.

It's important to take a close interest in the work on site so you're aware of what's going on, but you must do it without constantly getting in the way. Checking work as it progresses means you can nip problems in the bud – otherwise you risk only noticing that the walls have peculiar bumps in them weeks after moving in. Just like buying something in a shop, before handing over your cash you want to be happy with the quality. So if you see anything that looks a bit dubious, don't be shy about mentioning it to the contractor. If you think he's fobbing you off, seek the opinion of a surveyor or architect, or have a friendly chat with your Building Control Officer (they don't *have* to give an opinion, but it's always worth asking).

A firm of building contractors is basically just a bunch of guys with different skills. It's when they stray from the

Routine checks

- **Check the site**: A site unnecessarily littered with old materials and tools is a badly run site and a safety hazard.
- **Check the 'setting out'**: The position of the walls and doorways etc should correspond to the drawings.
- **Check Damp Proof Membrane** (DPM) sheets on ground floors are continuous and that there are no gaps to the insulation.
- **Check with a spirit level** that all vertical and horizontal surfaces are true.
- **Check details** like the heights of wall switches and sockets.

Recent changes to site safety laws means there is now a legal obligation for some homeowners to manage safety on site.

Failure to comply with these 'CDM regulations' (Construction Design & Management) can result in criminal prosecution.

The person required to manage Health & Safety on site is usually the Project Manager. So what exactly do you need to do? Legally having work done on your home makes you a 'domestic client' and in many cases you won't have to actively get involved in Health and Safety management. But if you are running even part of it yourself, you will have legal responsibilities – but much depends on which route you've chosen to get it built:-

Full Service route
If you're employing a designer as well as a main contractor for the whole thing they are automatically responsible for Health & Safety.

DIY route
If you doing all the work yourself the project is classed as DIY and doesn't fall under the CDM regulations

Project Management route
If you take on the role of designer or Project Manager, appointing and managing several trades, then in effect you become responsible for the overall safety planning for the works. This means you have to draw up a 'Construction Phase Safety Plan' which covers risk assessments, logistics and method statements for the works. This must demonstrate that you have taken the health and safety aspects into account. You can download examples from the book's website.

The commercial route
If you are developing the property to run for business purposes, such as a Bed & Breakfast or long term let, then you are no longer a 'domestic client' and the full CDM rules fall on your shoulders.

There is an additional requirement to formally notify the Health & Safety Executive (Form F10) before work starts for large projects totalling more than 500 cumulative days' labour on site (or that last more than 30 days and have more than 20 workers working at the same time at any point). But this is unlikely to apply because even very big home extensions are unlikely to take more than 450 person/days.

For all projects, whether you're legally responsible for Health & Safety or not, it's advisable to demonstrate the following:-
- Always make sure there's a basic first aid kit on site and buy a few hard hats and safety goggles to make available.
- Flag up any dangers (such as any asbestos-based materials or underground cables) and wear a hi-vis jacket and hard hat when on site to help reinforce the safety message for the workforce.
- Insurance – unless you have a main contractor don't forget site insurance covering all risks, employers and public liability

trade they know best, tackling something unfamiliar, that jobs tend to get botched. Specialist materials like lead, zinc, stone slates and marble normally require specialist skills, not a 'jack of all trades' learning on the job.

PROGRESS
Don't expect everything to run like clockwork all the time. Even the best builder in the world can be the victim of last-minute 'no show' deliveries or subbies going AWOL. So the occasional day with no one on site is to be expected, and a bit of slack needs to be built into the programme to take account of this. You need to allow your contractor some degree of freedom to manage the workload, so give him a little room to breathe. Larger firms will have several jobs running simultaneously, which can require skilled juggling of manpower. Inevitably an electrician or plumber will be urgently needed at two sites at the same time, just when he's disappeared for a week's holiday.

As project manager, you'll want to regularly compare progress on site to your original programme. But you need to be reasonable, as some things are not foreseeable. Delays due to severe weather aren't the contractor's fault (although they aren't necessarily an acceptable contractual reason for a project overrunning). It's therefore possible that the completion date may need to be extended. However, a site that remains spookily silent for days on end will soon mess up your programme, and you'll need to formally request that progress is restored. If the builders fail to respond then the matter may need to be treated as a dispute (see below).

Communication
The hardest part of a successful build is achieving good communication. Holding a brief site meeting with the main contractor perhaps every couple of weeks is essential. This means all parties, including yourself, can be regularly updated, thereby answering queries and preventing minor disputes from becoming major. Much as builders instinctively dislike 'wasting time' by turning up to tedious meetings, in the long run it will actually save time by minimising the chances of costly time-consuming mistakes.

Note that if you're employing a property professional such as an architect or chartered surveyor to manage your project, legally they are your 'agent' and all communications and instructions to the builder should go via them. The builder will get totally confused if you start telling him some things and the agent tells him other stuff, in which case he'll probably end up ignoring you both.

Fresh drawings
It may seem obvious, but everyone directly involved with the project – client, architect, contractor, subcontractors etc – should be singing from the same hymn-sheet. That means having the latest version of all drawings distributed and available for those working at the coal face.

Mark revisions clearly with the appropriate revision

identification, such as 'Drawing No.005/REVISION C', and be sure to remove all earlier drawings from circulation.

Keeping records

When the completion date finally arrives there are always going to be a few loose ends to sort out with the contractor. If the project runs late, the contractor will immediately give you ten good reasons why it wasn't his fault. Typically these relate to things like bad weather and undelivered materials, but a whole raft of personal problems may also be cited.

By the end of the project, everyone will have forgotten exactly what happened, or didn't happen, weeks ago on site. It's therefore worth keeping a simple daily site log of things like weather conditions (at least for the external work stages) and what labour and materials were present on site each day. Ideally take dated photos to prove it.

Site safety

The designer has a legal duty to minimise safety risks by drawing up a health & safety plan which is administered by the main contractor - see Boxout. If you are the client this should not be your responsibility, but if you're directly employing people on your site you must be able to demonstrate that you've taken reasonable precautions to prevent injury.

Either way, it's a good idea to specify aspects of site safety in the prelims and to encourage the builder to keep the site as tidy a possible at all times. For example, 240v power supplies are prohibited on building sites so contractors must only use 110v power tools, and it wouldn't do any harm to include a reminder of this in the documentation. You must also ensure that children are physically excluded from entering sites at all times by erecting suitable childproof barriers.

Building sites are renowned for serious accidents. Approximately half of all construction fatalities are due to falls, hence the recently introduced 'Working at Height Regulations' which, amongst other things, restricts the use of ladders. Where ladders are essential, their tops must be anchored to something secure. But these aren't the only worry. The risks from such routine objects as power tools, sharp blades, holes in the ground, bricks dropped from scaffolding, flame guns, toxic or flammable sprays and live electric cables are very real and need to be treated with respect.

It's never worth taking chances on site. Always wear a hard hat, steel-capped boots and a safety jacket. Look where you're stepping, and if you really must ascend the scaffolding notify the contractor first.

Keep your materials safe and secure.

Dealing with suppliers

Ordering materials

Managing the logistics of getting the right materials delivered to the right place at the right time can be a demanding task, one that clients using main contractors often take for granted. So if you've opted to buy the building materials and arrange deliveries yourself it means you'll be responsible for non-completion should work on site grind to a halt due to lack of materials. To help things run smoothly if you decide to source your own stuff, start by writing out a detailed shopping list of all your materials (known as a 'bill of quantities'). This is translated from your drawings and the information in your specification document, from which all the areas and volumes can be calculated with the help of a scale rule. Your specification should be clear about whether you want the trades to provide their own materials or just supply 'labour only'.

When ordering materials you often have to accept the nearest pack quantity size. Bricks for example are delivered in pack sizes (typically 360, 390, 400, 452, or 475 per pack) which may prove inconvenient if you only need a few. And don't forget to add an allowance for the materials that get wasted, or are surplus, perhaps to the tune of around 10%. Ordering more than you need may be expensive, but buying too little is probably more so.

Having worked out exactly how much of what you need to order, next select two or three major suppliers (usually builders' merchants) and give them your shopping list together with a copy of your drawings. Ideally show them samples of the specific bricks and tiles you require.

Most builders expect to pay substantially less than the list prices shown in catalogues, so there's no reason you shouldn't be able to negotiate a sizeable discount for such a large order. But you first need to open a trade account. You will be quoted keener prices if they know you're serious about buying, rather than just researching prices for estimating a job. Builders Merchants' prices normally include 'free' delivery although pallets are sometimes charged and refunded later after being collected.

Electric mixers are fine for mortar but not so good at mixing concrete.

You should qualify for at least a month's credit. By postponing a purchase beyond the end of the month you can often qualify for an extra 30 days' credit. Haggling over prices is standard practice at builders' merchants, but not of course at the big DIY sheds like Wickes and B&Q, where some prices can be as competitive as trade prices elsewhere although delivery is sometimes charged extra (N.B. some DIY stores now offer trade accounts with a 10% discount). To compare quotes from rival suppliers, ensure that you're actually comparing like with like and that the materials are the same. Also check that VAT is included, and that quantities and delivery dates are all clearly stated.

A single large supplier should be able to provide all of the big stuff you'll need, from cement and aggregates to roof tiles – one well-known firm's brochure even promises 'no unpleasant surprises'! Builders' merchants are normally most competitive on price when supplying bricks and blocks, timber, mass produced joinery, sand and cement, drainage and plastering materials. However, some components, such as double-glazed windows, bathroom fittings and kitchen units, may need to be ordered from specialist suppliers well in advance.

A useful alternative if you have implicit trust in your builder and his trade connections and you don't fancy your chances haggling with the stony-faced hardmen of the building supply world, is to strike an enterprising deal closer to home. You could offer to pay your builder to source the same materials at perhaps 5 to 10 per cent below your best supplier's quote. The attraction for the builder is that if he can then obtain the materials for a lower price through his contacts, he gets to keep the difference.

Plant hire

Just when you're starting to appreciate how much the main contractor does for his money, there's a third dimension to add to the equation: the curious world of plant hire. Just about everything can be hired, from JCBs, scaffold towers, cranes and cement mixers to angle grinders, power breakers, pumps and tarpaulins, normally on a daily or weekly basis. But hiring only really makes sense over short periods. Hiring for more than a few weeks often means you could have bought the tools for the same money. Be clear about whose job it is to arrange plant hire – there's a limit to how many excavators you can make use of at one time.

If you're employing subbies, it's a good idea to discuss each trade's requirements beforehand. Whereas some subbies tend to arrive fully tooled up (*eg* electricians, plumbers and carpenters) others, such as brickies, may only possess spirit levels and trowels, leaving you to fork out for cement mixers and scaffolding.

Scaffolding is normally priced for a hire period of 8 to 10 weeks, with a small surcharge levied for each extra week and is normally arranged by the main contractor. The price should include scaffolders making return site visits at different stages to erect the next storey ('lift') when needed. Erecting scaffolding is definitely not a DIY job, and must be carried out by a licensed specialist firm with plenty of insurance. Costs depend on complexity but most work is based on a simple metre price, typically £20 to £25 per metre run for each lift. Smaller local firms are usually cheaper and it's best to get more than one quote. Specify that it is erected in accordance with European Standard BS EN12811-1:2003 (formerly BS 5973) which will at least cover you in the event of an accident. Once the scaffolding is all in place, a 'handover certificate' will confirm it has been erected properly.

Deliveries

Delivery dates are crucial. But it's an unfortunate fact of life that materials sometimes arrive later than promised. Get this wrong and you could end up paying trades to sit around idle on site, and then have trouble getting them to turn up again next time. It's not unknown for crucial deliveries, like the concrete wagon, to somehow get mysteriously cancelled by suppliers despite having been paid for in advance, which can obviously mess up your programme. Correct ordering and punctual delivery of joinery, especially the windows, is always a critical element in any build. So if speed is of the essence, you'd be better off only ordering readily available products.

Never leave things to chance – it's best to double-check with a quick call to your supplier a day or so in advance to confirm the delivery date. When deliveries do arrive, where possible try to check the materials for damage before signing them off, although you rarely get much time to do this. If in doubt write 'unchecked' next to your signature, especially with deliveries of timber which is notoriously prone to bowing and twisting.

To avoid access problems, allow at least 3 metres width

Yee-haa! Dangerman delivers bricks.

for vehicular access, and make allowances for turning circles, parking, and space for off-loading from trucks.

Storing materials and site security

There's an art to managing incoming materials. The key is to plan ahead by considering which materials will need to be specially protected from the weather with covers, and to avoid blocking access routes. Then there's the matter of security, and of course the timing of deliveries – the longer you leave stuff piled up on site the more temptation there is for thieves to liberate it. Your site will need to be fenced off to deter intruders, using steel mesh fencing equipment. This can be hired.

Staggering delivery times can help avoid overcrowding the site with mountains of materials. Try to get deliveries stored away swiftly, covered up, and distributed around the site to where they'll be needed. Make full use of lockable garages and garden sheds.

Of course, it helps greatly if you've got a generously sized site with plenty of space for storage, so that materials requiring protection can be delivered days before they're needed. Things like bricks, blocks, and roof tiles can be stored for quite a long time, subject to being protected from the weather. Particular care should be taken with piles of sand – the local cat and dog populations will be just itching to make full use of them! Tarpaulins or plastic sheets weighed down with blocks should do the trick.

Materials like plaster and cement powder need to be delivered fresh, just prior to use. As note above, materials made of timber are especially vulnerable to distortion and warping, especially if allowed to get damp. Roof trusses must be stacked on a level base kept clear of the ground and covered.

Driveways and anything likely to be damaged should be protected. It may be useful to

take photos before the work starts as evidence of prior condition. Don't forget, it's essential for builders to have sufficient room to work, so be sure to leave plenty of clear space around the footprint of the proposed extension. A tidy site is a safe site.

Programming

To keep control of things, you'll need to prepare a written programme showing week-by-week what's supposed to be happening at each stage in the project. Obviously it's essential to co-ordinate the delivery of materials with the scheduled arrival of different trades on site – which is why it's vital you check the availability of stocks well in advance, particularly of materials like bricks and blocks which can be subject to shortages.

Having researched your material supplies and the availability of labour, you can then complete the various times and dates. Allow some flexibility for bad weather and the inevitable unexpected delays. Remember, these dates and times are only your best guess – they're not set in stone and you may need to fine-tune things as the project develops.

Cleanliness and protection

Never underestimate the amount of dust and mess that building a simple extension can create. Power sanders, demolition works, and angle grinders cutting chases in plasterwork can swiftly create an unpleasant swirl of gritty smog that rapidly engulfs your living space, clothes, food, children etc. If you're employing subbies direct, they have a reputation for being rather messy, regarding clearing up as the client's problem.

For many homeowners, this is the most disheartening part of the whole home extension process. But the problem can be minimised by good planning – keeping the newbuild separate from the main house for as long as you can by postponing 'breaking through' until as late as possible. It's also well worth stocking up on dustsheets to protect vulnerable surfaces.

Extras and changes

As noted earlier, if there's one golden rule above all it is to think through your plans very carefully at the design stage so that you don't keep changing your mind as the build progresses. If you do have to alter the design after the job has started, or you need to request some 'extras', always broach the subject first with your main contractor. Unless you're employing your own trades avoid making direct arrangements with individuals on site as this is outside the terms of the contract, and will seriously dismay your main man, resulting in a bad atmosphere and a lack of future co-operation.

In an ideal world, it shouldn't be necessary to vary the work as it progresses. But in reality there are four situations where this may happen:

You request additional work – As you watch your extension take shape, something will occur to you that you wish had been included but wasn't. Some builders make nearly half their profits from customers requesting extra works, because very often the client forgets to ask about the cost implications. You may therefore notice hands being rubbed with glee when you saunter up and ask your builder 'Could you just tile the basin splashback'. So, always be sure to get an estimate of the cost of any additional work before it's carried out, and then note how long the work takes and the materials used. It's very easy to underestimate extra costs and, as time goes by, to lose track, resulting in an unpleasant surprise when all the costs are finally totted up at completion. What can really cause trouble is issuing belated 'surprise' instructions, such as for extra roof work long after the scaffolding's all been taken down, or for an extra radiator once the system's already up and running.

The builders suggest extra work – Most builders have considerable experience of similar projects to yours, and as a result may have some genuinely smart ideas about how to improve the design, even saving you money by doing it another way. On the other hand, many are also highly skilled at the art of 'soft selling'. Friendly, casual suggestions, such as 'While we're at it we may as well replace those old ceilings', or 'It's no problem to just replaster the walls' may be perfectly pitched to illicit the required client response. It's fatal to assume there'll be no charge. Always ask how much it will cost.

Unforeseen circumstances – The builders stumble across something unexpected – rotten timber floor joists in the old house when breaking through, or the existing electric wiring isn't up to the job of supplying the new extension. This requires extra

Left: New interpretation of the traditional bathroom – 'alfresco-style'.

work that wasn't specified. But who pays the additional costs? It depends on whether such work was reasonably foreseeable and should have been built into the contractor's tender price. Or perhaps it should have been clearly specified by the client.

Items not specified – Basically, you expect to get what you asked for. If you specified 'guttering' but didn't specifically mention the extruded aluminium ogee style guttering that you really wanted, the contractor will price for fitting the cheaper standard half-round black plastic variety. If your architect leaves 'holes' in the specification that end up costing you extra cash, you may be entitled to claim a proportionate reduction in their fees.

Instructions

Another area shrouded in mystery and collective amnesia by the end of a project is 'who said what to whom'. For example, when you realise in horror that the kitchen walls have been painted a vile shade of slime green, the builder quite reasonably points out 'that's what it says in the specification, boss'. Your claim to have told his mate Dave to change it to magnolia some weeks ago is greeted with utter disbelief. The moral of this tale, of course, is *keep a written record of every instruction and change agreed*, with dates and details. Send a copy to the contractor, and if possible keep a folder on site that everyone can refer to. Any changes proposed by the contractor, such as substituting your first choice of parquet flooring because it's no longer available, should also be agreed in writing.

A written 'instruction' can allow the work to proceed where the cost isn't known, without holding things up. Instead, the cost implications are kicked into the future, to the 'final account' stage. But this can obviously be risky, so if possible costs should be nailed down in the form of a 'change order':

AGREED CHANGES		
Date	**Instruction**	**Contact**
2 Feb	Paint colour to kitchen walls changed to magnolia	Dave Amnesiac
1 Mar	Change main external door to 'Malton Glazed' hardwood 78x33in, ref 208-243	Mad Jack MacMad

Change orders

It's always better to hammer out a price at the time when the required extra works are requested. Then, to eliminate any possible doubt, a form known as a 'change order' (formerly known as 'variation orders') can be submitted, listing all the agreed changes. Change orders are written instructions from the client to the builder that authorise him either to omit work that was previously agreed, or to carry out additional work, together with the appropriate increase or reduction in costs (see below). It's also very much in the builder's interest for any extras to be confirmed in writing, since there's no legal obligation to pay for them unless they were formally agreed. It's surprising how memories can fade, so written evidence is important.

ref	Change Order	£
JB 1 20.7.08	Omit: external lighting system	(1,250)
BG 3 30.7.08	Add: Supply and fit 1 no. shower screen (B&Q ref 12345) to bath	105.00

So that you don't get fleeced for extra works, try to ensure that the builder sticks to the same profit margin as tendered for the original job. Of course it helps greatly if the builder's original quotation or tender clearly spelt out the labour rates charged, for example 'brickwork charged @ £X per square metre' so that additional work can be priced at the same rates. Similarly, you can base the cost of extra materials on the original prices pro rata.

An alternative method is for extra work to be priced using hourly or daily labour rates. It's best to agree such 'daywork' rates with your builder at the outset (e.g. 1 chippie at £190 per day). Labour charges can also be verified with trade associations, and the prices of materials researched online. You can then monitor roughly how long the extra jobs take. But bear in mind that the cost to a main contractor of bringing a subcontracted electrician back just to fit one socket will be disproportionately expensive. The total cost would need to also include materials and allow a profit margin. The obvious snag with daywork is that some less saintly builders could be tempted to devote excessive time to chatting, whistling and singing – time for which the client is paying.

Changes to the contract period

Requesting additional work not only means a bigger bill, but is also likely to have a knock-on effect on your completion date. The job may therefore need to run over a bit, and the delays to your programme should be agreed along with the costs. Confirm the revised completion date in writing so that the builder won't be hit with penalty clause for missing the original completion date. The builder may also incur extra hidden costs, such as hiring security fencing for a few more weeks, which he will have to pass on.

Money matters

Payments and retentions

The stages at which you pay your builder should be agreed in advance. For small projects that take up to 4 weeks he may accept one payment on completion, but for a typical home extension job 'interim payments' are made, often every four weeks, and certainly no more than once a fortnight. It's obviously important to keep clear records of each payment you make. To avoid 'double counting', each consecutive payment starts by totalling up all the work completed to date, and then deducting all previous amounts paid.

It's customary on all but the smallest jobs for the client to hold back a sum of money during the works, which must be agreed at the outset. The main purpose of this is to provide an incentive that will encourage the builders to return at later stages to fix any minor defects. Normally the contract permits the deduction of a small retention (say five per cent) from each payment. Half the retained money is released to the builder at the end of the build, at 'practical completion', and the remaining half is paid after a further three months, the 'defects liability period' (usually six months on larger projects).

If you insist on keeping too large a retention, the contractor will simply price the job higher. But if the retention is too small, they might consider it easier to lose the money than to physically come back and carry out any minor finishing tasks. If you're dealing with a trusted local firm you may not need to keep a retention.

There are two golden rules when it comes to payments:

Never pay for work in advance
If the builder goes bust halfway through the job, or if he's a rubbish builder and you want to terminate the contract, you'll be in a far stronger position. Also, if you pay for work that hasn't yet been done it removes much of the incentive for good quality workmanship to be completed on time.

Pay contractors promptly
Failure to pay is a breach of contract. You're normally obliged to pay within 14 days of the due date (or within 30 days of practical completion). No one is going to do their best work if they're not paid on time. Typically, builders are at their most financially vulnerable towards the end of a job, and paying promptly is an easy way to create a positive atmosphere of trust and co-operation.

Many subbies operate on a hand-to-mouth basis and expect to be paid promptly in cash, usually at the end of the week. If you don't have the money to pay them, they'll slip off to another job where they know they'll be paid. So if there's any doubt about funds being ready in time, don't wait until they're queuing up on a Friday afternoon with hands outstretched. Depending on your relationship, and how certain you are of having funds available in the near future, tell them in advance and leave the decision to them. At worst, if you anticipate problems consider calling a halt to the job until funds are available.

Making a payment

Normally you make a payment to the contractor for the value of work completed by each agreed date, say, on the last day of every month. The amount you pay is based on the price the builder quoted for each piece of work that's actually been completed. If a job is only half complete, then you simply pay a pro-rata amount of the price quoted for the full job. Valuing partially completed works is always going to be a bit of a guess, so it's not worth quibbling about the odd £50 here or there.

In addition you must include the value of any substantial materials stored on site, such as bulk deliveries of 'unfixed' bricks, blocks, tiles etc. Note that once you've paid for materials they are legally yours, so check they don't later mysteriously disappear.

So having totted up the total of all work completed to date, plus any large quantities of materials on site, you then add any completed extra work or changes that you've agreed – if you don't have a firm price, estimate it approximately. Finally, check that VAT is included. After deducting the agreed amount of retention (say 5%) and any previous payments you've already made, you should arrive at the actual sum due to be paid.

As a rule large quantities of bank notes and building sites don't make good bedfellows, although weekly payments to trades may be in cash as long as receipts are forthcoming. For main contractors a debit card or BACS bank transfer should be perfectly acceptable. But before making the first online bank payment it's a wise precaution to just pay a token sum, say £5, and check it came through OK the next day to guard against any risk of identity theft or hi-jacked bank account data.

The contractor may want to submit his own account listing the work that's been done, but to ensure you're not paying too much always carry out your own valuation.

An alternative method of payment is by making simple 'staged payments'. This is the way mortgage lenders like to release funds on self-build properties. Banks will normally advance moneys to you as each major element of the work is completed, once it's been verified by their valuer (guess who pays their fees?). So you can then pay the builders a previously agreed amount for work completed to key stages, for example upon completion of foundations, at DPC level, at completion of the main roof etc.

If you later need to withhold payment because of problems with workmanship or materials, it's essential to notify the builder in writing immediately, stating your reasons. If you fail to notify them and still withhold payment, you'll be in breach of contract and the builder can give you seven days' notice of his intention to stop work.

Practical completion and final payment

Towards completion of the project, the main contractor will submit his bill, the dreaded 'final account'. It's at this point that many a client has required the assistance of a stiff drink. But the final payment should not normally be made until the work is fully complete. This is the stage at which the client obtains full use of the building, although some small faults and minor finishing works may still be outstanding and will need to be rectified during the next six months – known as the 'defects liability period' (or 'latent defects period'). If you can schedule things so the final payment is going to be a substantial amount it means there'll be a greater incentive for the builders to fully complete the job. It's important to note that the Building Control definition of 'Practical Completion' relates to things like all the structural works, fire safety, insulation, stairs, electrics, smoke alarms etc being complete and may not include stuff like decoration, skirting, finished flooring etc. So although they may issue a 'completion certificate' if you're not keeping a retention, it's advisable to delay the final payment until any minor snags are sorted (See Chapter 17).

Penalties

Most contracts include a penalty clause, requiring the contractor to fork out money (known as 'liquidated damages') if the job isn't completed on time. This is stated in the contract as a maximum sum in pounds per week, agreed by both parties at the outset, for each week that the job overruns without a good reason. The client is in theory entitled to deduct this money from the builder's final payment. In reality, however, it can be hard to justify legally unless you can prove you've suffered real financial loss as a result, or that the delays were excessive and unjustifiable. Only larger firms of contractors are likely to accept such clauses. Nonetheless, this is a useful piece of ammunition in the event of delays and slow progress.

Guarantees

Construction work is traditionally guaranteed for a minimum period of 12 months against material and workmanship defects. Insurance-backed guarantees are preferred, since they'll still be valid if the contractor goes bust. But it's not just the building that's covered. Should your gleaming new oven promptly catch fire or the boiler conk out, it's worth noting that legally it's the responsibility of the supplier of the equipment to deal with the problem – which may be your contractor, unless you supplied it yourself. Always insist that contractors provide test certificates for fitting appliances as well as for all electrical, gas and heating work, to prove it all works safely.

Your have a legal right as the customer for the work to be carried out 'with reasonable care and skill'. If a significant defect becomes apparent soon after completion, you may reasonably claim that the workmanship was negligent. If a contractor fails to honour the guarantee, you must write informing them that you intend to appoint another firm, at his expense, and give him a final opportunity to sort it out himself. But talk to Trading Standards or a solicitor first.

Latent defects

In some parts of the structure, such as foundations and roofs, it may take quite a while for defects to become apparent, often long after the 'defects liability period' has expired. Only after the first heavy snowfall or severe storm might stresses cause structural cracking due to errors in the design or construction. Contracts normally allow you to take legal action for such 'latent defects' within 6 years of the appearance of problems. In some circumstances this can be extended to 12 years (such as where company directors sign the contract as a 'deed').

Dealing with problems

There's always a chance that your project will run super-smoothly all the way through. But the reality is that problems and misunderstandings of one kind or another usually arise, and when they do there's a right way and a wrong way to deal with them. Depending on how this is done the problem

"Of course the price we quoted doesn't include skips …"

"It's just a bit of shrinkage cracking mate."

will either be amicably resolved or will enter the dangerously expensive orbit of lawyers and tribunals.

On a personal level, it's important to avoid getting too emotionally wound up and resorting to angry outbursts. Take a deep breath and try to look at things objectively. Avoid the blame game, and instead focus on solutions and improving communications for the rest of the project.

To avoid frayed nerves and wrecked bank balances, the first step is to define the type of problem you're dealing with, and then take the appropriate measures to solve it. There are basically two types of problem: practical problems on site (*ie* unforeseen technical difficulties), and dissatisfaction with the builders' performance.

Practical problems

The first step is to identify the problem, for example the kitchen base units don't fit, because the available space is too short. Then consider alternative solutions, such as using shorter units, or cutting back the plaster on the walls. Contractors have a lot of experience at solving such problems, so don't automatically dismiss their suggestions. Finally, you need to agree a solution, and confirm it in writing, which should allow work to proceed subject to reaching agreement about cost. But defining who is responsible can often be tricky. Were the plans badly drawn? Should the contractor have noticed this detail? Hopefully it should be clear from the specification or brief who was responsible. Often small problems where responsibility isn't clear can be settled by agreeing to split the cost 50:50.

Dissatisfaction with the contractor

You may be unhappy with the contractor's rate of progress, or quality of work. Or both.

If so, don't waste time discussing it with tradesmen or subbies – arrange a meeting with the main contractor. If there's no improvement write a formal, but not unfriendly, letter requesting that the matter is rectified. Most disagreements with builders boil down to one of four things:

Poor quality workmanship

Any decent builder will know very well whether work is sub-standard or not, and should rectify it when requested. If not, the obvious answer is to simply say you're not paying for poor work. You may find keeping photos a useful record. Ultimately an independent contractor may need to be paid to make good the defective work (remember some builders love nothing better than to 'slag off' other builders, so surveyors are a more impartial source of advice).

Prolonged delays

The work has not been completed, or is way behind schedule. First check the contract and advise the builder that his inaction will put him in breach of contract, and that the breach must be remedied by him getting off his backside. Quote the relevant contract clause. If there's no response within a week, you may then need to go into 'dispute mode' (see below).

Charges for additional work

As noted earlier, to calculate reasonable charges for extra work they should be broadly comparable to the originally tendered work, or at least 'the going rate' in that trade. If all else fails you could refuse to pay any more than you think reasonable.

The extent of works required in the specification

You think a piece of work should have been included in the original price. The contractor does not. So that the entire project doesn't grind to a shuddering halt, for the time being you may have to 'agree to disagree', and later go with the opinion of a mutually acceptable third party professional.

Disputes

If you find yourself bogged down with a disagreement that can't be resolved, you may have a legal dispute on your hands. This means an independent third party capable of providing an objective professional opinion will need to be appointed to adjudicate, normally an experienced chartered surveyor or architect – but not the person who designed your extension, in case it turns out that some problems are due to bad design. Disputes should always be dealt with

promptly, as they only get worse if ignored. If the problem is due to building work that's below par, and the builder has refused to rectify it, then a good first course of action is to ask the Building Control Officer's opinion. A site meeting will need to be held to discuss matters. The final option of terminating the builder's contract is Big Potatoes, requiring legal advice. Once the dust has settled you'll need to appoint another builder to finish the job, for which they may well charge a premium. See website for further advice.

And finally...

If all this makes you feel a little queasy about going anywhere near a firm of builders, it shouldn't. The vast majority of projects succeed perfectly well, sometimes in spite of less than brilliant project management. Remember that what all the parties involved want most is a successful outcome. It's mainly just about applying a little common sense. So with no further delay, let's crack on and get that home extension built.

8 START ON SITE
Groundwork – foundations and ground floor

You've spent months preparing for this day, yet not a single brick has so far been laid. But the good news is that all the trouble taken preparing for the build should now really start to pay off, by helping avoid all those nasty mistakes, expensive conflicts and hidden dangers that are lying in wait to trap the unwary.

The site itself should now be as clear as possible, with obstructions like paving slabs removed and perhaps fences temporarily set aside (best tell the neighbours first!). Access routes need to be as clear as possible. The location of services such as electricity cables, gas, water and underground drainage pipes should have been identified and marked. Now it's simply a matter of transforming those carefully drawn plans into a 3D building. First however you must formally notify Building Control at least two days before work begins. True, they may choose not to visit at this stage, waiting instead until the foundations have been excavated, but that's their call, not your's. Failure to notify them is an offence for which you can be prosecuted.

NOTIFY BUILDING CONTROL 1
Start on site – two days' notice

Day One. Start on site is usually a fairly harmonious occasion. Everyone is full of the best intentions and wants to crack on and make it happen. The first phase, known as 'groundwork', comprises excavation for foundations, and usually also for the drainage. This is followed by construction of the below-ground footings and the main walls built up to damp-proof course (DPC) level together with the ground floor. The basic rule is 'the sooner out of the ground the better'. Once this essential phase is satisfactorily completed you'll be able to proceed with confidence onto the above-ground superstructure of your extension.

Disposing of waste

The first job is for all vegetation, shrubs, roots and topsoil to be removed from the whole area that's to be built on. This must be carried out to a depth that will prevent later growth, typically at least 300mm. But before enthusiastically ploughing into the ground with your JCB, it's important to consider what arrangements are in place for getting rid of the piles of muck that even a small building project will inevitably generate. The smaller the site, the more critical this is, as work will soon grind to a halt once you become inundated with mountains of spoil and rubbish.

All the excavated waste will need to be removed from the site at regular intervals. Not only is this essential from a practical viewpoint, but keeping the area tidy will also encourage tradesmen to be tidy and to do a good job.

Some waste can normally be recycled, saving money. Things like broken bricks, blocks and tiles can be set aside for later use, perhaps as hardcore for patios or drainage in soakaways, or it can sometimes be buried in the garden. Old half bricks can come in handy for garden walls. Clean timber off-cuts can be kept for burning in stoves or waste timber can be burned on site (subject to local smoke control laws).

Sending excavated spoil away is expensive so to keep costs down some can be used to make up levels especially on sloping sites. Or you may be able to disperse some around

the garden. Builders are not allowed to take waste to local household waste disposal tips. But there's nothing to stop you taking old paint pots, cardboard, timber etc in the car.

Skips and grab trucks

The time-honoured method of waste disposal is, of course, our old friend the skip. So much are skips part of our modern urban culture that economists have devised theories that measure the nation's economic growth rate by the number of skips present at any one time in a city's streets!

Overloaded skips won't be collected.

Think where you want your skips positioned, which should be in as convenient a location as possible for the builders to access them, ideally within your garden. Otherwise it may be necessary to park a skip on the road, for which the supplier should have a Local Authority licence. Note that you could be liable to prosecution if a skip is left overnight on a highway without appropriate lighting.

But be warned that weird nocturnal phenomena can sometimes occur when a skip is left empty overnight in the street. Next morning you may discover it filled with ancient sofas and old mattresses, which have mysteriously appeared out of thin air. To avoid this, it's best to arrange for skips to be delivered early in the morning, thereby giving you a good chance of using them before nightfall. Otherwise, take the precaution of covering them with a tarpaulin to reduce the temptation to flytippers. Calculating how many you're going

Grab trucks are the most efficient way to get rubbish removed, where access permits

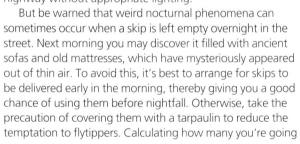

to need can be tricky as the amount of waste generated is usually a lot more than you would reasonably predict.

Excavated subsoil expands in volume once dug (as it is no longer compacted) swelling by at least a third. Clay is particularly prone to expansion as loose spoil and one cubic metre can weigh up to two tonnes. There always seems to be massively more of the stuff than you'd expect so to calculate the amount of excavated waste, work out the volume of the trenches being excavated and then add 50 per cent.

When it comes to getting rid of bulk excavated spoil skips are not always the cheapest option and suppliers limit the size of skip you can hire for this type of waste (see boxout). A better disposal option is to use tipper lorries co-ordinated to arrive with the excavation (the cost of 16 tonner is around £ 250 per load). Or you could dump the spoil in heap, and use a digger later to load the lorries. Alternatively it may be worth hiring a tipper lorry with a 'grab' which can be used to take soil and rubble to the local tip. These trucks can handle a large quantity of waste and can also be used to deliver bulk supplies such as ballast and sand.

Digging the foundations

As everyone knows, foundations have a very simple purpose in life – to transmit the load of the building safely down into firm ground. They need to provide a strong, level base for the new structure, spreading the load of the walls built on them. But they work the other way too: any movement in the ground gets transmitted back up to the building, and the foundations have to allow for this.

Before the long dry summers of 1975 and 1976 foundation depths weren't given a great deal of consideration. Victorian houses might have been built with brick or stone footings down to about 450mm or less. Over time, depths gradually increased as more modern concrete trenches became widely used from the 1930s.

Many pre-1980s buildings have remarkably shallow foundations by today's standards. Only when massive subsidence claims started to hit the insurance companies in the late 1970s was it finally accepted that to resist

Victorian stepped footings.

ground movement foundations needed to reach down to ground of adequate 'bearing strength'.

So it's essential to take great care when excavating in close proximity to old walls with shallow foundations. It's not unknown for builders to dig deep trenches alongside lengths of Victorian terrace walls robbing them of support, causing catastrophic collapse (the insurers then declining to pay out). Such excavations, where unavoidable, should be done in short strips at a time under professional supervision.

The type of foundations your new extension needs will depend on your local ground conditions, which vary greatly around the UK, each having different strength or 'bearing' characteristics. Some, like chalk, are excellent for building on and require relatively shallow foundations, perhaps only

Clay generally needs trenches at least 1.2m deep

700mm deep, to protect against frost which can damage buildings with very shallow foundations. Others, like sand and clay, have good load-bearing capabilities but clay has a worrying tendency to move about and cause subsidence. Your Building Control Officer will be familiar with the ground conditions in your area and has authority to dictate the required depth regardless of what's written on your drawings.

Good trees, bad trees

Because of their large size, oaks, willows and poplars are notorious for causing damage to buildings. These thirsty broadleaf species are the bad guys of the tree world. Their thirst is legendary, at least compared to well-behaved evergreens. But these aren't the only trees that can make trouble.

Because trees, such as plane, lime, and ash are more frequently planted close to buildings, they too have a bad record. Perhaps most notorious of all is leylandii which, along with eucalyptus, is a super-fast grower that can dry out the ground.

As a rule of thumb, damage can usually be avoided if the tree is no closer to the foundation than its mature height. With young trees foundation depths must be based on their mature height when fully grown. Less thirsty trees should be no closer to the building than half their mature height.

Tree	Elm	20–25m
Height[1]	Hawthorn	10m
Distance[2]	Leylandii / cypress	20–25m
Very thirsty		
Oak	16–23m	13–25m
Poplar	15–24m	15–30m
Willow	15–20m	11–25m
12–30m	Pear	12m
4–12 m	Cherry & plum	8m
8–13m	Conifer	20m
Fairly thirsty		
Plane	25–30m	15–25m
Lime	16–24m	8–18m
Chestnut	20m	15m
Beech	20m	10–15m
Ash	20–23m	10–20m
Sycamore / maple	17–24m	10–16m
Apple	10m	5m
6m	Elder	8m
8m	Hazel	
8m		8m
Not too thirsty	17m	7m
Hornbeam	14m	5m
Birch	10m	4m

[1] Typical mature height
[2] Typical minimum recommended distance from buildings with non-specialist foundations

Excavating to a decent depth should prevent your new walls cracking as a result of movement caused by seasonal ground changes, or the impact of nearby trees, or 'slope creep' if you're building on a hill. A required depth of at least 1.2 metres is fairly typical in clay areas. Elsewhere in Britain, on non-clay ground, the minimum depth of any foundation is around 700mm, or deep enough to avoid frost damage.

The problem with clay soil is that it's very susceptible to volume changes. The soil near the surface swiftly dries during the summer and becomes wet again in the winter, violently shrinking and swelling as moisture content changes with the weather. The effect of this can extend to around 900mm below the grass. Not surprisingly, the soil is driest towards the end of summer and wettest in early spring and the amount of ground movement will be greater in unusually dry years.

The presence of some notorious species of trees can require the digging of deeper foundation trenches or the use of special heavy-duty foundation types. But if you think cutting down such trees prior to construction will solve the problem, think again. Once thirsty trees are removed the clay ground may become freshly invigorated with all the water no longer sucked out by the trees, causing it to expand and 'heave'. Predicting the likely effects of trees on ground conditions is a specialised job. Because each site is different, Building Control should be consulted as to whether your foundations will need to be dug deeper to compensate. In more complex cases it's worth seeking the opinion of an arboriculturalist (a tree expert), but as a rough guide the NHBC's foundation depth calculator can be a useful tool: by simply lining up a tree's height and distance from a building you can work out the required foundation depth.

Of course, the great irony with home extensions is that while your main house may be sitting happily on its quaintly shallow original foundations, your extension will have to be built with nuclear-blast-proof boots deep underground. And having two such wildly different foundation depths on the same building means there's a real risk of cracking taking place at the point where the new extension and the old house meet. This is due to 'differential movement' – see page 153.

It's generally a good idea to get all the excavation done at the same time, whilst you've got diggers and labour available on site (see 'drainage'). If the footprint of your extension is very large, then the floor beams may require extra support at mid-span from mini 'sleeper walls' under the floor, which will also need foundations.

Basements

In recent years there has been a lot of interest in 'basement extensions'. But the problem with digging down directly under your house is that it's structurally very complex and enormously expensive. However if you're going to be extending your house, adding extra underground living space can make a lot of sense because some of the excavation work will need to be carried out anyway. The savings will be even greater where you have a sloping site.

Site suitability

To see whether your site is suitable a soil investigation is required. This is to reduce the risk from 'unknowns' lurking in the ground and to identify the location of service pipes and cables (which would have to be checked anyway for an extension). Digging an inspection pit is effectively a test run that helps predict what'll happen when you dig a much larger hole in the shape of the basement later. If it immediately fills up with water it means the water table is high and sites with poor-draining soil need more robust waterproofing, adding to cost and potentially making it uneconomic. The optimum type of ground is chalky soil which drains much better than clay, rather than soil that's very wet or crumbles readily. Once you know this you can design the basement.

Design

Basements usually occupy less than half the footprint of the ground floor of a typical house. So building one under a decent sized extension can provide useful space. Ideally it should sit directly under the new extension walls so the basement structure acts as the foundations for the extension above. The most economical shape is a square or rectangle because every additional corner adds significantly to the cost.

Two key decisions that need to be made at the design stage relate to fire and light. Any habitable room or bedroom needs fire escape windows ('egress windows'). As with loft conversions you also need to design an escape route, typically in the form of a staircase leading up to a 'protected hallway', such as an entrance hall with a main exterior door. Alternatively, stairs can lead directly to outside via a light-well doubling as an emergency exit. Light wells are open areas next to the basement, vertical shafts that allow natural light down to lower floors like sun tunnels. Or if you excavate a bit further they can be big enough to incorporate a sunken courtyard garden, perhaps with bi-fold doors leading out to it. Smaller light-wells can be made from prefabricated reinforced plastic (not in clay ground or high water table sites). In most cases however they're constructed similarly to the main walls, usually in concrete. As well as ensuring there's plenty of natural light you also need sufficient ventilation.

Semi-basements

Basements needn't be 100% underground. The traditional

Victorian 'semi-basement' for example overcomes many awkward design problems because the surrounding earth is excavated away, reducing the external ground levels. The clever thing is, by digging a deep trench at least a metre wide surrounding the basement walls, you don't need to worry about waterproofing. Instead, the outer sides of the trench need to be built as retaining walls, as they effectively hold back the garden. This design has the added advantage of allowing light and ventilation into basement rooms via conventional windows. Semi-basements work best on sloping sites because you don't have to excavate a trench to the front as you already have plenty of light on the downhill side, as it's already partially 'above ground'. So the living space is normally positioned at the front (downhill side) to maximise natural light, and in the darker end you can locate rooms where light isn't essential, such as utility rooms, stores, bathrooms or a home cinema.

Construction

Although conventional twin wall blockwork can be employed (with robust waterproofing treatment) there are various alternative means of construction:-

- ■ Pre-cast waterproof concrete panels manufactured off site and craned into place on a concrete slab foundation. Here the structure of the basement provides the waterproofing, and is generally considered a superior method.
- ■ Polystyrene ICF building blocks (Insulated Concrete Formwork). Once these hollow interlocking blocks are in place they are connected with steel reinforcing rods and filled with poured concrete.
- ■ 'In situ' reinforced concrete: Concrete pre-mixed with waterproofing additives arrives in a mixer lorry on site

Right: Basement excavation – poured reinforced concrete construction.

Below: ICF polystyrene blocks.

Pre-cast concrete panel basement

and is poured into shuttered 'moulds' containing steel reinforcement.

Waterproofing

Any habitable structure below ground needs waterproofing, so how you go about this is a fundamental decision. Essentially you can either opt for a totally watertight system where water is kept out (such as waterproof panels etc listed above) or a 'water management system'. This accepts that water may penetrate the structure (if the wall fails). Any moisture is channelled behind overlapping layers of thick waterproof membranes at wall and floor level down to an internal sump chamber. Here dual pumps extract the water out into a drainage system.

But when you're building an extension from scratch it's probably better to go for a more expensive concrete panel system, poured concrete or ICF; that way you don't have to worry about putting a screw through the waterproofing membrane when you hang pictures on the wall! You also don't have to worry about future maintenance of pumps and cleaning of drainage channels. But whatever method you choose it's essential that the walls are carefully integrated with the flooring, and special care must be taken to ensure floors and walls are well insulated. Where your contractor is building the structure in blockwork (known as 'shell & core') it's a good idea to appoint a specialist installer to do the waterproofing so you get a warranty.

Costs

Costs vary enormously depending on build quality and the ground conditions (typically from £2k/m2 to £4k/m2). The cost also depends on things like having good site access, and how easy it is to excavate and remove soil and divert any services. For larger projects it's best to appoint a specialist firm to design and install the basement so that it's fully covered by a guarantee – because if basements go wrong they go wrong bigtime, becoming underground swimming pools!

Setting out trenches

It's not unknown for a bloke with a mini digger to take a bit of a guess and start excavating roughly where the plans suggest the walls might be built. That's if anyone bothered to give him a set of plans in the first place.

Supervision of this crucial stage is often minimal. One muddy patch of land can look pretty much like another, so it's all too easy for mistakes to occur, especially if everything's been left up to a harassed digger driver.

Trying to change the position of foundations once the concrete has been poured is obviously going to be both troublesome and expensive. So accuracy is crucial at this stage to ensure the walls are built in the right place, are square and structurally sound, which in turn depends on precise measuring. Having double-checked all dimensions on site with those shown on your approved plans, the position of the trenches should be clearly marked out. The traditional method used for setting out trenches is one that Bob The Builder's great-grandfather would have recognised.

Tools required for setting out
- ■ A large spirit level
- ■ Some builders string line (hi-vis)
- ■ A datum peg
- ■ 4 profile boards
- ■ A builder's square

A 'datum peg' need be nothing more exotic than a chunk of wood (roughly 400mm long and 50mm square) hammered into the mud to mark levels on site. Its top must be level with an agreed point on the existing house, usually the DPC or ground floor level. Place the datum peg into the ground at the far side of the proposed new extension, about 1.5m further out than the position of the new wall (so it doesn't get booted over). Getting it level with the existing DPC or floor is done by running a string line from the DPC on the main house and checking it with a spirit level. Additional pegs can then be positioned around the site as required, and should be regularly checked.

'Profile boards' are used to mark the positions of the trenches and walls. A profile board is basically a horizontal strip of wood about 1m wide with four nails or screws lined up along the top. The space between the two outermost nails (about 600mm) represents the total width of the trench to be dug, and the narrower space between the inner pair

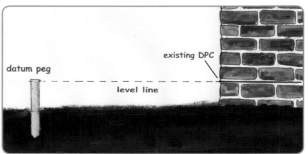

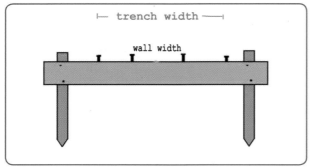

⊢ trench width ⊣

wall width

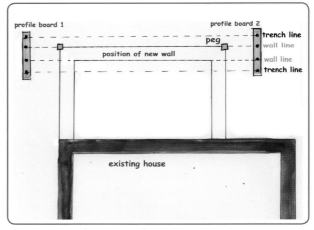

profile board 1   profile board 2

peg   trench line
   wall line
position of new wall   wall line
   trench line

existing house

foundations have been laid, in order to guide the bricklayers up to DPC level. The profile boards can then finally be removed.

of nails shows the planned wall width (about 300mm).

Each board has two vertical stakes for legs so it can be hammered straight into the ground. The tops of the boards must be level with the tops of the datum pegs. There should be one board at each end of the planned foundation trench. To actually mark the position of the trenches, run some builders' line between the two boards at either end of the trench (outer nail to corresponding outer nail etc), thereby creating 'tramlines' with the two inner string lines showing the finished wall positions and the two outer string lines the foundations. The new walls will normally be parallel to (or in line with) those of the main house. Additional boards and lines can be installed, one pair for each new wall. A builder's square is used to ensure adjoining walls meet at a perfect 90° right angle.

Having double-checked all measurements so that the string lines perfectly correspond to the position of the new walls shown on your drawings, they should then be marked on the ground. Starting with the outer line, this was traditionally done by sprinkling a line of sand directly over the strings, although a can of spray marker paint may prove more robust. When a clear outline is marked on the ground, all the string lines can be removed. But the boards should remain in place, so that the inner wall lines can be put back once again after the concrete

Excavation

NOTIFY BUILDING CONTROL 2
Excavation of foundations – one day's notice

Digging foundations by hand is about as close as you're ever likely to get to the true meaning of 'hard labour'. Indeed, so arduous can this activity be that the nineteenth-century Russian mystic Gurdjieff actually sought out such work – having discovered that the sheer strain could send him into a stress-induced trance (history does not record whether the resulting foundations were straight).

If handling pickaxes, shovels and wheelbarrows really isn't your thing, then the alternative for all but the smallest jobs is to hire a mini-digger. Select the 600mm width bucket (rather than the narrower 450mm one) and you're away. But just when you're making rapid progress doing the work of ten men at the push of a lever, crunch! – the time you've gained is lost by chopping through the electricity supply, or severing a gas or water pipe or fracturing the drains. Which is why a lot of fuss was made earlier about locating the routes of underground services. Armed with such advanced information you can carefully excavate by hand around the sensitive pipe and cable areas, and use the digger for everything else. But even where soil investigations have already been undertaken, sites can still throw up something unexpected like an old pond or air-raid shelter, hence the need for contingency funds. If you come across soft spots or bad ground you may have to go deeper.

Of course, before deciding to employ mechanical diggers you'll obviously need to check there's sufficient space on site as well as suitable access. Fortunately you can now hire 'micro diggers' which at only 720mm wide are capable of negotiating entrance doors and tight alleyways, so they can be used for terraced house extensions.

The vast majority of extensions use conventional trench / trenchfill foundations (see next page) and it's important that the trench bottoms are as level as possible (to avoid all the wet concrete sliding down to one end). So as the digger driver works his way round it's a good idea to keep checking depths with a laser level and staff. The trench sides should be cut square with the base. As a precaution, the stringlines are sometimes set up again to make sure no trench has 'wandered' offline and the walls can be positioned centrally. On sloping sites small steps can be cut at intervals to maintain some consistency of depth, but don't make them too big or the walls may later settle and crack due to the different depths. Several small steps are better than a few big ones, with the height of each step no deeper than about 200mm (check on site with Building Control), and overlapped horizontally by the concrete above by about 1m.

Once dug the trenches may need to be 'crumbed out'. A good digger driver will smooth out the teeth marks as they dig but it may be necessary to get into the trench to clear loose debris or fall-ins, which requires great care. Trench work is usually fairly safe down to about chest height but the deeper you go the greater the risk of trench collapse, so it is wise to shore up deep trenches. The second most common cause of injury on building sites (after falls from height) is from unguarded holes and trenches so any left unattended must be covered or cordoned off. Trenches should be left unfilled only for the shortest possible time, to minimise the risk of accidents and problems like trench collapse and filling with water. Health & Safety 'CDM' regulations require contractors to erect barriers around any open trenches or holes more than 2m deep, and to lay stout boards over the top of them, or make similar 'protection from falling' arrangements.

Trees, roots and slip membranes

Tree roots can exert considerable pressure on buildings so deeper foundations may be necessary depending on how close the tree is, its mature height and water demand (see page 107). It's advisable to extend your foundations below any visible root hairs in the trench to a further 300mm, where the ground is not so prone to drying out.

A common dilemma when excavating is what to do with protruding tree roots. Slicing through live roots more than 50mm thick can destabilise the tree, with potentially lethal consequences. If you have to build close to a tree, it may be possible to bridge over roots allowing space for future growth, but you'll need to seek advice from an arboriculturalist.

Removing a tree may not help if the subsoil is shrinkable clay, as the ground can then become waterlogged and swell up causing 'heave'. It is however possible to build in anti-heave precautions at low cost by lining the sides of the trenches with compressible polystyrene anti-heave 'clay boards' designed to be soft enough to absorb ground pressure. But you need to ask advice on the optimum thickness (from 50 to 300mm thick). They must be positioned to within 500mm of the bottom of

the trench so have to be pinned or supported until the concrete is poured. Alternatively, where foundations could be affected by tree roots (or their removal) it's a common precaution to line one or both sides of trenches with 'slip membranes'. These are made of dense but flexible heavy gauge polyethylene sheeting designed to counteract any pressure from expansion in the ground by allowing some degree of movement without affecting the concrete foundations.

Final checks

Once you've finished excavating, it's essential that Building Control inspect the trenches before the concrete is laid. Apart from checking whether they've been dug to the appropriate depth, the officer will also want to be sure that the trench base is firm and secure and that the sides aren't about to collapse. You may be asked to provide temporary support to the trench sides or they may want you to dig a little deeper. Building Control have the right to request such modifications even if it means going beyond the foundation depths shown on your plans that they've already approved. This is in order to make sure the foundations are compatible with the actual ground conditions on site. But this only works one way – you're allowed to increase foundation depths, but not to reduce them. Of course, this might well throw out your careful calculations for ordering the correct volume of concrete, so it's best not to finalise your ready-mix order until after the inspection. However if it turns out you need a larger quantity of concrete than ordered, it's worth renegotiating the price per cubic metre with your supplier based on the additional volume.

Where mesh reinforcement is required, it's usually positioned 50mm up from the bottom of the concrete and 50mm down from the top. The lower layer can be laid on cut concrete blocks placed on the base of the trench, while the top layer can be pushed into the freshly poured concrete.

Before filling the trenches with concrete, it pays to plan ahead and calculate where you want the level of the concrete surface to stop. The DPC should be at least 150mm above the finished external ground level. Foundation blocks are normally laid in courses of 225mm (215mm + 10mm mortar joint) or laid flat in courses of 110mm (100mm + 10mm). Brick courses are 75mm (65mm + 10mm).

Alternatively, to help calculate the number of courses of bricks or blocks, you can make a simple tool called a 'gauge rod'. This is basically a giant ruler, a length of wood about 2m long marked with the heights of brick or block courses, including the 10mm mortar joints.

Measuring downwards from your DPC line you can calculate the ideal place where the top of the concrete strip should finish. One way to mark this is to drive wooden stakes into the bottom of the trench about every 2m with their tops level with

Celcon cavity foundation blocks.

Temporary timber shuttering used to shore up trenches in potentially unstable clay

the desired surface of the concrete. Setting up a laser level so it can point at the pegs can be a useful aid to improving accuracy.

Foundation types

So far we've assumed you'll be using conventional 'strip' or 'trench-fill' foundations. Both require the same sort of trench to be excavated as described above, although trench-fill is now the most common type of foundation for home extensions.

But trenches have their limits. Any deeper than about 2.5m is not normally acceptable, whereupon special types of foundation designed for use on difficult terrain may then be needed (such as on filled ground or where there's a serious threat from large trees). The downside is that special 'raft', 'piled' or 'pad and beam' foundations will always cost significantly more than traditional trenches, plus they usually require a specialist engineer to design them.

Hopefully the foundation method best suited to your site will have already been determined from a survey of the ground conditions. In reality, however, ground conditions can be very localised. Everyone else in your street may have been perfectly OK using traditional foundations, but sod's law dictates that there'll be a localised soft-spot just where you want to build. And bang goes that contingency budget.

Strip foundations
In many cases, a simple strip footing is all that's required. Also known as 'deep strip' foundations, these are the least expensive type and traditionally the most widely used where ground conditions are normal. A trench is dug, normally to at least 1m depth and a width of about 600mm (sometimes 850mm wide on sand, silt or soft clay). Concrete is poured into the bottom of this to create a concrete strip, sometimes reinforced with steel mesh. The concrete should normally have a depth (thickness) of about 300mm, certainly never less than 150mm.

This means you'll then need to build several courses of brick or blockwork on the foundation strip to reach above ground level (calculating how many courses are required as described above). Where underground drainage pipes have to pass through, it's often easier to build around the pipes in brick or blockwork with a concrete lintel placed over the pipe (see 'footings' below).

Trench-fill foundations
Trench-fill foundations are similar to deep-strip, except the excavated trench is filled almost to the top with concrete. Although more expensive than strip foundations in terms of using more concrete, this method gets you out of the ground quicker and is widely favoured because it avoids the labour costs and hassle building deep brick or block walls in awkward trenches below ground. This form of construction has become increasingly economic as labour costs have increased, and as mechanical excavators and ready-mixed concrete have become widely available.

Trench-fill is also often used where soil is loose or where the water table is high, and in areas with heavy clay soil with trees nearby, because such foundations can be taken deeper than strip.

Whereas for strip foundations the minimum practical width is at least 600mm because of the difficulty laying bricks or blocks in a very narrow trench, with this method trench widths can be 600mm or narrower (e.g. 450mm) in normal ground conditions, with consequent savings in concrete.

With this method the sides of the foundation play as much a part in supporting the load as the bottom. This suits stable ground where trench walls are capable of bearing loads, as well as the base. Chalky and clay soils are ideal. Unless the soil is firm, mesh reinforcement may be required for additional strength and the trench sides might need to be lined with a slip membrane.

Where drainage pipes have to pass through trench-fill foundations they mustn't be engulfed and trapped in the concrete. Pipes have to be positioned when the concrete is poured and protected by being wrapped, creating space to allow for future settlement without fracturing

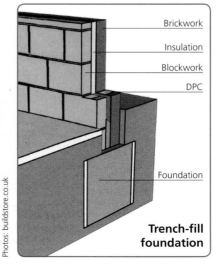

Blockwork
Insulation
DPC
Brickwork
Blockwork
Foundation

Strip foundation

Brickwork
Insulation
Blockwork
DPC
Foundation

Trench-fill foundation

Photos: buildstore.co.uk

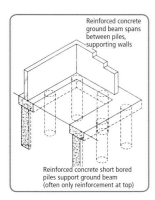

Reinforced concrete ground beam spans between piles, supporting walls

Reinforced concrete short bored piles support ground beam (often only reinforcement at top)

the pipes.

Builders often pour the concrete right up to 75mm below the finished external ground level, equivalent to one 225mm course of blocks below DPC or 3 courses of brick. Or if the foundation stops a little lower at say 225mm below ground, you'd need one course of blocks up to ground level then 2 courses of brick up to DPC (150mm). Bear in mind that for the visible wall surface above ground, brick usually looks nicer than concrete block!

Pile foundations

Piles are concrete columns drilled deep into hard bedrock to securely anchor the building, aided by frictional resistance from the surrounding ground. They've become much more common in housebuilding since the advent of cheaper short-bored systems installed using hired mini-piling rigs and also due to the rising cost of soil removal and concrete. It's now the most widely used foundation type after conventional trenches.

This method is used in unstable ground where good support can only be found at very deep levels, or where physical site restrictions (such as in cramped town centre gardens) make other forms of foundation impossible. They are often specified in shrinkable clay soils affected by trees, steep slopes, or geological faults. But they're only likely to be cost-effective where trenches would otherwise have to be dug deeper than about 2m. Piled foundations are usually designed and installed by specialist contractors. Mini steel-cased or precast concrete piles are driven down in sections to a given depth, making it quicker than digging deep trenches.

Piles are placed about every 2.5m under the main walls, and at corners and intersections. Once firm ground is reached, they can be topped with mushroom-like 'pile caps' on to which horizontal reinforced concrete ring beams (aka

'ground beams') are installed, spanning from pile to pile like large lintels to support the main walls. There are four main types of mini-piling ('micro pile') systems:-

- **Augered piling** is widely used in clay subsoil and involves drilling holes (200mm to 600mm in diameter) as deep as 24m with an 'auger' (a rotating shaft with cutting blades). Once drilled, the auger is withdrawn and the hole filled with steel-reinforced concrete. This is the least expensive and most common method, and is virtually vibration free. On sites with very restricted access, lightweight hand auger tripods can drill with a diameter of up to 300mm and to a depth of 13m.
- **Continuous flight auger (CFA) piles** are used in unstable or water-bearing ground. The main difference from augered piling is that the drilling pieces are hollow, so concrete can be pumped directly to the bottom of the hole as the auger is withdrawn.
- **Driven piles** use a steel casing and are suitable for wet, unstable or contaminated ground. More economical than the CFA method, these piles come in sizes varying from 150mm to 320mm. The casing is first placed in a small pilot hole and then pushed into the ground using a suitable weight on a hydraulic pile driver. One benefit of this method is that it creates little or no spoil, saving on transport and disposal, thus also reducing the carbon footprint.
- **Screw piles** (also known as helical piles) akin to giant wood screws — these hollow tubular steel piles are wound into the ground by machine with no prior excavation. The main benefit is fast installation and minimal soil displacement and disposal.

Raft foundations

Rafts are basically large reinforced concrete slabs, rather like thick, super-strong solid concrete floors. Because they spread the load over a larger area, they're used in poor quality soft or weak filled ground that may be prone to subsidence, or where there's groundwater on site.

They require a level site, but because they can 'bridge across' weak areas they're often appropriate on clay that's prone to excessive shrinking and swelling, or where there are unpredictable conditions deep below the surface that might lead to future ground movement, such as underground streams or old mineshafts. If subsidence occurs, the raft should absorb the movement.

Rafts have the advantage of needing only a relatively shallow depth of excavation (except that you may have already dug down to a great depth before discovering the trenches were unsuitable). Construction may entail excavating to about 650mm across the whole floor area, and then laying a bed of consolidated hardcore, with the foundation concrete being poured on top, together with the floor slab concrete. The structure is reinforced with steel fabric mesh laid in sheets and the process repeated with a final top layer of concrete. This consumes large

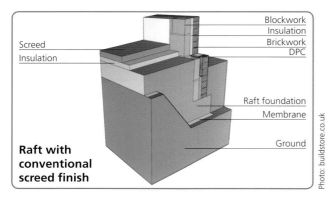

Blockwork
Insulation
Brickwork
DPC
Screed
Insulation

Raft foundation
Membrane

Ground

Raft with conventional screed finish

Photo: buildstore.co.uk

amounts of concrete of a relatively high strength mix. 'Flat rafts' are of uniform thickness under the whole of the building (at least 150mm thick) whereas 'wide toe' rafts have their edges constructed thicker and deeper and reinforced with metal bars or 'cages'. Both leaves of the main walls are built upon these edges which are stepped down (aka 'wide toe edge beams'). Any areas that have to support the internal walls of the building are also stiffened in this way.

When the extension is finally finished the only visible difference is where the slab projects out about an inch or so at the sides beyond the brickwork, or it may be buried entirely so no one will ever know all the extra trouble and expense you went to. However one consolation with this method is that, in effect, it doubles as your new floor structure, just awaiting a layer of insulation and floor screed to finish it off.

Pad and beam foundations

Pad foundations were traditionally designed to carry individual 'point loads' suiting buildings with skeletal structures, with steel or timber posts sitting directly on the pads. But today in most cases they carry reinforced concrete beams spanning like long lintels between them, in a similar fashion to piles making them suitable for supporting lightweight panel timber frame buildings. It's a similar concept to piles, but instead of being driven

very deep into the ground, here large holes are dug and filled with concrete. But they need reasonably good load-bearing ground. The holes are normally dug using a simple mechanical post hole borer that can drill down to a depth of around 1.4m. Pads may be circular, square or rectangular, located at corners and regular intervals in between. They avoid problems with piledriving such as damage from ground vibration. One advantage of this system is that the construction process is within the capabilities of competent DIY builders.

Concrete mix

Having concrete delivered ready-mixed and poured directly into your trenches from a mixer truck will take a lot of the hard work out of the job. One person struggling with a cement mixer can mix about 1m3 of concrete in an hour, so although ready-mix is probably only cheaper when you need more than a couple of cubic metres, it's normally well worth the extra expense. It also provides a more consistent, higher quality mix. Mixers are more suitable for mixing bricklaying mortar. However, if you're building a very small extension or porch, or if lorry access is restricted, the mixing may need to be done by hand. You really need two people – one to mix and one to pour, as continuously as possible.

Ready-mix is ordered by the cubic metre and a full truckload comprises about 6m3. To calculate the volume needed, multiply the depth x length x width of the trench or slab. As a rough guide, a strip foundation in a trench 10m long x 600mm wide would need about 2m3 of concrete (assuming the concrete strip will be 300mm deep in a 1.2m deep trench). The same trench-fill foundation would need more than 6m3 (or 5m3 for a 450mm wide trench). When calculating the amount needed always allow a little extra – better too much than not enough. Any spare can be driven away or spread thinly on a plastic sheet and broken up for use as hardcore.

A typical foundation mix would be 1: 3: 6 Portland cement/sand/gravel (sand premixed with gravel is known as ballast). But when ordering it's best to just explain what it's for and let the supplier work out the optimum mix. Also mention the trench dimensions, and whether it is to be poured direct or barrowed. Standard foundation mixes are known as 'GEN 1', whereas a stronger 1: 2: 4 floor slab mix is 'GEN 3'. Other specialised mixes are available for reinforced concrete and driveways etc. The lower the GEN number the less it should cost, but the price also depends on the delivery distance and how much of the truck's capacity is utilised - and of course greater quantities should translate into lower prices per cubic metre.

Speed is of the essence when pouring concrete. Concrete cures (sets) fairly rapidly, so avoid pouring one load then waiting a day or more for the next one. If there's a long delay between batches the first lot will start to harden and the new load won't bleed in with it, leaving a join that'll become a weak point in the foundation. A full truckload can take about 15 minutes to pour (or a little longer where you need a pump).

The ideal situation is to excavate the trenches and pour the concrete the same day. Before pouring, ensure the trench bases are clean, level, dry, and free of any loose material. Where there's room for the concrete lorries to pull up alongside or near the trenches, the concrete should be poured directly into them down a chute from the lorry. But very heavy vehicles need stable ground and you don't want a monster 20-tonne concrete wagon parked too close to those fragile trench sides. Fortunately they come equipped with extension ramps which can

reach up to 4 metres. It may be possible to extend these by rigging up a temporary 'slide' out of spare timber lined with plastic sheeting to help guide the mix into the trenches. A better solution if site access is restricted is to hire a concrete pump, saving the need for laborious time consuming wheelbarrowing of batches of fresh concrete around the site or using dumper trucks. (If you're hell-bent on barrowing tell the supplier in advance to add some retarder to the mix, which will delay the drying out time to a couple of hours). Pumps are invaluable where delivering large amounts of ready-mix concrete into a complicated network of trenches with restricted access. Savings in time and labour should offset cost of £400 – £500 per day. Pumps needs to be booked and the concrete supplier advised so their mix can be adjusted to facilitate a continuous pour.

Normally the mix should be of a 'thick lumpy custard' consistency, not too wet, requiring just a little encouragement from rakes or shovels to pull it along the trenches. The use of concrete pumps helps achieve an even spread. Alternatively, special 'self-placing' foundation concrete mixes are a recent innovation that flow easily around the trenches. Note that ready-mix should not be watered on site, as this will interfere with the mix, and watered concrete is a major cause of foundation failure. The concrete should be levelled out and tamped to the previously positioned pegs or markers. The more level the top of the concrete is the happier your bricklayer will be.

NOTIFY BUILDING CONTROL 3
Concreting of foundations – one day's notice

Working with cement – wise precautions
- Wear protective gloves and boots – concrete burns the skin.
- Check the weather forecast before concreting – overnight frost can ruin concrete. Foundations poured in winter conditions should be covered over.
- Be prepared. Note the location of your nearest plant-hire firm in case of urgent problems, such as the need for a water pump in the event of flooding.

'Footings' – the below-ground walls

The term 'footings' has a rather quaint, old-fashioned ring to it. Way back before the widespread use of concrete, the main walls of Georgian or Victorian houses might have only had five or six courses of brick below ground level. As they got deeper, the brickwork would gradually be 'stepped out' to

Braided nylon builders line and pegs used to set out wall position on concrete.

Standard below ground cavity wall which will need backfilling.

Celcon full width solid foundation blocks don't need backfilling.

Mix of class B engineering bricks and concrete blocks suitable for below ground walls.

spread the load, like a big pair of feet protruding either side, each course being about quarter of a brick wider than the one above. But brick or stone footings were superseded in the early twentieth century by modern concrete foundations which spread the load adequately without resorting to stepped brickwork. However, the word 'footings' persists as a description for underground masonry.

After allowing two or three days for the concrete foundations to cure, the below-ground walls can be laid in brick or blockwork up to DPC level. If planned in advance, this should fit a multiple of courses rather than having to cut them to get the DPC at the right level.

The first task is to set out the wall positions on the concrete foundations using profiles. In the case of strip foundations the walls must be built up more or less centrally, so that a typical 300mm wide cavity wall built on top of a 600mm wide concrete strip should have 150mm of concrete strip projecting out on each side. If at this point the builders suddenly realise the trench location doesn't actually correspond to that shown on the drawings, they may be tempted to build off-centre, which can later result in structural instability, so monitor this stage carefully.

With trench-fill foundations the concrete is substantially thicker, so strictly speaking it's possible to build off-centre, even near the edge. This is why trench-fill is often used where space is limited, such as where main walls need to be built close to garden boundaries, or where awkward neighbours won't permit even temporary access.

The architect should have specified bricks or blocks that are suitable for damp underground conditions, such as hard 'Class B semi-engineering' bricks. Not only must bricks and blocks be approved for use below DPC level, but so should the mortar, normally employing sulphate resistant cement. If the wrong materials are used, such as some types of aerated lightweight block (unless they are special 'trenchblocks') they can erode very swiftly, with serious structural consequences.

The inner leaf of wall is built up to DPC with concrete blocks or bricks and the external leaf built up to just below the finished ground level then stopped. The level of the DPC and the base of the external doors will need to take account of the depth of floor insulation (say 100mm deep) plus the screed (typically 65mm) and floor coverings.

For extra strength the below-ground cavity in this lowest part of the wall is traditionally filled up to ground level with a 'sandwich filling' of lean-mix concrete or mortar. The external ground level is normally 150mm below the level of the DPC (where the outside ground is much lower fill the void up to at least 225mm below DPC). The fill should slope slightly outwards so any trapped water can drain away through weep holes in the outer leaf. This often gets skimped on site so a useful short-cut is to simply use special modern full-width foundation blocks, which saves having to fill below-ground cavities (typically 300mm wide but available in widths up to 350mm for wider walls).

Where drainage pipes pass through the foundations concrete lintels will normally be needed to bridge over

Above and right: Once periscope vents are fitted (for beam & block floors) the lower walls can be built up.

Wider outer leaf designed to accommodate thicker traditional brick plinth (also needed for stone walls).

them. A space of at least 50mm must be left around pipes, and a flexible pipe surround fitted, to discourage uninvited guests in the form of insects and subterranean creatures (see next chapter).

Airbricks

Check if your existing house has suspended timber ground floors, very common in period properties and pre-WWII houses. If so, there should be a number of airbricks built into the lower walls to provide a crucial through-flow of ventilation under the old floors. This allows any damp to evaporate and helps prevent rot and beetle infestation to floor timbers. Great care must therefore be taken not to block them with the new extension.

If you opt for a solid concrete ground floor in your extension you don't need air bricks but you may need to run ventilation

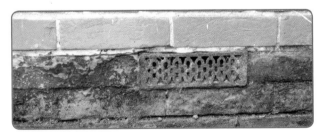

Above: Existing airbricks must not be blocked.

Right: Periscope vent with traditional terracotta airbrick inset.

ducts through your new floor so that the existing floor can still breathe (unless the floor in the main house is solid). New plastic or terracotta airbricks can be built in to the extension's lower walls, ducted to the existing airbricks in the old external main walls. There should be a plastic sheet (cavity tray) placed above sleeves running across cavities.

If your chosen ground floor design isn't of solid concrete it'll be of either modern beam and block suspended concrete (see below) or traditional suspended

timber. In both cases you'll need to install airbricks below DPC level, spaced no more than about 2 metres apart, sleeved through both the outer and inner leaves and the cavity of your new walls. These vents allow any build up of gas beneath floors to escape harmlessly.

DPC – the damp-proof course

The purpose of the DPC is to prevent damp from the ground rising up the walls and making life a misery with rot, mould, blown plaster and unpleasant smells.

Once the foundations have been concreted and the walls have been built up to DPC level, the DPC itself can be laid. It should be positioned at least 150mm above the finished external ground level (2 courses of brick). Normally a long strip of black plastic will be bedded along both the outer and inner leaves onto a full and even bed of fresh mortar. Laying the DPC is a key stage that requires Building Control to pay a visit and inspect it before it's covered.

NOTIFY BUILDING CONTROL 4
DPC level – one day's notice

A bed of mortar is then laid over the DPC followed by courses of bricks or blocks. The DPC should cover the full width of the masonry and project out very slightly beyond the external face (but not into the cavity). Joints between strips should overlap by at least 100mm. DPCs are sold in a range of widths from 100mm (for a single leaf wall) up to 450mm plus. Using a wider one on the inner leaf should allow sufficient 'spare' to be left projecting on the inside to later overlap with the DPM flooring membrane by a minimum of 50mm, forming a continuous barrier. Avoid having earth or flower beds banked up against the outer walls, otherwise additional protection with vertical plastic sheets or tanking can be required to stop damp penetrating.

Now work on the ground floor can begin. The area within these new 'dwarf' main walls is known as the 'oversite'. If it hasn't been done already, all topsoil here

Left: Laying the DPC.
Above: The DPC
must overlap later
with floor DPM
sheet.

should be cleared, together with anything that could grow or rot affecting ground stability, such as roots, bits of wood etc. The actual depth removed will vary, but in plots subject to rampant plant growth may need to be 300mm or more.

Ground floors

In Victorian houses the ground floors largely comprised timber floorboards suspended above the ground by timber joists resting on supporting walls. But their relatively high cost and potential vulnerability to damp and rot led to timber floors being gradually superseded by cheaper solid concrete.

Today, you basically have three choices for the construction of your extension ground floor. If you're a diehard traditionalist there's nothing to stop you building traditional suspended timber joists and boarding, but this is the least efficient and probably the most expensive option. The type of ground floor almost universally used today for newbuild housing is 'suspended concrete', made from concrete beams and blocks. The third option, and still the conventional choice for many home extensions, is the solid concrete floor slab.

All three types have their pros and cons, but whichever method is chosen, measures must be taken to keep damp out of the building and to keep the house warm by minimising heat-loss. And as noted earlier, suspended floors of either type will require airbricks inserted in the walls below DPC level.

Regardless of the type of construction, you normally want the finished floor level (FFL) in the extension to turn out perfectly level with the adjoining floor in the main house. Nothing looks worse than a noticeable slope you could toboggan down! But to get ground floor levels to

Timber frame construction

Foundations and ground floors

Foundations for timber frame panel construction are the same as for masonry walls – ie traditional strip or trench-fill, sometimes piles or rafts. However, greater accuracy is required than with conventional brick and block walls, where discrepancies can usually be made up for by the brickies. Unlike standard brick and blockwork

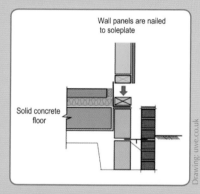

you can't easily modify large timber wall panels on site to accommodate substructure walls that are out of true. So accurate setting out of the foundations and construction of the substructure or 'underbuilding' (ie the masonry walls below DPC level) is vital. To be confident that the panels will all fit together properly this should be level to within 20mm and square to within a 12mm tolerance. Once the substructure is complete, a treated timber sole plate is fixed to it, using either steel brackets, special anchors, or shot fired using a nail gun. The sole plate sits on a DPC to protect it from damp.

For more on timber frame construction see Chapter 10.

match up seamlessly requires considerable care to ensure that all the construction layers in your floor 'sandwich' are positioned at just the right levels. It's best to work backwards from the finished floor level and calculate the required depths for each layer - e.g. floor coverings, underlay, screed, insulation and the structure beneath. There can also be knock-on effects higher up the building so at this stage it's a good idea to take a fresh look at your drawings working down from the highest point of the roof and noting the room heights and the depths of ceilings and floor joists upstairs.

Beam and block 'suspended concrete' floors

Imagine a Victorian suspended timber floor made instead from reinforced concrete and you'll have some idea of how a modern 'suspended concrete' floor works. Special concrete beams are laid like traditional timber floor joists spanning above the ground from wall to wall. But instead of nailing floorboards to them, the spaces in between are filled with concrete blocks.

Beam and block flooring became popular during the 1990s for use on sites with ground problems caused by subsidence, clay heave, sloping land, or contamination. Bridging across difficult terrain is a simple way to overcome such difficulties. Today, nearly all new houses use beam and block construction for their ground floors, regardless of ground conditions. But for home extensions, traditional solid concrete floors are still widely used, because they are cheaper for small floor areas and because builders are familiar with them – 'that's the way it's always been done'.

But beam and block isn't at pole position with budget-conscious mainstream housing developers for nothing. It offers serious benefits over other types of floor structure, and significant savings elsewhere in the build. It can be laid very quickly, even in adverse weather, and can span greater distances than timber joists without support, plus the void is a handy place to run the service pipes. Compared to solid concrete floors, 'B&B' is not only easier to install but is less prone to defects.

To ensure the correct beams are used for the required span the manufacturers can custom design and deliver the beams to fit your extension if you supply them with a set of approved plans. Your drawings should show the location of any internal walls that need to be supported by the floor, and the details of any service pipes coming up through the floor, such as soil pipes for loos. But you may need to order 4 to 8 weeks in advance.

Another important benefit is that ground preparation is minimal, with significant savings in labour. Provided the ground isn't prone to being waterlogged, the soil under the floor requires no oversite concrete. All you need to do to prevent the risk of any future plant growth is clear the topsoil and vegetation and lay some thick polythene sheeting over the ground, weighed down with sand (Building Control may also require a quick spray with weedkiller in any areas harbouring aggressively pervasive species like Japanese knotweed).

As with all suspended floors, the weight is taken largely by the wall foundations, rather than direct to the ground as with a concrete slab. The main limitation is the span of the beams, but they can normally manage up to about 6m ('Rackhams 225' beams can span up to 8m). If the dimensions of your extension are greater than this you may need to construct an additional load-bearing internal 'sleeper wall' for the beams to rest on (with proper foundations).

The void beneath the floor should be a minimum of about 150mm, and should be ventilated with air ducts. This is particularly important if mains supply pipes are run within the underfloor space or in areas at risk from radon or methane. These air ducts are of an odd-looking 'periscope' shape (known as 'cranked ventilators') that zigzag from the outside wall down into the void. This allows a free passage of air under the floor without letting light in, creating a microclimate as inhospitable as the surface of the moon, thus prohibiting plant growth.

The special pre-cast concrete floor joist beams have a profile rather like an inverted 'T' and are manufactured reinforced with steel. Size-wise they're typically 150mm deep, but are also commonly available in 175mm and 225mm sizes which, being thicker, can manage longer spans without support. They can take the same standard 100mm deep building blocks used in walls.

Constructing B&B floors on site could hardly be simpler - at least in theory. To form a supporting base the inner leaf blockwork first needs to be built up to the level of the bottom of the floor beams, with the outer leaf stopped at least one course of blocks lower than this. Concrete beams are extremely heavy, although for smaller spans it should be possible for two strong people to lift a shorter single beam into place without requiring a small crane. Builders sometimes adapt mini-diggers to offload and position beams around the site cradled in fabric slings hung from the digger bucket.

First, the beams are laid in rows with their ends resting on the inner leaf of the main walls, over the DPC (the DPC on the outer leaf may be a little higher). It's important that the supplier's drawings are followed carefully with correct intervals left between the rows, so the blocks can simply be placed in the gaps between the beams. Then Hey Presto! – you have your floor structure. The blockwork infill between the beams can be done quickly and cheaply with standard 100mm thick concrete blocks (215 x 440mm) laid in either length or width direction. For very large spans the floor can be made stronger by simply laying more beams closer together with the blocks laid sideways.

At the floor perimeters, smaller sized 'slip bricks' (normally provided by the beam supplier) can be used to infill around beam ends, or blocks can be cut to fit. Holes for services should be made at this stage to avoid subsequent cutting. The level of the DPC and the base of the external

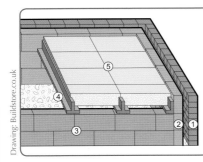

Drawing: Buildstore.co.uk

Beam and block floor
1 Outside wall
2 Concrete block inner wall
3 Sleeper wall
4 Concrete beam
5 Concrete blocks

doors will need to allow for the depth of floor insulation (say 100mm deep) plus the screed (typically 65mm).

To prevent movement once all the blocks have been fitted, the floor surface should be grouted with a 1:4 cement/sand mix brushed into the joints between the blocks.

But why use ordinary concrete blocks when it's easy to beef up your insulation by fitting large purpose-made floor blocks? These contain integral thermal insulation, which can reduce heat loss through the floor by as much as 40 per cent compared to solid floor slabs. Laying larger blocks (560 x 440mm) of the same thickness can be done twice as fast as for normal-size blocks. Or you could fit high performance 'jet floors' that use expanded polystyrene (EPS) infill

blocks between the beams. They are about 10% more expensive than standard, but you don't need to provide an added layer of insulation, just a screed (which must be placed immediately to protect the 'soft' infill blocks from damage). Or as a compromise you could specify standard size thermal blocks with good insulation properties suitable for infilling floors.

Insulating
There are two common methods of adding insulation and floor finishes above a standard beam and block floor, normally done at a later stage once the building is weathertight (see page 232):-

■ Insulation boards made from rigid polyurethane (or thicker polystyrene) foam are placed over a thick polythene DPM sheet laid over the surface. These are then covered with a floor screed (either conventional cement/sand, approx 65mm thick or a thinner liquid screed). The joints between the boards should first be taped to prevent wet screed running down between them. At the edges of the screed, the insulation boards should be extended up to form a 'warm' barrier with the cold wall surface. Once the screed has fully dried out the floor can be tiled or finished with wood flooring or carpet etc (See Chapter 15.)
■ Alternatively, dispensing with the need for a later wet screed, special highly insulated composite 'floating floor' panels can be used. These are made of insulating material bonded to a base of either plywood or chipboard. Before laying the floor panels, a 500 gauge polythene sheet is laid as a vapour control to protect subsequent floor finishes from any damp in the structure below. The floor panels are then laid, with their tongues and grooves glued with a PVA adhesive. Alternatively conventional floorboards can be set on battens over insulation boards, instead of a screed.

Busy grouting – Milbank floors.

However It's important to note that pre-stressed beams are not perfectly level, having a distinct camber (around 13mm on a 4m long beam) which is not a problem if you plan to later insulate and screed the floor, giving a nice level finish. But if you want a screed-free dry finish or floating floor, the use of a levelling compound may be required prior to laying the floor finish.

Concrete slab floors

Ground floors built exclusively of solid concrete were the standard form of construction in most new housing from the 1950s until superseded in recent years by suspended concrete. They are a tried and tested method, still popular with many small firms of builders and although relatively labour intensive, they are quite cheap on materials. But unless built with considerable care, solid floors can suffer from serious defects. If the preparation isn't right, floor slabs easily settle and crack up. Indeed, floor slab settlement is one of the most common problems with new construction. This may arise due to poor 'compaction', where the hardcore base hasn't been property compressed and instead starts sinking years later, leaving a cracked, hollow floor surface. Or problems may be down to poor preparation of the oversite ground, which later sinks, taking the floor with it. But sinking isn't the only problem. Solid floors can also suffer from 'sulphate attack' where they arch and bulge up, causing cracking. This is due to chemical reactions in damp hardcore expanding the concrete. 'Slab doming', as it's known, can be so severe that it even pushes out the bricks in adjacent walls.

Solid concrete floors are built straight off the cleared oversite ground in layers comprising hardcore 'rubble', sand 'blinding', damp-proof membrane, insulation boards, concrete slab, and sand/cement screed topping – not necessarily in that exact order. Depending on ground conditions, the slab may need reinforcing with steel mesh prior to adding the concrete.w

NOTIFY BUILDING CONTROL 5
Oversite concrete – one day's notice

Laying a concrete slab floor

Preparation is key. Once the ground level has been reduced to remove any organic rottable surface topsoil you should have a nice clean, inert base to build on.
First, a layer of clean hardcore or aggregate minimum 150mm thick is laid over the prepared oversite ground (that's after it's been compacted, so aim for about 180mm laid loose). The maximum thickness is 600mm). This should be spread out evenly across the site. Clean broken bricks, roof tiles, concrete or crushed stone (washed) can be recycled for this purpose, as long as there's nothing measuring more than about 100mm (roughly half a brick). Or you can have aggregate delivered, e.g. concrete crushings or ballast. Getting

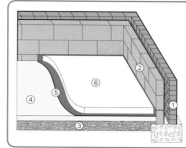

A solid concrete oversite
1 Outside wall
2 Concrete block inner wall
3 Hardcore infill
4 Sand blinding
5 Damp proof membrane
6 Min 100mm concrete oversite

Drawing: Buildstore.co.uk

this right is important because many defects in slabs are caused by the wrong sort of hardcore or not compacting it properly.

This hardcore base needs to have good drainage qualities and be well compacted so that it doesn't start sinking or expanding years later. It should also not be affected by water or be prone to chemical reaction. Unless it's 'clean' (ie has had the rubbish sifted out) demolition rubble isn't suitable, since old bits of plaster, wood, metal etc can hold moisture and rot or rust. Avoid materials such as soft lightweight concrete blocks, shale, loose chalk and tarmac road planings.

For this reason, 'ready-made' loose granular material such as MOT type 1 granular sub-base is a popular choice, since it's fairly fine, of consistent quality and compacts well. It can also be used as a surface layer applied to ordinary hardcore and can be ordered from builders' merchants and delivered direct to site.

The hardcore base must be compacted so as not to leave pockets of air. Whereas some materials, like 'granular sub-base' and gravel, tend to self-compact, only requiring a quick going-over with a roller, others, like broken bricks, need to be specially compacted. For this you can hire a vibrating roller or a plate compactor 'wacker plate'. The hardcore should be compacted in layers no thicker than 225mm at a time.

Solid floor sub-base compacted using a vibrating wacker plate.

Left: MOT type 1 granular sub-base hardcore.
Right: Compacting the hardcore.
Below: Sand blinding over hardcore with snazzy blue DPM, but no DPC or insulation yet.
Below Right: Damp proof membrane in place, awaiting insulation and screed.

The hardcore is then levelled with a layer of sand 'blinding' having first removed any large protruding sharp bits. The sand should be raked to an even depth of about 20mm and either rolled or trodden down to compact it.

To prevent dampness from the ground getting through, a hefty 1200 gauge (0.3mm thick) plastic sheet damp-proof membrane (DPM) is laid. If one sheet isn't large enough, the joints in the DPM must be overlapped by at least 150mm and taped. This can be placed above the sand blinding, which prevents the plastic DPM sheet being punctured. Alternatively it can be placed higher up on top of the next layer, the concrete slab. The lower option is preferable where the ground is damp or where there's a risk that chemicals in the ground could rise up and damage the layers of insulation (see next page). Leave a generous amount of spare DPM sheeting around the edges, sufficient to be joined up with the DPC in the walls, so as to form a continuous barrier against damp. In granite areas where there's a higher risk of radon the DPM and DPC should be taped together, or you may need special measures such as a sump chamber embedded in the layer of fill to vent any gas safely away from the dwelling. Radon cavity trays can be installed in the main walls, sealed to the DPC on the inside leaf, and dressed down into the lower level of external blockwork to form a barrier.

Next comes the solid concrete slab or 'oversite concrete'. As with the foundations, the concrete can be delivered ready-mixed down the chute of a cement truck, or for a very small project such as a porch you could instead produce it on site with a cement mixer. The concrete for the slab is normally a stronger 1:2:4 'GEN 3' mix. As the concrete is poured it should be raked level to a depth of at least 100mm taking care not to puncture the DPM (most slabs are 100mm to 150mm thick). It then needs to be 'tamped' down using a long horizontal strip of wood called a tamping board. By applying a sawing motion over the surface this will remove air bubbles and release excess water as well as levelling the surface by skimming off any high points. The surface is normally left rough if a screed is to be added later, but some builders dispense with the screed, opting instead for a smooth finish on the concrete slab itself (assuming the insulation layer has already been placed under the slab). Once it's started to cure, the surface can be smoothed using a steel trowel. Or if you like gadgets, the slab can be levelled by 'power floating' – but don't get too carried away; take care not to slice through the projecting plastic DPM sheet. The DPM should extend up around the sides of the floor slab as described above, and needs to be 'dressed-up' around service pipe entry points. It will also be necessary to run a strip of insulation material around the edges before pouring the concrete, to protect against 'cold bridging'.

If your designer has specified that the slab needs to be reinforced (normally where ground conditions are a bit dodgy), special sheets of steel mesh can be sandwiched within the slab at the midpoint. Set the mesh above the insulation, temporarily secured in place (e.g. with broken patio slabs) and then wire all the sheets together. You need to ensure that the upper layer of concrete is poured swiftly so that it bleeds into the lower layer and the reinforcement when still wet. Where slabs are thicker than 150mm, even where ground conditions are good, the addition of reinforcement will add strength, helping to avoid settlement cracks. The most common steel reinforcement used is 'A142' anti-crack mesh. It is usual to lay it within garage floor slabs and should be located towards the bottom of the concrete layer. Concrete contracts slightly during the curing process, so don't be alarmed if small surface cracks appear. Later, when set, concrete will also expand and contract very slightly with room temperatures. In very large slabs (about 6m x 6m or larger) movement joints are needed to allow for expansion. However some designers play safe by including movement joints in non-reinforced slabs at a spacing of about 30 times the slab thickness. So, for a 150mm thick slab, this would be 4.5m. Joints can be made of bitumen impregnated fibreboard joint filler such as flexcell. No joint should be wider than a maximum 30mm.

Waiting for the concrete to cure typically takes two to three days, during which time it will be very vulnerable to damage from frost or heat (more than foundation concrete, which is not so exposed). Where it has been
laid on a plastic DPM it can take longer to cure. It's best to plan the job so that concrete is not laid when temperatures are likely to drop to zero. Otherwise in very cold weather the exposed surface must be protected with suitable sacking, straw, or loose polythene sheeting material while it cures. Conversely, in hot weather concrete can dry too quickly causing it to weaken, crack and shrink, and you must keep it shaded and moist (but not soaking), giving it a periodic light sprinkling of water during the curing period and covering it with damp hessian sacks or old carpet.

Insulating
Ground floors can be cold underfoot so they need to be insulated to minimise heat-loss, achieving a U-value of 0.22 or better. Insulating solid floor slabs can either left until a later stage, or done now by placing rigid foam boards on top of the DPM before the concrete slab is laid. Obviously the insulation boards used must not be 'squashable' under the weight of the slab so they need a high compressive strength (which is why wall insulation is not suitable) as well as good moisture resistance. This requires purpose-made floor insulation boards (Polyurethane PUR or polyisocyanurate PIR perform better than EPS polystyrene - Kingspan and Celotex are well-known manufacturers). Typically you might need at least 75mm depth of rigid foam boards with a decent thermal conductivity K-value of around 0.022. Most heat is lost around the edges of floors so whatever material you use, to prevent 'cold bridging' the insulation should be lapped up around the edges of the slab and continued up the wall level with the top of the screed (applied later). These short upstands around the edges only need to be about 25mm thick, sufficient to fully encase the screed in a nice warm 'overcoat'.

Above and below: GEN 3 concrete poured directly from truck without the need for a concrete pump

Delivery of 100mm thick rigid 2400 x 1200mm phenolic foam floor insulation boards awaiting storage

In most solid floor extensions however the insulation is placed on top of the floor structure, similarly to beam & block floors, prior to screeding (see page 232). This job is left until the building is weathertight so the insulation doesn't get wet or damaged. Laying the DPM is also left until later as it needs to go higher up, under the insulation and on top of the concrete slab rather than below it. The insulation boards will then be placed over the DPM and lapped around the edges as described earlier. Where you plan to install Under Floor Heating it's essential to do it in this order.

Laying a screed
To finish a concrete floor and form a suitable surface

Oversite concrete being poured over DPM.

for the usual floor coverings like carpets, tiles, laminate, engineered wood flooring etc, a 65mm deep sand/cement screed, or thinner poured liquid screed, is normally applied over the beam & block floor structure or concrete slab. This is normally put in place by the plasterers once the building is dry and weathertight. (See Chapter 15.)

Suspended timber floors
Timber floors are traditionally constructed from timber joists clad with floorboards or chipboard panels. At ground-floor level, extra protection is needed from damp, and the void below the floor timbers must be well ventilated. Unlike their Victorian forebears, modern timber ground floors must be thermally insulated to reduce heat-loss.

Today, this is the least popular method of floor construction due to the expense and work involved in first having to clear the oversite vegetation and earth, and then effectively having to construct a concrete slab as ground cover. Plus there's the drawback that timber joists may only be able to manage relatively short spans (not much more than 4m) requiring additional 'sleeper walls' for support - see span tables on website.

Today stronger manufactured I-beams or eco-joists are often used in preference to traditional softwood joists. Otherwise, the ground floor construction is pretty much as per the upper floors – see Chapter 11 for construction details.

Briefly, these are the key requirements for new suspended timber ground floors:

- Joist ends on exterior walls should normally be supported in metal joist hangers, but in some cases can rest within 'cut outs' walls (e.g. in the walls of the old house which will now be internal).
- The oversite ground must be cleared and covered with a concrete slab, minimum 50mm thick, laid over a 1200 gauge polythene DPM and a hardcore base.
- An air space of at least 150mm is required between the surface of the ground below the floor and the underside of the joists.
- A good cross-flow of ventilation air is required to the void beneath the joists, from airbricks built into the walls below DPC level to prevent vegetation growth and disperse moisture (minimum vent area is 550mm^2 per metre length of wall)

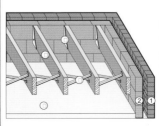

Suspended timber floor
1   Outside wall
2   Concrete block inner wall
3   Concrete oversite
4   Wooden joist
5   Metal joist hanger
6   Herringbone strut

Drawing: Buildstore.co.uk

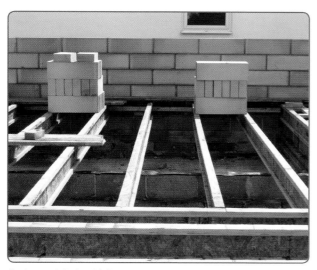

Engineered timber I-joists.

Mineral wool insulation suspended between joists on plastic netting.

- The timber plates on which the joists rest must have DPCs placed under them (i.e. on top of the supporting sub-wall)
- To prevent the risk of ground water entering and 'ponding' under the floor, drainage points may be required, such as surface water gullies in the garden.
- Floor insulation is especially important to reduce heat-loss, given the need for a flow of (cold) air below the

Above: Floor joists positioned on sleeper wall prior to DPC being fed under joist ends. Metal hangers should be used for main walls.
Below: Joist hangers fixed to old wall.

boards. It's best to fit rigid boards between the joists (e.g. PUR) minimum 100mm thick, cut to size and supported on battens fixed to joist sides. Alternatively 150mm deep mineral quilt 'loft insulation' can be supported from plastic netting but these tend to sag over time.

It's essential for your design to specify the correct size and grade of timber floor joists for their span (normally spaced 400mm apart). This must be calculated by your architect or engineer in accordance with Building Regulations. See Chapter 11.

If the main reason for wanting a suspended timber floor is the lure of traditional 'stripped pine' floorboards you'd probably be better off laying pine boards over battens fixed to a concrete floor.

Main trades needed on site
- **Groundworkers:** Excavation of trenches and drain runs.
- **Bricklayers:** Building the walls up to DPC level.
- **Labourers:** Mixing and pouring mortar for walls and concrete for smaller foundations/floor slabs.

Materials
- *Floor slabs*: Use Ordinary Portland cement (OPC), not masonry cement. Sand must be sharp sand (coarse concreting sand) mixed with 20mm gravel aggregate. Specify sulphate-resisting cement where sulphates in hardcore such as brick rubble, or in subsoil, could attack the concrete.
- *Beam and blocks*: To BS 8110, with minimum half-hour fire resistance.

www.home-extension.co.uk

9 DRAINAGE

Don't plan on hanging up your shovel and mini-digger just yet. The groundwork isn't finished until the below-ground drainage system is all done and dusted. Of course, you don't have to do it right now, you may well opt to leave the drains to the end of the project. In fact, the only option you can't choose is to install the drainage halfway through your build, because scaffolding and materials will be in the way. But it makes sense to get all the excavation done at the same time while the equipment and labour is already on site, and before things get too busy.

Photo: Hepworth

Drainage falls into two categories, foul water and rainwater. Foul water from toilets, bathrooms and kitchens is sometimes subdivided into 'black water' (from toilets) and 'grey water' (everything else) – but you'll also need to provide a suitable dispersal system for surface water, the relatively clean rainwater that collects on hard surfaces like roofs and paving.

Even if your extension isn't going to need a new bathroom, kitchen or WC, you may still need to carry out some work on the underground drainage system, for example if any existing pipework to the main house needs to be diverted from where you want to build. Your approved plans should show how this is to be achieved.

NOTIFY BUILDING CONTROL 6
Draining commencement – one day's notice

Building Control will take a close interest in your drainage.

Top right: New rainwater pipework.
Below: Inspection unit awaiting burial.
Right: How to lay foul drains. photo Hepstore.com

Ever mindful of the typhoid and cholera epidemics in the nineteenth century caused by raw sewage from dodgy drains seeping into people's drinking water, any proposed alterations to your property's existing drainage system will require Building Regulation approval and the Building Control officer will want to come out, inspect and probably test any new work.

Drainage works

Foul water is normally dispersed to sewage treatment plants via public sewers. Although some older urban districts may have a combined system that can take both foul waste and rainwater through the same pipes, most properties have totally separate systems. Others may have no provision for surface water disposal at all. So unless you have approval to connect to a combined system, you must not mix these systems up by, say, inadvertently connecting rainwater downpipes to a kitchen gulley. If the system isn't a combined one, in severe storm conditions a sudden tsunami of rainwater cascading through the sewer system could overpower it, causing a deluge of liquid excrement downtown.

In some rural areas where there are no public sewers, the job of dealing with people's foul waste may instead be down to private cesspits or septic tanks, which require periodic emptying by specialist contractors. Most home-extenders will not need to worry about such matters, so the wonders of private sewage works are explained on the website.

Where there's no surface water system to connect to, rainwater will often discharge via soakaways buried in the garden. So if one fine day your lawn starts furiously frothing

New rainwater gulley and flexi-bend connected to underground pipe.

and bubbling, it may be because your systems have got inadvertently mixed up, with a washing machine waste pipe connected to a rainwater downpipe.

Common failings

There tends to be something of an 'out of sight, out of mind' attitude to drains, and dodgy workmanship has often been covered up quickly and buried without a trace.

The most common cause of failure is bad joints between pipes. Joint failure may not sound too serious, but it can set off a chain of potentially catastrophic events. Small leaks only get worse over time, and where drainage pipes crack, they are an invitation to thirsty tree roots nearby to seek out water and start growing into them. The result: blocked drains and leakage of foul effluent into the ground. Persistently waterlogged ground can risk localised foundation failure, with the potential to cause structural damage to the main walls of the house.

Conversely, if you live in an area with a high water table, groundwater from the surrounding land may seep into a drainage system that's not fully watertight, and the pipes will act in reverse like a land drain, dispersing water from your garden instead of your bathroom.

Common causes of cracking to shallow drains include crushing from heavy vehicles parked above, and seasonal ground movement, particularly in clay soil that swells in wet weather and then shrinks in summer. Old inspection chambers may have been 'jerry built', perhaps of only thin (115mm) brickwork, or clumps of old rendering or mortar may have come loose causing blockages. In many cases old chambers are buried under turf or patios, unknown to you until you start excavating foundations (hence the importance of checking the ground first). Also, hidden soakaways may silt up and overflow, and if built too close to the house may increase the risk of damp

Be especially vigilant for builders lazily chucking building rubble and paint down newly laid drains.

It's important when installing drains to 'go the extra mile' to ensure that new pipes are 100 per cent watertight before backfilling and leaving them in peace, hopefully forever.

Excavation

In some ways, adding an extension to your home can be more difficult than building on a greenfield site where everything is 100 per cent new. Your new extension drains are basically a small addition to the existing system, which may itself not be too brilliant. Many drain runs on older properties are not particularly deep, which makes it harder to achieve a reasonable depth and gradient for your new drainage pipes. Plus of course great care must be taken when excavating close to old walls with shallow foundations.

To help calculate the required levels of new drain runs, architects' drawings normally show the levels of manhole covers along with 'invert levels' (the depth of the channel at the bottom of a chamber) at key points. The trenches should be as narrow as possible, allowing about 150mm space either side of the new pipes, which normally means a trench about 450mm wide (a digger's narrow bucket). There are no set depths for pipework in the Building Regs but going much deeper than a metre means trenches can start to become tricky to work in. However, they need to be dug about 100mm deeper than the required pipe level to allow for the granular bedding that the pipes will rest on.

Your approved Building Regs drawings should clearly show the proposed new drain runs for your extension, and will also specify the type of materials to be used.

Existing waste pipe remains in place during works.

Photos: Hepstore.com

Pipe materials

New underground drainage pipes are either flexible (plastic) or rigid (clay or concrete). Rigid pipes have an inherent strength but can be damaged by movement, whereas flexible pipes can resist movement but may deform if overloaded so require good support when laid. These days most extensions use standard orange coloured 110mm PVC pipes.

To avoid damage, careful storage and handling of pipes on site is important. If proper protection is overlooked and pipes are stacked without support, plastic pipes can become bent and distorted, and clay pipes may easily fracture.

Pipes made from vitrified clay date back to Victorian times but are still used today. However, most modern drainage pipework is of the heavy-duty plastic type, manufactured in an orangey terracotta colour to resemble traditional clay. Plastic is much easier to work with than clay, being both lightweight and simple to cut with a saw, plus they're very resistant to the kind of chemical attack that can fatally erode pipes made from other materials. Plastic pipes are commonly of 110mm diameter or sometimes 160mm. They are available in generous lengths of 3m, 6m and even 9m, minimising the need for joints.

They're connected to each other with integral flexible synthetic rubber seals that allow for a small amount of movement whilst remaining watertight. To ease the connection at these push-in 'snap joints' use silicone lubricant. Don't use washing-up liquid, oil, or grease, as this will damage the seal, causing it to leak.

DIY stores stock a wide selection of push-fit couplings; probably the most commonly used fittings are straight socket couplings, junctions in 'T' and 'Y' shapes (87.5 and 45 degree triples) and various bends (e.g. 10, 30, 45, and 87.5 degrees or flexi-bends that can adapt from 0 to 90 degrees). As usual with plumbing materials it's best to stick to one brand because rival products of the same nominal size are not always readily compatible.

When the day comes to join up your gleaming new underground pipework to the old existing system, be prepared for some possible surprises. Victorian cast iron pipes may still exist, along with some made from innovative materials popular in the post-war years, such as concrete, asbestos cement fibre and pitch fibre. This may cause a degree of head-scratching. See 'Joining it up' on page 131.

Pipe laying

Normally new pipes are laid starting at the highest point, *ie* the point nearest the new extension.

Once the trench is dug, the first task is to ascertain the height difference between the point where the waste water will leave the property (typically at the base of a soil stack) and the point where the pipe will join the existing system or (if you plan to bypass the existing drains) the public sewer in the road.

The objective is to achieve the correct fall (gradient) so that the waste will be sent speedily on its way. If the

Above and right: New extension drain runs may need to be fairly shallow.

pipes are laid too shallow, the waste will hang around and the pipes will be prone to blockage. On the other hand, if pipes are laid too steep the water can be evacuated so swiftly that the 'solids' get left behind, again risking blockage. A gradient of about 1:40 (equivalent to a drop of 25mm on a 1 metre pipe run) is normally desirable, as consistent as possible along the full length of the pipes. Plastic pipes benefit from very smooth internal surfaces, so although gentler falls may technically be acceptable they're best avoided, as you need to allow for settlement occurring at a later date. In reality pipes are generally laid to an actual fall on site of between 25mm and 90mm per metre run. To find the recommended figure for your system, check with the pipe manufacturer.

Once the trenches have been prepared, but before laying the pipes, the gradients (shown on your plans) can be checked on site against a string line run between pegs set at each end of the trench, adjusted to the correct angle. Then a bed of fine gravel or pea shingle can be laid to this gradient, to a minimum 100mm depth, compacted along the bottom of the trench. The pipes should be carefully laid on top. Sharp inclines should be avoided, although a few gentle radius bends may be permitted provided they don't prevent rodding.

Next double-check the gradient, using a spirit level adjustable to pre-set levels (or alternatively you can take a standard 1m spirit level and attach a 25mm block of wood under one end).

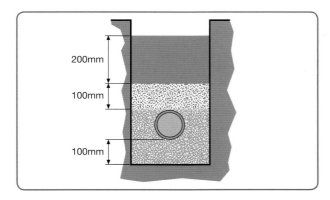

Note that it's essential to keep gravel out of the collar joints, since if one of the rubber seals becomes displaced the joint will not be watertight. The connections should be a tight fit, and before fitting them together the end of the pipe should be smeared with special collar lubricant, to help prevent damage to the rubber seals.

Deep pipes/shallow pipes
Where your new drainage trenches are deeper than the foundations of your existing main walls and the pipes pass within 1m of the foundations (or those of the neighbours), there can obviously be some risk of structural damage. So the Building Regs sensibly require that such pipes must be encased in concrete, at least up to the level of the base of the nearby foundations. Should the pipes collapse in future, this precaution means there won't be an ensuing seismic shift in the ground, robbing the foundations of support.

It's not just deep pipe runs near foundations that need extra protection in the form of concrete. Very shallow drain runs may need similar treatment to protect them. This is especially important for pipes run close to the surface, ie within about 600mm. Here a hard surface covering such as paving slabs would be required. Where they are run beneath driveways, or subject to unusual loadings – like cars parked over drain runs to the side of semi-detached houses – any depth less than 900mm will need a concrete capping over the drain.

Where only a very shallow fall is possible to your extension, perhaps because the existing system is so close to the surface, using larger diameter pipes will allow water to flow more easily at gentle gradients.

Pipes through foundations
Probably the most critical point of the whole exercise is where pipes cross under the foundations of a building. Pipes passing through walls or under buildings must be specially protected. This is normally achieved by installing a lintel above the opening, leaving a gap of at least 50mm around the pipe to allow for settlement. The pipes are surrounded by granular bedding (pea shingle etc), but the gap around the pipe can be an invitation to burrowing

Joining it up

creatures, and a flexible sheet material should therefore be fitted around the opening to stop them getting through. Such openings also need to be sealed against any localised risk of potentially lethal gases (radon or methane) seeping through and accumulating in confined spaces. The choice of material will depend on local conditions, so ask Building Control what they recommend.

Plastic pipes running through foundations may need to be supported on a bed of concrete, or even fully encased in concrete. But here a gap of about 12mm must be formed in the concrete at each pipe joint, or the flexibility will be lost.

At the precise point where pipes enter a building (or join an inspection chamber), there may in some cases be a serious risk of movement between the pipe and the structure that it's passing into. To prevent the pipe fracturing, one solution is for the piece of pipe running up to the building to be kept short, say about 600mm, with a joint at each end. In effect this makes the pipe 'double jointed'. Because both the joints are flexible, they act like a pair of hinges allowing the pipe and the building freedom to move independently of each other.

Joining up the new and existing systems inside your garden boundary can be done in a number of ways – by simply joining one pipe directly to another, or by connecting at an existing manhole, or by building a new inspection chamber.

Although the amount of new pipework required for an extension should be very limited, as noted earlier you may encounter old pipes made from unusual materials that they need to be joined to. This can be a specialist task, particularly when confronted by decrepit asbestos cement pipes. These must never be cut or altered without wearing protective masks etc, since breathing in asbestos fibres is dangerous and professional advice should be sought. But it's not just the materials used for old pipes that can pose problems: modern metric pipes commonly need to be connected to old imperial sizes, normally of 4in or 6in diameter. This can present various difficulties, such as how to connect modern rubber collar couplings to old 'spigot-and-socket' pipe joints. Fortunately the manufacturers of modern drainage systems take account of such eventualities, and a wide variety of adapter couplings are available so that metric can be successfully joined to imperial, and modern plastic to old glazed stoneware etc. Only where old pipes are misshapen or damaged are you likely to encounter difficulties, when the only solution may be to excavate and replace the old pipes. And bang goes the contingency budget (again).

First you need to identify the point at which the new pipe will hook up with the old one. This should then be carefully excavated. With luck, your addition to the existing drainage system may only consist of a single new pipe, requiring a simple 'saddle' connection. If the existing pipework is plastic it should be relatively straightforward to cut and insert a standard 45° 'Y' connector or an 87.5 degree 'T'. But it can be difficult to connect to old pitch-fibre pipes if they've become deformed after years of being squashed in the ground.

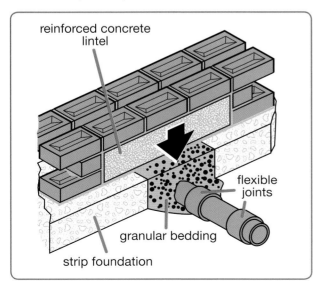

reinforced concrete lintel

flexible joints

granular bedding

strip foundation

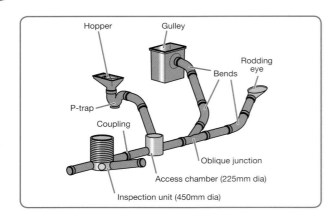

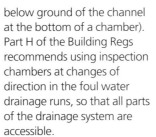

Rodding eye.

Where it's not possible to connect pipes directly to each other, a new underground junction will normally need to be constructed with a suitable access chamber.

Manholes, inspection chambers, and rodding eyes

A manhole is a large underground drainage chamber big enough for a person (of either sex) to physically clamber down like a small mineshaft. They aren't usually found in gardens, where instead you usually come across more slender inspection chambers which are still sometimes referred to as manholes despite being much smaller (rectangular metal covers typically measuring 600 x 450mm). These are designed to provide limited access for unblocking underground pipes by giving them a good 'rodding' (ie inserting lengths of special drainage rods through them). It was the Working In Confined Spaces legislation that sounded the death knell for old school manholes. Just to add to the confusion, there are two smaller modern alternatives – rodding eyes and inspection units (aka 'drain access chambers').

Inspection chambers of all descriptions serve two main purposes: first, as a junction where several underground pipes can join up into one main outgoing drainage pipe; and second, to provide access for clearing blocked pipes.

Your approved drawings should clearly show where new inspection chambers are to be located, and should also note their depth or 'invert levels' (the distance

below ground of the channel at the bottom of a chamber). Part H of the Building Regs recommends using inspection chambers at changes of direction in the foul water drainage runs, so that all parts of the drainage system are accessible.

Ready-made circular polypropylene units are suitable for drains up to 1m deep. These mini-inspection units are lightweight and easy to install. Available in diameters such as 250mm, 300mm or 450mm they typically have five inlets and one outlet. Anything deeper will require a full-size rectangular 'manhole' type inspection chamber. For depths up to 2.7m, the minimum internal dimensions for a rectangular manhole are 1,200 x 750mm. Traditionally these were built of brick, but today they've been largely superseded by preformed concrete sections or in-situ concrete poured around a plastic liner. Anything deeper than 2.7m is a major project best left to professional drainage contractors.

These heavy 'manholes' can be prone to settlement, so pipes entering the chamber should be fairly short, say 300–600mm in length. These 'rocker pipes' allow slight movement of the chamber or drainage system without imposing any stresses on the joints.

Underground drainage systems should be accessible without the need to enter buildings. So indoor chambers should be avoided. Indeed, Building Control may have already asked you to redesign your extension or re-route the existing drainage purely to avoid such an unsatisfactory arrangement. But if there is simply no other option, and Building Control permit it, special care needs to be taken with internal covers, so that they remain accessible and aren't hidden beneath washing machines or cookers. The covers must be double-sealed and screwed closed to prevent noxious stenches and 'solids' from seeping out and enlivening your dinner parties. Special deep recessed covers can be fitted which can be screeded along with the floor surface and tiled to match (or

Inspection unit connected up.

paved to blend in with patios etc).

When connecting pipes to new or existing chambers, it's important to note the direction of flow. Your new incoming branch pipe should merge via a side channel and should follow the existing flow direction, with the 'streamlined' angle of entry ideally not exceeding 45°.

Where space is very limited, Building Control may accept small plastic 'rodding eyes'. These are short branch pipes that come up to the surface with an airtight cover through which drain rods can be inserted for clearing blockages (by pushing the blockage along the pipe and into the nearest full-size inspection chamber).

And now for a quick moan about lids. In the good old days, inspection chamber covers were made of durable, virtually bullet-proof cast iron. Well OK, they may have cracked now and again when driven over by the occasional artic, but on the whole they did their job well. Today, however, many driveways are afflicted by flimsy light steel chamber lids, which are notorious for becoming dented and bending underfoot, with self-destructing handles to boot. If by some miracle they survive, rust will soon eat through and corrode them. So be

Right: Internal inspection cover in kitchen, best avoided
Below: Inspection chamber with dented lid and loose surround – after just 6 years.

sure to select covers that are tough enough for their purpose, especially if there'll be any vehicles in the vicinity.

SVPs – soil stacks

An important element in the overall design of a drainage system is the above-ground soil stack, usually referred to as the 'soil and vent pipe' (SVP). If your house is 1960s or older, this commonly takes the form of a large vertical pipe running up an outside wall. More modern houses usually have them run internally and boxed in.

Older SVPs are usually of cast iron, whereas modern ones are of 110mm diameter plastic. Their main purpose is to connect to upstairs WCs for dispersal of foul waste (euphemistically referred to as 'soil' or 'solids'), but they're also a handy way of collecting 'grey' waste water from pipes serving baths, basins and sinks, which connect to the SVP with special collars. Branch pipes connecting to the side of the SVP should normally be no longer than 3m with provision for rodding access to clear blockages, and must be properly supported with clips every 750mm. External waste pipes are usually run in grey plastic which is UV-resistant (*ie* it shouldn't become brittle as a result of ultra-violet sunlight).

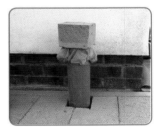

Foul waste pipes awaiting internal connection must be protected from debris (and to prevent foul smells!)

This is the only part of your drainage system that is vented, being open at the top, at roof level. This helps prevent the dreaded problem of 'siphonage', which can occur when large deluges of waste water surge down the pipes pulling along all the air in their slipstream. Without ventilation, this can literally suck the water out of traps and gullies behind, thereby allowing the sweet aroma of drains to waft up into your bathroom. So if you detect a malodorous stench in the air, don't automatically blame the kids – it may be down to siphonage. Talking of essence of ordure, the top of your SVP should project at least 900mm higher than any nearby window, otherwise

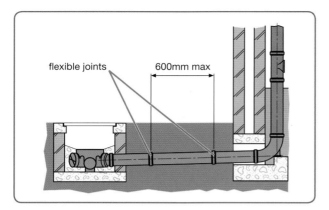

flexible joints   600mm max

you risk foul odours seeping through any nearby windows or vents. This means they normally need to terminate well above eaves level. At the very top, fitting a 'bird balloon' may save you the job of having to pluck old birds' nests and dead pigeons from your drains at a later date. Venting internally via special roof tiles can be a neater solution.

A simpler alternative is to fit an 'air admittance valve' (commonly called 'Durgo valves') connected to the top of an internal soil pipe terminating within the bathroom or loft. These have a special one-way valve that prevents siphonage but keeps smells in. However, they must be located above the flood level of the highest sanitary fitting in the same room (e.g. higher than the overflow of wash basins). 'Durgo' valves are normally only fitted to serve a secondary bathroom, where the house already has one main SVP. In other words, they're ideal for extensions. See Chapter 14.

Meanwhile, down underground, the soil stack is connected to the main drainage system. Here there must be a gentle bend at the underground base, to prevent foaming from detergents and the accumulation of solid waste.

New soil pipes in extensions are normally run internally, so the pipe will need to pass under and out through the

'Durgo' valve
in loft

main wall or foundations. To allow for different rates of settlement between the house and the drainage system, the two should be independent of each other. One way of achieving this is to fit a large diameter circular plastic duct in the foundation structure. The pipe can be run through this duct with a minimum clearance of 50mm all round. Alternatively, a small opening for the pipe can be left with lintels supporting both leaves of the walls above, as for a window or door opening. In each case rigid sheet material must be placed around the pipe to exclude undesirable visitors.

When fixing new soil pipes in place, they should be secured to the wall by pipe clips spaced no more than 1.8m apart.

Rat attack

Readers of a nervous disposition look away now. If there's one thing that can spoil the thrill of a lovely new extension, it's sewer rats putting in an unwelcome appearance. Vermin such as these may have been disturbed as a result of all the unsettling demolition work, and upwardly-mobile sewer rats love nothing better than to take up residence in nice fresh drainage pipes. So to deter possible ingress into your new system, all pipes and sewers should therefore be kept closed during the works as much as possible. Pipe ends should be temporarily stopped up, and manhole covers left in place. Disused drains, abandoned sewers and deceased cesspools should be excavated and completely removed, and old dead-end pipes packed with concrete.

Testing times

Building Control will need to inspect new drainage work before it's covered up, in order to ensure that all joints and seals are secure with no leakage. It's very much in your interest for the new waste system to be thoroughly tested, having first been checked by the builders who installed it. The simplest way to do this is simply by filling it with water (for systems down to a maximum depth of 2m).

NOTIFY BUILDING CONTROL 7
Drainage completion and ready for testing
– one day's notice

Now listen up. Here's a fun way to spend a few minutes. Buy or hire a donut shaped 'expanding rubber bung' or, better still, a device that looks like an inflatable football with a long stem. Open the inspection chamber serving your new pipework and firmly place the bung or 'football' into the pipe leading from the extension / house. Expand the bung by turning its central lever or inflate the football with a car pump until the pipe is fully sealed off. Next, run all the taps in the extension until the sinks and basins etc are about half full. Keep a close eye on this (making sure no one needs the loo in the meantime!). If the water levels don't drop for about 5 minutes, congratulations! – no drop in pressure means the system should be leak-free and you can happily extract your bungs.

Alternatively, an air test involves pumping air into sealed-off sections of pipework via a nozzle in a special bung, and checking that the pressure remains constant without dropping (by attaching a pressure gauge, or a U-tube filled with water). Smoke tests can be a useful alternative method of demonstrating leaks in exposed pipe runs visually.

There's another reason for doing this now. Building Control may wait until completion before choosing to conduct a similar test. But leaving trenches exposed for weeks on end is to invite accidents and damage. So ideally, if you can grab your Building Control Officer next time they're on site, and demonstrate your pressure test, it should lay this one to rest.

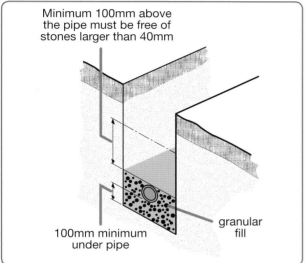

Minimum 100mm above the pipe must be free of stones larger than 40mm

granular fill

100mm minimum under pipe

Backfilling

Once Building Control have approved the new drainage work, the trenches can be backfilled. To protect flexible pipes, they must be fully surrounded by about 100mm depth of pea shingle/gravel. To get pipes well and truly 'tucked in' and protected from harm, no gravel stones larger than 40mm should be used, especially in the area immediately above them. This is followed by 300mm of soft soil which must be free of rubble such as rocks and bricks. The earth excavated from the trench is generally used for backfilling. The remaining topsoil is less critical but it will take many months for the ground to regain its stability. Heavy compaction should not take place until there's at least 600mm depth of soil over the pipe.

In areas where there could be damage from loadings above, such as parked cars or fence spikes, the pipes should be protected by concrete. Backfilling on top should not commence until at least 24 hours after concreting and traffic loads should be avoided for a minimum of 72 hours.

Gullies

Ready-made plastic gullies are fitted at ground level outside the house where rainwater downpipes connect to the underground surface water system. Similarly, where a ground floor kitchen sink has to discharge 'grey water' into a gulley (rather than being connected to a handy nearby

INSTALLING A GULLEY

SVP), a back-inlet gulley should be used. This is so the dirty water discharges directly to the drain and not over a grating that could get blocked by leaves etc.

Gullies are similar to traps under basins and baths. Their U-shaped bend retains water at the bottom of the 'U', forming a very effective barrier that stops foul odours coming back up from the drainage system. Traditionally the problem with gullies was clearing blockages since unlike bath traps you couldn't just unscrew them and rinse them out. Enter modern 'back inlet gullies' with built-in rodding access. These are covered with a grid, and when located level with the ground can provide additional drainage from the surrounding surface water, such as from patios (where permissible).

When extending to the rear or side of an existing kitchen, there will often be old gullies and pipes to deal with. Ideally, completely new drainage connections should be formed and the old pipes can then be blocked off and

Installation of toilets at 2nd fix stage relies on accurate positioning of the cold water supply and foul waste connection at first fix stage.

filled with concrete – taking care to first stop up the far end of redundant pipes, so that the entire drainage system doesn't get concreted!

Old rainwater pipes are usually straightforward to divert or substitute with new ones. But in some cases it may be necessary to leave an existing gulley in place, typically one serving a kitchen sink, so it can continue in use. This then becomes an internal gulley, which like internal inspection chambers is not an ideal arrangement and should normally be avoided. Otherwise it will need to be fitted with a screw-down sealed cover at floor level, for access purposes. First check any such proposed arrangement with Building Control.

Fitting a new WC

One of the many attractions of extending your home is the relief that an extra loo or bathroom can bring to a busy household. The Building Regs take a keen interest in such matters, particularly the need for good ventilation. The regulations on positioning of cloakrooms have relaxed in recent years. If you really wish, there's no reason why you shouldn't amaze your guests with a toilet that opens directly to your reception rooms or kitchen (without an intervening lobby area, as was formerly required) as long as there's a wash basin installed along with the WC. Windows aren't essential to a cloakroom, so there are many ingenious locations where they can be installed, such as within former under-stairs cupboards. But even where you do have window ventilation, extractor fans are still required to achieve the necessary three air changes per hour with a 15 minute over-run timer.

Modern WC pans are normally of a 'P' trap design, ie the pan waste outlet projects rearwards horizontally (rather than old 'S' traps that pointed down through the floor) ready to be mated into 'multikwik' or 'supersleeve' connectors.

Trees

In an ideal world there wouldn't be any massive trees growing near your proposed drain run. This is because trees are the enemies of drains. The roots of some species, such as willows and poplars, can be ruthlessly efficient at seeking out moisture, literally breaking through the tiniest of hairline fractures in drainage pipes in search of a drink. And when you start excavating near trees, or cutting through their roots, it can destabilise them. It's a hard problem to solve since, as noted earlier, cutting them down and removing them completely can cause ground 'heave', which is also potentially damaging.

In reality, there may be no option but to run the new pipes within fairly close proximity of trees (for example if the trees happen to belong to the neighbours). If so, there are some useful precautions that can help preserve your new drains:

- Where pipes are most at risk, they can be encased within concrete, with flexible jointing material applied around pipe joints within the concrete casing.
- Excavate drainage trenches by hand rather than using a mini-digger, to avoid cutting through roots larger than 50mm diameter.
- If possible, plan your drains so that the pipes run above or below any large tree roots.
- A 'root barrier' can be constructed as a shield in the ground to protect pipes, in the form of a deep, very narrow trench filled with special thick plastic sheeting, located between the pipe run and the trees.

Water recycling

There's no reason you can't save on water bills and do your bit for the planet by simply reusing all that relatively clean rainwater that otherwise disappears off into the ground. 'Harvested' rainwater, once filtered, can be put to good use watering the garden or supplying loos and washing machines. You can even recycle 'grey water' from baths and basins for flushing WCs. This is obviously more relevant if you're building an entire new house rather than extending, but it may be worth enquiring about diverting rainwater to water butts and then having it pumped to a separate water tank that serves your bathroom. You can even buy small purpose-made on-site treatment and filtration systems.

Rainwater drainage – soakaways

In most areas the water authorities discourage surface water from being combined with foul drainage to prevent overloading public sewers with water that doesn't require treatment. But rainwater needs to be taken well away from walls and foundations otherwise it may eventually cause damp or structural problems. In most properties connecting to the main system is prohibited so the best solution is to divert rainwater from the house into a handy ditch or nearby stream. If there are none, then a simple alternative is to construct a soakaway, assuming ground conditions allow.

Soakaways are the traditional 'hole in the ground' method of dispersing rainwater, and in recent years they've become more widely used in urban areas (where space allows). They're either made as conventional pits filled with rubble or as ready-made concrete chambers with holes in the walls, and must be designed to store the water run-off from roofs and hard surfaces, and to then disperse this stored water into the surrounding soil.

Trench-type soakaways should have at least two access points, including one at each end of the trench. To be most effective, soakaways work best in non-clay, low water table areas (otherwise ground water can fill the soakaway instead of the other way around). First, you need to arrange for Building Control to check the soil and advise on the required depth and distance from the house (normally at least 5 metres from the extended house and 2.5 metres from neighbours' fences). This may involve digging a trial pit and filling it with water three times in succession to monitor the rate of seepage. The chosen site should also avoid any risk of waterlogging to downhill areas. In most cases where the soil drains well, and the roof area is less than 100m2, you should be able to construct a traditional type of soakaway. (See website for details).

But if a soakaway isn't built correctly there can be problems with overflowing or silting up. Maintenance can also be a problem – the main one being how to find it! Some form of inspection access should be provided (but often isn't) so that suction emptying and jetting equipment may need to be used to clear them. The good news is you may qualify for a reduction in your water bill which includes a charge for surface water discharge, which is now done via your garden.

Main trades needed on site
- **Labourers:** Excavate trenches, backfill.
- **Plumbers:** Lay and connect pipes.
- **Bricklayers:** Build inspection chamber.

Workmanship
- Requirements for workmanship to drains are covered in the code of practice BS 8000-14.

www.home-extension.co.uk

10 THE MAIN WALLS

Now's a good time to stand back and take stock. The walls are built up to DPC level and the ground floor structure is in place. In most cases, the drainage works will also be largely complete. So far so good.

Photo: David Davies

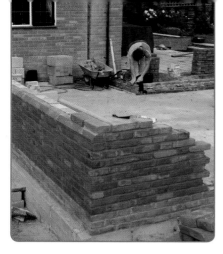

Left and right: Traditional brick plinth to lower walls gives appearance of Victorian solid wall, but is modern cavity construction with thicker lower outer leaf infilled with blocks.

The opportunity should now be taken to get the site tidied up and to backfill the remaining trenches around the walls up to ground level with earth and rubble. This will set the stage for the next major phase – construction of the main walls.

Although this chapter focuses predominantly on masonry walls, much should still be relevant to non-conventional construction (see Chapter 4) because the outer leaf will most likely be built in brick, stone, or blockwork. Modern timber frame construction is explored in detail at the end of this chapter. But regardless of your chosen method of construction, a strange thing can happen at this stage. You notice that the floor space appears incredibly small. Thankfully this uneasy feeling that the rooms have somehow shrunk should pass once the walls are all nicely plastered and decorated, at which point everything should magically resume its rightful proportions.

The external finish

Nothing will affect the appearance of your extension as much as the choice of materials for the walls. Planners often stipulate that the new walls should match the 'visual character' of the existing house, whereas Building Control will want to see highly-insulated modern construction, not some quaint medieval throwback. The type of external finish designed to achieve these twin goals will have been specified on your drawings and priced accordingly by the builder.

The vast majority of home extensions are built of traditional cavity masonry, the method of construction used in most British homes since the 1930s. Today this commonly comprises a decorative outer wall of brick and a separate inner wall of thermal blocks, with an air cavity between. These two 'leaves'

Manufactured clay bricks designed to imitate traditional handmade styles.

(or 'skins') are tied together with small stainless steel wall ties across the cavity, the inner leaf normally taking most of the load. Finished main walls typically measure a little over 300mm with 100mm wide cavities which normally suit ties 225mm or 250mm in length.

But there are several possible variations on this basic theme and local historic architecture can be a great source of inspiration. The outer walls could be of concrete blockwork finished in cement render. Or perhaps traditional lightweight 'shiplap' timber cladding, or decorative tiling. The premium material for walls is of course natural stone, but this is expensive and necessitates building the outer wall a little thicker, at least 150mm, to help match traditional local building styles. Modern 'reconstituted stone' blocks (made from stone dust or aggregates bonded with cement or polyester resin) cost half as much as real stone. Exotic two-tone designs, such as brickwork with infill panels of flint or traditional lime render can look great. Flint is either laid as whole stones or

It's hard to beat real knapped flint for period charm. But ready-made flint wall panels are easier to construct on site.

Right and below: Reconstituted stone mimics real stone and can be offset with brick detailing .

'knapped' with the cut insides facing, although ready made flint blocks are an easier option. But it's worth noting that mixing materials normally means increased complexity at junctions, which will inevitably bump up the cost.

If you're adding to a period house, your extension might be designed to echo some original decorative features, such as string courses of dark engineering bricks or contrasting red bands. At roof level a skilled brickie may relish the challenge of trying to match the original pattern of projecting corbels or dog tooth detailing under the verges.

Victorian solid walls were normally laid in either Flemish bond or English bond. English bond consisted of layers of bricks laid lengthways (stretchers) alternating with courses

Above left: Traditional plinth with engineering bricks.
Above right: New decorative arch complements Victorian house but new brickwork not in matching Flemish bond.

of bricks laid crossways to show their heads (headers), but by far the most common style was Flemish bond, in which stretchers were alternately punctuated by headers.Modern cavity walls make exclusive use of 'stretcher bond' with all the bricks laid lengthways. This can make blending a new extension to an old building quite difficult, so the planners may have stipulated that your modern cavity walls should be built to imitate Flemish bond, with the outer leaf using alternate bricks cut in half, known as 'snapped headers'.

Brick selector

Choosing bricks sounds like fun, but the problem is that if you get it wrong you're stuck with them. Unlike emulsion, you can't simply return the wall to B&Q if you don't like it. Bricks typically comprise around 5% of the build cost, yet they can account for as much as 70% of its appearance, so it's obviously critical to get this decision right. You may even find that picking more expensive handmade bricks will enhance the extension's 'kerb appeal'. Fortunately,

most manufacturers can now supply 'sample panels', equivalent to about half a square metre of the wall's surface area, made from thin brick slips. Alternatively, once you've narrowed the choice down to two or three types of brick, you could buy about 50 of each and get your brickie to construct a small sample wall. This should provide a pretty good feel for what the finished wall will look like.

Brick-supply specialists have libraries you can visit to obtain a match – but be aware that photos may not always faithfully reproduce the subtle hues of 'real-life' bricks. Ideally, take a sample with you of the ones you are hoping to match. If the bricks you want are no longer made, there are companies that will make replicas – at a price. If you're extending an historic building, local salvage yards can turn up hidden treasures, although old reclaimed handmade bricks can be surprisingly irregular in shape, driving bricklayers to distraction. Even bog-standard bricks have changed shape over the last 25 years, from old imperial sizes to metric, and this can make it virtually impossible to neatly line up extension brickwork with the existing courses.

The standard UK metric brick is 215mm long x 102.5mm wide x 65mm deep, and you need 60 of them to build one square metre of wall. Most bricks are also available in greater depths of 73mm, and some as large as 80mm. To avoid the inherent problems associated with the use of fragile porous reclaimed bricks, you can buy tough modern ones that look very realistic. Manufactured with a traditional appearance, these ancient-looking bricks – such as small 50mm 'two-inchers'– are perfect for extensions to some 'Olde Worlde' period houses.

However, getting a precise match with the walls of your existing property may not be too easy, because you need to take into account how things might look after a few years' exposure to the weather.

Luckily, the choice of bricks currently available is extensive, with hundreds of imported and home-grown varieties. Choose from colourful buffs, yellows, tawneys, or red Durham multis. Or how about bucking up your neighbourhood with some drag-faced or sand-faced styles? To blend in with an older house, there are historic-looking pre-war commons and stock bricks, not forgetting

White powdery 'efflorescence' – harmless salts in new brickwork should brush off.

Victorian style single bullnose, double cants and squints for specialist detailing.

Handmade bricks have a pleasing natural variance in colour and texture, with a wide range of bespoke shapes, sizes and blends. One recent trend is for longer, thinner 'Roman bricks'.

Wirecut bricks are a more affordable option and are still the most commonly used facing brick in UK. The name relates to fact they are mechanically extruded and cut by wire. These give a more uniform appearance, although some types have applied weathering/ageing techniques to make them resemble handmade ones.

Common clay bricks can normally be used for internal load-bearing walls although blockwork is more common. Toughest of all are dense 'Class A' engineering bricks. Traditionally of a distinctive semi-gloss blue/black or blood red colour, these are so hard and water resistant that they were employed in the construction of 19th century railway bridges and even for DPCs. Today structural engineers sometimes specify them as padstones for supporting steel beams. 'Class B' 'semi-engineering' bricks are often used in below-ground walls.

But appearances aren't everything. Bricks are technically rated for both frost resistance and salt content. Frost can attack damp bricks, expanding the moisture by 10% and causing the faces to crumble. Salts within bricks can chemically react with cement mortar and expand, causing cracking and spalling. In most parts of the country 'M rated' bricks should be sufficiently frost resistant, but if building in severe frost areas or mountainous regions go for the harder F (or FR) variety. Salt ratings are either N (normal) or L (low) and in very exposed, or wet locations, such as some coastal districts, the vile weather may require the use of L rated bricks along with sulphate-resisting cement.

Masonry needs to be protected as much as possible from the onslaught of the elements. Good design should ensure that the wall surfaces are spared the persistent passage of rainwater, by the construction of overhanging roofs, such as big umbrella-like eaves and projecting bargeboards, large sills on windows and doors, and generous coping stones on parapet walls.

Achieving the right 'character' isn't just about selecting the right materials. Good brickwork is taken for granted, so poor quality workmanship will ruin the whole appearance of a building. In case anyone tries to persuade you otherwise, brickwork should be uniform, with the mortar joints of equal thickness in each course (normally 10mm) and of equal width at the vertical side joints (the 'perpends'), plus the mortar

texture and colour should be consistent throughout the wall. Different batches of facing bricks can vary slightly in colour, so wise brickies pick from mixed batches. This avoids 'shading', where it's obvious half the wall comprises an old batch of a different shade that the supplier has had kicking around for a year or two. To prevent staining, always keep stored bricks covered and dry on site.

Blocks

Concrete blocks are normally used to construct the load-bearing inner leaves of cavity masonry walls as well as many interior ground floor dividing walls. If your walls are going to be rendered or clad externally, then the outer leaf will in most cases also be made from blocks. The standard size is 440mm long x 215mm wide x 100mm deep, the equivalent of 6 bricks. You need 10 blocks to build one square metre of wall. Their strength is expressed in Newtons per sq mm ('N') and for most straightforward extensions the basic 3.6N strength should be sufficient (as opposed to stronger 7.3N). Your structural engineer's calculations will have specified the required strength.

You may think a block is a block, but actually the type chosen is very important. Dense aggregate blocks have high strength but are poor insulators. They're used for foundations, external leaves of some rendered walls, and for internal load-bearing partitions. Lightweight aerated blocks which, as the name suggests, look a bit like an Aero chocolate bar inside, aren't so strong but have excellent insulating properties, and are widely used for inner leaves and partition walls. So you can't just use any old blocks left over from the last job. The drawings will specify blocks of the correct compressive strength (eg 7.3 N), density (eg 1,000kg/m^3) and thermal efficiency (e.g. K-value 0.20W/mK) designed to support loadings and meet energy targets. Some have a rippled or 'striated' face, ready for rendering. Others have a warm buff stone-like colour. Well-known brands of lightweight 'aerated' thermal blocks include H+H Celcon, Forterra Thermalite, and Tarmac Hemelite. However, because of dire shortages of blocks in recent years new clay-based blocks such as Plasmor Fibolites are making big inroads (made from expanded clay nodules rather than 'pulverised fuel ash' coal waste used in conventional aerated blocks). One problem with aerated 'thermal' blocks is they're very prone to shrinkage cracking when drying out on internal faces after being plastered. Although not usually of any structural significance, this can appear quite dramatic and tends to greatly alarm homeowners. For this reason it's not unknown for builders to be tempted to switch them for more robust but 'colder' dense blocks when the architect's not looking. Fortunately, to pre-empt such problems, finished interior walls are now normally lined with plasterboard, achieving the twin goals of concealing any shrinkage cracking and minimising heat-loss.

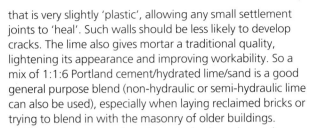

Mortar

Where would we be without mortar, that trusty mix of sand and cement that magically glues buildings together? Simply take a shovel-full of cement, add four shovels of soft sand, mix it all up with a little water, and Bob's your Uncle. Sounds easy, doesn't it? But if the mix is too weak, with excessive sand, your mortar joints will eventually erode and crumble. On the other hand, if the mortar is too strong with too much cement, the joints will crack and the wall could fracture; too wet and it'll dribble away before the bricks can be placed; too dry and it may fail to bond properly.

This is where experienced brickies are a godsend. They'll know how to vary the mix so that it's just right for the strength of the bricks and the type of sand being used, as well as how to compensate for the effects of weather on drying-out times.

The colour of sand can vary considerably depending on the region from which it comes, so where consistency of appearance is important this should be taken into account. The type of sand used for brickwork is 'builder's sand', as opposed to 'sharp sand', which is coarser and more suitable for making concrete or rendering.

Mortar can be mixed on site, or for very small quantities you may prefer to buy dry pre-mixed bags where all you have to do is add water. If you plan to make your own, remember not to mix too much at a time, as the shelf-life of cement mortar is normally only about two hours. Also,

it should not be re-wetted after mixing.

A typical mortar mix for new work above ground would be 1:4 or 1:5 Portland cement/sand (a stronger 1:3 mix would be used in masonry that gets very wet, such as underground work). This produces a strong mix with good frost resistance when set. However, it can also be fairly brittle. Adding a small amount of lime produces a less rigid mortar

that is very slightly 'plastic', allowing any small settlement joints to 'heal'. Such walls should be less likely to develop cracks. The lime also gives mortar a traditional quality, lightening its appearance and improving workability. So a mix of 1:1:6 Portland cement/hydrated lime/sand is a good general purpose blend (non-hydraulic or semi-hydraulic lime can also be used), especially when laying reclaimed bricks or trying to blend in with the masonry of older buildings.

The performance of mortar can also be enhanced by additives (brickies seem to rate a brand called 'Feb') although some types of cement come ready-modified with additives to improve workability. In place of traditional lime many bricklayers mix in liquid plasticiser, which adds tiny air bubbles to the mix, making it 'creamy' and easier to work. It also provides a degree of frost-resistance during the setting period, which is helpful when building in winter. A suitable mix which includes plasticiser would be 1:5 or 1:6 Portland cement/sand. Although 'anti-freezing' agents can be added to the mortar, bricklaying should really only be carried out when temperatures are above 2°C, and fresh work must be protected against frost, especially overnight.

Special sulphate-resistant cement can be used for below-ground walls, or those with particularly high exposure to aggressive weather. Colouring agents can be useful for blending in extensions to old houses, such as those with historic 'black ash mortar'.

If you want decent brickwork, a good start is to ensure that the materials are protected when stored on site so they're clean and dry. Cement should be stored safely off the ground, and loose piles of sand should be covered over when not being used. Taking truck deliveries of sand in one-tonne bags may be more manageable.

Striking and pointing

Although the word 'pointing' is widely used to describe the finish of mortar joints, strictly speaking the word 'striking' is more appropriate for most new work.

'Striking' describes the process of finishing the mortar joints between newly laid bricks. Bricklaying should be stopped at convenient stages so that the striking can be done. First, any small surface voids in the mortar are filled using a small pointing trowel. Then the mortar is 'struck' in the style required, doing the vertical 'cross joints' first, then the horizontal 'bed joints'. Finally, any crumbs of mortar from the wall are brushed away. If there are large pieces of mortar on the face of the brickwork, wait for about 12 hours until it has gone off before rubbing it away.

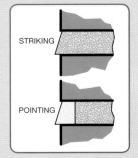

STRIKING

POINTING

Above: Once the brickwork has been completed the joints are finished using a special pointing tool (here in 'bucket handle' style) and any loose particles removed with a bristle brush.

Styles of finishing

Flush
Flush finishing is achieved by drawing a strip of wood about 12mm wide, 6mm thick and 100mm long along the joints.

Bucket handle
Formed by pulling a suitably shaped piece of metal (or a bucket handle!) along the joints. Also known as the 'hollow key' style.

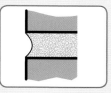

Weathered
A weathered finish is good for throwing off rainwater from a wall, and is considered to be fairly durable. It is sometimes used on stacks to improve weather resistance. The vertical joints can be struck to the left or the right but must be kept consistent, otherwise the wall will look peculiar!

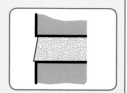

Struck
Struck jointing is not ideal for most exterior facings as it leaves the upper edge of the lower brick exposed to the weather.

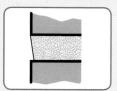

Recessed key
Recessed key jointing suffers from the same drawback as 'struck'. Here the mortar is raked out and is then pressed back evenly using a special 'chariot' jointing tool.

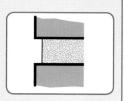

Finishing mortar joints
Mortar makes up around 20% of the area of a brick wall, so getting the finished joints looking right is vital to the appearance of the entire building. At regular intervals the rough mortar joints on fresh brickwork should be carefully finished before the mortar gets a chance to harden. But this isn't just about getting your walls to look good. Most of the seepage of rainwater through outer walls actually occurs through the joints rather than the bricks. Good workmanship will help prevent this.

Once the new brickwork has been completed the joints between the bricks are finished using a special pointing tool or a smooth piece of wood.

But what style of finish to choose? Don't be seduced by snazzy 'inverted arrow head' and 'recessed key' indented pointing. These are usually best avoided, since rainwater can collect and pond on the exposed ledge of each brick, which can lead to damp penetration and frost damage.

Depending on the style of the main house brickwork, it's often best to go for a simple, traditional style, such as a plain 'flush' finish. If you're using reclaimed or handmade bricks which are uneven in appearance, traditional 'bucket handle' joints (which are recessed in a curved shape) should suit the weathered character of the bricks.

The true masters of pointing and bricklaying were the Georgians and Victorians, who equated thin joints with top-quality construction. Incredibly fine joints (called 'tuck pointing') are especially evident on brick arches above many Georgian doors and windows. Today, trying to match such fine quality work may prove difficult. Modern finished mortar joints are typically about 10mm thick.

Brickies

It may sound obvious, but the secret to getting good quality brickwork it is to employ a good, experienced local bricklayer. Sir Winston Churchill famously stated that *"every man should build a wall"*. But good bricklaying is an art that can take years to perfect. It is also one of the world's oldest professions, along with stonemasonry and prostitution.

It's important to have a clear understanding at the outset about what is, and what is not included in the price, especially if you're employing trades directly for a fixed

Above and right: When bricklaying, string lines and pins are continually in use to ensure joints are straight and level

Related jobs that are also done by the bricklayer

Included
- Setting out the walls on the new foundations.
- Fitting air bricks.
- Laying the DPC.
- Building in templates or frame ties to door and window openings.
- Installing cavity insulation.
- Fitting lintels.
- Building in restraint straps.
- Bedding on the timber wallplate at roof level.

Not included*
- Erecting scaffolding or towers.
- Supplying materials.
- Constructing timber templates for windows and doors.
- Plant hire.
- Cutting indents into existing walls and opening existing cavities for vertical DPCs.
- Fixing profiles.

Unless agreed as an 'all-in-rates' package.

price. There are a number of related tasks that also need to be done. Avoid prima donna brickies who consider it's someone else's job to do anything other than placing one brick on top of another.

Communication at this stage is paramount. Remember, your prized extension is just another job to your brickie, so make sure your requirements are clearly understood and that he's equipped with a copy of the final approved plans, especially if there have been changes. Knowing in advance exactly where each opening is supposed to go is obviously crucial.

It's also essential that all the materials are available on site at the right time. If future visits have to be made after the main walls are built to complete any unfinished work there may be an extra charge.

Cavity walls can be built very quickly. Some highly motivated brickies, if well supplied with the raw materials, can steam ahead at a staggering rate. A team of two brickies plus a labourer should normally be able to lay up to 1,000 bricks a day or 30 to 40m2 of blocks, or more likely a mix of the two.

To get things moving, the bricks and blocks are usually loaded in small stacks up to a metre high at roughly 1.5m intervals around the walls, set back from the face about a metre or so. On uneven ground a 'foot scaffold' may be needed or the ground back-filled. Bricklayers can then set up string lines and build up the corners one block high in each direction. This allows them to check the square of the building. They then run a string line from corner to corner and infill along the line, checking levels and uprights and building in the wall ties as they go. The two leaves of each wall are, strictly speaking, supposed to be built up more or less together at the same rate. But in real life, in the race to the top, brickies often like to crack on with one leaf first, before catching up later with the other. Some prefer to build a few courses of the inner leaf blocks ahead of the brickwork, others favour a brickwork first approach. Either way, blobs of excess mortar should be scraped off the inner cavity walls as work progresses, as such obstructions can later risk rainwater bridging across the cavity onto the inner wall. To keep cavities clear of mortar droppings (known as 'snots') it's good practice for a protective batten to be placed over the cavity as work progresses above.

Where window and door frames aren't being installed as the walls take shape, dummy timber templates or 'profiles' can instead be built in, knocked up by s carpenter in 100 x 50mm timber with batten diagonals.

Insulation should be added as the wall is built. In walls that are to be fully-filled with insulation, such as 100mm glass mineral wool batts, it's common practice to lead with the outer leaf as the batts are largely self-supporting (but to pre-empt any risk of insulation stuffed into cavities pushing out fresh brickwork, brickies sometimes build cavities a bit wider).

Where they're only to be partially-filled, e.g. with 75mm mineral wool batts or 50mm rigid foam boards, the inner leaf tends to lead so the insulation can be secured to the blockwork with wall tie retaining clips (small plastic discs known as 'collars' or 'dollars') before the outer brickwork is built up. Where the two leaves aren't built up together, a maximum height difference of 18 courses of bricks or 6 courses of blocks (about 1.35m) is acceptable. Finally, at the end of each day's work the bricks should be cleaned so that they're free of mortar splashes.

Render

As well as excelling in the field of mortar pointing, the Georgians also knew a thing or two about using render to disguise cheap brickwork so that it looked like expensive dressed stonework. 'Stucco', a hard external lime plaster that predated modern cement render, was applied to amazing effect. Render is a bit of a fashion thing, coming back into vogue now and again, such as on Regency and Victorian seaside terraces and many 1930s semis. It also

has technical benefits, providing good weather protection and improved insulation, whilst at the same time allowing the use of cheaper materials for the main walls, which today means using concrete blocks instead of bricks.

For your new extension, you may rather fancy a smooth, clean, white-painted cement render finish. Or to match your existing house you may opt for pebbledash or roughcast render. Modern, sophisticated hard-wearing renders reinforced with alkali-resistant glass fibre are available in a wide variety of colours and finishes. You can even order render to be supplied premixed so that all you need do is add water. Even better, special through-coloured, single coat 'monocouche' renders are claimed to be easy to apply and never need painting, but are relatively expensive. (See Chapter 16.)

Cavity walls

Walls made of traditional solid brick, much favoured by the Victorians, are today extinct in new construction. Even if you're building an extension onto an old period house, no way would they be permitted. In fact, it was already realised way back in the nineteenth century that problems with dampness penetrating through walls could be massively reduced by constructing two separate thinner walls with an air cavity sandwiched between them, rather than one big thick wall. If driving rain penetrated the outer brick wall, at least it wouldn't be able to bridge the gap and reach the inner leaf. Except, of course, that it can. Since the 1990s it has been common practice to stuff cavities full of insulation, either during construction or later by injection-pumping it through small drill holes. What wasn't foreseen at

Base 'scratch' coat applied to suitably rough faced blocks.

Mineral wool insulation batts stuffed into cavities – needs to be protected from weather asap.

Photo: The Insta Group

Above: Granular cavity fill pumped in once wall is complete

Above and left: 50mm rigid insulation cavity boards secured to inner leaf thermal blockwork with 'collars' clipped over wall ties

the time was that, in some cases, this could allow moisture to cross the void, causing damp patches and mould in the rooms of the unlucky occupants.

Cavity insulation

As noted earlier, there are two principal ways of installing cavity insulation in new walls, 'total fill' and 'partial fill'. But where cavities are totally filled up there's a potential risk of rain penetrating through the outer wall, sneaking across the cavity and soaking through inner walls, at least in houses exposed to very severe weather. Because insulation works by trapping air within its body, to work well it needs to remain dry, so having your cavities crammed with a lot

Rubbish workmanship! – giant lumps of mortar and loose wall ties block cavity.

of limp and soggy insulation can actually make your home colder.

This may all seem slightly odd since most types of insulation are perfectly waterproof. Indeed, if you place a batt of standard mineral wool on a pool of water it will quite happily float for hours without absorbing a drop. But inside the lonely world of a cavity, in extreme conditions, it can potentially act as a bridge conveying water from the outside wall through to the inner leaf, and over time it may becoming virtually waterlogged.

This problem can be aggravated if careless brickies allow mortar droppings to fall down the cavity. When mortar 'snots' land on wall ties, or start to accumulate at the bottom of the cavity, you have the classic conditions for damp to bridge the cavity.

So seriously is this problem taken that 'total fill' is now only acceptable in more sheltered parts of the country (some newbuild warranty providers require it to be avoided altogether). The UK has 4 different levels of 'exposure zones' for wind-driven rain (see website) and fully filled cavities should only be considered in 'sheltered' and 'moderate' parts of the county (ie zones 1 and 2 which cover much of the east and south of Britain). But with ever stricter thermal insulation standards to meet, what are you supposed to do? The obvious solution is to construct bigger cavities, now routinely built 100mm or wider so they can accommodate a thick wedge of insulation whilst still leaving a decent-sized air void. In most cases this means the overall wall thickness is a little over 300mm. This should leave you with a clear 50mm or so 'defensive space' between the insulation and the outer leaf – which is exactly what original uninsulated cavity walls used to have in the first place. In 'severe' exposure zones 3 and 4, partial fill with a generous air void of 75mm is recommended.

An exception to this may be seen on some new housing developments, where cavities are completely filled with tiny lightweight water-repellent polystyrene granules blown in once the walls have been built. Despite fully filling the void, major housebuilders are confident these will not allow damp to pass, even in the most dire weather. But much depends on where the property is located.

Left: Worrying lack of wall ties and collar clips to secure insulation boards.

Below: Traditional 'soft red' brick soldier course over window – will contrast nicely with white render.

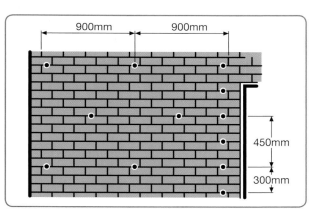

Traditionally, it's the bricklayer's job to install the insulation in the cavities as walls are built, continuing all the way up to the top (not forgetting gable walls to any rooms at roof level). As mentioned earlier, with rigid insulation the inner leaf tends to lead so the boards can be secured to the blockwork with wall tie retaining clips. It's important that this is executed carefully because to be effective the boards must be firmly attached and not left hanging limply where the sun don't shine. Some types of rigid foam insulation are designed to be interlocking, others may need their joints taped. To protect the insulation from the weather, the cavities in unfinished walls should be covered over at night. Also, any unused material stored on site should be kept dry and clean.

There are some additional factors to consider when deciding which type of cavity wall insulation to use. Insulation made from traditional mineral wool will offer good protection from fire and noise transmission, whereas modern foam-based materials will provide better thermal efficiency. If you prefer an organic home extension, natural cellulose fibre made from recycled newspaper or sheep's wool can be blown into the cavities once the walls are completed. But the most widely used materials are high performance polyurethane type rigid boards (PUR, PIR etc) or mineral wool batts.

In recent years remarkable progress has been made towards achieving super-low heat-loss U-value figures in modern houses. Apart from improved cavity wall insulation,

this has primarily been down to the development of lightweight insulating blocks for use in the inner leaf of cavity walls. But the warmest ones can be so full of air bubbles that their compressive strength is relatively poor and drilling into them to fix screws and wallplugs for shelves or cupboards can reveal their soft crumbly nature. So dry-lining the walls internally with plasterboard means you can fix things to the plasterboard-lining rather than direct to soft blockwork. For extra grip it's a good idea to fix strips of plywood prior to plasterboarding in areas where you want to install wall units etc.

But there are some more traditional ways of making the walls of your new extension walls super-snug. Applying traditional weatherproof timber boarding, tile hanging or cement rendering to beef up the outer walls has been standard building practice for centuries, in coastal districts or places exposed to regular battering by Mother Nature. Wrapping your home in an external 'raincoat' will provide an essential extra line of defence against driving rain and howling gales whilst also helping to further reduce your U-values. See Chapter 17.

Wall ties

For cavity walls to be stable and strong, the two leaves must be joined together with wall ties that bridge across the void. In fact the walls won't last long without them, so it's essential for wall ties to be fitted properly. Where lazy or incompetent builders have omitted to include them, or where old ones have rusted and failed, walls have been known to crack or even collapse.

To achieve structural stability, the ties must be placed at regular intervals and fully bedded a

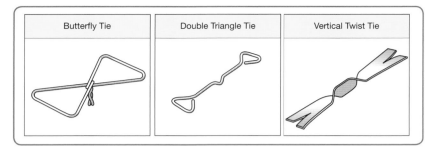

Butterfly Tie	Double Triangle Tie	Vertical Twist Tie

minimum of 50mm into mortar joints, sloping at a slight gradient downwards and outwards so that any moisture heads out and not into your bedroom. The first row is inserted at ground level. As a general guide, ties are fixed in the wall about 900mm apart horizontally and about 450mm vertically, staggered in a 'domino five' pattern. Around door and window openings the density is normally increased and the ties are spaced vertically about every 300mm, positioned no more than 225mm in from the edge. You need at least three wall ties per m² (4 per m² for timber frame) – see box out.

Until fairly recently the cheapest and most widely used wall ties were the 'butterfly' type. Looking a little like tiny coat-hangers contorted into a figure of eight, they have over the years proved adequate for the job in normal conditions. But today, 'double triangle' wall ties are the most widely used type. These typically comprise a 225mm long strip of stainless steel wire about 2mm thick with a small fold at each end. Small retaining clips are slotted over their stems to secure insulation to the inner leaf. The squiggly bits in the middle of ties are known as 'drips' (because any water travelling along it should drip off before it can do any damage). The drip should be positioned roughly in the centre of the cavity. Of course, being covered by big blobs of bricklaying mortar will mess things up, so it's important that ties are kept clean. However, wall ties are designed to suit particular cavity widths, so where cavities exceed 100mm, longer 250 or 275mm ties can be used, while for walls in exposed locations stronger flat 'vertical twist' types are recommended.

Thermal bridging

The more insulation you stuff into the fabric of your house, the greater the relative importance of any remaining cold areas where the walls can 'leak heat'. The weakest link when it comes to insulation is normally around windows and doors. It was common until quite recently for the sides of the cavities round wall openings to be 'closed off' with bricks or blocks, effectively creating a solid wall with the outer and inner leaves of the wall joined together. This created a 'thermal bridge' crossing from the cold outer wall to the inside walls of rooms, resulting in 'cold spots'. Cold spots in rooms can also occur where gaps are left in the cavity insulation, or where poorly fitted steel wall ties poke through into the plaster of the inner walls.

At this juncture, you might be thinking 'So what?' After all, just how life-threatening can a cold spot on a wall really be? The answer is, no one wants to live in an unhealthy house with damp, mouldy walls. Cold spots on the walls will irresistibly attract the warm, moist air circulating around a typical home. This will then promptly condense back into water on the cold wall, causing damp patches which can eventually grow black mould.

Fortunately there's a simple solution. The problem of thermal bridging around openings for windows and doors is prevented by installing special insulated plastic strips known as 'cavity closers' which fit snugly into the ends of cavities, neatly sealing them off. Cavity closers can double as a DPC thereby tackling the problems of damp penetration and heat loss at the same time. When the frames are fitted, the cavity closer should overlap them by at least 25mm. No longer is it acceptable to just stick a course of 'cold' bricks or concrete blocks to close off the two wall leaves around openings.

The other part of the solution in most newbuild construction is for the inner face of walls to be dry-lined with plasterboard, making their internal surfaces warmer, reducing the risk of damp caused by humid air in the room condensing (whilst also providing a handy void behind the boards to run pipes and cables).

Nothing has escaped the attention of the energy-efficiency

Below: Wall with full-fill mineral wool insulation awaiting cavity closer.
Right: Cavity closer fitted.

Below: Lintels now come ready insulated.

police, so the lintels you fit above openings now come ready-packed with insulation. Indeed, you can even compare different brands of lintel according to thermal efficiency by their respective 'R' values (a mirror image of U values – the higher, the more they resist heat leakage). Even so, the cold underside of some beams or lintels may still require an insulated lining to be applied.

Apart from door and window reveals, the other high risk areas for cold spots are where the walls meet the roof, which is why it's not unusual to see mould staining to some upper bedroom walls. The solution is for loft insulation to be carried over the wall plate to link up with the top of the cavity wall insulation. To prevent ventilation air paths at eaves getting blocked, small plastic 'rafter vents' or 'eaves protectors' can be installed around the edges of the loft. A similar 'cold bridging' problem can arise at the bottom of the building where the floor screed meets the walls, which is why the floor needs to be sealed from the cold wall by a strip of insulation around its edges.

Ventilation

If you reckon the rules on insulating your extension are a bit OTT, then you'll be delighted to know that Building Control pay similarly close attention to its breezy bedfellow, ventilation.

The problems began when sealing out draughts from our homes became a national obsession in the 1970s. Fireplaces got boarded up and rooms hermetically sealed with double glazing. At the same time, gas appliances would eat up valuable oxygen leaving occupants gasping in the over-warm centrally-heated atmosphere. Steam from kettles, baths, washing and cooking with nowhere to escape then caused an epidemic of condensation, often manifesting itself as unsightly damp black mould.

The fact is, when the warm, moist air in your house hits a cold surface it will cool and condense back to water, causing damp. The source of all this water vapour is simply such ordinary human activities as breathing and sleeping. Add to this tumble driers, washing machines, sweaty pets, power showers, gas heaters and houseplants and you'll

find an average home produces well over ten litres of water vapour a day – and it has to go somewhere.

The solution is to do exactly what you do in the car when it steams up: wind down the windows and turn up the blower. In other words, improve the ventilation.

The objective when designing a new house or extension is to provide controllable ventilation. This means that in addition to having openable windows and doors ('rapid ventilation') some element of permanent 'background ventilation' which can trickle through all the time is needed to reduce the risk of condensation. So small 'trickle vents' positioned in the heads of new window and door frames are now required. But because most water vapour comes from kitchens and bathrooms these rooms must be equipped with extractor fans that automatically expel steamy air before it can cause trouble. Finally, if you fully insulate your walls and reduce emissions of water vapour in the first place – for example cutting down on boiled food – the problem should be solved. See Chapter 14.

Beams and lintels

Lintels are horizontal beams placed in the walls above openings for windows and doors etc. The purpose of lintels or beams is to safely transfer the loads from above down onto the walls either side of the opening (a simpler solution than building traditional brick arches).

You may be slightly surprised to hear that lintels

Below: To support heavier loadings over openings (e.g. bay windows) engineers may specify steels & padstones instead of standard lintels.

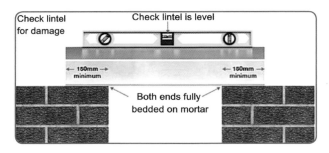

were omitted in the outer leafs walls in many housing developments from the 1940s through to the 1970s, often relying instead on metal window frames to take the loading. This wasn't a particularly brilliant idea, as many replacement window contractors have belatedly discovered amidst showers of falling bricks.

Traditionally made from timber or stone, lintels are now normally of either lightweight galvanised steel or pre-cast reinforced concrete. They are installed as the leaves of the wall are built up by being bedded on mortar.

Steel is the preferred material for bridging openings in cavity walls; brands commonly specified include Catnic, IG, Keystone and Birtley. Most have an inverted 'V' profile with a slanted top and protruding feet designed to sit on each leaf of a cavity wall; they are factory-insulated inside the 'V' (a 'thermal break') and can be neatly hidden within the brickwork. Steel 'box lintels' are another type more often used for openings in solid walls. Simplest of all are concrete lintels which, apart from not looking too pretty can suffer from cold bridging, so their use tends to be restricted to internal walls or for pipe openings etc in outer leaves. The exception to the almost exclusive use of steel or concrete can be found on some contemporary designs, which have dipped into the past with manufactured 'stone' lintels , some made from granite mixed with cement. Others have reverted to using large timber beams. These chunky 'railway sleeper' type hardwood timbers are extremely robust and are reminiscent architecturally of period cottages, a style briefly revived in the 1930s, though unlike those in Victorian houses these are not hidden away behind brick arches. The whole point is

Exposed hardwood lintels impart traditional period house style.

to display them as a prominent architectural feature above windows and doors on the outer leaf.

At the design stage your structural engineer will have calculated the loadings (both imposed 'live' and permanent 'dead' loads) and specified beams and lintels that can safely take the weight. Or if you're designing your own extension, it's a good idea to make use of the free design and specifying service provided by lintel manufacturers.

Regardless of all the complex desk-calculations, some builders on site always know better and prefer to stick with the same familiar types of lintels they've used for years. Funnily enough, these usually happen to be the ones that are cheapest and most easily available. Worse, when a lintel doesn't fit, out comes the angle grinder. But cutting to reduce the length can significantly weaken them, plus the exposed steel ends will be prone to rust. It's not entirely

unknown for DIY builders to put them in sideways or upside down – one possible clue to such an error is that you have to stand on your head to read the markings.

Suitability for purpose depends on the required loadings and spans. Steel cavity lintels are widely available off the shelf for

Standard steel lintels are designed to support each leaf of the wall above eg 100mm thick blocks to be bedded on mortar. Never build on top of the lintel's central 'pokey hat'!

standard masonry wall construction in lengths from 750mm to 3,900mm, with a range of sizes in between in jumps of 150mm. It's essential that each end of a lintel extends sufficiently (normally 150mm bedded on mortar) onto the supporting walls either side (known as the 'end bearing'). Where the realities of working on site mean that a lintel is not perfectly level, a small amount of packing, such as with metal plates, may be permissible.

Things get trickier where your design dictates that the end of a large beam needs to rest on top of a lintel at a T-junction, for example where the end of a ceiling beam is supported on a main wall just where there happens to be a window below. Such 'point loads'

Thick oak beam rests on dense concrete block padstones specified by engineer to help support load.

Above and right: Padstones are essential at beam end bearings.

Above and right: Steels often need to be pre-drilled so they can be bolted together or for fixing timber plates.

must obviously be checked early in the design stage by a structural engineer. In addition, Building Control will need to be satisfied that the type of lintel used matches those shown in the approved plans.

Many metal lintels for use in cavity walls not only come ready-insulated, but are also designed with a slight slope down to the front and their ends raised with special 'stop ends'. This helps direct any water in the cavity away and out through weep holes in the outer walls that the brickie will hopefully have remembered to incorporate (see 'Cavity trays' below).

Steels

Steel beams are specified where you've got extra large openings in walls, super-heavy loads to support, complex roof structures or you need to bridge across wide open-plan spaces internally. Referred to on site simply as 'steels', or by designers as 'UBs' (Universal Beams) or 'UCs' (Universal Columns) they are similar to traditional RSJs (Rolled Steel Joists) which have now been phased out. Steels are manufactured in a wide range of lengths and cross-sections

Up she rises! Twin chain-driven hand winches used to left monster steels into place.

but most have an 'I' profile, hence the term 'I- beams'.

When ordering steels, to save drilling on site it's a good idea to specify where you want holes pre-drilled to accommodate timber plates which will later need to be fitted on top or alongside. Ditto for any welding of projecting lips etc, a job best avoided on site as the quality can be a bit iffy as well as posing a potential fire risk.

The Building Control Officer will refer to the drawings you submitted for your Building Regs application and will want to know what section size of beam is being proposed together with the grade and weight of steel, along with structural engineer's calculations to demonstrate that it's capable of supporting the imposed load. With very wide openings, the weight transferred at each end of a beam can be so great that it can crush ordinary bricks or blocks, so the ends of the steels need to sit on 'padstones'. These 'end bearings' will also have been designed by the structural engineer usually comprising dense concrete blocks or Class 'A' engineering bricks, sometimes with steel plates inserted to help spread the load.

Another way to help spread the load is by increasing the amount of the beam that projects onto the walls at each end beyond the minimum shown in your approval drawings. The need for padstones will, of course, depend on the precise load that's being carried, unlike relatively small openings for standard doors or windows where a masonry wall can normally support the weight of lintels unassisted. Where site access is restricted it may be possible to specify 2 or 3 shorter beam lengths which can be bolted together on site (known as 'splicing') before placing the complete beam into position. The end bearings on which the beams rest should be built several days prior to placement to allow the cement time to harden.

The required length of any heavy duty beam is always going to be at least 300mm longer than the opening, needing a minimum 150mm bearing either end.

Where a beam is installed at 90 degrees to a 100mm thick wall, rather than having to increase the wall thickness to accommodate the required 150mm end bearing, the load factor can instead be reduced by fitting a suitably sized padstone. In some cases engineers may accept a shorter 100mm bearing for smaller lintels with lighter loadings.

Despite their tough image, steels are not indestructible, reacting to fire by buckling, warping and bowing with potentially lethal consequences. Without some serious fire-protection measures you might not get a chance to escape before the walls start collapsing on top of you. So standard procedure requires them to be encased in special pink-coloured fire-resistant plasterboard (12.5mm or 15mm thick). Alternatively, special intumescent paint can be applied which expands to many times its normal volume when exposed to fire, protecting the surface of the steel.

If your extension design is fairly complex or has an exotic flavour, perhaps boasting galleried landings and mezzanine floors, there may be a need for a steel beam to be supported where there's no suitable wall to do the job. In such cases one solution is to construct new supporting columns, such as brick piers or steel columns, but these will need their own special concrete pad foundations, also designed by the engineer. This is a fairly common solution when extending at first floor level over old garages with weak existing walls and inadequate foundations.

When it comes to the back-breaking job of getting steels physically raised and placed, it's fair to say that it's an inexact science (putting it mildly). The process usually commences with sporadic bursts of morbid cursing from those tasked with doing all the heavy lifting (engineers are routinely accused on site of 'over-engineering' and specifying unnecessarily huge steels). Where beams can't be comfortably lifted then they can be shoved along the ground using a primitive system of rollers and levers. To get them airborne, one tried and tested method involves raising one end of the beam at a time onto substantial steel tressles until it's at a height where it can be lifted into position by a few strong blokes and a lot of 'grunt power'. But to comply with CDM safety requirements rather than struggling to manually lift beams into position it's a lot easier and quicker to hire a small crane. A few hundred pounds of additional cost should be more than justified by the time saved and the serious potential safety hazards avoided.

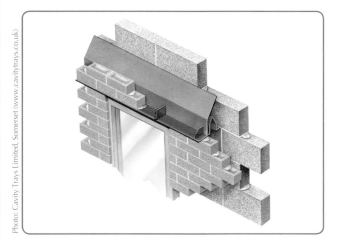

Photo: Cavity Trays Limited, Somerset (www.cavitytrays.co.uk)

Cavity trays and weep holes

We've already established that moisture can, in adverse circumstance, get inside a cavity. It can penetrate from outside if severe rain soaks through small cracks in mortar joints, or from inside in the form of condensation. The problem is, once it finds its way in, how do you get rid of it?

Enter the cavity tray. Modern practice is to fit purpose-made plastic trays over window and door lintels, so any water that runs down inside the cavity will be caught and dispersed out of the wall through 'weep holes'. These are small vertical gaps left between a few bricks (at their vertical 'perpend' joints). They act as tiny drainage outlets, usually with small plastic weep-vents pushed into the holes. Weep holes should be installed no closer together than 900mm intervals, with at least two provided to drain each cavity tray above openings. They should also be placed near ground level so that any moisture that accumulates at the bottom of the cavity (on the concrete infill at the base) can escape.

Basically, trays should be provided over anything that interrupts the cavity – lintels, ducts, even recessed meter boxes – since these can all potentially direct rainwater onto the inside wall. Cavity trays are normally stepped at least 140mm from the outer leaf up into the inner leaf, and may have their 'tails' left projecting out slightly through the outer brickwork. Where the side of a roof slope joins a wall, a series of small stepped trays are usually provided.

To save time, some 'intelligent lintels' are now designed with built-in DPCs that function as their own cavity trays (but in walls exposed to extreme weather you still need to fit a 'proper' tray). Alternatively, thick plastic sheets (damp-proof membranes) laid over the lintel and turned up at the sides should, in effect, act as trays, collecting any moisture and directing it to the outside.

Remedial cavity trays

Building a single-storey extension against a cavity wall of the existing house can pose an interesting potential problem for the occupants. The original outside wall of the main house will now be enclosed downstairs by the new extension, in effect becoming an internal wall. But at first floor level it's still an external wall, exposed to all manner of foul weather and driving rain. The worry is that any rain that penetrates through the old brickwork upstairs could now seep down the cavity and cause nasty damp patches downstairs.

Thankfully there's a solution to prevent such a dispiriting and unwelcome intrusion. The builders will need to insert a new plastic cavity tray into the cavity of the old main wall, just above the point where the new roof joins it. This 'remedial tray' sits across the cavity and catches any water that penetrates, neatly diverting it out and away through new weep holes in the outer wall.

The insertion work is done from outside. First a single course of brickwork needs to be temporarily removed in the old wall using an angle grinder (in some cases a second course may also need to be removed). About four to six bricks are removed at a time, enough to allow the tray to be fed through, piece by piece. Obviously, the tray needs to be at least as wide as the new extension roof below it. The bricks are then replaced, leaving a few small weep holes. Ideally this job should be done before breaking through internally from the main house into the new extension.

Joining to the existing house

When it comes to joining your new extension walls onto those of the existing house it's important to get the detailing right to avoid worrying future problems developing in the form of cracking and movement. Traditionally the two structures were married together by neatly 'toothing in' the new extension brickwork to the old, continuing an existing wall surface as seamlessly

Skilled 'toothing-in' new brickwork to old looks neat but the joint is relatively weak and can risk 'differential movement' cracking (top right).

as possible. To make an invisible joint, a brick would be cut out and removed from every other course in the old wall, and the new ones stitched in. To look right your new bricks would need to perfectly match the originals and be laid with the utmost care. But even if the finished job looked wonderfully neat, there could still be trouble in store.

Although extensions are built to be structurally independent, there is a potential risk of cracking occurring between the main house, resting on its old, shallower foundations, and the new extension with its deep bomb-proof boots. These two structures, although now joined together, are likely to be affected differently by seasonal ground movement. This typically results in a phenomenon known as 'differential settlement', where the old part of the house settles in response to the ground beneath at a different rate to the extension. This in turn puts intense pressure on the junction between the new and the old. Result – vertical cracking. A similar problem can be caused where the materials used to construct the extension are radically different from the main house. For example a new timber frame extension will move differently to an existing masonry building. Fortunately any movement is likely to be cosmetic and limited, as the new structure has its own foundations. But no one wants the enjoyment of their gleaming new extended home to be ruined by the appearance of cavernous cracks. So what to do?

To help accommodate these forces, flexible wall-tie methods were developed. Thin vertical strips of steel known as profile plates (or 'crocodiles') are fixed to the existing wall with expansion bolts, one for each leaf of the new cavity wall. The brick or block courses of the new walls are then built up against the profiles with a metal clip attachment bedded into each course and slotted onto the next 'rung' of the profile. This method can accommodate approximately 10mm of movement. When done, the visible vertical joint to the outer brickwork will need to be filled with a suitable compressible material (capable of being squashed down to half its original thickness) such as flexible cellular polyurethane or foam rubber. To resist water penetration joints also need to be sealed with a suitable silicon mastic sealant, such as polysulphide or low modulus silicon (brown is a popular colour). Visually the appearance of such a joint may be further improved by camouflaging it with a strategically placed downpipe, or by cladding the outer walls. A handy back door opening can sometimes be designed at this point so that the door frame disguises much of the joint.

Stainless steel 'crocodile' wall starters for tying-in new walls to existing masonry. Can accommodate slight movement with vertical expansion joints (right).

Another potential design issue with timber frame extension walls is they're likely to be 50mm or so thinner than the modern cavity brick or blockwork equivalent. This can sometimes create a practical problem ensuring a consistent extended wall line (except where it abuts the old wall at 90 degrees). One solution is to thicken the extension walls with extra insulation or external cladding. Or where the planners want extensions designed so they're set back a bit, that can be a handy way of disguising the difference in wall widths.

From a practical point of view, if your new wall joins the old one at a 90 degree right angle (ie a 'T' junction rather than continuing an existing straight run) the old wall will now effectively form a bridge across the new cavity. Consequently there's a risk that rain could also bridge from outside across the cavity, so a vertical DPC must be installed where any part of an existing outside wall becomes a new internal wall. This is done by cutting a vertical line in the outer face of the old wall with an angle grinder, roughly centrally between the two new profiles, and feeding a new plastic strip (vertical DPC) into the slot. It is then lapped behind the new outer leaf in order to bar the path of any rain trying to bridge across at this point. Ideally the old cavity should be cut open a bit wider so it joins the new cavity, but this could have structural implications and weaken the bolt fixings to the profiles. Ask Building Control for their opinion.

Thermal movement

All building materials are subject to movement. But this isn't necessarily a result of heavy structural loadings. Another common cause of movement is expansion and contraction due to heat and moisture. So it's rather surprising that the two most common materials used in wall construction, bricks and blocks, have violently different reactions when exposed to heat and moisture. Bricks made of clay are subject to long term expansion.

Concrete blocks, on the other hand, are very prone to shrinkage, especially the lightweight aerated type. These conflicting forces of expansion and contraction within masonry walls need to be accommodated by building in movement joints, otherwise the build up of stresses can cause cracking. South-facing walls are more susceptible to thermal movement because of their greater exposure to the sun. The general rule is you need a vertical movement joint every 12 metres in a straight run of clay brickwork containing window or door openings. Happily, for all but the largest extensions this is unlikely to apply. But your architect or engineer should take this into account in their design and manufacturers of blocks and bricks can advise on recommended distances and joint widths. Expansion joints need to be filled with purpose-made compressible materials and sealed with mastic, as described above.

Templates for windows and doors

Fitting expensive new windows and doors into the walls as construction progresses can all too easily result in them becoming damaged. So it's normally better to make up simple 'dummy window' templates from timber which can be temporarily built into the walls. Later, when the walls are complete, the templates can be removed and the new frames fitted. In the meantime the templates can be boarded over for security. Even tough UPVC frames are now generally installed at a later date, with special 'cavity formers' being built in as work on the walls progresses.

Great care must be taken to ensure the template sizes are accurate to avoid the anguish and frustration of trying to later squeeze frames into openings that are too small. An alternative is to install the frames without the glazing as the wall progresses, ensuring of course that they're temporarily protected from staining and disfigurement.

There are, of course, other openings that will be required in the walls, such as for pipes, flues, and various vents, but with the exception of those for meter boxes, they tend to be cut through the wall at a later date, rather than trying to build in fiddly small holes as you go. Pipes run through walls will require compressible packing around them to protect them from bending and cracking.

Above and below: Window frames can be fitted as walls are built, or templates used instead.

Lateral restraint straps

To be structurally strong, walls need a little extra support. This is provided by tying the new walls in to other parts of the structure. So, at each floor level horizontal L-shaped steel restraint straps are built in to the inner leaf blockwork. These are later fixed across floor and ceiling joists as well as roof rafters from any gable end walls. Now, you may wonder how a few thin-looking steel straps, only 30mm wide and 5mm thick, could possibly make much difference, but they do. The Building Research Establishment (whose job it is to test houses to destruction in a massive airship hangar somewhere in Bedfordshire) have simulated extreme hurricane-force wind-load conditions, conclusively proving their importance. At particular risk in high winds are gable end walls, which particularly benefit from being tied to the roof structure.

Scaffolding

When construction of the walls has progressed to a height beyond the reach of human hands, scaffolding will be required. It's important this is ordered well in advance so it can be erected in good time for the bricklayers setting-out the first-floor walls. Scaffolding must be supplied, erected and maintained by specialist companies who hold their own insurance, and is usually arranged by the main contractor. But for small single-storey extensions a less expensive alternative can be to hire scaffold towers, with decks made from planks. This is a much cheaper solution for short-term tasks where the required height is less than 2.5m. Your bricklayer may be willing to supply and erect a suitable access tower himself (for a small fee).

The world of scaffolding has a terminology all its own. Ask what stage of construction a building has reached, and you may get a response like 'second lift'. This might seem a trifle odd given that stairs are normally the preferred method of ascending, but here the term 'lift' refers to the height that the build has reached. 'First lift' is the lowest scaffolding platform, where the walls are built up to about 8 block courses high, or just over half way up the ground floor windows. If you happen to be walking underneath this is perfectly positioned at forehead height for denting your cranium on sharp bolts, so be sure to wear a hard hat. The scaffolders will later return to raise it up to 'second lift' , which is about half way up the first floor windows, so the brickies can continue. This will also provide a platform for roof work, fixing guttering and painting fascias, although scaffolding isn't always required for fitting windows which are often installed at a later date. 'Third lift' is only needed for gable ends, chimneys or buildings more than two storeys high.

During the course of the works, check from time to time that it hasn't sunk into soft ground, and that ladders are securely tied and set at an angle of about 75°. The vertical tubular poles ('standards') must rest on substantial base plates. With masonry outer walls it's standard practice for shorter horizontal poles with flattened ends

Left and opposite: Wall plates must be bedded in mortar and clamped with restraint straps no more than 2m apart.

('putlogs') to be temporarily embedded in open joints in the brickwork as it progresses (but are not supposed to rest on the DPC). These cross-members sit at right angles to the main scaffolding and support the boards.

There are obvious health and safety dangers with erecting and dismantling temporary working platforms at height, and spectacular collapses have occurred from time to time. Scaffolding has to support a considerable weight, not just loads of burly builders but also lots of heavy bricks and roof tiles stacked up, making the possibility of overloading a real danger. So all lifts must be fully boarded out and have hand rails and ladders firmly fixed. There must also be edge-guarding with an upstand board fixed along the side of the walkway to stop material falling off. Where people are likely to be passing underneath, such as a pavement, there should be protective netting to catch falling debris.

If you need to build close to the boundary with next door and can't come to an amicable arrangement with the neighbours about entering their garden to help build your house, some of the scaffolding may have to be erected internally. This is because there is no automatic right of access to next door's land for the purpose of building (although there is for carrying out maintenance – the Access to Neighbouring Land Act 1992).

Wall plates

When wall construction finally reaches roof level, a strip of 100 x 50mm softwood is normally bedded in mortar along the top of the walls. This is the wall plate, and its job is to provide a secure base for the roof timbers to rest on. In order to hold the wall plates in place, they're clamped vertically to the walls below using 30 x 5mm L-shaped galvanised steel restraint straps. The straps should be placed no more than 2m apart, and no further than 450mm in from the ends of the walls, extending at least 300mm down the wall. It's normally

the brickie's job to fit wall plates and strap them in place, the carpenter having cut them to the correct size.

However, there's one part of the job that, with the best will in the world, the bricklayer cannot always finish until later. This will only apply if your pitched roof has been designed with a triangular gable end, rather than a sloping hip (see Chapter 12). Here, the gable brickwork may need to be completed only once the end roof rafters are in place. This is because the brickwork needs to be accurately cut to fit the profile of the roof (if it's to be left naked without bargeboards to disguise the joints under the verges). You may therefore need to programme an agreed date for the brickie's return visit to finish the job.

Internal walls

If your extension is going to have more than one room, you'll obviously need to build internal partition walls to divide the space. On the ground floor, blockwork dividing walls are

generally preferred since they're relatively cheap to build and also provide good sound insulation between rooms. These are normally no thicker than 100mm, the width of a single concrete block, and not usually load-bearing. Lintels tend to be of the simple reinforced concrete type.

While you've got your brickies on site, it's a fairly simple job to build the partition walls along with the main walls, or soon after. Where they meet main walls, they should be well bonded in – something Victorian builders often shamelessly botched. Any load-bearing 'structural' internal walls will need their own foundations and DPC, although the width of the trenches can normally be less than for main walls.

If you've opted instead to have your partition walls built of timber studwork, the plasterboarding will obviously need to be done later when the structure is fully dry and watertight (see Chapter 13). Use treated timber if there's any risk of studs being exposed to the weather. Upstairs,

Load-bearing internal blockwork wall.

it's no longer acceptable to build walls of loadbearing blockwork supported on doubled joists or timber beams because of the shrinkage movement when drying out, both in the blocks and the timber. However it's normally possible to build straight up from the wall below or from a steel beam (subject to confirmation by Building Control). Otherwise it's generally considered better to build in timber studwork upstairs, since it is less than half the weight of a solid masonry wall. See page 203.

Party walls and noise pollution

If your neighbour already has an extension that runs along the garden boundary right next to where you're now building, or if they're planning to build one, you might want to share this boundary wall between you. If this is to become your party wall, there are two key technical issues to consider – the risk of fire, and the possibility of noise pollution.

Achieving one-hour fire resistance shouldn't be a problem – a standard masonry wall should easily exceed this, especially if it's dry-lined with plasterboard. Sound insulation is a little more complex. Noise pollution is defined as 'unwanted sound', which comes in two varieties. Airborne sound such as loud music or shouting and screaming is one type. The other is 'impact sound', such as the thud of boots walking, although this tends to be more of a problem when designing floors, such as in flats with noisy neighbours upstairs.

Airborne sound is carried by vibrations in the air, like ripples in water. An effective barrier would be a thick, heavy wall, such as one made of concrete blocks. Stopping impact sound is a little harder, as you need some kind of separation in the form of a physical air-gap. A wall with a cavity can act as a barrier that sound can't track across. Dry-lining such a wall with plasterboard will improve it further, ideally incorporating an extra air void behind the plasterboard, partially filled with a layer of dense mineral wool. The edges will need acoustic sealant to block air paths. If all else fails, special composite acoustic sound-deadening panels can be fixed to floors and walls.

Main trades needed on site

■ **Bricklayers:** Build the walls up to wall plate level.
■ **Carpenters:** Build templates for window and door frames and cut timber wall plates.
■ **Scaffolders:** Erect and later dismantle scaffolding.
■ **Labourers:** Cut indents into existing walls, and fix profiles.

www.home-extension.co.uk

Timber frame construction

We last took a peek at building a modern timber frame extension back at the foundation stage (see also Chapter 4). Now we're going to focus on the overall process from erecting the wall panels right through to completion of the structure. We've chosen to feature it all in one go rather than spreading it out over the coming chapters because the order of construction is quite different from conventional masonry.

Erecting wall panels

The factory-made wall panels arrive on site rather like a giant flat-pack furniture kit. Before they can be erected a treated timber sole plate is fixed to the lower wall substructure over a DPC, as shown in Chapter 8. The wall panels can then be lifted into place and nailed to the sole plate, before being nailed to each other.

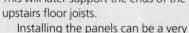

If all goes well the panels should all be in position within a remarkably short time, hopefully plumb and square, with nice tight joints. Before any strong gusts of wind have a chance to rearrange your carefully planned room layouts, a 'head binder' needs to be nailed across the top of the panels to help keep them in line. This will later support the ends of the upstairs floor joists.

Photo: UK Timber Frame Association

Installing the panels can be a very quick operation. It should be a two-person job to fix one storey of panels in a day. This is amazingly quick compared to blockwork construction, which can take a week or so to reach the same stage. Of course, this assumes there have been no errors in the factory with regard to panel sizes. It's worth remembering that when it comes to accommodating any imperfections of 'fit', conventional blockwork is more forgiving than timber frame. So when you get to the upper floors, the rate of progress will depend on whether the walls that you've just built down below are perfectly square.

Erecting large ready-made panels may sound like child's play, but there are some key things you need to get right:

- Always consult your drawings before assembling wall panels – this will be a lot quicker in the long run than steaming ahead and relying on guesswork!
- Don't cut notches or drill the panels, unless shown in the drawings.
- Don't leave holes in the vapour control layer, *eg* when installing services. Similarly, take care not to damage the breather membrane covering to the sheathing.
- Be sure to install all necessary cavity barriers in the correct position for fire-prevention.

Insulation

Where manufactured timber panels are not pre-insulated at the factory, it's a fairly easy job to fit insulation on site once they're assembled and the inner leaf wall structure is in place. Mineral wool (similar to loft insulation) is still the widely used despite being significantly less thermally efficient than thick polyurethane foam boards. Nonetheless, standard 140mm wall panels with mineral wool stuffed between the studs should easily be able to achieve even the U-value target for extension walls of 0.28W/m2K. If you want to go one better, you can reduce U-values further by additionally fitting insulated plasterboard on the walls, although you'd lose an extra 50mm or so from the main walls of each room. It's technically possible to get timber panel walls down to an extremely respectable 0.10W/m2K, which could make all the difference to your extension's 'area weighted' average score if you want to fit large areas of glazing.

Wall cavities in timber frame buildings are typically only 50mm thick and should normally be left uninsulated. In theory you could partially fill the cavity as long as there's a 25mm air space. But unless the quality of workmanship is scrupulous, there's always the risk of hidden defects occurring over future years – for example, if bits of insulation come loose air paths can become blocked, allowing damp to cause timber decay. So cavities are best left empty. Above all, cavity fill should never be squirted in retrospectively as a 'home improvement'.

Vapour control

Modern timber-frame house construction was dealt a massive blow in 1983 when a damning *World In Action* TV programme caused a major scare that set the industry back almost an entire decade. The programme exposed cases where defective workmanship on site had allowed damp to enter the load-bearing timber structure with predictable results – over a number of years, mould and rot had caused serious structural defects. It also claimed that jerry-built timber framing was at the heart of a recent house fire. (See 'Fire precautions' below.)

This is why modern designs go to considerable lengths to prevent airborne moisture within rooms penetrating plasterboard-lined timber panel walls. Once water vapour from steamy kitchens and bathrooms is allowed to seep into the wall structure, it can find its way to the cold outer face of the sheathing and condense back into water. Hidden in the darkest depths of the wall, dampness from condensation can prove very damaging to timber wall panels.

To prevent such nightmare scenarios occurring in the first place, a vapour control layer is sandwiched behind the plasterboard and the insulated inner wall panels to form a

moisture barrier. Polythene sheeting is normally the preferred material, with generous laps at the edges, or you could instead specify foil-backed plasterboard, always ensuring that the joints are properly sealed. Openings for sockets, switches and pipes should have additional sheeting to prevent cuts. Any that do occur should be sealed, and cable/pipe runs are best contained within accessible ducting.

High-performance breather membranes are normally factory-fitted to the cavity side of the sheathing. Similar to the underlay sheeting fitted beneath roof tiles, these protect the timber frame from any incoming damp. Any moisture that does penetrate and condenses into water should be

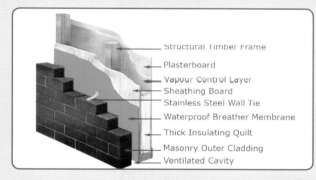

- Structural Timber Frame
- Plasterboard
- Vapour Control Layer
- Sheathing Board
- Stainless Steel Wall Tie
- Waterproof Breather Membrane
- Thick Insulating Quilt
- Masonry Outer Cladding
- Ventilated Cavity

able to escape through the sheathing on the outer face of the wall, evaporating into the ventilated cavity or out through weep holes in the outer wall.

Upper floors

The upper floors of timber frame houses are supported upon the wall panels below (no building loads are carried by the masonry outer leaf). As with standard brick and block extensions, floor joists are now commonly made from composite I-beams or manufactured eco-joists rather than traditional '8 x 2' softwood. The main difference from conventional masonry buildings is that the floor joists are supported on the 'head binders' running across the tops of the wall panels, instead of resting in metal joist hangers hung from blockwork walls. Also, because of the potential fire risk with timber walls, once all the floor joists are in place the voids between them need to be closed off where they meet the wall panels. This is done by fixing a 'header joist' to the outer part of the head binder, running along its full length.

The flooring itself usually comprises nothing more exotic than standard chipboard panels nailed to the tops of the joists, although sometimes OSB or plywood sheets are used, or traditional softwood floorboards. So far so conventional. But one major difference with timber frame is the way the

upstairs flooring is laid – *ie* across the full width of the floor *including* the edges over the main wall panels. This means the next lift of wall panels is built off the chipboard (or OSB etc) floor, which acts as a convenient platform or deck.

Clearly this could make things a bit tricky if one day in the future you need to lift the floor boarding near the edges of a room. So some timber frame systems use a more conventional arrangement where the upstairs wall panels don't sit directly on the floor deck, but are instead fixed to a sole plate nailed along the tops of the joists.

Once all the upper storey wall panels are fully erected, work can commence on building the roof. (Roof construction is the same as for masonry buildings.) Constructing the outer leaf of the walls is normally left until the roof is in place and the structure is weathertight. Leaving the building half-naked in this way while the roof takes shape is one of the biggest differences with traditional construction, where both the leaves of the walls are slowly built up together before starting roof work – taking considerably longer to get the shell weathertight.

Internal partition walls

Internal stud walls do more than just separate rooms – they also help stiffen the building. Where stud walls are load-bearing they need strengthening to provide 'racking resistance' (to prevent them twisting) by applying diagonal bracing and cladding one of the faces with a layer of ply or OSB sheathing.

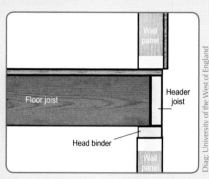

The Building Regs also require that any room next to a bedroom or WC must provide adequate sound insulation against airborne noise, which can normally be achieved by stuffing the frame with mineral wool or glass fibre quilt, which is very effective at deadening sound waves. Partition walls are usually finished with 12.5mm plasterboard both sides with a skim plaster finish.

Fire precautions

It doesn't take a genius to work out the combustible connection between fire and wood. So timber frame buildings need to be designed from the outset to cope with such potential risks. For a start, all internal surfaces are clad with (naturally inert) plasterboard with a skim plaster finish that should provide a minimum of 30 minutes' fire resistance before flames could reach the wall panels.

To slow down the passage of fire and smoke should it reach the cavity, special 'cavity barriers' are required vertically at regular intervals around all openings such as doors and windows, as well as to eaves and verges and at roof level. Cavity barriers around windows are usually

Diag: University of the West of England

formed in timber; elsewhere they're generally made from inert fire-resistant mineral wool. These should also provide a minimum of 30 minutes' fire resistance.

Openings

Window and door openings in the timber panels are normally pre-cut in the factory according to your drawings. However, if you later decide that an extra window would be nice, before cutting an opening it's essential to check with the timber frame supplier (as well as with Building Control). Openings must be strengthened by being 'trimmed', ie framed with timber studs. Where the greatest loads have to be supported – ie at the top (lintels) and the bottom (at sill level) – the studs are usually doubled up or even tripled. Lintels are relatively lightweight and can be fixed with restraint clips, or screwed or nailed to the timber frame.

As we saw earlier, to provide fire protection within the cavity it's standard practice to fit timber battens around openings to act as cavity barriers. But because they touch the outer leaf, these battens need to be protected from damp with a DPC, which should also prevent any risk of moisture crossing to the inner leaf.

Windows are fixed into the opening using metal straps or cramps made from galvanised or stainless steel. A small window might only have two fixings either side, while wider windows could have three cramps either side plus four at the top. To allow for a small degree of movement between the window and the wall panel, the bottom of the window is not usually fixed. A small gap filled with flexible sealant should be left below the window to the outer masonry wall, to allow for slight timber frame shrinkage.

Frame around window

Lintel

Extra studs support lintel & sill

Timber battens (50 x 50mm) around window opening form cavity barriers. Batten size depends on cavity width. DPC protects inner leaf from damp

Diag: uwe.ac.uk

Wall ties and weep holes

Wall ties on modern timber frame buildings are different from those used in brick and block construction. For a start they need to be suitable for relatively narrow cavities – at around 50mm these are typically half the width of those in ordinary masonry walls. Wall ties should be made from flexible stainless steel and fixed to the panel studs, not just the sheathing. The ties are laid sloping outwards at a slight gradient so that any subsequent shrinkage in the frame doesn't cause them to settle and slope back towards the rooms, attracting damp.

Ties are normally required at the rate of 4.4 per square metre. In practice this means that horizontally they're placed at stud centres. Vertical spacing should be at five or seven brick courses, depending on whether the studs are at 600 or 400mm centres. At window and door openings, wall ties are required every third course either side of the jambs.

Photo: uwe.ac.uk

Weep holes should be provided at 1,500mm centres. They're required below the DPC and above horizontal cavity barriers.

The shrinkage factor

As everyone knows, timber used for construction can be prone to shrinkage as it dries out once the building is occupied (and especially once the central heating is turned up full whack). In most cases this simply results in the odd minor inconvenience, such as a wobbly floorboard. But what if the entire load-bearing structure of the building is made from timber?

The fact is, modern timber structures do tend to suffer slight shrinkage during their early life. The marriage of a brittle outer wall to a relatively flexible inner frame means you need to take special precautions so that the structure can manage these initial growing pains. For a start the moisture content of the timber panels as they leave the factory should be no more than 20%. It also helps if they're kept as dry as possible during construction. Obviously the larger the building, the more important it is that all interfaces between the timber frame and other rigid materials can accommodate movement.

When it comes to physically constructing the outer walls, there are some subtle but crucial differences compared with conventional brick and block. First, the wall ties spanning the cavity between the outer brickwork and the inner timber panels must be able to accommodate movement. Second, when constructing the outer leaf of the main walls your brickies will need to incorporate suitable movement joints.

Most shrinkage occurs across the grain of the wood. Vertical shrinkage will therefore occur in the horizontal timbers, ie the joists, plates and rails. Shrinkage tends to be most evident at the top of the building and could be as much as 20mm in a two-storey house. To allow for the load-bearing timber frame 'dropping' slightly, the outer brickwork should be kept clear of the roof structure sitting above it by at least this amount. You also need to include horizontal movement joints at verges to gable walls and around internal soil stacks projecting from roof slopes.

Most important of all, you need to allow for future movement at windows. So when the outer leaf is built, a small gap should be left below each window opening to act as a movement joint to accommodate timber frame shrinkage (about 3–5mm for ground floor windows and 10–12mm for the first floor). This gap should be filled with compressible sealant.

For example, where you've got a large 'Victorian-style' projecting concrete outer sill, and a UPVC or timber window with its own small integral sub-sill set within the opening, a movement joint should be left between the integral sill and the larger concrete sill below.

Gap for shrinkage
Diag: uwe.ac.uk

Wall cladding

Constructing a brick outer leaf isn't the only option when it comes to cladding your freshly assembled timber-framed shell. After all, why disguise your high-performance walls so that they look like every other bog-standard home extension? Weather protection can equally be provided by tile hanging, weatherboarding or rendering. This can be added to an outer leaf of blockwork, or directly applied to the timber panel inner leaf, dispensing with the need for a conventional cavity, subject to achieving wall insulation U-value targets.

Tile hanging and weatherboarding

Both tile and timber cladding can be applied to a framework of battens nailed to the newly installed timber panel inner leaf. For reasons of appearance, traditional small plain tiles are generally preferred to larger, bulky-looking interlocking ones. Alternatively, you could pick from various styles of 'barn conversion' timber cladding – see Chapter 17. In both cases vertical battens are first nailed through the outer layer of sheathing to the main vertical panel studs. An additional layer of insulation can be incorporated over the sheathing to boost thermal performance. Then rows of horizontal battens are laid across them, forming a cavity. Tiles or timber weatherboarding can then be nailed to battens. Any water that penetrates the tiles or cladding should be able to harmlessly drain down the face of the breather membrane in the cavity and out a strategically placed weep hole.

Render

It isn't possible to render directly on top of the breather membrane, so some form of galvanised or stainless steel

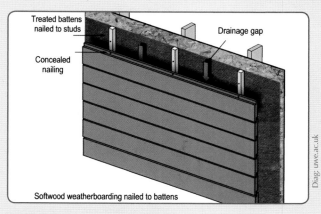
Treated battens nailed to studs
Drainage gap
Concealed nailing
Softwood weatherboarding nailed to battens
Diag: uwe.ac.uk

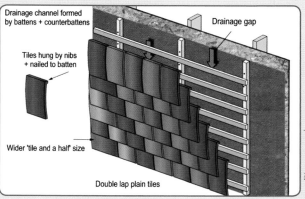
Drainage channel formed by battens + counterbattens
Drainage gap
Tiles hung by nibs + nailed to batten
Wider 'tile and a half' size
Double lap plain tiles
Diag: uwe.ac.uk

mesh is required. This mesh is usually fixed to vertical battens nailed to the studs (extra studs may be required in the panels to carry the load). It's normal practice to protect the battens with a vertical DPC in case the render becomes saturated. Render thickness depends on the nature of the render, the type of mesh and the building exposure, and can vary between 6mm and 20mm. A horizontal movement joint is usually required at each floor level to accommodate frame shrinkage.

Alternatively, you might want to consider modern insulated render systems, which are cheaper than brick and provide excellent thermal insulation. These comprise thick insulation boards (typically polyurethane) fixed to a framed background with a drained cavity at least 15mm wide. A synthetic render is then applied directly to the boards.

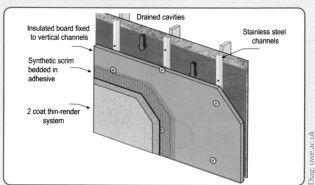
Drained cavities
Insulated board fixed to vertical channels
Stainless steel channels
Synthetic scrim bedded in adhesive
2 coat thin-render system
Diag: uwe.ac.uk

11 UPPER FLOORS, WINDOWS AND DOORS

As the main walls take shape, the upstairs floor joists can be fixed in place. With a little help from some temporary boarding, these can provide a useful work-platform as your new extension grows ever taller.

One key decision that needs to be made by this stage is whether to go ahead and install your expensive new windows and doors as the walls are built. The problem with this, of course, is the potential risk of damage as the build progresses on site. All it takes is a falling roof tile or a wayward scaffold pole and you could find yourself having to reluctantly fork out for replacements. So for many home extenders, only once the roof is on, and breaking-through to the main house successfully completed, will the time be right for the eyes and soul of the new building to put in an appearance. Until that day, you may wish to keep them safely stored away, or simply delay their delivery.

Above left and above: Windows are not normally fitted until the shell is complete.
Below: Metal web floor joists designed to accommodate pipework.

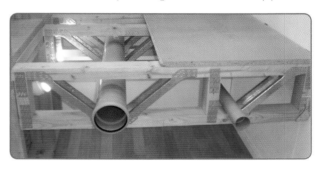

Upper floors

The upper 'intermediate' floors are traditionally constructed from timber floor joists spanning between the structural walls of the building, though the floorboards themselves will only be fixed at a later stage, once the building is dry and completely weathertight.

Treated timber should be used because the building is still exposed to the elements. In the meantime, a few sheets of thick 18mm plywood or OSB are sometimes flung over the joists to provide a temporary deck. This can pose a danger for unwary homeowners taking a leisurely after-hours stroll around the works, so take care not to come a cropper by stepping on overhanging edges.

The floor joists are one part of the structure where times are changing. Although many home extension builders stick doggedly to using traditional 195 x 45mm 'eight by two' softwood joists, others are following in the footsteps of the mainstream housing developers and using factory-made

timber 'I-joists' that look rather like steel beams made of wood. Despite their thin appearance they're actually incredibly strong and light and are able to span larger distances without support (over 6 metres using 300mm or deeper joists at 400mm centres or closer - see website tables). One of main problems with ordinary joists is that they tend to shrink, causing creaks and squeaks in floors. I-joists have greater rigidity and don't shrink. Although more expensive, these 'thin webbed' joists manufactured from engineered timber are quicker to install, some even having preformed 'knock-outs' for pipes and cables. Another option is metal web floor joists (aka 'Eco' / 'Easi' / or 'Posi'-joists' etc). These are recognisable by their distinctive curly metal webbing connecting the top and bottom softwood flanges with spaces large enough to accommodate waste pipes, so they also don't require notching or drilling for pipes and cables. Apart from their expense, the main drawback of manufactured joists is that the top and bottom flanges shouldn't be cut as this can critically

Far left and left: Traditional '8 x 2' softwood joists can be cut to fit on site and fixed with nail guns.

Right: Manufactured I-joists prevent shrinkage problems and squeaking but must be accurately specified.

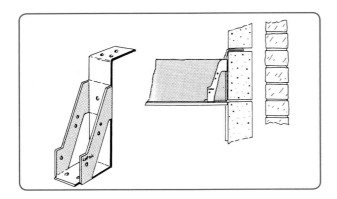

Timber-to-timber hangers

diminish their strength (although holes can be drilled centrally in the webbing of most I-beams). Also, they may need to be ordered a few weeks in advance. Manufactured joists of the right size aren't likely to be available 'off the shelf' because home extensions aren't all built in standard dimensions like much new-estate housing. And it's essential to specify precise dimensions when ordering because unlike traditional softwood joists they can't be cut to size on site.

Spans and joist hangers

Joists are normally laid across the narrower span of the room. In most home extensions, the main walls will carry the floor load at either end. But once a room becomes wider than the maximum span for a conventional floor joist (about 4.5m – see span tables on website) or for longer-spanning manufactured joists, extra support will be required, either from a structural beam (typically a steel) or a load bearing internal wall, which will add to the cost. Steel beams are not in themselves that expensive. They can either be hidden within the floor void, so the timber joists are hung off the steel, or placed below the ceiling, in which case they need boxing in with plasterboard.

On external walls, the floor joists ends should be slotted into galvanised steel joist hangers (small purpose-made cradles) fixed to the walls. This overcomes the problem in many older houses where joists bedded directly into solid outer walls could become damp and at risk from rot.

Joist hangers are usually an inverted 'L' shape with protruding upper 'tongues' at the back for slotting into mortar joints (they also need bolting/screwed to the wall). They're normally built into the blockwork inner leaf as the walls are constructed, in a similar way to the restraint straps.

Left: Hangers built into new blockwork.

Right: Joist ends cut into web of steel – solution if old walls too weak to support new loads

This is preferable to using angle grinders to retrospectively cut slots for the hanger tongues to be wedged into. Other types of hangers are designed to be nailed or screwed directly to lengths of timber, such as wall plates, or 'timber-to-timber' connections to other joists. There are also double width hangers to support pairs of joists.

In new house construction it's no longer acceptable for joists to just be slotted into the walls because it poses problems with air tightness and sound transmission. Although this restriction doesn't apply to extensions, it's still advisable to use joist hangers. If there's no other option and Building Control approve, the embedded joist ends must be protected from the risk of damp by strips of plastic DPC. They must also be pre-treated with preservative, and cut so as not to project into the cavity.

Joists not only have to provide a perfectly horizontal floor surface but are also responsible for creating a nice level ceiling in the rooms below. So it is essential that the hangers are carefully fixed in place to get them perfectly level, although some joist ends may still need packing underneath with slim wedges of slate or plywood etc.

Where joist hangers have to be fixed to an existing wall, a horizontal timber wall plate can first be bolted in place using expansion bolts (e.g. M10 size). Steel hangers can then be fixed to this. Alternatively, special 'face fix' hangers with wide ears can be used which are designed to be expansion-bolted direct to the wall surface. Another option with floor joists is to cut slots in the existing wall which are pointed up with mortar once the joist end has been inserted.

Of course, the floor structure does more than support your feet. As we saw in the last chapter, it also plays

Left: Joists supported in openings cut into old main wall, which will now be internal

Right: Double joist hanger – all holes must be nailed!

a crucial role in holding the main walls of the building together (called 'lateral restraint') with the help of horizontal steel straps, thereby preventing structural movement.

Fitting floor joists

Timber is rarely perfectly straight, and whereas a slight bow over the length of a joist isn't necessarily a problem, any badly twisted material should automatically be rejected upon delivery, since it will only tend to get worse over time. Prior to fitting, all the joists should be compared and the straightest ones located near the edges of the room. Any that 'hump up' slightly should be positioned near the middle of the room (avoid placing them the other way so they sag over the ceiling). This is because any slight rise should gradually be compressed by the weight of furnishings in the room, and revert to a reasonably flat surface.

Floor joists traditionally comprise 195 x 45mm treated timbers set apart at either 400, 450 or 600mm centres. 'Centre' measurements are taken from the centre of one joist to the centre of the next. The precise dimensions will vary depending on spans, so check on your plans (and see website). Structural timber like softwood for floor joists is supplied 'dry-graded'. Under the Building Regulations, the permitted moisture content is restricted to a maximum of 24 per cent (much higher than this and timber can become attractive to wood-boring beetle and fungus). Low moisture content timber is defined as 'below 20 per cent', but the final moisture level in modern houses is only about 10–12 per cent, so shrinkage problems are still a real possibility. To help prevent this, new joists and floorboards are normally supplied 'kiln dried'. However twisting and warping is still the curse of much cheaper timber (See 'Grading timber' on the next page).

Although NHBC no longer require interior joinery to be treated, when it comes to building floor structures they should be factory vacuum-impregnation with preservative to protect them against rot and beetle attack. This is especially important where you have suspended timber ground floors since they are likely to be more at risk from

damp. The timber undergoes 'vacuum impregnation' treatment by being immersed in a pressure tank and is either 'tanalised' - a water based treatment that lends the wood a faint green or brown shade, or 'protimised' - a spirit based process that leaves the wood uncoloured (or sometimes dyed red).

Strutting and trimming

No matter how carefully the timber floor joists are installed, it's likely that some slight twisting will take place as shrinkage occurs. This can lead to distortion of the floorboards and may even damage ceilings below. To minimise this, some form of additional bracing is needed between the joists. The traditional solution is to fit small timber struts between the joists in an 'X' pattern known as herringbone strutting. For spans between 2.5m and 4.5m, one line of strutting is adequate, but for every additional 1.5m further struts are needed. Modern construction makes use of purpose-made steel 'herringbone struts'. An alternative solution involves wedging a series of small timber off-cuts called 'noggins' between the joists which also helps prevent 'rotation'. In some cases both strutting and noggins are applied.

But where you need to make space in the floor structure for a staircase or a chimney breast to come through it, you'll need to construct a special framework of joists around the new opening. This is known as 'trimming'. Here, the joists that would otherwise be in the way of the stairs need to be cut short and 'teed off' (trimmed) with trimmer joists.

Below left: Ready made herringbone struts.
Below rRight: Floor structures must be strapped to main walls.

Above: 'I-joists' trimmed at stair opening.

Left: Steel to support wall above.

These are special joists that are butted at right angles across all the ends of the shortened main joists usually doubled up and bolted together. The main joists either side of the opening are also doubled up for strength. Special steel joist hangers can be used to join the trimmer timbers together. For floorboards, see Chapter 12.

Grading timber

Timber is an indispensable natural building material, but treat it badly and it will exact slow revenge, finding ingenious ways to retaliate by splitting, twisting, buckling and warping over the years. So ideally timber should be dry and well-seasoned before coming anywhere near a house. Victorian buildings and inter-war properties with their naturally slow-grown air-dried timber are often in better shape today than many 1970s houses, where wet rot has long ago devastated the windows and eaves.

Internally, some modern houses have suffered from extreme shrinkage cracking, due to the speed of their construction. Timber that's still green and fresh from the tree may continue to season after the house is occupied, especially with the central heating on full blast, causing it to shrink and bow. Soon after occupation floor joists may shrink back from walls, and large gaps appear at staircase walls and at the edges of ceilings. So to minimise the risk of shrivelling and buckling, timber used for structural purposes such as floor joists and roof rafters is kiln-dried to reduce the moisture content. Even hardwood beams should be specified as 'well-seasoned'. Nonetheless it's advisable to allow new timber to adapt to the relatively dry atmosphere of the room before cutting and fixing it, by opening up packs and letting

them become conditioned so that any severe shrinkage will hopefully occur before it can do any harm.

Hardwood is the timber that comes from broadleaf trees such as oak, birch and beech. Softwood comes from conifers like spruce, Scots pine, firs and yew. As you might expect, most hardwoods (mahogany, oak, teak etc) are inherently more durable (as well as more expensive). However Douglas fir is a widely available resinous softwood that can perform as well as many hardwoods.

Most construction grade 'carcassing' timber is spruce, (known as whitewood). Joinery grade wood is usually pine (known as redwood) and is used for windows, skirtings, floorboards etc, often sold with a planed finish.

As you pore through the left-over lengths of timber at your local DIY store, bear in mind that the pieces you select should ideally have straight grain with no knots or drying splits ('shakes') – which is precisely why all the old knotty and warped bits are left on the shelf. To save builders having to waste time judging every single piece of wood they use, timber comes ready strength-graded, the supplier having already assessed these features. For structural purposes new timber is supplied in strength classes that determine the allowable working stresses:

Photo: UK Timber Frame Association

Timber strength class

C14	C16	C18	C22	C24	C27
weaker	--------	--------	--------	--------	stronger

The best known and most widely available grades are C16 and C24. Engineers tend to specify stronger C24 which can be used over larger spans and doesn't costs much more than C16. The strength class depends on both the species and the grade of the actual piece of wood. In all there are 16 strength classes ranging from C14, the lowest softwood strength, through to D70, the strongest hardwood strength class. Softwoods are more difficult to assess than hardwoods, and there are two overall visual strength grades used as guidance for structural use: GS (general structural use) and the stronger SS (special structural use).

Timber joists – points to check
- Stress grade as specified.
- Free from bow, twist, rot and woodworm.
- Depth and width as specified.
- Tops of joists level.
- Joists correctly spaced apart.
- Joists doubled up where supporting upstairs walls or trimmed around stair openings.
- Joist ends built tightly into brick/blockwork with no gaps (on inner walls).
- Joist ends securely fixed to joist hangers (outer walls) fixed tight to wall.

Basically all you've got to do is check that the material is stamped with its grading, and make sure you purchase the type that's specified in your approved plans. But be aware that unless you or your builder personally select prime cuts from the supplier's yard some of the lengths loaded onto the truck for delivery may be badly warped and need to be returned.

Nails
The best types of nails to use in timber are 'twist nails'. True to their name these have a twisted shank which give them a better grip. They bite hard into wood and are more difficult to pull out than conventional 'wire' nails or 'cut' nails. These are recommended for fixing structural items such as joist hangers. One thing that Building Control sometimes check on site visits at this stage is that all the fixing holes in steel joist hangers and metal plates have been nailed, with none left empty!

Similarly, for a 'permanent grip' when fastening plywood, or MDF etc 'annular ring shank' nails are widely used - they look a bit like screws with jagged rings on their shanks.

Carpenters and joiners
The difference between a carpenter and a joiner is that traditionally carpenters do all the big structural timberwork (often called 'first fix'), mainly working outdoors, whereas joiners come along later to carefully perfect the finished appearance of the property using smoother, planed

timber. Joiners tend to largely operate indoors, installing such things as architraves, panelling, fitted kitchen units, and staircase mouldings (often called 'second fix'). Joiners see themselves as craftsmen, sometimes regarding carpenters sawing and nailing lengths of wood together in rather the same way that portrait artists might perceive interior decorators. The reality is that both are highly skilled trades. Many carpenter/joiners perform the full repertoire. But there's one important difference: whilst poor quality joinery is annoying, poor quality carpentry can threaten the very structure of a building.

It's said that the test of a good carpenter/joiner is how neatly they can hang a door. Although not exactly 'rocket-science' this does allow you to easily note the degree of care and attention to detail.

Floor insulation
Upstairs floors don't require thermal insulation against heat-loss except in rare cases where the ceiling underneath

is open to the exterior, such as over an unheated space like a passageway or an integral garage. Either way, insulating timber floors as they are built is simple and inexpensive. Thick slabs of insulation can be cut and slotted between the joists, if necessary supported by timber battens nailed to the lower part of the joists. In addition you can use thicker insulated plasterboard for the ceiling below.

Although this won't be necessary for most extension floors, you still need to provide sound proofing. This is all the more important because of the trend for naked floor surfaces that can make rooms resemble echo chambers, not helped by ceiling downlights which serve as pathways for noise to penetrate through floors. The Building Regs Part E2 deals with sound transmission within the home (as opposed to noise from outside). The current requirement for 40dB (decibels) of sound reduction in internal floors and walls isn't very demanding. You should be able to easily exceed this target by stuffing mineral wool insulation between the joists - see page 125. You may even want to go beyond the call of duty and specify 15mm thick blue acoustic plasterboard and fit recessed lights within a lower 'dummy' suspended ceiling.

Windows and doors

If there's one part of the build that's likely to spark a heated debate it's your choice of windows and doors.

Some folk harbour a slightly cynical view that any

design that displays even the slightest artistic flair will inevitably be doomed, strangled at birth by the Council planning department. To be fair, the planners will understandably want to prevent problems such as windows that very evidently overlook the neighbours and may also be keen to preserve the architectural character of the local area.

If your windows survive that process, Building Control will doubtless take a dim view of anything that allows undue heat-loss. Indeed windows are now the most regulated element of the build – with thermal, fire, ventilation, child safety and security standards to comply with. Conflict between the respective standards is more likely to arise with listed buildings or in conservation areas, where simultaneously trying to preserve the old and enforce the new may prove incompatible.

Windows

The choice of available new windows is extensive. You

can buy anything from quaint replica box sashes to conventional side or top hung casements or even zany tilt-and-turn jobs. These are available in a variety of materials such as softwood, hardwood, uPVC, coated aluminium or galvanised steel, as well as in a range of colours and glazing styles. Then there's the question of whether to opt for 'off the shelf' or custom-made. Bespoke windows are likely to cost at least 20% more than standard sizes, and since you're building from new in most cases it makes sense to design standard sized openings.

Taste is a personal matter, but as a general rule it's worth trying to emulate the original window architecture of the house you're extending, especially with pre-war or older properties. Sticking cheap plastic windows in an extension to a Jacobean cottage with traditional leaded lights, isn't

Standard frame sizes normally correspond to multiples of masonry courses.

going to do a lot for the property's resale value. uPVC can suit many modern houses but isn't as long lasting as is sometimes believed. Despite the magic words 'maintenance-free' it is hard to repair and can't be repainted so it gradually loses its finish and often becomes discoloured with a useable life of only around 30 years. Research shows that in the long term timber windows actually turn out to be the cheapest option if regularly painted or stained every 10 years or so. Engineered timbers such as 'Accoya' manufactured from modified solid wood are a recent innovation offering outstanding durability and need considerably less maintenance. Alternatively, you might plump for contemporary grey aluminium which can look sleek and stylish with slim lines to maximise natural light. For improved energy efficiency frames with a polyamide thermal break are recommended. Then there's the option of 'deco' style hot dipped galvanised steel with polyester powder coatings which should last more than 60 years and shouldn't need redecorating for 30 years .

Most modern windows are 'casements' which simply means they open on hinges (rather than sliding like sashes). Casements can be side or top hung, or pivoted in the middle. A window that doesn't open at all is known as a 'fixed light'. If you feel the need to add that elusive quality known as 'character', there are endless choices of 'cottage style' and 'Georgian' glazing bars as well as 'swept head' curved top inserts .

As a rule of thumb, your windows will cost twice as much per square metre as the walls they sit within. Should you choose to buy custom-made windows in non-standard sizes, they could set you back up to three times the price of bog standard mass produced units. Most windows have to be ordered in advance, so plan for a 4 – 8 week delay. Perhaps the commonest size in new housing is the 1,200 x 1,200mm 'double casement' but there are a wide range of 'off the shelf' sizes.

The standard height options are:
450, 600, 750, 900, 1,050, 1,200, 1,350, and 1,500mm (sizes rising in 150mm jumps, equivalent to 2 brick courses).

The standard width options are somewhat less logical:
488, 630, 915, 1,200 and 1,770mm

Mass produced timber windows are commonly made from Scandinavian redwood, factory vacuum-treated with preservatives. Locks are now fitted as standard, and opening casements are ready-draughtproofed. Windows and other joinery items are supplied with a base coat of wood stain which you can later choose to stain (or paint), or else a white primed finish for painting.

To compete with UPVC, timber windows are now normally delivered ready glazed as well as pre-finished.

From a technical viewpoint, new windows need to comply with Part L1 of the Building Regulations for thermal insulation (Part J if your extension is Scottish). To provide background ventilation, habitable rooms must have opening windows fitted with small trickle vents in the heads of window frames.

There are minimum size requirements for window openings. For all habitable rooms, the Building Regulations require the openable area of the window(s) to be equivalent to at least five per cent of the room's floor area. Perhaps due to their more northerly location, Scottish standards are formulated to allow in more daylight, stipulating a minimum glazed area in each room equivalent to 15 per cent of its floor area.

But apart from looking good and keeping your home warm and bright, there are other factors that need to be considered:

■ Escape from fire, especially on upper floors.
■ Security, especially to ground floors and windows facing flat roofs.
■ Danger from broken glass.

If windows are located on a wall within 6 metres of next door's house, there are likely to be restrictions on their total size. This is to control the risk of fire jumping from one building to another. The Building Regs also restrict the use of materials that are not fire-resistant close to a boundary, such as plastic and timber.

In the event of having to escape from a fire, the minimum 'clear openable area' that most people can realistically squeeze through is 450mm wide x 750mm high. So Building Control will normally want to see a minimum clear opening width of 450mm on upstairs windows to bedrooms. To achieve this you may need to specify wider fire egress hinges (or it's a simple job to swap standard scissor hinges on casements). That's all very well but what about the nightmare scenario where you're trying to escape from fire and the window is locked? Trying to smash your way out through sealed unit double glazing in an emergency can be virtually impossible, so locks must be easily accessible. One other point to bear in mind is the height of 'egress windows' which must be no higher than 1100mm above floor level to the bottom of the opening, and no lower than 800mm for child safety.

Reveals

The vertical sides of the walls around window and door frames are known as reveals. Even quite modern houses can suffer from damp and mould around the reveals

Left and below: Windows are one of the most highly regulated parts of a building, especially security and escape from fire

because of those twin evils discussed earlier – cold spots and thermal bridging. But inserting special foam-filled plastic 'cavity closers' into the cavities not only breaks the cold bridge, but also doubles as a vertical DPC and provides a fixing point for the window frame itself.

Frame fitting

Something that will greatly affect the look of your house, and yet is sometimes overlooked, is the question

Frames are commonly fitted using metal brackets, often improvised on site

of where exactly to position the new window and door frames within the wall openings. It's often left to the blokes on site to make this key decision on your behalf. The Victorians set their windows and doors well back into the brickwork, but this necessitated fitting huge masonry sub-sills underneath projecting well clear of the wall, adding to

Photo: eddystoneselfbuild.co.uk

Self-fixing frame screws .

Use of metal strips to fix windows potentially risks thermal-bridging and cold spots (even with insulated cavity closers).

the cost. Recessed joinery not only looks better, but a softwood window that is sheltered from the weather by being set back in its opening can ultimately perform better than a more exposed hardwood one. However, modern volume-produced windows are generally designed to fit just 25mm or so back from the outside face of the brickwork, which on the plus side leaves space for a nice big window ledge inside. This makes it difficult to match the pattern of the existing windows in extensions to many older properties where they will need to be set fairly well back. This decision will affect the outer sills, which must project out sufficiently from the wall in order to disperse rainwater. So when ordering you may need to specify longer sills where the standard ones are too short.

Before fixing, the frames must be checked for correct positioning with a spirit level, to ensure they've been fitted square and plumb (upright and level). This is where using small ribbed plastic wedges (aka 'shims' or 'packers') can be invaluable, gently hammering them in to make small refinements until the frames sit just right.

Various methods can be used to anchor the frames into the surrounding masonry. Traditionally, galvanised steel 'frame cramps' were screwed to the sides of the frames and bedded into the mortar courses in the masonry as the walls were built up around the frames. But today window installation is often left until a later stage when metal brackets are fixed to the sides of timber windows and screwed into the inner leaf masonry reveals. Builders sometimes improvise with metal strips cut from surplus steel wall ties. Although acceptable to Building Control these sorts of metal brackets

could potentially act as 'cold bridges' crossing cavities, despite the reveals being lined with insulated cavity closers. A better alternative may be to use special frame-fixing 'hammer-in' screws with integral long plastic wallplugs, or self-fixing concrete screws (which don't need wall plugs). These can be installed by drilling holes in the frame and then keeping on drilling into the wall (using a masonry bit), finally hammering or screwing and tightening them. But whatever method is used, take it easy with the power-driver as overtightening can cause distortion to the frames.

It may sound obvious, but always check that lintels have been correctly fitted above all openings. It is not unknown for builders to omit these, instead relying on the reinforcement in the frames themselves to hold up the brickwork above. But even robust-looking uPVC

Left, below and right: Shims and packers gently hammered into position help get frames true and plumb before fixing and filling

frames aren't sufficient to take the place of a lintel. Above the lintels, cavity trays should be installed (or an equivalent sheet of plastic DPM angled up at the sides) to protect the lintel from condensation in the cavity.

Finally, to banish draughts for ever, frames need to be completely sealed, by injecting a suitable silicone mastic between the outside frame and the reveal. Any small gaps on the inside can be sealed with a few blasts of expanding polystyrene foam (wear gloves!).

Standard pre-insulated steel cavity lintel

Window fixing – points to check

- The sills have a protruding lip or thin 'drip groove' set back a few millimetres from their outer underside front edges.
- The sills project well clear of the wall, so rain can drip off freely.

- Timber frames are protected by DPCs or plastic cavity closers.
- Where the outer wall below the window is to be tiled or timber clad, a lead flashing 'apron' should be fixed under the sill (to be dressed down over the cladding).

Glazing

Double-glazing as a product has something of a chequered history. Many units have been bedevilled by high failure rates within a few years of being fitted. The mysterious phenomenon of 'misting' commonly manifests itself as a result of moisture condensing inside the (supposedly) sealed units, due to wet edge seals breaking down. Fortunately, modern units are much improved, thanks to drained and vented bottom rails in the frames that allow moisture to drain away or evaporate, rather than accumulate. Timber windows with deeper glazing rebates have also helped, and being delivered already factory glazed has cut out the risk of 'Friday afternoon' fitting on site.

To meet the requirements of Part L1B of the Building Regulations new double-glazed windows must have a U-value no higher than 1.6Wm2/K. One of the problems with U-values is the difficulty of comparing different windows – because frames and glazing have separate U-value ratings. The BFRC rating system (British Fenestration Rating Council) uses Window Energy Ratings (WER) that take account of the performance of the whole window, including heat gain through the glass. Ideally aim for a high A or B energy rating, but not lower than C. In fact many windows on the market today are A-rated or have U-values of 1.2 or better and the best triple glazing is now down to below 0.9 Wm2/K.

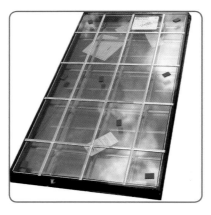

To reduce heat-loss most sealed double-glazed units have vacuum-sealed cavities with generous air gaps of 16mm, 20mm, or 24mm. Special 'low-E' glass has a microscopically thin coating applied to the inside of the inner pane that allows the sun's rays to pass through but reflects infra-red radiation back into the room (check the label to confirm the panes are fitted right way round!).

'Low-E' coatings are available either in a 'hard' form or as the more efficient 'soft' variety.

Specifying cavities filled with argon or krypton gas further slows the transfer of heat across the cavity because these inert gases are more 'syrupy' than air. And you can even specify solar-controlled glass that can reflect away unwanted sunshine to help overcome summer overheating (the 'G factor')

To prevent condensation

forming on cold winter mornings around the perimeter of windows, where the glass is cold at the edges, special 'thermal break' spacer bars are fitted. These separate the cold outer frame from the warm inner parts, with a layer of resin or plastic sandwiched between the inner and outer sections.

Perhaps surprisingly, when it comes to the subject of noise reduction, secondary glazing is actually superior to double-glazing. With an optimum space of 150mm between the secondary glazing and the glass in the main window, this can provide effective insulation against noise at high frequencies, as well as deadening low frequency sound, such as road traffic.

Broken glass

To anyone with young children, danger from unprotected glass at low levels can be especially worrying. So to cut the risk of accidents the Building Regs require safety glass to be fitted in critical locations, as defined in Part K of the Building Regs (formerly in Part N). That means any glazing within 800mm of floor level. And if you have windows next to your doors (ie within 300mm) then any glazing within 1,500mm of the floor must also be made from safety glass. Ditto for panes of glass anywhere that are wider than 250mm, and for internal doors with pane sizes greater then 250 x 250mm.

But what exactly is safety glass? There are two common forms of strengthened glass that comply with BS 7950. The type used in car windscreens is 'laminated safety glass', which is over 6mm thick and shatters into tiny pieces on impact rather than into big sharp shards. To achieve this, an invisible clear plastic sheet is sandwiched between 2 layers of ordinary glass, so that it all holds together on impact. When fitted in house windows, it gives glazing the added strength to resist intruders.

Safety glass also comes in the form of 'toughened glass' which is baked hard to five times the strength of ordinary float glass. Toughened glass is harder to break, but when it does break it shatters into relatively safe small nodules that hang together, but can be knocked through afterwards. Toughened glass costs about 50% more than standard glass. Of the two, it is reckoned that laminated glass is more secure, although it costs twice as much as standard glass. Small panes in doors etc may instead be made from tempered or annealed safety glass.

Security compliance now also dictates the need for

Door dimensions
The world of doors remains a stronghold of imperial measurements, the most common off-the-peg sizes being 78 x 33in (1,981 x 838mm) and 78 x 30in (1,981 x 762mm). For taller, wider folk 80 x 32in (2,032 x 813mm) doors are available. The standard exterior door thickness is 44mm. Including the frame, most uPVC exterior doors are available sized 82 x 36in (2,085 x 920mm), or 82 x 47in (2,085 x 1,190 mm) for French doors.

laminated safety glass that's 'P1A rated' to all windows that are 'easily accessible to intruders'. P1A refers to a lab test where a 100mm diameter steel ball is dropped onto the glass from a metre and a half height without breaking through it. 'Easily accessible windows' are defined as those within 2 metres of the ground, a balcony or a flat roof or pitched roof less than 30 degrees. Preventing burglars breaking-in is of course child's play compared to keeping kids safe because children are naturally attracted to anything life threatening. For this reason any part of your upstairs windows less than 800mm above floor level must not be openable. This is a part of the building where you may find potential for conflict within the various regulations. For example, windows that are firmly lockable for security purposes must also be easily openable for escape in the event of fire. 'Juliet balconies' or external railings protecting French windows upstairs must extend a minimum of 1100mm above floor level to stop people falling out; but this could impede escape from fire, so the windows need to open sufficiently wide to allow 'fire-egress' (see page 169). Similarly, skylight windows in new loft rooms should allow escape from fire, but at the same time mustn't be easily openable by children intent on playing 'roof-exploration' games; a suitable compromise in such a situation might be reached by fitting special high-level childproof handles.

Doors
Choosing the doors for your extension provides a great opportunity to add real character to your home. Fitting cottage style ledge & brace doors or some stylish French windows or super-wide bi-fold doors could be just the thing.

It pays to take a little time when picking a new door as fitting a cheap one may leave you vulnerable to leaks as well as break-ins. Doors manufactured from uPVC are usually supplied as a complete unit with an integral frame. Their major advantage is that they're virtually maintenance-free, although they're not as attractive looking as traditional wooden doors, which are still the most popular choice. Fibreglass (GRP) can do a fairly convincing impersonation of timber and may be worth considering. Steel doors are a serious modern alternative, popular in North America.

Door frames
It may sound obvious, but before attempting to fit a frame spare a thought for the direction you want the

door to open. Entrance doors should open into the house, as do 'French windows' although balcony doors sometimes swing outwards. To save space internally, you might want a kitchen door, for example, to open outwards. If so, extra precautions should be taken to prevent possible injury (eg kids running past just as someone flings open

the door) and to protect the frame from the weather.

Timber door frames are usually of 100 x 75mm softwood and can be fitted in the same way as window frames (described earlier). Frames are normally pre-treated and primed. Once fitted, the joints between the frame edges and the walls need to be sealed with mastic.

Rainwater is prevented from entering under the door by means of the 'threshold', a hardwood sill positioned centrally to the underside of the door, incorporating a thin steel strip known as a 'water bar' or 'weather bar'. The threshold will need protecting against damp with a DPC strip underneath. It must also be installed at the right height in relation to the floor inside and normally two brick courses above the ground outside. Once fitted, timber thresholds should be temporarily covered over until completion, to protect them from damage.

Traditionally a small section of wood needed to be cut out from the bottom outer edge of new doors using a circular saw to form a stepped rebate so that when the door was closed it smoothly dovetailed over the threshold weather-bar. This modification isn't always necessary,

Below: Door awaits weatherboard.

depending on exposure, but the metal weather bar in the sill can't keep all the rain out just by itself. It needs to work in conjunction with an overhanging weatherboard projecting from the base of the front of the door. Some modern weatherboards simply comprise small, curved metal strips that just require screwing into place on the door.

Fitting doors

New timber doors should be allowed a little time to acclimatise before fitting to minimise the risk of bowing, warping and sticking. The new door frames will have been specified to accept your precise choice of door, so

Juliet balconies must be min 1100mm above internal floor level and gaps between vertical rails no wider than 100mm.

theoretically it should all slip daintily into place. In actual practice, however, some planing may still be required to achieve a good fit.

As a rule, hinges should be positioned about 150mm from the top of the door and 200–225mm from the bottom. Because exterior doors are relatively heavy, particularly those containing glazing, a third hinge is required mid-way between the other two. Brass hinges are preferable since they aren't susceptible to rust. The hinges should always be fitted to the door first, before the frame.

The new door is fitted by first being placed on some thin strips of wood to achieve a 6mm clearance between the bottom of the door and the sill, so the hinge points can be marked on the frame. This may seem rather a wide gap, but it allows for the fact that the door will tend to drop slightly over time. A clearance gap of around 3mm at the top and sides is recommended. When any necessary trimming has been done and the hinge positions chiselled out, the door is temporarily wedged in the open position so the hinges can be screwed to the frame.

Finally, your door furniture and locks can be fitted. Mortises may need to be cut into the side of the door by drilling out and then chiselling. Timber doors should be painted or varnished soon after installation so that they don't get a chance to absorb moisture and swell.

Bi-fold doors and French windows

When is a window not a window? Answer: when it's French. Windows in *La Belle France* open inwards (great for cleaning and painting) and are often very tall extending to the floor and arranged in pairs. So back in the day our Georgian forebears nicked the idea and reformulated it as pairs of hinged doors at the back of the house. These typically comprised several panes of glass set in frames of wood or steel. Today fully glazed pairs of French windows are now a popular addition to bedrooms, contained behind iron, steel or glass Juliet balconies.

The fashion for wider patio doors became mainstream from the 1970s comprising 2 large glazed panels, one fixed, the other sliding along fixed tracks. More recently, bi-fold doors combined the best of both worlds by sliding on a track but also being hinged together so they could concertina into the smallest practicable space, minimising the barrier between garden and house. Which is why they're also known as 'folding sliding doors'. Extensions are ideally suited to wide bi-fold doors (costing from around £2k). Sometimes the track is built flush with the internal finished floor level and external patio for an 'unbroken' feel (but to check damp problems you need to install a drainage channel at the base of the doors on the patio). The current fashion is for slim frame or frameless glass doors to maximise light.

Security

Police statistics tell us that the average British home suffers an attempted break-in once every 12 years, of which more than half are successful. It's also a fact that around two-thirds of all break-ins take place through the rear of the house. But since this is the part of the property where most extensions are built, you may now have an excellent opportunity to beef up your home security. But what do burglars find at the rear of a typical house? Often it's the easiest doors to break in through – sliding patio doors and externally hinged French windows (aka 'French doors'). Patio doors are currently rather out of fashion and it's unlikely you'd be fitting new ones, but any existing ones should be fitted with special locks so they can't be lifted off their runners. If you plan to fit new French doors, specify additional locking slide bolts.

One obvious precaution with newly glazed windows and doors is to ensure that the beading that holds the glazing panels in place is fitted internally, so intruders can't simply prise it off and remove the glass from outside. Fortunately glazing now normally comes factory-fitted, delivered as complete units often ready-painted.

Security measures for doors and windows are now covered by Part Q of the Building Regs. Entrance doors need to meet PAS 24 security standard. The NHBC newbuild standard is to fit 5-lever locks to all external doors (plus a cylinder rim/night latch to the main entrance door) and locks to all windows. Locks should be specified to comply with BS 3621. The easiest locks to use are mortise types with lever handles that automatically operate a latchbolt and deadbolt. To make escape easier in the event of fire, doors should be readily openable from inside without a key.

> ### Main trades needed on site
> ■ **Carpenters:** Making templates for the window and door frames. Fitting upper floor joists, doors, and windows.
>
> *www.home-extension.co.uk*

12 ROOFING

And now to the crowning glory of your extension. Not only will the new roof make a big design statement, but when the building finally has its 'hat' on you'll at last feel that the end of the project is in sight. You know you're on the home straight when a dark, damp shell open to the elements is magically transformed into a dry, weathertight space – a home in the making. To mark the occasion in style, you may even find an excuse to enjoy a little celebration as the final roof tile is placed – the traditional 'topping out ceremony'.

Softwood cut timber roof construction with ridge plate, rafters and ceiling joist collars.

Rafters must be doubled either side of roof openings. Here lead flashing was pre-fitted later to be dressed down over slates.

First, there's the small matter of constructing one of the most complex parts of the build. Not only will it have to look good and perform well, it also has the added complexity of needing to marry up neatly with your existing building.

For most extensions there's a simple choice of roof styles: pitched or flat. Strictly speaking, a pitched roof is defined as one with a slope steeper than about 12°, although in reality 17.5° is about the shallowest slope some roof coverings can manage. Flat roofs have something of a patchy reputation technically and are rarely acceptable to the planners for multi-storey extensions. There are, however, some intriguing possibilities that mix and match the two styles. You could opt for part-flat and part-pitched. Or perhaps an ultra-shallow lead-clad roof.

On the ground, the most obvious sign that your project is entering a major new phase will be the change of personnel on site, with the bricklayer handing over to the carpenter, shortly to be followed by the roofers.

The first thing the carpenter will need to check is that the building has so far been constructed square and that it's level on all sides at the wall plates, not forgetting to ensure that the scaffolding has been safely installed up to roof lift.

Even if you've succeeded in getting the roofing works

Below and opposite page: Traditional oak Kingpost roof structure. Dry run at ground level to check components all fit prior to installation on roof.

scheduled for the (hopefully) dry summer months, until the breather-membrane has been draped over the rafters for weather-protection it's a good idea to keep tarpaulins handy in case of a sudden downpour.

If you're planning to employ your own roofing contractors, it's worth remembering that roofing is a trade that has a reputation for attracting rogue operators. Cowboy roofers tend to pop up after severe storms offering 'maintenance services'. They know that, safely out of sight, all manner of botched jobs can be carried out with impunity. So look for firms registered with the National Federation of Roofing Contractors (NFRC), who provide an independent warranty. Go and view some of their previous jobs and check out details like the neatness of pointing to verges and mortar bedding to ridge tiles. This is a good test, since messy pointing tends to be indicative of slap-dash workmanship. Always discuss the materials to be used with the roofer in advance, and try to inspect the work as it progresses, when it's safe and convenient to do so.

Safety and scaffolding

Roofs need to be treated with respect. Never try to carry out work in windy or poor weather conditions. On isolated sites, it's advisable not to do roof work alone.

A high proportion of building site accidents arise from

poor erection of scaffolding or temporary work platforms. This should normally be the responsibility of the main contractor. Because of the real danger of serious injury and fatalities, scaffolding is the subject of much health and safety legislation. To help weed out cowboy scaffolding firms, it's worth quoting this little phrase when confirming instructions in writing:

'The scaffolding shall be erected and maintained in accordance with BS 5973 and 5974 "Access & working scaffolds and special scaffold structures in steel" and The Construction (Health, Safety & Welfare) Regulations 1996.'

Pitched roofs

As everyone knows, the basic structure of a roof takes the form of a simple triangle. The two main roof slopes meet on top at the ridge, whilst the base of the triangle is formed by the ceiling joists acting as collars.

Roof slopes are constructed with timber rafters. Depending on the roof span (ie how wide it is) these are

Above and below: Simple cut timber roofs, note birdsmouth joint at wall plate

commonly made from 47 x 150mm timbers which are typically spaced apart at 400mm or 600mm centres. The specific sizes and spacings of the rafters will have been determined by your structural engineer. The tops of the rafters normally meet at a horizontal timber ridge plate that runs along the top of the roof, although steels are sometimes used for the ridges in larger structures. At their feet the rafters are fixed to the timber wall plates (the wooden beams running along the top of the walls). To stop the rafters spreading and pushing the walls outwards, they are tied together by the ceiling joists.

This describes a traditional custom built 'cut' roof structure. However, most roofs today are constructed using factory-manufactured 'trussed rafters'. The question is, are ready-made, standard-sized roof trusses likely to be at all suitable for your individually designed home extension?

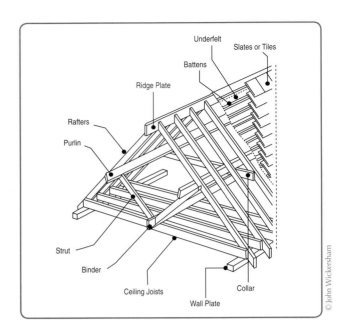

© John Wickersham

Trussed rafters

The roofs of most new houses have been built from prefabricated trussed rafters since the 1970s. Because some can span over 8m without needing extra support from internal structural walls there are big potential savings elsewhere in the build. Although they're relatively expensive to buy they're quicker to install, with consequent savings in labour costs – except, of course, when it comes to non-standard designs, like most home extensions. Here your carpenter might have to spend a considerable amount of time customising them to fit, pushing up the labour costs, possibly making them uneconomic. In fact trusses should not be modified on site without authorisation, as cutting bits off can drastically weaken the structure. So manufactured trussed rafters are only likely to suit large, simple, rectangular-shaped extensions, and in most cases your chippie will need to construct a traditional 'cut roof'.

If you do decide to use trusses, they need careful handling to prevent damage. They must be stacked well clear of the ground on bearers and sheltered from the weather.

Building the roof is essentially an assembly operation with trusses normally spaced at 600mm centres. But because some larger ones can weigh 30kg or more, lifting them into position at a great height can sometime require the assistance

of a hired crane, making the job a lot quicker and safer. Once the trusses are lined up, they can all be connected together with binders and straps, and twice skew-nailed to the timber wall plate.

Another drawback of conventional trussed rafters is that the resulting loft space cannot easily be used for living accommodation due to the intricate network of struts and bracing timbers. A good way round this is to specify 'room-in-roof' (RiR) trusses which are specially designed to provide a ready-made shell for a loft room, making it a relatively simple matter to complete the interior finishing at a later date. For an extra couple of thousand pounds or so, this

can provide a very cost-effective solution, but their extra weight means you'll also need to budget-in a decent-sized crane. Trussed rafters in themselves are rather weedy looking things, held together with

'Room in roof' trusses invite possible future loft space conversion.

primitive metal connecting plates. So beefing them up with some extra bracing is now required as a result of some early unbraced examples collapsing like rows of dominoes. This means a number of additional horizontal and diagonal 100 x 25mm timber strips and binders need to be nailed in place.

Straps and clips

We've already encountered 'restraint straps', used to anchor down the timber wall plates that run along the tops of the walls (see Chapter 10). The wall plate defines the point where the roof structure sits

Ends of lateral 'L' straps built into blockwork inner leaf.

on the house. Without such measures to hold them down, severe gales have caused roofs to lift off, a phenomenon known as 'wind uplift'.

But straps have other uses. 'Lateral restraint straps' are fixed horizontally, tying in the roof timbers to gable or party walls, as well as being fitted lower down the structure, at ceiling and first floor levels. Each horizontal restraint strap should be secured across at least two rafters with plated screws (as well as being fixed to timber noggins or packing strips between the rafters) and downturned tight against the inner leaf blockwork. It's the bricklayer's job to build the lateral restraint straps into the cavity of the walls at rafter, ceiling and first floor levels, rather than regarding them as an optional extra – which makes this a good test of a competent tradesman. The straps are left sticking out ready for the chippie to screw to the rafters or joists.

As well as needing extra bracing, roofs built from trussed rafters also require small metal 'truss clips' to secure the trusses to the wall plates below. Then there are special 'vertical anchor straps' with distinctive twisted necks designed to tie the rafter feet of the trusses to the wall below.

Cut roofs

Because of the relatively small size of most home extensions, and the need to custom-build the new roof where it joins up to the existing house, traditional 'cut' roofs are widely used. Here, the carpenter cuts all the various timber components to length on site. It's important this is done in accordance with

Lower roof slopes need thin marine ply (or similar) covering to support underlay and prevent sagging.

Extension roof with new valley between old and new.

Above: Double check all roof slope angles and dimensions as the structure is erected!
Left: Traditional oak frame roof structure with horizontal tie beams nailed to wall plates rather than conventional rafters.

your approved drawings and structural calculations, which will have taken into account all possible anticipated loadings, such as from heavy roof tiles, severe gusts of wind and drifting snow etc.

A traditional cut roof with two main roof slopes is known as a 'close coupled roof', essentially comprising a pair of lean-to roofs propped up against each other.

Erecting the roof

One of the most perilous parts of your entire project is now about to begin. The skeleton of the extension roof first takes shape starting with the horizontal timber ridge board placed in position to mark the highest part of the roof structure. This is attached at one end to the existing house, and at the other end to a highly trained volunteer in a hard hat holding it up in thin air! Alternatively, a large timber triangle can be knocked up and secured to the wall plates to

Left: Breather membrane secured with battens – now it's dry inside!
Below: Extension ridge plate fixed to existing hipped roof.

provide a more reliable form of temporary support while the first rafters are carefully positioned in place to take the load. The carpenters can now complete the roof structure, filling in all the missing rafters. At this point you might want to quickly check that the degree of pitch as built matches that shown on your plans.

The rafters are typically spaced 400mm apart and rest at their base on the timber wall plate. So that they're securely connected, a small V-shaped cut known as a 'birdsmouth' is made, joining neatly to the wall plate. At the top they're nailed to the ridge board.

But the job's not over yet. In larger roofs, additional support may be required about halfway up the rafters in the form of large horizontal 'purlins'. The problem with purlins is that traditionally they often needed to be propped up in turn with timber struts, and the load transferred to internal load-bearing walls. Not only was this expensive (requiring the building of additional 'structural' internal walls with their own foundations) but it took up valuable space. So today large steels are sometimes employed, either at the apex as ridge plates or lower down as purlins that don't need any extra support. The steel beams will then need timber plates bolted to their top surfaces (so should be ordered pre-drilled).

A currently popular traditional-looking design might feature low roof slopes swooping down around bedroom dormer windows. Inside, the first floor rooms encroach into the roof space so that the ceilings slope around the edges of the rooms. Here you'll often find the rafters strengthened with steel purlins above the ceilings.

It's often been said that a good roof structure is a work of art, so it seems a shame to hide it behind giant sheets of plasterboard. Given that you're paying for a skilled carpenter to custom-build the roof at considerable expense, why obliterate all that craftsmanship behind ceilings? Your designer may have already recognised the potential for a bit of 'wow factor' here, leaving some of the structure on display for all to admire – in which case you'll need to take special measures with the insulation (see below). If your chippie

Steel ridge beams are now fairly common; end bearings needs to rest on padstones .

New hipped roof awaits hip tiles

is really good he might even be working on a traditional 'kingpost' roof structure, the perfect backdrop to that suit of armour and stag's-head trophy you've always promised yourself!

Lean-to roofs

The most common type of roof for a typical small ground-floor extension is the simple lean-to. This is just a single-slope 'mono pitch' roof where the tops of the rafters are propped up against the wall of the main house. Construction involves first bolting a horizontal strip of timber to the wall of the existing house, onto which the tops of the lean-to rafters are secured. At their feet they connect to the timber wall plate on top of the main walls. As described earlier, the ceiling joists prevent them pushing out the walls. If your new extension has a gable end wall or, in the case of a lean-to roof, half a gable to its side, then it may be only once the rafters are in place that the brickie will be able to finish building up the gable end wall. So don't be too hasty making that next big payment – you may still be due a return visit.

Hipped roofs

If you like pyramids this is the style for you. Instead of just having two roof slopes propped up against each other and the triangular space in between at the gable end infilled

with brickwork, hipped roofs have a third roof slope. Hips were especially popular on 1930s houses.

However, hips are more complicated to construct than a bog-standard 'close coupled' design. The difficulty is that the carpenter needs to make a lot of tricky angled cuts to all the different-sized 'jack rafters' near the angled hip corners where the roof slopes meet. The corners themselves are made from special 'hip rafters', usually clad with round 'hip tiles' (similar to ridge tiles) or with perkily upturned 'bonnet tiles'. Due to their weight, hip tiles normally need a protruding metal strip called a 'hip iron' at their base, to discourage any loose ones from slipping off and maiming innocent passers-by. Neatest of all are 'close mitred hips' where the tiles either side are precision cut to meet over a hidden lead soaker, creating an 'invisible' join.

Felt and underlay

Roofs should have a secondary barrier beneath the tiles to keep out severe weather. This defence against wind-driven rain getting under the tiles has traditionally comprised a layer of thick felt, used in most new housing since the 1950s. But the days of heavy, bitumen-soaked hessian underlay, drooping ponderously between damp rafters, are now long gone. Today, modern high performance lightweight roofing felts such as 'Klober', 'Permo' and Dupont 'Tyvec' are normally specified. Rather like high-tech mountaineering clothing, these 'breather membranes' cleverly prevent rainwater from getting in, yet allow water vapour to escape outwards from the loft

Left: Hipped roof designs require a lot of complex cutting.

Right: Battens need to be sized and gauged / spaced correctly to suit the type of tiles or slates .

by permeating through the material. They are thinner yet tougher than the old felt, which was always prone to being ripped and torn on installation. Most important of all, modern underlay doesn't rot.

As soon as the basic roof structure is complete the breather membrane underlay can be installed, unless you want to insulate the roof at rafter level (see below) rather than laying conventional loft insulation above the ceilings. It is secured to the rafters with treated softwood roofing battens, starting near the bottom at the eaves and working upwards. An overlap of at least 100mm must be allowed where one sheet joins another. This has the advantage of swiftly providing a temporary waterproof cover so work can proceed in relative comfort down below.

In Scotland the rules are different. Rafters must first be covered with rigid 'sarking boards', a traditional form of timber cladding.

Battening

The roof tiles or slates are hung from rough-sawn timber battens running horizontally. These are fixed to the tops of the rafters with galvanised steel round wire nails through a layer of breather membrane underlay. Battening also helps improve the lateral stability for the roof structure. Tiles are commonly hung from 25 x 38mm battens whereas slates need fatter 25 x 50mm ones to accommodate nails. However it's best to specify 25 x 50mm pressure treated graded softwood regardless of coverings. Avoid cheap battens which can split when roofers walk on them! In terms of quality they must be BS5534 (ignore any other BS numbers). The original

idea behind coloured 'graded' battens often dyed red or blue was to make them stand out from 'ungraded' ones, which usually have a greenish tinge due to the preservative. But then some producers of cheaper battens started copying this practice, so the colour alone doesn't tell you much.

Before setting out the battens you first need to know the required spacing between each row. This is known as the 'gauge', and the precise figures will vary according to the specific type of slates or tiles you're using. It depends on a tile's recommended lap (how far the tile above overlaps the one below) in relation to angle of roof pitch.

Gauge, pitch, and lap figures can found on the manufacturers' websites. The gauge will be equal between all the battens except usually for the bottom one, where shorter eaves tiles are fixed.

Once all the rows of battens are nailed in place they can double as a sort of giant roof ladder that tilers make good use of when scampering up and down roof slopes.

Cold roof, warm roof

The conventional way to insulate a loft is to lay at least 270mm depth of mineral wool or fibreglass quilt between (and over) the ceiling joists to achieve the required U-value of 0.16 W/m2K. This means the roof space above is left cold, with a cross-flow of air from the eaves dispersing any rogue condensation and damp. This is known as a 'cold roof'.

But increasingly, extension designers trying to make the best use of the limited available space need the bedrooms to encroach into the roof space. Normally, the tops of the walls should rise at least 1.5m above the bedroom floor level

Left and below: Warm roof: vertical counter battens under horizontal tile battens.

Photo: Helicalsystems.co.uk

Photo: Helicalsystems.co.uk

Above and below: Sheets of multifoil insulation laid over rafters.

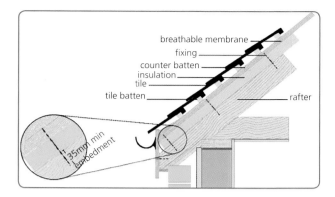

before meeting the sloped ceiling. But so that loft rooms don't become freezing damp garrets, the insulation needs to be moved higher up to rafter level. This is then known as a 'warm roof'. Here, the best approach technically is for the insulation to be laid on the outside of the roof structure, so that the whole house, including the loft space, is kept warm. However because this has the effect of raising the height of the roof it can potentially pose planning problems or cause design issues at junctions etc. So instead, the insulation is often placed between and underneath the rafters (as with loft conversions).

Where warm roofs are constructed with the insulation laid on top of the rafters, this usually comprises thick sheets of rigid polyurethane foam boards (PU or similar PIR or PF etc) to achieve the slightly less demanding U-value of 0.18 W/m2K. As a precaution, first a vapour control sheet is laid under the insulation (on the warm, inner side) in case any water vapour from the rooms below should get into the insulation and condense into moisture. On the outer side of the insulation boards, timber 'counter-battens' (minimum 38mm x 38mm) are nailed down the line of each rafter to create an air space above the insulation. These are fixed through the insulation boards into the rafters below using special helical fixings (except where nailing into rigid structural boards under the insulation). Finally, a breather-membrane is spread over the top of the counter-battens, held in place by conventional horizontal battens on to which the tiles or slates are hung.

Alternatively, where the insulation is laid between the rafters, a fairly typical arrangement might comprise 120mm rigid polyurethane foam boards cut to size and placed between 150mm thick rafters. It's easier to fit the insulation between

the rafters working from above once the roof structure is built rather than the (more usual) approach of pushing them up from inside later. You need to leave minimum 20mm ventilation 'droop space' between the upper side of the insulation and the breather membrane which will later be draped over the rafters prior to battening and tiling. Next, the undersides of the rafters should be lined with a vapour control sheet (e.g. 500 gauge). This is followed by an additional layer of rigid insulation boards, later to be plasterboarded. Or you can combine both layers by using insulated plasterboard fixed under the rafters using dry wall screws (typically 42.5mm thick comprising 30mm insulation + 12.5mm plasterboard).

There are various other materials that can be used to insulate a new roof. For example, thin sheets of 'multifoil' that look a bit like a BacoFoil and Kleenex sandwich can instead be laid over the rafters. Despite being only about 30mm thick, these shiny 'radiant heat barriers' are claimed to provide the equivalent of more than 200mm of loft quilt insulation. N.B. Some local authorities may not accept certain brands of 'radiant heat barrier' insulation – so check with Building Control at the design stage.

In terms of fire-resistance, the fact is most insulation materials are potentially combustible when exposed to fire. The notable exception is mineral wool insulation (rock or stone based) which has excellent fire-resistant properties and is available in semi-rigid batt form to stuff between rafters, although you may need a thicker depth to meet heat-loss targets. Either way it's reassuring to note that standard plasterboard ceilings with a skim plaster finish should provide minimum 20 minutes fire resistance.

Ventilation

Until fairly recently, the subject of ventilation was widely ignored by the building trade. Today, however, Building Control take a close interest so it's important to get the detailing right. Damp from condensation can ultimately rot timbers, so in a conventional 'cold' roof space having a decent amount of loft insulation as well as a good cross-flow of ventilation is key to preventing damage. A traditional roof design with a loft must therefore incorporate an effective method of passing air through the roof space. This is conventionally done with vents in the soffits under the eaves (equivalent to a 10mm continuous

gap along their full length) on opposite sides of the building. The good news is that if you've specified a warm roof incorporating an appropriate breather membrane, ventilation is less

of an issue than it used to be with traditional thick roofing felts. However you still need to leave a slim continuous air space underneath breather membranes, usually vented via the eaves. Achieving the required 'through-flow' of air may not be so easy with lean-to extensions because a single roof slope propped up against the wall of the main house means you haven't got eaves on opposite sides of the roof. So instead, you could fit special roof tiles or slates with inbuilt vents rather than ugly 'mushroom vents' sprouting from the upper roof surface. These will allow air entering at the eaves to flow up through the roof and out again. Vented ridge tiles or roof tiles can also make useful outlets for soil stacks and extractor fans. Alternatively, if your design has gable ends, or small 'half-gables' either side of a lean-to roof, then extra ventilation can be provided via a vertical I-shaped slot, which can look quite fetching in a churchy kind of way, or perhaps a terracotta airbrick in each gable. But be sure to fit insect mesh over vents unless you relish the prospect of playing host to swarms of wasps, birds or bats.

Joining it up – valleys and flashings

Where a new roof joins with the existing one at right angles, the roofers will first need to strip a few tiles or slates from your existing roof to expose the structure around the area to be joined, so that new valleys can be formed. Valleys are found where one pitched roof joins another at an internal angle (so you shouldn't need to worry about them for most single-storey extensions or where simply building straight out from a side gable).

If your old roof isn't underfelted, which is perfectly normal in many older houses, you'll be left with precisely zero weather protection once the existing tiles are stripped away, so tarpaulins should be kept handy to prevent pouring rain damaging ceilings and clouds of dust intruding into bedrooms and bathrooms below. If you can schedule the roofing process for the dryer summer months so much the better – just don't assume it won't rain!

Mitred valleys now usually 'dry fix' with central GRP valley trough visible.

Having stripped the tiles from the immediate part of the old roof, new timber 'valley boards' or 'layboards' (typically 250 x 25mm 'scaffold plank' size or exterior grade plywood) are then nailed diagonally to the existing rafters, creating valleys where the two roofs meet. Your structural engineer will have calculated whether the existing roof timbers are likely to need any additional support as a result of the extra load imposed on them.

Before tiling can start, a lead lining is laid over each valley board in strips no longer than 1.5m and a minimum of 100mm wide. The lead used should be 'code 4' or thicker 'code 5'. The strip higher up should be lapped over the one below by at least 150mm (225mm for shallow roofs of less than 30°). Modern fibreglass (GRP) valley linings and flashings are a cheaper alternative to traditional lead and easier to fix, although good old-fashioned lead is superior and longer lasting. Traditional 'open valleys' such as these have the adjoining tiles or slates cut around them, with the sides of the valley pointed up with mortar.

Cutting & fixing a lead flashing.

TYPES OF VALLEY

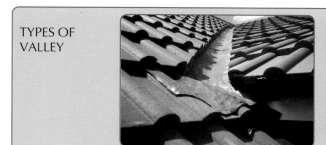

Open

Mitred

Curved

Above left: Layboards used to form valley base.
Above right: GRP valley trough for traditional 'wet fix' mitred valley.

Lead is notoriously prone to expansion, and needs to be carefully nailed so as not to restrict thermal movement which will cause it to crack. Special copper or stainless steel clout nails are used since they don't react with lead.

But there's more than one type of valley. A more desirable arrangement than using 'open valleys' is to fit purpose-made curved valley tiles on plain tile roofs, very popular on 1930s houses. These are less prone to maintenance problems over time. Another traditional method, similar to an open valley, is the 'mitred valley'. Here the tiles down the facing edges of the valley are accurately cut (mitred) to butt up against each other to achieve an almost invisible join, protected underneath by long strips of lead 'soakers' bedded in wet mortar, or GRP valley troughs (or 'trays'). But because over time these could potentially become blocked with moss and leaves, they have now largely been replaced with modern 'dry' mitred valleys. These are lined underneath with special

Below (left to right): Lead soakers cut to size and folded into place before tiling over. Then covered with lead flashing strips 'bossed' into shape. Flashing then tucked into cut groove, secured with lead wedges

'pointed hat' GRP valley troughs with their distinctive central ridge that pokes up all along the join to stop muck getting in. But at the end of the day your choice of valley will largely be determined by the design of your existing roof which you may want to match as well as your chosen type of tiles or slate coverings.

Coverings

The planners will have already taken a keen interest in your choice of roof coverings, possibly even requiring you to submit samples for approval before starting on site. But whatever materials you choose, there's a good chance that you'll want them to match your existing ones as closely as possible. For example modern artificial slates can blend in reasonably well complementing an older roof clad with natural slate. On the other hand, contrasting materials can also sometimes look good, such as orangey-coloured terracotta plain clay tiles pitched against a grey slate roof, or vice versa.

But good looks aren't everything. There are important technical factors to consider when choosing roof coverings. Some may not be suitable for use on very shallow roofs. And when comparing the pros and cons of tiles or slates, their weight is another key factor to bear in mind. The loading they impose on the structure must be carefully considered at the design stage.

The lap factor

One crucial piece of information when selecting coverings is the amount of 'lap' required, ie how much the heads (tops) of one row of tiles or slates need to be covered by the tails (bottoms) of the row above in order to successfully keep the weather where it belongs, on the outside.

As far as the lap factor is concerned, there are basically two kinds of products – 'single-lap' and 'double-lap'. Deciding

PLAIN TILES

Plain tiles are rectangular shaped and relatively small. Most have a slight camber to assist water discharge off the roof. They are available both in natural clay and manufactured concrete.

Sizes: A typical size would be 265 x 165mm. But being fairly small, the pitch of plain-tiled roofs cannot normally be much less than 35° (typically 40 to 45°).

Coverage: Around 60 to the square metre. Typical weight: 60kg to 78kg/m2

Lap: Typically 65mm+.

Tiles are manufactured with projecting 'nibs' so they can be hooked over battens. Traditionally, every fourth or fifth course might be nailed, or every course in exposed windy areas or on steeper pitched roof slopes above 45°. But today, all tiles should be nailed.

PANTILES

Pantiles are traditional large tiles of Dutch origin with a wavy S-shaped profile, traditionally popular in the counties around East Anglia.

Sizes: Typically range between 342 x 252mm and 406 x 330mm.

Coverage: About 15 tiles per sq m.

Lap: Typically around 75mm.

Like plain tiles, pantiles are hung by their nibs but are lighter (per square metre) and can be laid to a shallower pitch – some as low as 22.5°. They are relatively quick and easy to lay. Pantiles overlap with each other at their sides, and so only need one short lap from the row above (single-lap).

INTERLOCKING TILES

One of the most cost-effective roofing materials, these large, low-profile tiles are similar to traditional Roman tiles and are quick and easy to lay. They are single-lap, with consequent savings on labour and battens.

Sizes: Typically 380 x 230mm or 420 x 334mm.

Coverage: 10 tiles per sq m. Typical weight: 40kg to 50kg/m2

Lap: Typically 75mm+.

Constructed from coloured concrete, or dearer clay, some can be laid to a very shallow 17.5°, but they can look clumsy. The interlocking sides provide weather resistance without needing extensive overlapping like plain tiles, so the weight over a given area is lower. However, they are considerably heavier than slates. They're generally cheaper than plain tiles and work well at low pitch angles and in exposed locations. Worth considering where they match the original coverings to your property.

NATURAL SLATES

Photo: David Snell

Natural slate is one of the most hardwearing of all roofing materials, being lightweight, frost resistant and durable, with a lifespan well in excess of a hundred years.

Sizes: A 'Countess' is the traditional 512 x 255mm standard size, along with the 560 x 305mm 'Small Duchess'.

Coverage: Typically 18–30 per sq m.

Lap: Typically 65mm.

Some can be laid as shallow as 20°. Each slate needs to be nailed through holes in their centres or their heads (tops). Nails are usually of copper or aluminium. They're double-lapped, and laid in different grades of thickness, starting with the thinnest on top. Natural Welsh, Cornish or Cumbrian slate is the ideal covering, but is relatively expensive. Reclaimed slate is a good compromise as are imported Spanish ones although the quality of some Chinese or Brazilian slates can be patchy. To assess reclaimed slates tap them with hammer; a ringing sound shows the slate is okay, but a dull sound could indicate it's cracked. For compliance with NHBC Standards slate should achieve a T1 grade – the higher the grade the less 'oxidising pyrites' it contains which cause rust-coloured staining (and the dearer it is). Slates are also graded by how water absorbent they are, e.g. W1 grade means low absorption and hence a longer life because the more water they absorb water the softer they will be. S1 grade means they're resistant to acid rain.

ARTIFICIAL SLATES

Modern artificial slates are a popular, cheaper alternative to natural slate and can look authentic. They are made from composite fibre and cement, or moulded with a mixture of 50 - 80 per cent recycled slate dust and glass fibre resin.

Sizes: Typically 360 x 340 mm.

Coverage: Typically 12 per sq m.

Lap: Typically about 75mm.

Some can be laid to a very shallow pitch, even as low as 15°, and most are lighter than real slate. Some are manufactured with interlocking sides to create an easy-to-lay single-lapped roof. Now often the budget material of choice.

STONE SLATES

These are actually not slates at all, just heavy slabs of natural stone, in fairly irregular sizes. The most expensive of all roof coverings, stone slates are commonly seen in areas like the Cotswolds and the Pennines. For those working to a budget, it may be worth investigating modern artificial concrete moulded imitations.

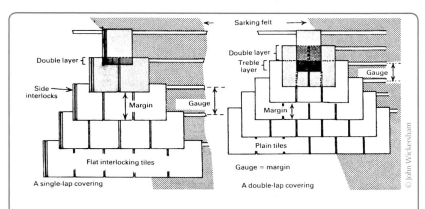

Single-lap tiles are made with interlocking side grooves. Double-lap slates and plain tiles do not have these grooves, and need to attain a treble thickness at their heads to keep out the rain. This necessitates many more battens.

which type to use will dramatically affect not only the weight of your roof, but also the cost of labour to build it.

Traditional 'double-lap' coverings like small-sized plain tiles and natural slates can't be overlapped at their sides, so the only way to cover the joints between them is to overlap them from above. They are traditionally laid in rows (courses), starting at the bottom of the roof slope and working upwards with the vertical joints staggered, like the bonding of brickwork. To keep out the rain at the joints between tiles in the same row, each gap must be covered by the tile above it and protected underneath by the tile below. This means that at certain points there'll actually be three layers, a triple thickness, which in turn necessitates using a lot of battens.

If this sounds like hard work, you're right. It's a lot easier to fix jumbo-sized 'single-lap' tiles or modern artificial slates, specially designed with grooves at the sides so they can 'interlock', overlapping each other sideways. This means only a short single lap over the head of each tile is needed to make them instantly watertight, resulting in a much quicker job requiring fewer tiles and battens.

Laying roof tiles

Start with the first row of tiles at the lower edge, above the gutter. Mark the centre of the lowest batten then loosely place a row of tiles onto it. To ensure the roof looks properly balanced, start at the mid-point of the batten either with the first tile centred, or with a joint between two tiles. Then spread the tiles symmetrically out from the centre in each direction, and reduce the gaps to create a perfect fit. Aim to get them finishing equally on either end of the roof slope. At the end verges special 'one and a half' width tiles are normally placed every

other course to achieve a neat finish at the edges, and at the eaves shorter eaves tiles are used. Tiles around the perimeter of the roof now need to be twice nailed or clipped, and elsewhere should have at least one nail fixing (BS:5534).

Should tiles need to be cut in order for a row to fit neatly, the trimmed tile is usually placed in the next-to-last position along the row rather than at the end, so the outer tile doesn't have a cut edge exposed at the side. Subsequent rows above are fixed with staggered joints lapped according to the manufacturers' guidance.

But whatever type of tiles or slates you choose, the amount of lap is generally less on a steep roof (of more than about 45°) because the rain will run off more quickly. However, lower down near the eaves, the pitch is sometimes made shallower (with 'sprocket eaves') in order to slow the rainwater for a safe landing into the gutter. Conversely, on very shallow roofs the rainwater runs slower and tends to 'fan out' dispersing at an angle, getting drawn upwards and sideways by 'capillary action'. So a greater headlap and sidelap are needed to stop it seeping under the edges.

Another problem with modest slopes and exposed sites is that the flatter the roof pitch, the more risk there is of 'wind uplift' allowing wind-driven rain to penetrate under tiles – an additional reason for a greater lap. It's important to ensure that the correct size and type of tile has been selected for the angle of pitch and laid to the correct lap, or else rainwater may well track-back underneath. Manufacturers can provide comprehensive information. To top it all off neatly, special purpose-made tiles are also available for ridges, hips and verges.

Blending in

Most of us don't want our new extensions to stick out like a Las Vegas casino Heliport. But getting a new roof to blend in naturally with an old one requires a fair bit of care and thought, especially when building to the front of the house. Nothing is guaranteed to make your extension look more glaringly obvious than vast expanses of shiny new roof tiles sitting self-consciously next to the mature, subtly shaded and weathered old roof. But how to instantly tone down those dazzling, bright new tiles?

There are those who claim that the natural weathering process can be speeded up by spraying your new roof

tiles with liquid fertiliser. These are probably the same people who swear by other slightly dubious instant-ageing concepts, such as painting fresh stonework with organic yoghurt to help it 'acclimatise', or coating new brickwork with boiling linseed oil for a supposedly better match with old walls. Fortunately, if you prefer not to become the laughing stock of the entire neighbourhood, there's a more reliable solution. Because achieving exact colour matches using new tiles can be an impossible task, one obvious remedy is to instead use matching old ones. You might well ask 'Where do I find those?' Easy – by simply stripping a suitable number of tiles or slates from your existing rear roof slope, the front can be clad to perfection, the less visible rear roof slope then being re-clad with the gleaming new coverings. You'll be amazed at the results.

If using reclaimed materials from your own house or from any other source, always be sure to remove any broken, cracked or frost damaged tiles or slates. Alternatively, if you find that your old roof is actually on the way out it may be cost-effective to carry out a complete re-roofing job, as much of the necessary labour and scaffolding will already be on site.

Slates or tiles?

Tiles, in all their many varieties and styles, comprise the majority of British roof coverings. A quick zoom back in time a couple of centuries would find many roofs clad with handmade plain clay tiles secured with small timber pegs

(known as 'peg tiles'). In Victorian times lightweight natural slate roofs became pretty much universal, until manufactured plain clay tiles with projecting 'nibs' (that simply hooked over the battens) took centre stage later in the century, persisting through the Edwardian era and into the 1930s as the roof covering of choice. The advent of cheaper manufactured concrete tiles and easy-to-lay interlocking tiles has ensured their continuing popularity in more recent years. Today, natural slate and clay tiles are relatively expensive, and similar looking cheaper alternatives such as artificial slate are widely used. The problem with some concrete tiles is that after about 10 years they can start to look rather washed out – one reason you never find them in salvage yards. However some are now manufactured 'through coloured' to resist discoloration. Clay is more expensive than concrete, but it's often worth paying the extra for a quality product. The dearest coverings tend to be stone slates, natural Welsh slate, handmade clay tiles and thatch.

Less common types of hip covering: Bonnet tiles (above left) and purpose-made corner tiles (above right).

Ridge and hip tiles

The most exposed part of the roof is at the very top – at the ridge. This therefore needs to be well protected and waterproofed, which is traditionally done by being capped with special half-round or angled ridge tiles bedded in mortar. Hipped roofs have similar hip tiles laid along both 'corners' of the side roof slope. However, over the years the bedding mortar can become loose, allowing storms to dislodge them – and being hit by a flying ridge tile is no joke. Modern 'dry-ridge' tiles have overcome this problem by using special screws and fixing wires that tie them to the ridge timbers below (now required by BS:5544); traditional mortar can still be used when accompanied by a mechanical fixing to help anchor them. Some incorporate vents to enhance airflow within the loft space.

If you're of an artistic persuasion, this could be the perfect opportunity to embellish your design – by topping off the roof with an antique cast iron finial or a glorious terracotta crest. Salvage yards may stock some irresistible reclaimed items.

Verges

The verges are the projecting edges of roof slopes found above triangular gable end walls (or lean-to roofs). They typically project about 60mm or so over the wall, the end roof tiles being tilted up slightly in order to keep rainwater away from the edges. This is achieved by wedging purpose-made 150mm wide strips of fibre-cement boards (known as an 'undercloak') below the batten ends (spare tiles or slates or are also sometimes used).

The verges are traditionally pointed up with mortar and often decorated with a wooden bargeboard fixed underneath or perhaps some fancy 'dog's tooth' brickwork. However, the exposed mortar pointing often develops cracks

Below left: Tiling upwards and inwards from roof edges
Below right: Traditional pointing up of verges

or erodes over time. A modern 'dry-fix' alternative uses plastic cover strips secured with clips, or special one-piece tiles called 'cloaked verges' that wrap over the edges. The only snag is that modern maintenance-free materials can look architecturally inappropriate (ie a bit naff) on extensions to older buildings. However BS:5544 now requires mechanically dry-fixed verges.

To achieve a neat finish at the verges, the rows of tiles at the edges require specially wide 'tile-and-a-half' tiles on every other row. Similarly, to complete the roof at the bottom edge along the eaves, shorter 'eaves tiles' are used. These bottom rows of tiles are covered by the overlapping ones above, and sometimes raised ('kicked up') with tapered wooden fillets fixed over the joist ends, in order to slow the speed of rainwater.

The roofline – eaves, fascias, soffits and bargeboards

The term 'roofline' refers to the detailing at the edges of roofs – *ie* at the feet of the rafters and at the verges.

There's no question that the external walls of a building are better protected from the weather if there's a certain amount of roof overhang, and this presents an interesting architectural opportunity to give the building some real character. So at the design stage, quite a bit of thought will have gone into choosing one of the various possible decorative facings around the roof's perimeter. The style that you finally plump for here will have a marked effect on the final appearance of your extension.

Fascia boards are horizontal boards of timber or UPVC that run along the eaves at the feet of the rafters, or they may sometimes be fixed directly to the brickwork. Normally the rafter feet project out beyond the main walls, so the roof overhangs the walls by between 50 and 200mm. The most widely adopted standard eaves style in housing since the 1930s has been 'box eaves'. Here, a traditional fascia board is fixed along the ends of the projecting rafters, in turn supporting the guttering. This leaves a gap underneath which is filled with a strip

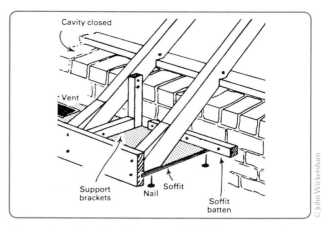

The overhang offered by a box eaves design helps to protect the brickwork below.

of plywood or fibre-cement board forming a box shape, hence the name. This narrow ceiling or 'soffit' closes off this entrance to the roof void, yet provides ventilation, usually with integral grilles or small vents fitted at intervals.

Today, however, there's a distinct preference for more traditional eaves methods. So you may instead opt for your projecting rafter feet to be left quite naked, and not to be boxed-in at all. Consequently, in order to prevent a mass influx of birds, wasps and creepy crawlies into your loft, the bricklayer will need to fill any gaps between the rafter feet on top of the wall, and any necessary loft ventilation must be provided with insect-proof wire mesh. Sheets of plywood are laid over the lower rafters extending at least a metre up the slope. The projecting rafters at this stage will be too long and need to be cut back, so consider what length looks right and synchronise it with the tiling and guttering. Once painted or stained the gutter brackets can be fixed direct to the rafter feet.

There's another traditional eaves style that can also create a roof overhang without the need for any timber fascia boarding. If you're adding on to a Victorian house, you may want to match the decorative brickwork eaves. Here the upper wall brickwork is 'corbelled' in a projecting pattern, perhaps with protruding bricks alternately stepped outwards.

Bargeboards are similar to fascias, but instead run along the edges of gable roofs, under the verges. Once again you're confronted with various options. Most modern houses simply leave the plain pointed up verges projecting over the wall, although the brickwork detailing below needs to be very carefully finished. Some designs may better suit fancy 'Victorian' brick corbelling under the verges, as described above. Otherwise simple bargeboards fixed to the brickwork can look just right. Or you might want to make a bold

Below left: Traditional exposed rafter feet eaves with brick infill, but needs ventilation gap.
Below right: Conventional box eaves in uPVC with ready-made vents.

Right: Timber strip to make slope shallower at eaves to slow rainwater

Timber frame 'ladder' projects over gable end to create roof overhang

design statement and build your roof verges projecting assertively over the gable end wall with big overhanging 'Edwardian' bargeboards. If so, you'll first need to answer an important technical question; namely, how do you prevent the overhang drooping and sagging under the weight of the tiles? Fortunately the Edwardians had a ready answer, which was to build a gable 'ladder'.

When the overhang reaches more than about 150mm the structure needs beefing up, so to extend the roof outwards rows of timber noggins are placed across the gable end wall like rungs in a ladder. On the inside, these are fixed to the end rafter, and on the outside to the new

Above: Traditional decorative brickwork courses under verges
Below left: Timber bargeboards under verges
Below right: Cement fibre undercloak tucked under battens to raise edge slightly

outermost external rafter. The decorative bargeboards can then be fixed to this outer rafter.

Fascias and bargeboards are commonly made from 25mm thick timber. When extending an older property timber is normally the best choice architecturally. But exposed or unprotected roof timbers need regular decorative weather protection to stop them rotting and to preserve their appearance. So builders will often fit 'maintenance-free' uPVC fascias, bargeboards and soffits secured with special stainless steel fixing nails, which can be disguised with small coloured plastic caps to match the colour of the board (usually white). Resin-based fibreboard is also a popular choice. If you don't like decorating but want the look of real wood, then red cedar is a more expensive compromise since it is naturally weather resistant and doesn't require painting or staining. Or engineered timbers such as Accoya are extremely durable.

Dormer windows

Rooms built into roof spaces often have small 'cottage' dormer windows projecting through the roof slopes. Dormers can be set back slightly, with the timber frame structure built up from the rafters or floor joists with a framework of upright timber studs. Alternatively, they can be built straight up from the wall below, Victorian style. The dormer sides are known as 'cheeks' and are traditionally clad in materials like lead sheet, timber boarding, or are sometimes rendered or hung with tiles. At the junctions to the roof it's common to have 'soakers' hidden under the tiles. Like valleys, these 'secret gutters' are formed from strips of sheet lead.

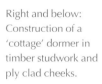

Right and below: Construction of a 'cottage' dormer in timber studwork and ply clad cheeks.

Tapered timber 'firrings' fixed above horizontal joists create the required roof fall.

Flat roofs

If you fancy the idea of stepping out of your bedroom on sunny mornings to enjoy a spot of breakfast on your private roof terrace, then a flat roof might be just what's needed to enhance your lifestyle. Assuming the planners haven't already torpedoed such an idea, there are however some key differences between building a standard flat roof and one that's 'habitable'. To be fit for purpose, the designer will need to carefully consider matters like the type of surface treatment, the strength of the supporting structure, and how best to stop friends and family plummeting off the edges.

Flat roofs are, of course, not actually flat. By definition, anything up to about a 12° pitch counts as flat. They need to be built with a decent 'fall' because the slow rate at which rainwater discharges from the surface poses a greater threat to this type of roof than to a pitched one. The steeper the slope, the greater the self-cleansing effect as rainwater passes over its surface. The Building Regulations encourage a fall of 1:40 or steeper (the minimum permissible is 1:80), but that hasn't stopped some roofers actually building them totally flat. If built correctly however, rainwater should discharge efficiently into the gutters without stopping en route to cause damaging 'ponding' on the surface.

Hitting the deck

Flat roofs have had something of a bad press in recent years. Lifespans can be alarmingly short, often only 10 to 15 years.

But if built with care, using the correct materials, they can perform perfectly well. Construction involves two main elements – the supporting structure, and a protective covering.

When building a new flat roof structure, the joists spanning from wall to wall are actually set perfectly level, so that the ceiling below will also be level. To create the required fall for the decking, tapered strips of timber the same width as the joists, called 'firrings', are nailed along the tops of the joists (timber merchants can supply firrings cut to the correct fall).

But before ordering your roof joists, you first need to consider the required size, grade and length (which should already be specified in your plans). Common joist sizes are 200 x 50mm, 175 x 50mm, and 150 x 50mm. But here, as elsewhere, manufactured I-joists are starting to replace traditional softwood.

Where a new flat roofed extension (normally single storey) meets the existing house, a horizontal timber wall plate is first bolted to the wall of the house. Metal joist hangers can then be nailed to this wall plate, and the ceiling joists slotted in to the hangers (or supported by the wall plate). The joists will span to the outer wall of the extension, normally spaced apart at either 400mm or 600mm centres. The precise dimensions of joists and their respective spacings will have been calculated according to the loads imposed on them. As with pitched roofs, the support structure joists rest on timber wall plates on the tops of the main walls.

To complete the structure, a deck of 18mm or 25mm thick marine grade plywood or OSB3 is then laid over the joists and secured with screws or galvanised nails. Ordinary chipboard is not recommended as it can disintegrate when damp. If there's any delay at this stage make sure it's protected from rain with temporary sheeting. A polythene vapour control layer (min 1000 gauge) should fully cover the deck. Next the rigid insulation boards are placed on top (typically PUR, around 100mm thick or as required to achieve min U-value of 0.18). Although the roof covering can then be laid directly on top of the insulation, it's better to cap the 'sandwich' by

Below left: Roof joists with tapered firrings 1:40 slope.
Below centre: 18mm OSB deck covered with vapour barrier and 100mm rigid insulation.
Below right: 9mm ply top deck over insulation ready for covering.

boarding over the insulation with a top layer of 9mm OSB3 or 12mm plywood secured with long screws to the joists or deck beneath. Finally, the roof covering, such as EPDM synthetic rubber or mineral felt, can be laid on top. Upstands at adjoining walls need particular care to prevent leaks and should be overlapped with flashings. To keep rainwater from spilling over the edges, the sides of the roof surface can be built up slightly with triangular pieces of timber called 'tilt fillets' nailed to the edges of the decking, except, of course, for the lowest edge by the guttering.

Coverings

When specifying flat roof coverings, the designer will need to consider key factors such as whether anyone is likely to be walking on the structure, as well as taking account of the direction the property faces, since south-facing roofs are more likely to fail early. One major reason for flat roofs having short lifespans is the sun's intense heat on dark surfaces, effectively cooking it in summer and freezing in winter. The continual expansion and contraction this causes is very damaging.

Historically, flat roofs (including the timber decks of sailing ships) were waterproofed using asphalt, a black, gooey, bitumen-based substance. It occurs naturally in liquid form (in asphalt lakes etc) or can be distilled from some types of limestone rocks and shale, or manufactured from petroleum distillation. Tar is a compound with similar properties produced by the distillation of coal or wood (or cigarettes). Today the cheapest and most common covering material for domestic flat roofs is mineral felt. This was traditionally laid in triple layers bonded together and to the deck with hot bitumen tar, and a solar-reflective covering applied to the surface for protection against damaging ultraviolet radiation. However modern 'torch on' roofing felt (see boxout) comprising two or three layers of high-performance glass-reinforced polyester, doesn't need to be covered with mineral chippings or solar-reflective paint. Synthetic rubber sheeting is dearer than felt but longer lasting.

If your extension design means that people are going to be stomping around on the roof, the surface layer will need to be formed from a hard-wearing material. Rather than traditional asphalt, purpose-made, 'promenade' paving slabs are now widely used; these are designed to be light but strong, often made from composite glass reinforced concrete (GRC) or in the form of interlocking rubber tiles. These

are normally placed above small raised supports to allow rainwater to disperse invisibly away under the paving, along the waterproof sub-surface.

Other materials traditionally used for covering flat roofs include metals such as lead, zinc and copper which provide a more durable, if more expensive, solution. Of these, lead is the most realistic for home extensions, being less expensive than copper and more durable than zinc, lasting 100 years or more.

Lead sheet with plenty of 'rolls'.

In today's metric world it's heartening to find that lead is still specified traditionally in pounds per square foot, varying from 3 to 8 psf (Code 3 to Code 8). The higher the code number, the thicker and more durable it should be. Code 4 lead is the one builders tend to use unless instructed otherwise. Flashings should typically be made of Code 4 or 5 lead (1.8mm or 2.24mm thick). Flat roofs and valley gutters need to be of heavier Code 6 lead (2.65mm thick) or higher.

However, lead is notoriously prone to expansion in hot weather, so any large areas without expansion joints will eventually cause splits and buckling. Expansion cracking can be prevented by building in expansion joints known as 'rolls' and 'drips'. Rolls are formed from a strip of lead wrapped around a wooden pole (like a broom handle) running parallel to the direction of roof slope. Drips are basically steps in the flat roof covered with overlapping sheets. Individual sheets should not exceed about 2.25m length between drips and 675mm width between joints or rolls. Lead is also prone to 'creep' – extremely slow movement downhill – so the roof pitch or fall needs to be laid just right, between 25–60mm per 2.25m run. At joints with walls, the sheets should be turned up and lapped over by a separate lead flashing.

Insulation

To comply with the Building Regulations, flat roofs over habitable rooms must include thermal insulation. Traditionally there have been two methods of insulating the roof – a 'warm' or a 'cold' roof – depending on exactly where you place the insulation. Today, however, 'cold roofs' are banned in Scotland and are frowned upon in the rest of Britain.

So the obvious choice is to build a warm roof, which is the simpler option anyway. Here purpose-made rigid foam insulation boards are placed on top of the deck protected with a vapour control layer of polythene sheeting, as described on the previous page. This is far more efficient than the old 'cold roof' method, which involved placing loft insulation above the ceiling leaving a ventilated air space above, like in a conventional loft.

With warm roofs it's not the end of the world if a little moist, warm air from the room below percolates up through the plasterboard into the void between the ceiling joists because there's no cold surface for it to condense

Flat Roof Coverings

Torch-on felt

Traditional 'pour and roll' felt has now been replaced by modern hot flame applied torch-on felt, made from a more reliable material with a more robust finish. Applied hot in 2 or 3 layers, this is normally the cheapest option. Construction usually consists of a vapour control layer, then 2mm reinforced felt plus a 4mm top layer 'cap sheet'. The surface is finished either in black bitumen or coloured mineral fleck.

Pros: Cheap to buy, quick to install, cost around £50/m^2 fitted

Cons: Relatively short lifespan, although some have 20 year guarantees

EPDM rubberised roofing

Widely used and relatively easy to install, comes in cut-to-measure synthetic rubber rolls with its own flashing strips. Usually bonded to the substrate with adhesive.

Pros: Installed in one single layer so no joins and less risk of leaks. Light, durable, expands and contracts easily, so ideal for larger roofs expanses. Should last at least 30 years.

Cons: Can look wrinkled if done badly. More expensive than felt at around £80/m2 fitted.

PVC single ply membranes

Fitted by approved installers, well known PVC roofing brands include *Sarnafill* and *Bauder*. Like EPDM is glued directly to substrate base.

Pros: Good longevity around 50 years. Longer guarantees than EPDM. Can be shaped easily. Some mimic appearance of metal.

Cons: Can look wrinkled if done badly, more expensive than EPDM

Fibreglass GRP

Liquid fibreglass can be laid wet and built up with matting. Most are laid in one layer.

Pros: Suits complex roof shapes, very resistant to damage, 25 year guarantee. Can be coloured.

Cons: Not as flexible as EDPM or felt, so may not suit some very large roofs with greater expansion. More expensive than single ply or felt at around £90/m^2 fitted.

Metal

Metal cladding is a superior traditional covering – in lead, zinc, copper, steel or aluminium.
Suits roofs with a shallower pitch (e.g. around 5 degrees for zinc).

Pros: Very long lasting (think church roofs), fire-proof, low maintenance, good looking

Cons: Expensive

Mastic asphalt

Potentially one of the longest lasting materials, used under roof terraces that are walked over, as a base layer beneath paving slabs.

Green roofs

Plant based 'living roofs' can look wonderful, but are complex to construct. A root barrier is needed to stop roots interacting with the waterproofing beneath, plus a drainage layer to retain water and edging features to stop vegetation leaking away.

Pros: Positive impact on appearance, good for absorbing rainwater run-off.

Cons: Very heavy so structure needs reinforcing, high maintenance, very expensive.

---

against (although some degree of ventilation is still considered desirable).

If you're feeling really lazy, for smaller extensions you can buy ready-made 'composite' decking that combines a triple sandwich of plywood, insulation and felt covering all bonded into one.

Single sheet of EPDM rubber sheeting glued to ply top deck

Joining it up

The biggest weak point on flat roofs is normally where the roof meets a wall, typically to the main house. Here the roofing felt should be dressed at least 150mm up the wall (known as the 'upstand') and fixed into a chased out mortar joint and bedded in mortar. The sharpness of the 'corner' where the felt is folded up the wall is reduced by fitting a small strip of timber or plastic 'angle fillet' under the felt. Finally, a lead flashing cut into the wall above is dressed down over the joint, finishing no closer than 75mm above the roof surface. Any pipes or ducts passing through the roof are another point to watch, so the joints to any soil pipes or skylight roof windows poking through the surface must be carefully waterproofed.

Combination roofs

If you like the simplicity and economy of flat roofs, but don't like the way they look, don't despair. One way to disguise a flat roof is to hide it behind a small 'pretend' pitched roof.

Pair of small flat roofs inset into pitched roof allow light to windows.

Rainwater fittings

When the roof is complete, and whilst the scaffolding is still in place, it makes sense for the gutters to be fitted and the downpipes connected to the waiting surface water drain connections below. But first, the fascia boards or rafter feet that the gutter clips will be fixed to should be painted.

There's a wide variety of guttering on the market, and you'll probably have already considered the style that best suits the character of your extension. Most popular is good old half-round 112 x 52mm black PVC, which is relatively cheap and adequate for most purposes. But you could equally opt for traditional cast iron, or low-maintenance cast or extruded aluminium, galvanised or stainless steel, zinc or copper. You'll need to decide between the various shapes, such as deepflow (115 x 75mm), squareline, or period-style moulded, ogee or 'foundry finish' (in PVC but looks like cast iron). Not forgetting the choice of colours – black, white, grey, brown etc. And of course you'll need downpipes in compatible styles and materials.

But remember, your new guttering will normally need to match the existing system, so think carefully about compatibility before selecting your preferred choice of bright orange extruded aluminium. Given safe access, installing a rainwater system should be a relatively simple task – see box.

The Building Regulations stipulate that rainwater systems (*ie* your gutters, downpipes and gullies) should be able to cope with at least 75mm of rainfall per hour – in other words, they have to be capable of putting away a full 3 inches per 60 minutes. This means making sure your gutters are carefully fitted so that they're fully supported by brackets and don't sag, and are set to the correct falls. They must also be served by sufficient downpipes so rainwater will glide smoothly away. It's worth noting that dormer windows, unless set well back, tend to cause complications with the rainwater system, often needing a separate gutter and pipes either side.

One possible downside of having swish new guttering is that it could make the adjoining old fittings on the main house look less than impressive, not to say embarrassingly outmoded. In which case you may decide to go the whole hog and fit new replacements all around the house. Otherwise, it may prove a little tricky connecting up the new guttering with the decrepit old stuff, although universal adapters are available. If the extension is built right up to the neighbour's boundary, and your gutters overhang next door, you might also want to check your legal rights of access for routine maintenance and cleaning out. Finally, when it comes to buying guttering, try to stick with one brand because, frustratingly, different manufacturers seem to design their products to be incompatible with others despite being the the same nominal size and type.

Note that intricate details of rainwater fittings can be found in Haynes *The Victorian House Manual* and *The 1930s House Manual*.

With such 'false hip' roofs, the visible lower part is built as an apparently normal pitched roof, but the upper central part that you can't see from ground level is actually flat.

Designing a single-storey rear extension can be tricky because a lean-to pitched roof may cover the existing bedroom windows. One solution is to go ahead with the pitched roof, but cut away the parts outside the upstairs windows, instead building them flat. So you basically have a mini flat roof outside each window within the overall pitched design.

EPDM rubber roofing lapped up around roof lights and under adjoining tiles.

Another solution is to build a roof that defies description either as flat or pitched. Actually it's a lean-to roof of an extraordinarily shallow pitch of around 10°. But instead of being covered in cheap felt, it could be clad in fabulous, long-lasting leadwork. This is a good compromise, being shallow enough to allow freedom at window level, yet steep enough to look attractive and to efficiently disperse rainwater.

Left: Dormers need downpipes either side.
Below left: Swan neck bend.
Below: Downpipe connected to underground system.

Installing a rainwater system – key stages

■ Guttering needs to be laid to a slight slope (fall) so rainwater will run along it and disperse easily. Aim for a fall of about 10mm for each 3m run of guttering.

■ If there's a fascia board, make sure the board is perfectly level so that you can use it as a guide for setting the gutter fall.

■ Start at the highest point of the run, marking the position of the clip, and do the same at the lowest point by the downpipe. Run a string between the two marks to get the right fall.

■ Gutter brackets can be screwed to the fascia. Where there's no fascia board, special brackets are available for fixing to rafter feet, or into the brickwork. Brackets should be fixed about 900mm apart, closer where there are junctions to bays etc.

■ At their lowest point, the gutters should be no more than about 50mm below the edge of the tiles. Also at the bottom edge of the roof the membrane underlay should lap down into the gutters (to guide rainwater) – so don't trim it back. Some roofers prefer to fit more durable strips of plastic DPC here.

■ Assemble the sections of guttering and fit them to the brackets, connecting up corners and stop ends etc.

■ Connect the gutters to outlets, bends and downpipes. Because the eaves normally project out, overhanging the wall below, upper downpipes often need a 'swan neck' double bend to bring them back near the main wall. This may also be needed again lower down the wall if the upper wall projects out with tiles or timber cladding.

■ Plastic downpipes should simply slot together, requiring support-brackets every 2m or closer.

■ At their base, the downpipes will either discharge over a gulley or connect directly into the underground drainage system, ideally via back inlet gullies (for easy clearing of blockages).

Chimneys

Most home extensions don't have chimneys. But if your existing home doesn't have the benefit of a fireplace, or you have your heart set on a fabulous showpiece living room, it might be worth constructing one or installing a woodburning stove.

Fireplaces and flues

Although it's a lot of extra work and expense, a new fireplace can transform an ordinary extension into something quite extraordinary. Far be it for us to try and dictate taste, but if you don't want run-of-the-mill pseudo-Victorian, you could cause a stir by fitting a cool Art-Deco fireplace, or perhaps a surreal living 'flame and stone' contemporary feature.

But the decision on whether or not to include a fireplace needs to be made at the design stage, since the foundations may need to accommodate a large external chimney breast, especially if you're tempted to build a massive inglenook cottage fireplace. The chimney breast and flue can be constructed at the same time as the walls. Alternatively, some modern living flame gas fires only require a balanced flue through the wall (similarly to wall-mounted boilers). But the major drawback with conventional fireplaces is that around 75% of the heat disappears straight up the chimney, so a installing a modern stove will be far more effective at room heating. Note that in many urban areas if you plan to burn wood or coal you may be legally restricted to using 'clean' fuels.

Building a new fireplace will normally necessitate the insertion of extra air vents in the walls. This is because air for combustion is drawn from the room's atmosphere, and an open fire needs at least six changes of air in the room per hour to burn well. In fact you need an astounding $110m^3$ of air supply per hour for rooms harbouring any kind of solid fuel appliance.

New stacks and chimney breasts can be built incorporating ready-made concrete flue liners inserted section by section. These liners are easy to construct, being simply pieced together and the joints sealed with special fire-cement. The resulting space between the liner units and the surrounding brickwork is then back-filled with a weak mortar mix.

At chimney pot level, there are a

Photo: eddystoneselfbuild.co.uk

Photo: capitalfireplaces.co.uk

Above: Concrete flue liners built within new external chimney breast (right) serving inglenook fireplace

Below: Stainless steel twinwall flue for woodburning stove. Regulations on roof exit positions very restrictive. Internal flues need clear 50mm safety space around.

whole range of caps, cowls and hoods available to protect flues and stop rain from pouring down. Specialist advice is useful here, as the wrong choice of cap may affect the way the fire draws, causing it to smoke.

Detailed advice about stacks, flues and fireplaces can be found in Haynes' *The Victorian House Manual* and *The 1930s House Manual*.

Woodburning stoves

Installing a woodburning stove is a very popular option, because they look good and give off incredible warmth. The fun part is choosing from a huge choice of designs, ranging from traditional Olde-Worlde cast iron through to super modern curved glass woodburners hung from walls, some featuring 3 glazed sides to optimise the view of the fire. On a more practical note, stoves can achieve over 80% efficiency (ie how much heat energy is produced for the amount of fuel put in). Heat output is measured in kW, as it is for boilers.

Stoves and flues must be fitted by a HETAS registered engineer, and Building Control will want to see their

Good chimney design

Stacks should be built so that rain driving against them in severe weather is dispersed, to prevent damp in the structure below. Some good design features are:

- The chimney should terminate at least 900mm above the main roof ridge to avoid turbulence, downdraughts and 'smoke blow back'.
- Lead flashings should protect the joint where the stack meets the roof, around the base. Flashings are fixed into a mortar joint in the chimney brickwork about 150mm above the level of the roof covering. They should be embedded at least 25mm into the masonry, fixed in place with metal wedges, and sealed with mortar.
- The top brick courses should project about 30mm so they overhang to throw rainwater clear of the main stack. The flaunching (the big lump of mortar at the base of the pots) should slope outwards.
- To prevent water soaking through the masonry and down into the roof structure there should be a damp-proof course (DPC) through the chimney approximately 150mm above the roof, and another one below the brickwork head.

Woodburning stoves – key decisions

Location

Stoves can't be plonked down just anywhere in the home. For example Building Regs prohibit them within kitchens. You can install it *near* the kitchen but the stove may need a ducted external air supply so that the cooker extractor fan doesn't impact on airflow to the stove. The main restriction on the stove location is determined by where you can run the flue out of the roof or walls.

Fire-prevention is a major consideration so it's important to leave space around the stove to allow room for air to circulate. The recommended minimum is 150mm either side of stove. There must also be at least 300mm of non-combustible material in front of stoves to act as a hearth.

What size of stove?

It can be tempting to opt for a stove with a large output. However stoves work best operating at higher temperatures, close to maximum output. So too large a stove could find you constantly having to cut the air supply to dampen it down and cool off.

A useful rule of thumb to determine the optimum size is to first calculate your room size in cubic metres (LxWxH). For example a 5m long x 5m wide room with a standard 2.4m ceiling height would be 60m3. Then divide by 20 (this assumes fully insulated newbuild construction). So here the stove heat output would be 3 kW (before deducting the output of any radiators). Another reason for not buying

one that's unnecessarily big is that cast iron stoves are incredibly heavy. But it's also worth considering the maximum length of logs your chosen stove can hold.

Technical features

The latest stoves have the option of external air supply connection (like boilers), so only air from outside the house is used for combustion, not air from the room. This should prevent you having to knock air vents through the walls to keep Building Control happy. Most stoves have an 'air-wash' feature to help keep door glass clean and clear. Here pre-heated air is introduced at the top of the fire and flushed down the inside surface of the door glass. This passage of hot air keeps the glass clear of soot and smoke, reducing cleaning. In smokeless zones you will need a 'clean burning' DEFRA-approved appliance with reduced emissions.

Maintenance

Modern wood burning stoves need very little cleaning due to the complete combustion of the wood which leaves minimal ash. Sweeping the chimney or flue periodically is recommended to keep it clear, and also visually checking seals and grates. If it's burning properly there should just be a small amount of dry dust on the door glass that can be wiped off with a paper towel when cool. It also helps to ensure the wood you burn has been properly dried, ideally with moisture content under 20% (logs can take a year to season).

installation certificate to prove it's safe, along with a fitted CO detector. A mid range stove is likely to cost around £1k (excluding fitting) plus the same again for the flue. Stainless steel 'twin wall' flues can either be run externally up the outer wall or internally through the roof structure (either freestanding or encased in a new chimney breast and brick stack). But the rules on where you can stick steel flues through roofs are very restrictive (e.g. there must be at least 2.3m between the flue and any bedroom windows - see website). So the position of the flue needs to be decided at the outset, otherwise you may end up with monster exhaust pipe running all the way up the side of your home looking rather like a chip shop! This will also have a bearing on where you can position the stove internally.

And finally...

When the roofers have all finished, the rainwater fittings are in place, and the carpenters have completed all the eaves and bargeboard details, the scaffolding may no longer be required.

But don't be too hasty. The 'snagging' process (see page 256) may yet reveal defects at roof level, such as leaking skylights, loose flashings, or leaking gutter joints.

Also, fitting upstairs windows and decorating the external joinery will be a lot easier whilst direct access is still possible. So hang on to the scaffolding while you can.

Main trades needed on site

- **Roof tilers:** *Included* – laying breather membrane underlay, battens and tiles, forming valleys and bedding ridge tiles and pointing up verges. Most will also do small amounts of leadwork, like fixing valley linings and lead flashings, but work to flat roofs and large valleys is a specialist trade.
- **Felt roofers:** *Not included* – inserting cavity trays or fitting lead flashings.
- **Carpenters:** *Included* – building the roof structure, except for battens which are fixed by the roofers, cutting and fixing timbers to form valleys, stripping existing tiles from the old roof where the new roof will join it. Fitting fascias and soffits. Fitting the guttering is *not included*, unless specified.
- **Bricklayers:** Building up gable ends walls after the carpenter has fitted the rafters.

www.home-extension.co.uk

13 BREAKING THROUGH AND INTERNAL WORKS

Well that's all the big stuff done. But before officially pronouncing the building 'weathertight', it might be wise to wait until the first rainy spell has passed without the need to erect umbrellas indoors. Roof leaks tend to manifest themselves fairly swiftly.

Next comes one of the messiest parts of the entire project – the moment of truth when the building work comes crashing into your private life.

What used to be your garden will now be looking like a war zone, but it no longer needs to. Surplus materials should be removed, and drain runs covered up. This will help set the scene for the next phase. As the internal works start to take shape, you should finally begin to see the fruits of your labour.

But first it's worth taking a few moments to sit down with the contractor and assess whether the programme is realistically still on course for the agreed completion date. Your timetable may need to be amended if, for example, unusually vile weather has held up progress. The good news is that from now on bad weather can no longer be an excuse for delays, as the remaining work will be largely indoors. It's also a good time to take stock of your finances, particularly if there have been any 'extras'. So get your calculator out and update all those overly optimistic projected expenditure figures.

Looking back to the design stage, you may have included some approximate figures in the specification for things like kitchen units and bathroom fittings if the prices weren't known at the time. Although a useful way of buying yourself some time early on in the project, there inevitably comes a day of reckoning, and you'll now need to firm up any such estimated costs. Right now, it's especially important to check if any potentially crippling delivery delays are in the pipeline for big ticket items on order, like glazing and kitchen appliances. High value items need to be delivered in good time so as not to delay things, yet not too early because of the risk of theft.

Mineral wool provides effective acoustic insulation in stud walls

The masterplan

From now on there'll be a bewildering number of trades buzzing around the site, hopefully not getting under each other's feet. As a result it can be fairly easy to lose track of precisely who's supposed to be doing what, and when they're meant to be doing it. Some events are time-critical and must be done in the correct order, some less so. A rough guide to the order of internal works would be as follows:

- External doors, windows and glazing fitted & protected.
- Breaking through.
- Upper floors boarded.
- Internal partition walls.
- First fix – plumbing, heating, electrics.
- Plasterboard ceilings and walls.
- Plastering and ground floor screed.
- Second fix – plumbing and bathroom fittings, heating and electrics.
- Second fix internal joinery – doors, skirting, kitchen units, architraves, floor coverings.
- Loft insulation.
- Tiling, painting and decorating, external finishing.

One of the busiest trades at this stage will be the chippie, fresh from earlier triumphs building the roof structure and fitting floor joists. He'll shortly need to start installing the windows and doors, if not already in place, followed by construction of internal stud walls, and fixing floorboards and door linings. Unlike most other trades, the chippie's work is spread over much of the build and isn't always rigidly programmed. There are also a couple of internal joinery jobs that may possibly be required, such as preparing loft hatch openings and, in some extensions, installing the staircase. The more intricate joinery works will be left until all the plastering and floor screeding is complete.

When all the windows and external doors are fully fitted, and the extension is secure, it's time for another milestone in your build. One of the messiest parts of the entire project is about to commence – breaking through the wall between the new building and your home.

Of course, it helps if your builder has bothered to run this past you in advance, rather than for example finding your viewing of *Coronation Street* rudely interrupted by a giant demolition ball. It's surprising how often otherwise good client–builder relationships are suddenly ruined at this stage, causing simmering grievances to flare up into outright warfare. So it pays to plan this highly intrusive phase carefully, so your home and loved ones don't get caked in dust and debris, spoiling an otherwise professional job.

External doors, windows and glazing

Until now, the builders may have managed to get in and out of the extension via an ingenious temporary door knocked up out of a bit of old plywood screwed to the door frame. However, before your home is opened up to the extension you'll want the reassurance of decent security, in the form of a robust new entrance door. On the other hand, you don't want your expensive new portal to be hideously scarred by paint and plaster splashes or damaged by trades coming and going. So once hung, be sure to retain the protective plastic coverings until completion.

We covered the installation of windows and doors in Chapter 10, because some builders will want to install the frames as the main walls are built, rather than using templates, but for most projects it's a safer option to wait at least until all the major roof works are done, to minimise the risk of damage.

Most external timber doors are of the traditional 44mm thick solid timber panelled variety. Hardwood is still the most popular choice. Cheap flush doors with a plywood finish over a lightweight frame are best avoided. But whether you opt for timber or UPVC, you'll normally want to match the style of the other doors on the rest of the house. Having said that, you might want to add a bit of 'cottagey' character, perhaps with a split top-and-bottom opening stable door to the rear or side of the house. Fitting brand new doors and frames is always a lot simpler than messing about with peculiar-sized ancient items salvaged from reclamation yards.

Regular viewers of Channel 4's *Grand Designs* may have noticed that one of the most common reasons for

disastrous delays is the late delivery of the windows and glazing. This may have something to do with the fact that the architect specified a unique triple-glazed design, hand-crafted in Iceland from titanium alloy. But the point is that by placing your window order early you should hopefully avoid holding up the entire project further down the line.

The days of messing about with putty and metal 'sprigs' to fix a bit of ill-cut glass into its frame are, thankfully, now long gone. Windows are normally supplied with factory pre-fitted double-glazed sealed units able to meet or beat the Building Regulations heat loss target of 1.6 W/m²K (or min WER band C). Obscured glass will be needed for bathroom and cloakroom windows, and safety glass for any at low level. However, for custom-made windows the services of professional glaziers may still be required.

Breaking through

Knocking an opening through the wall of your house directly into your living space obviously won't do a lot for dust allergy sufferers in the family. So before work starts, it's essential to protect furnishings and floors with sheets and to close off the doors to the rest of the house.

The least messy way of breaking through is to use an angle grinder to cut most of the way through the wall from the extension side. Then, when you're sure everything of value is protected, finish the job off from inside the house with a bolster and chisel, which makes less dust than using power tools. But unless your builders are advised of this approach, they'll automatically use the quickest method and blast straight through in one go.

Building a two-storey side extension can mean double trouble when it comes to knocking through. One of the all-time classic home extension mistakes may only become evident once the builders break through upstairs. The plan may have been to construct a door opening leading from the new side extension bedroom to your existing landing. But strange as it may sound, the somewhat inconvenient fact that the stairs are smack in the way can sometimes get overlooked! The Building Regulations don't allow new doorways to open straight out onto steps – for obvious

Above: Now you see it...
Below: ...now you don't.

reasons there must be a clear landing. This is the kind of problem you may encounter if the drawings and design stage are rushed, and if you don't get this right you can forget about Building Control issuing that all-important final certificate upon completion.

The job of breaking through and creating a new doorway will be considerably easier if you only need to adapt an old window by converting it into a full-height door opening. Simply cutting out the section of masonry below the window means there's no need to mess about fitting new lintels. But where a new, or wider, opening is necessary, structural work will be needed. Where beams are inserted into an existing wall it's vital that they're placed tightly so they firmly support the wall above to avoid cracking. This is achieved using props and packing under the ends with slate. Building Control will want to inspect this to ensure the work matches that shown on the approved plans and calculations.

'How I broke my neck' – unacceptable opening onto staircase.

Making an opening

The wall above must be supported temporarily while a slot is cut for the new lintel. This is done by first cutting holes about every 600mm just above the position of the proposed new lintel.

Steel or timber 'needles' of about 150mm x 50mm are then placed through these holes in the wall, and are supported each side by adjustable steel 'Acrow' props, in turn resting on thick scaffold planks placed on the ground to spread the load. (On weak timber floors, the joists must be checked first to improve support.) Be careful not to overtighten the props – they just need to support the wall, not jack it up!

The new lintel is inserted in the wall and must extend either side of the proposed new opening by at least 150mm. To spread the load, additional support will be needed under the ends of the lintel, usually in the form of concrete padstones or engineering bricks (specified by your structural engineer along with the type and strength of lintel or beam).

The lintel is bedded in mortar onto padstones at each end and the masonry above built up. The space between the top of the new lintel and the brickwork or blockwork above it must be packed with mortar. It's important that there's minimal shrinkage in this mortar as it dries out, otherwise the brickwork above will 'drop' onto the beam – a surprisingly common sight in the walls of houses where patio doors have been replaced. The solution is 'dry packing'. This is normally a 1:3 cement/sand mix which isn't actually dry, but is dampened with a small amount of water. The mix should be rammed hard into the space and allowed to dry for at least 24 hours before the props are removed.

The new opening below the lintel is marked out on the wall, then the plaster is chopped out vertically with a bolster and the masonry cut and removed. The side reveals (jambs) can later be made good with plaster. Alternatively a timber frame liner can be screwed to the reveal. Finally, the surrounding masonry and gaps to the floor are filled and levelled.

Internal walls

Before the electrician and plumber can start working their special magic, all the internal walls and floors should first be in place. As noted in Chapter 10, if your extension comprises two or more rooms then simple non-structural partition walls may be all that's needed to perform the basic task of divding up the space. If your internal walls are built of concrete blockwork, they'll probably have already been constructed by the bricklayer at the same time as the main walls. But internal walls built of timber studwork will now need to be erected – see below.

If you have an eye for interior design you might want to add a little glamour to your internal walls, perhaps in the form of glass blocks. These are best encased in a surrounding timber framework within the wall. But you don't need to go mad and glaze every square metre. Just one or two strategically placed blocks can do wonders to brighten an otherwise plain bathroom or kitchen.

Blockwork or studwork?

People generally tend to prefer 'solid walls' inside the house, perhaps because hanging stuff off them is easier. Non-structural walls made from concrete blocks can be built very rapidly and provide better sound insulation than stud walls. However they're normally confined to downstairs because movement in upstairs floor structures can cause cracking in relatively heavy brick or blockwork.

Structural walls

When it comes to load-bearing 'structural' internal walls, these are only likely to be needed in larger home extensions. In most cases where the floor joists only span up to 4 or 5 metres they shouldn't need any extra support. Load-bearing internal walls obviously play a key role holding up the building and the type of brick or block used to build them will therefore need to be specified by your structural engineer (so check that the builders aren't just using any old blocks they had left over!). These walls should be clearly shown on your drawings since they may need to support loads from the roof, floors and/or walls above, and hence need proper foundations. Even where they're not supporting anything above, they may play a structural role buttressing lengthy runs of main walls which typically need internal support every 7 metres. Internal door openings in load-bearing walls must employ lintels (usually the concrete beam or steel box variety).

Upstairs, it's no longer acceptable to build internal load-bearing walls out of blockwork supported on doubled up joists or timber beams because of shrinkage movement when drying out or deflection – both in the blocks themselves as well as the timber floor. However they can normally be supported on steel beams bedded in the main walls. Where you've got steel or timber beams supporting walls or floors above need fire protection by lining with pink 12.5mm fire-rated plasterboard with a skim plaster finish.

Load-bearing internal walls can sometimes also be built from timber studwork, but it needs to be strengthened. To stiffen the wall and turn it into a structural element normally requires an additional diagonal length of studwork in each 'bay', and the faces of one or both sides lined with plywood or PSB screwed and/or glued to the studs. Such load-bearing walls on upper floors should be built directly above doubled-up joists bolted together to provide strong support.

Bear in mind also that any new party walls between dwellings need to achieve 60 minutes fire resistance,

Steel box lintel on internal wall with space left for door lining below

normally achievable with standard plastered masonry. The same applies to walls to internal garages, although doors to garages from inside only need 30 minutes fire-resistance plus a self-closer.

Stud partition walls

If the upstairs internal walls don't need to carry any weight, as noted earlier it should be possible to simply divide the rooms with inexpensive timber stud or lightweight metal frame partition walls. Upstairs partition walls don't need to be built directly up as a continuation of a ground floor wall below and are sometimes supported instead on doubled up floor joists. Stud walls are cheap and easy to build, and their perceived drawbacks, such as poor sound insulation, can be overcome.

Lightweight timber frame walls normally comprise 47 x 100mm or 47 x 75mm softwood studs, clad on both sides with plasterboard sheets. Upstairs, stud walls can be securely fixed to the floor joists below and the ceiling joists above. At ground floor level they can be built directly off a beam and block floor or off a concrete slab. Equally they can be built off the finished screeded floor surface (sometimes reinforced with steel mesh along the line of the wall).

But at what stage should partition walls be built? They definitely need to be in place before the electricians and plumbers run their pipes and cables, which in turn has to be done before plastering, so the partition walls are generally built soon after the structure is weathertight. Floor screeding is normally done later, along with the plastering (being a 'wet trade'), so where the timber base plate has already been fixed to the concrete floor slab, it must be

protected with a plastic DPC underneath, lapped up the sides so that the wet screed doesn't soak the untreated timber.

Steel stud partition walls are popular with developers but are relatively thin and potentially prone to noise transmission

Building a timber stud wall

- To build a stud partition, you first need to mark out its top and bottom position with lines on the ceiling and floor. Horizontal timbers can be fixed along the lines, to make the header plate and base plate respectively (also known as the top plate and sole plate). For added strength, nail through the floorboards to joists where possible. Fixing to concrete floors is done with screws and plugs.
- Where the wall is built on an existing timber floor, such as to upstairs rooms, fixing is straightforward if your new wall runs at right angles to the floor joists. If it runs the same way as the joists then unless it's directly above a joist you'll need to provide extra support for the new base plate in the form of strips of timber 'noggins' (minimum 50 x 38mm) between the joists. The same applies at ceiling level.
- Next the vertical timber studs are fixed in place, normally at 400mm or 600mm centres. But the precise spacing should match the size of plasterboard used. Standard plasterboard sheets are 1200 x 2400mm or smaller 1200 x 900mm, so the studs should be placed to allow the boards to join over a timber stud.
- To provide strength, you need to fit at least one row of horizontal studs (noggins), between all the main vertical studs at about half height, which also provides an essential fixing point for the plasterboard sheets. Pipe and cable runs should be through small diameter holes drilled centrally through the studwork. When constructing the frame 'skew nailing', with nails hammered in at an angle, is the quickest method of joining the various pieces. It helps to drill a pilot hole first.
- If you know you'll later need to hang stuff off this wall, such as kitchen wall units, basins or radiator brackets, now is the time to fit extra rows of noggins at the appropriate height so that you'll have something substantial to drill into. Or you can line the studwork frame with sheets of plywood.

A quicker modern alternative widely used by mainstream housing developers is the galvanised steel partition system wall. These tend to be thinner at around 50–70mm but can also be clad with plasterboard. You can even buy 'off-the-shelf' ready-made plasterboard sandwich partitions with a cardboard cellular core, which just need cutting to size.

Once the framework for the stud walls is complete the door linings can be fixed in place and the wall left awaiting any cabling and pipework runs before being plasterboarded. Instead of a skim plaster finish, the boards may be left unplastered with the joints professionally taped and jointed ready for decoration, although a skim plaster finish is normally preferable, particularly in kitchens and bathrooms because of their moist atmosphere.

Sound insulation

One drawback with stud walls is the perceived problem of sound travelling through them, which is of particular importance for bathroom walls. But it's a fairly simple task to pack the hollow voids with thick sound-deadening mineral wool acoustic quilt before plasterboarding at second fix stage a little later.

The Building Regs only require internal walls to bedrooms and rooms with a toilet to be insulated for sound (minimum 25mm thick, but best to fully fill the void). Although not strictly required to kitchens, reception rooms or walls between bedrooms and en-suites, it's good practice to do the whole lot while you've got easy access. However, because solid masonry is usually a better barrier to sound, you might want to specify blockwork partitions anywhere downstairs this is especially important. On upper floors studwork walls can be given added resilience by lining with blue coloured 15mm acoustic plasterboard before skim plastering. Acoustic performance can be further boosted with anti-reverberation quilt placed within the studwork.

Door linings

Openings left in internal walls for doors will need door liners to be fitted. These are essentially simple planks of MDF, softwood or hardwood rather than the purpose-made door frames used for external doors. Door 'casings' are similar except they're already rebated to accommodate the door (rather than nailing timber door stops on later). Door linings however are the most widely used method and can either be fixed in place now, or left until the floors have been screeded or boarded. But they should be installed before the walls are plastered.

Linings traditionally comprised some handy leftover floorboards, but today ready-assembled kits are available in differing sizes to fit walls of varying widths. MDF is preferable as off-the-shelf softwood is often badly warped and distorted. Or you could specify dearer hardwood where a visible wood finish is desired.

Door linings are sold in standard sizes designed to accept internal doors manufactured to predetermined heights and widths (standard internal doors sizes are 1,981mm high by either 686, 762 or 838mm wide and 35mm thick). They are deliberately wider than the wall

Traditional square edge pine boards. T&G or chipboard are more common.

structure in order to accommodate the depth of plasterboard and plaster (typically adding about 15mm either side, so you need studwork + about 30mm). There are a wide range of sizes, typically 27.5mm or 32mm thick with widths of 94mm, 108mm, 120mm, 132mm, usually just over 2 metres high. Or they can be made in custom-sizes to suit non-standard doors.

Timber liners are easier to fit to stud partition walls since they're screwed or nailed directly to the timber sub-frame. Where the internal walls are built from blockwork, liners are sometimes fixed to them using cut nails driven directly into the masonry. However, it's better to use special frame ties, or screws driven into wallplugs. The screws should be fitted in pairs to prevent frames from twisting as doors are opened and closed.

Fitting doorstops is normally done later, towards completion, at the same time as the doors are being hung. Remember that the door linings have decorative surfaces that will be on view in the finished extension, so protection from damage will be needed, especially if they're later to be varnished or stained.

Timber flooring

Now that the building is dry inside, the timber flooring can be safely laid once they and the upstairs joists have had time to acclimatise and are nice and dry. This has the additional benefit of strengthening the floor structure.

The general idea is to get this level with the adjoining floors in the main house, but in many extensions even a blind person would have little trouble pinpointing the boundary of the new extension, thanks to the pronounced 'hump' in the floors where this was badly judged. To be fair, achieving an 'invisible' join to the existing floors isn't easy. The way to get this right is by regular measuring and checking at the floor joist stage (or by breaking through a lot earlier).

Of course, the aesthetic appeal of traditional timber flooring will be somewhat diminished by blobs of plaster, paint, mastic and heaven knows what raining down, so once fitted take care to keep them protected during the next few gruelling weeks.

Photo: realoakfloors.co.uk

Real oak flooring is hard to beat

Floorboards versus chipboard panels

You have two main choices when selecting your timber flooring: floorboards or chipboard panels. For a traditional floor that you can leave exposed with an attractive stain or varnish finish, pine floorboards are hard to beat, or you might want to push the boat out with dearer hardwood ones. Standard chipboard panels are cheap and quicker to lay, although they need to be covered – perhaps with laminate, wood flooring or carpets – which obviously adds to the cost. Plywood sheets are a possible third option, often used in bathrooms. Whichever type you choose, a 10mm expansion gap should be left at the edges by the walls that can later be concealed under the skirting. Redwood or whitewood planed tongued-and-grooved (PTG) or traditional Victorian style square edge (PSE) floorboards are commonly sold in widths from 119-150mm and thicknesses from 18-25mm.

However, unless the timber has been slow-grown and well-seasoned, or has been carefully reclaimed, wood floors can suffer from shrinkage between the boards. Even expensive solid hardwood floors can develop unsightly cracks. So it's best to first let the new boards dry out before laying by storing them for as long as possible in a centrally heated environment. By the time they have acclimatised, the moisture content should ideally be down to around 15 per cent or less.

Softwood floorboards were traditionally fixed to the joists using special large flat nails called brads, typically 55mm in length, the heads being easily embedded in the boards without the need for punching-in afterwards. But in less well seasoned modern timber these can cause splitting, so it's preferable to use special super-thin 'lost head' countersunk hex screws.

The ends of boards should be staggered at different joists. For added strength the tongues can be glued into the grooves. Softwood boards can then be sanded and sealed.

Flooring grade chipboard is widely used by most mainstream housebuilders, largely because it's cheap. Chipboard panels are manufactured with tongued-and-grooved edges and are sold in various sizes, such as 2,440

x 600mm. The 18mm thick panels can span 450mm between joists, and the thicker 22mm ones can manage 600mm. Although chipboard is unlikely to shrink, it has been known to disintegrate when wet, so it's best to select the moisture resistant 'green' type. However, unless fitted with scrupulous care, over time chipboard is very prone to creaking as a result of panels springing away from shrunken joists. It's also very difficult to lift and replace intact should access be required for future maintenance to pipes or cables.

When laying, the boards can be PVA glued at the joints, and then secured using purpose-made screws or special lost-head round 'ringshanked' nails at 75mm centres. Chipboard is notorious for blunting tools because it's so dense, so it's worth drilling pilot holes first. The tongued-and-grooved edges of the panels can become easily damaged, so never hammer directly onto it near the edges without first protecting them under an offcut. Also, beware sharp particles that can often fly out when sawing, so eye protection is essential.

If noise transmission is an issue, special sound-deadening acoustic floor panels can be fitted instead of conventional chipboard Made from high density cement-impregnated chipboard, these look similar to standard 19mm tongued and grooved panels. Sound insulation can be further improved by placing thick mineral wool batts between the joists and double plasterboarding ceilings below where required by Building Regs. The upstairs floor voids can be a handy place to dump all those offcuts of spare insulation that would otherwise fill a skip.

Timber floorboarding can also be fixed to concrete ground floors onto battens over a vapour membrane, instead of a conventional cement screed finish. Whilst on the subject of floor finishes, note that most laminates and parquet timber floor coverings are not sufficiently moisture-resistant for use in kitchens and bathrooms. Where underfloor heating is installed, tiles or engineered timber are popular floor finishes.

Stairs

How many home extensions need stairs? Very few. You might need an extra staircase for a granny annexe, or perhaps your design boasts spiral stairs leading to a cool galleried mezzanine landing. Whatever the reason, the stairs are one of the most complex parts of the internal joinery, but because of their lack of relevance to the vast majority of home extenders, readers are referred to the website or the Haynes *Victorian House Manual* for more detailed descriptions. If you are planning to fit a staircase, note that once the carcass is in place at this stage it is best to leave it devoid of banisters and balustrades for the time being so that they don't get damaged.

Complete stair kits can be ordered online, with the main carcass delivered pre-constructed to your specified sizes. The key dimensions to measure are the finished floor level (FFL)

Stairs and the Building Regulations

Briefly the requirements are:

- Landings should be at least the width of the stairs (both in length and width). No doors should open outwards onto a landing.
- The pitch of the staircase must be no steeper than 42°.
- Headroom: there must be minimum 2m clearance above each step.
- The tread of each step must be minimum 220mm deep (strictly speaking this refers to the 'going', which is the tread without its 'nosing', the bevelled front bit that sticks out); maximum is 300mm
- The height of each 'riser' must be a maximum of 220mm (the riser is the vertical part of each step); minimum is 150mm.
- Handrail height should be between 900mm and 1000mm measured to the top of the handrail.

downstairs to finished floor level upstairs, plus the width of the stair opening between the joists, and the headroom from the lower steps. Remember to allow for future floor finishes (such as tiling, including adhesive) and be sure to double check all measurements before ordering!

Stairs are potentially dangerous places, a prime location for accidents in the home, hence the eagerness with which the Building Regulations cover the subject. So it's a little surprising that they can be rather relaxed about stair widths. Although standard widths are normally a minimum of 800mm, you're allowed to reduce it in some circumstances. In restricted spaces, such as access to lofts, a 600mm width may be acceptable.

Space-saving loft stairs are even permitted with 'paddle shaped' treads that alternate from right to left on each tread, forcing you to descend back down them facing forwards as if on a ladder.

Handrails need only be provided to one side (normally the outer side) unless the stairs are unusually wide (over 1m), in which case both sides need one. Handrails and banisters are normally fixed at a convenient level, between 900mm and 1m above the 'pitch line' of the treads, but the bottom 2 steps can normally be left open at the sides so the newel and rail can start a little higher up.

The banister spindles known as 'balusters' mustn't have a gap between them bigger than 100mm, to prevent small children from plunging to their doom. 'Ranch style' horizontal balustrades should be avoided, not least on the grounds of good taste. Building Control also take a dim view of '70s style open tread stairs (with no risers).

Externally the rules are different. For added safety, parapets to external steps or balconies need to be placed a little higher, at a minimum of 1,100mm above floor level.

Spiral stairs

Spiral stairs are a great way to add some instant style, but before you're temped to splash out on a wonderful cast-iron antique masterpiece remember that it may not comply with current standards for internal use. Check compliance with BS 5395: Part 2.

In fact the Building Regs are not at all kind to spiral stairs. Designers like them because they don't need support from an adjoining wall, being reliant instead on a giant central newel post. This clearly offers the freedom to do something wacky, like appearing to be freestanding in the middle of the room. The simplest option is to specify off-the-shelf spiral 'loft stairs', which come in kit form. One final thought from bitter experience – be sure to tell the builders whether you want your spiral stairs erected clockwise or anticlockwise. Or they may just bollix it in their own special way.

Photo: Wooden Hill

Integral garages

For those whose first love will always be the car or bike, moving it into the house with you isn't an unreasonable idea. But sadly, the truth is that vehicles don't always make very good housemates. For a start there's the exhaust fumes, then there's the potential for oil and fuel spillages, and the risk of explosions and fire.

As a result, the Building Regs take a close interest in the safety of integral garages. First, they demand that the garage floor surface must be a minimum of 100mm lower than the house, and second, that any door from the house into an integral garage has at least 30 minutes' fire resistance.

To get the floor down this low the garage floor slab should ideally have been built lower than the rest way back at foundation stage, although you should gain at least 65mm by not needing a screed finish. Another solution may be to fit a raised concrete threshold to the new garage/house doorway, which in effect raises the immediate floor height at the crucial point.

A fire door with 30 minutes' resistance ('FD 30') can be identified by a small plastic marker (a blue circle with a white centre) embedded in its side. It's worth paying careful attention to fire door requirements, as you may

need quite a few of them if you're also doing a loft conversion (see Haynes *Loft Conversion Manual*).

Fire doors to garages need to be self-closing, so special door-closing devices need to be fitted. But it's no good having a fire-resistant door if the flames can simply lick their way around the frame. So fitting purpose-made fire-resistant frames is the best option. These have special intumescent strips indented around the frame. Alternatively you could specify fire doors with integral intumescent strips. These will resist fire since they react to extreme heat by instantly expanding and sealing the gap between the frame and the door, thus delaying the advance of lethal smoke and flames. It's worth noting that the gap between the door and the frame shouldn't exceed 3mm and you need seal sizes of 15 x 4mm for 30 minute fire doors or 20 x 4mm for 60 minute doors.

For garages it's a good idea to fit a combined intumescent strip and smoke seal that does two jobs for the price of one, providing an additional protective barrier against cold smoke and poisonous exhaust fumes.

As far as the walls between the garage and the house are concerned, a standard brick or blockwork wall should have no trouble stopping the spread of fire, but timber stud partitions must be boarded on both sides with pink fire-rated plasterboard with a skim plaster finish. The same plasterboarding solution applies to garage ceilings. The floors above integral garages also need insulating to minimise the chill factor in the bedroom above, and this is normally achieved by laying loft insulation quilt between the joists.

Other areas that are vulnerable to fire include any exposed beams, which will also require boarding and skimming, and the joints between walls and ceilings may need extra 'fire-stopping' with insulation material to protect nearby joists or roof timbers.

One final thought. Adding gas supply pipes to this already heady mix may sound like a dubious idea, but because of all the fire protection garages are actually excellent places to site boilers, and are increasingly the location of choice on new developments. Boilers should be safely positioned well away from potential car impact zones, at a reasonably high level.

Left: Fire door with self closer.

> ## Main trades needed on site
>
> ■ **Carpenters:** Building studwork walls, fitting door linings, loft hatch, and doors and windows.
> ■ **Bricklayers:** Making good around openings.
> ■ **Labourers:** Demolition.
>
> *www.home-extension.co.uk*

14 FIRST FIX
The Services

The time is now right for 'first fix'. This means routing all the new pipework and electrical cables through the building whilst its skeleton is still exposed.

Photo: designer-radiators.com

Photo: eddystoneselfbuild.co.uk

Mixed copper and plastic pipes run above ceiling – will later need lagging in loft.

Pipes supplying hot and cold water to bathrooms, kitchens, loos and utility rooms will now need to be tucked away behind wall surfaces and in ceiling voids. The central heating pipework and some of the waste pipes also need to be installed at this stage. But, as the name implies, these jobs will actually be completed later in the build, so don't be too alarmed when you notice lots of disconnected pipes with their tails poking forlornly out of the walls. Similarly, the electrical cables are only run as far as new boxes fixed in the walls, with their ends left loose and drooping (but obviously not live). These unfinished services will then spend several weeks awaiting 'second fix', which will only take place once all the messy 'wet works' (such as plastering and screeding) have been completed and the new pipes and cables concealed behind sheets of plasterboard.

One piece of good news is that compared to building a whole new house, you'll save a huge amount of expense and aggravation because all the incoming mains supplies – electricity, water and gas (or oil or LPG) – will already be in place. Which means the utility companies can't charge a king's ransom for the privilege of connecting a new supply.

Thankfully, you should only be faced with the relatively simple task of extending the existing systems from your main house into the new extension. But just when you thought the gods were at last smiling upon you there may be a shock in store. It's not unusual at this point to make the unwelcome discovery that your existing electrics and central heating are, frankly, getting a bit past it. At best

they would struggle to cope with the extra load imposed by having to serve the additional accommodation. This is always fertile ground for builders seeking profitable 'extras' in the shape of unanticipated upgrading of old systems, which is why it's very useful if you can price extra work on the same basis as the competitively tendered prices for the main job.

Electrics

Electricity is the biggest killer in the house. At least a thousand fires and more than 50 deaths each year are due to electrical faults. So electrical work is not really an area for novice DIY enthusiasts. Anything with a risk of death attached isn't normally worth saving a few quid over. On the other hand, if you know what you're doing there's a fair amount of wiring that isn't restricted under 'Part P' of the Building Regulations - see Boxout.

Electricians

It's slightly worrying that just about anyone possessing a pair of hands and a functioning brain is entitled to call themselves an electrician. No licence or formal qualifications are required, which is a little surprising given the risks of being fried to death from a moment's absent-mindedness. However, if your extension is being managed under the terms of a building contract it will require that the individual employed must be at the very least a 'competent person' (which legally means 'someone capable of signing a BS 7671 installation certificate'). This is, in any case, a requirement of the Building Regulations.

So what should you look for when picking a suitable electrician? It's essential that they're registered with an appropriate organisation, such as IET (Institute of Engineering and Technology), the ECA (Electrical Contractors Association) or, probably the best-known of all, NICEIC (National Inspection Council for Electrical Installation Contracting). If employing trades directly, as always get more than one quote, and make it clear that payment for the job will be subject to first receiving the test certificate.

Registered electricians are required to register their completed work at an online database after testing and commissioning it. This generates a paper certificate of Part

P compliance that's posted to you and an email notification sent to Building Control (who won't sign off the completed extension without it).

Sockets and switches

Now is the time to decide where you want all the socket outlets, light fittings and switches - don't wait until everything is all beautifully plastered. It's best to give the electrician a set of clearly marked coloured drawings showing what you want and where you want it. Then walk round the building together pointing out what's required. If you don't do this they will most likely apply his own skill and judgement – ie do it the easiest way.

Most electricians 'supply and fix', providing all the materials. But when it comes to choosing light fittings it's often best for clients to agree that they supply the kit. This should give you (and your partner) the freedom to change your minds without incurring extra charges!

The electrician's first job, after checking your plans, will be to route all the cables around and fix the boxes in place. He'll return at a later stage to do the second fix work, installing covers to the switches, sockets and ceiling roses once the plastering of the walls and ceilings is out of the way. Electricians need to work closely with dry liner/plasterers and keep accurate records and photos to avoid a lot of baffled head-scratching at second fix when it's all covered over.

You'll need to clearly communicate any special requirements, although there are limits to what you can request. Remember that the Building Regulations require that new power sockets must be positioned between 450mm and 1200mm above finished floor level, and light switches similarly no higher than 1200mm from the floor. Also, no sockets are allowed in bathrooms. And consumer units now have to be accessible at height of between 1350 and 1450mm.

Adding style

This is a perfect opportunity to add a little creative lighting to your design. Features like discreet LEDs embedded in floors, parapet walls and kitchen units, or outdoor uplighters can all make the new extension feel super-stylish. Why stick with standard-issue white plastic sockets and switches when there's a choice of brushed aluminium, brass, or chrome? If you prefer something less contemporary, there are distinctive antique designs

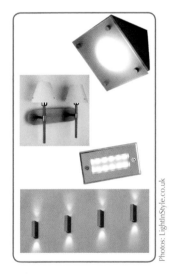

Photos: LightInStyle.co.uk

making something of a comeback – repro versions of deco uplighters and rounded bakelite-style switches.

How many sockets?

One of the most common complaints amongst house buyers is the belated discovery upon moving in that there are insufficient power points for all the various phone chargers, playstations, printer-scanners, foot spas, toasted sandwich machines and smoothie-makers that modern life requires. So be generous with the DSSOs (double-switched socket outlets) in your new rooms, since the cost of adding a couple of extra ones here or there at this stage is peanuts.

Depending on room size, a modern household requires about three or

Cable run holes in joists should be drilled centrally

four DSSOs for each bedroom, five or six each for kitchens and living rooms, and a couple for halls and landings. But in the bathroom, only shaver sockets are allowed (run from the lighting circuit).

Running cables

Traditionally, cables running along masonry walls would be buried in 'chases' gouged out of the walls to maintain a flush surface for plastering. Today, with dry lined main walls, cables are normally surface run, often shielded with protective flat steel or plastic channels which are pinned to the bare walls and then plastered over. In studwork, small holes are drilled centrally in the timbers through which cables can be routed, safely out of range of plasterboard dry wall screws.

Cables must be run either vertically or horizontally from the outlets they supply, within permitted safe zones at 90 degrees to fittings and shouldn't wander in wavy lines across walls. Straight lines are essential so that the following trades (and people living there) know where not to drill holes. For ground floor sockets it's advisable to drop the cables down the wall from above rather than run them up from below (saves running cables through ground floors, and protects circuits from flood damage). Any outdoor cables must be run in special external grade protective conduits.

Having gone to so much trouble at the design stage carefully calculating that your extension would be structurally safe, you don't want the joists to now be seriously weakened by having huge chunks cut out of them for the various pipe and cable runs. Timber-frame houses are particularly vulnerable to insensitive cutting, so don't allow your electrician to hack away at load-bearing timber studs in order to neatly recess his socket boxes. Any holes or cuts made in the timber frame's vapour barrier must be sealed, using special adhesive tape.

Electricians normally need to run cables through upstairs floors, which means drilling holes in timber joists and feeding them through. The critical points structurally in joists are at their centres and ends, so there are strict rules about how to do this without weakening the joists:

■ Holes should be drilled about halfway down the joist (including some manufactured I-joists).
■ Don't drill near the joist ends – not within the first quarter of the joist's span from the wall (optimum is within the zone between the first quarter an a third of the length from either end).

- The size of holes should be no bigger than quarter of the depth of the joist.
- Don't drill holes too close together (no closer than three times the hole's diameter).

Note that electric cables run within thermal insulation, such as loft quilt, can potentially be at risk of becoming overheated. If there's no other option in a loft, use a higher capacity cable than necessary and run them immediately on top of the plasterboard ceiling or on the surface, rather than being totally encased within thick layers of quilt. Or you could run them in wide-bore tubing.

Consumer units

The first question to ask when extending an electrical circuit is whether your existing consumer unit (aka 'fuse box' or 'distribution board') is capable of coping with the additional load. Most houses have electrical systems that are unsatisfactory in some way, either due to poor-quality alterations or just through sheer age. Even many modern systems won't comply in some way or other with the latest wiring regulations which are frequently updated. So now may be a good time to update or replace your consumer unit, especially if it has ancient re-wireable fuses.

When it comes to testing the finished job the electrician has to test the whole circuit, including any existing parts of the system as well as the new 'add ons'. In other words they aren't allowed to simply test and certify their own new bit of an extended circuit in isolation. So any faults in the older parts (such as an old fuse box without RCD protection) will need to be upgraded, adding to the cost.

For larger extensions you will need to install a new secondary consumer unit (e.g. supplied by splitting the existing consumer unit tales using a 'Henley block') rather than just extending the existing circuits in the house. Modern consumer units provide greatly increased protection against electrocution with integral RCDs (Residual Current Devices, sometimes called 'earth leakage circuit breakers'). RCDs are designed to prevent you from getting a fatal electric shock if you touch something live, such as a bare wire. They protect most individual circuits or groups of circuits including all the wiring and sockets and any connected appliances, although they tend to be very sensitive, cutting out whenever a lightbulb blows. This is in addition to

MCBs (Miniature Circuit Breakers) for individual circuits. These special fuses automatically switch off when they sense a fault or overload, thereby potentially saving lives. When they 'trip', you can simply reset the switch (rather than the traditional method of struggling in the dark to replace bits of blown fuse wire). Non-combustible metal consumer units have now replaced the standard plastic type, some with the benefit of RCBOs which combine MCBs and RCDs.

The basics

The power circuits that supply the socket outlets in the walls are arranged as 'ring mains', usually with one circuit per floor. The 2.5mm^2 'twin and earth' cable connects from the 32amp MCB in the consumer unit, looping round all the

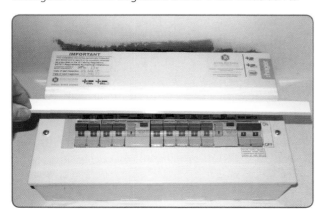

> ## How much can you do yourself?
>
> Some electrical work is covered by the Building Regs Part P – but not all. Work covered is known as 'notifiable work' and must be carried out by an electrician who is registered under the 'competent person scheme'. You can check whether an electrician is Part P registered with their institute (NICEIC, or ECA or NAPIT etc) or online with the Registered Competent Persons Electrical website electricalcompetentperson.co.uk
>
> If an electrician is non-registered they can still do it as long as they submit a separate Building Regs application for notifiable electrical works. Building Control will then inspect at 1st fix and 2nd fix stages, test and certify the work upon completion.
>
> ### Notifiable work includes:-
> - Installing a new circuit
> - Installing a new consumer unit – or replacing an old one
> - Any work in bathrooms / shower rooms to circuits inside the zone 600mm from the edge of the bath or shower tray (or 1.2m from the shower in wet rooms) and within 2.25m height above floor level
> - Any work to circuits in rooms with swimming pools or saunas
>
> You are allowed carry out minor 'non notifiable' electrical work such as replacing socket covers, switches, ceiling roses and replacing cables from a single circuit (eg if damaged), and adding extra lighting points to existing circuits. But it should be tested by a competent electrician.
>
> So in a typical extension with a new dining room and bedroom for example, the power and lighting circuits can often be extended from the existing circuits, and hence are not 'notifiable'.
>
> But adding an en-suite to a bedroom and fitting a light or fan within the zone would be. So would any new kitchens because they need their own power circuits, and any new circuit from the existing consumer unit is notifiable.
>
> But there's a potential catch: you might set out intending not to do notifiable works but then discover that your existing circuits have inadequate earthing, or the old consumer unit needs replacing if it doesn't have RCD (residual current device) protection. So it's best to employ a registered electrician just in case.

13amp socket outlets on one floor in series and then back to the MCB. One circuit can normally serve a floor area up to 100m² (an average semi having roughly 50–60m² floor area for each storey) but any number of power points can be provided within this. The kitchen, being a high demand area, has its own circuit. Also, electric cookers and immersion heaters have separate 45amp and 20amp MCB fuses respectively but use 'radial circuits', where a single cable is run from the MCB direct to the unit. Cables run to outdoors should have separate RCD protected circuits.

Electricity will always head for earth, taking the easiest route (normally along its circuit). But in the event of a fault, leaking current could pass to earth through you, the floor and the walls, and especially through anything wet or metallic. So to protect against electric shock, all exposed metal components should be connected with an earth wire (green and yellow sleeved) to prevent them becoming 'live' and retaining any dangerous shock current. The requirement is to bond metal items such as incoming service pipes (water, gas, oil etc), central heating pipes, hot and cold water pipes, and all metal in bathrooms. New copper piping for heating and water normally needs to be earth bonded to the electrical system. However, pipework run exclusively in plastic shouldn't need to be bonded.

Photo: LightinStyle.co.uk

Each floor of the building will normally have its own lighting circuit. But unlike power circuits, these are not run in a loop or 'ring' that returns to the consumer unit. Instead, the lighting cable (thinner 1.0mm² or 1.5mm² 'twin and earth') connects from the 6 amp MCB fuse in the consumer unit to a series of ceiling roses or wall lights in turn. Each room switch is wired directly to a rose via a single cable (e.g. 3 core and earth). New lighting circuits may also need to incorporate smoke alarms and shaver points.

Special locations

Bathrooms, shower rooms, pools and saunas are all defined as 'special locations' due to the increased risk of electrocution from water (but cloakrooms/WCs without a shower are not). In such high risk areas, nothing electric should be touchable from where a person could be in contact with water at the same time. Only specially protected fittings are allowed in bathrooms and light switches should be of the pull-cord type or else located in the landing/hall outside the bathroom door. Electrical fittings such as lighting need to comply in terms of safety, defined by 'IP Ratings' (Ingress Protection). The numbers relate to how waterproof and dustproof a fitting is (the higher the numbers the more resistant). For example bathrooms are split into 4 different safety zones (see diagram) and the minimum IP Ratings are:-

■ Zone 0 - IP67 (totally immersion-proof)
■ Zone 1 - IP65
■ Zone 2 - IP44

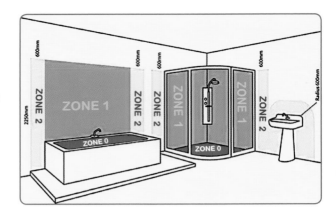

Similarly, most outdoor lighting will be IP rated 67 or 68, although a lower rating of 44 will be suitable for general outdoor use where not very exposed to driving rain.

Extractor fans

Today's Building Regs demand that kitchens, bathrooms, cloakrooms and utilities are fitted with extractor fans and that all other rooms should be ventilated (see Boxout 'Room Ventilation').

There's a good reason for all this official consternation. To get rid of all those litres of humid, moist air swirling around the atmosphere of modern homes, effective ventilation is needed to prevent problems from condensation and black mould. And nowhere is it needed more than in kitchens and bathrooms where steamy air from laundry, showering and boiling food will do the most damage, condensing against cold surfaces, such as loo cisterns, and then dripping into puddles on the floor.

In kitchens the most effective fans are ducted cooker hood extractors that suck out steamy stale air direct from the source and expel it outside. Building Control won't be fooled by a posh-looking, designer cooker hood only housing a charcoal 'recirculation' filter that's not actually vented to outdoors and just recycles stale air.

Bathroom fans can be less powerful, typically needing to extract 15 litres of air per second, whereas kitchens need at least 2 to 4 times that amount to cope with condensation from cooking. In bathrooms, fans must not be located anywhere someone using the bath could touch them, and away from the risk of shower spray. If the bathroom is so small this isn't possible, consider fitting special low voltage bathroom units. Ideally fans should be sited on the opposite side of the room to the windows, to encourage a decent through-flow of air.

Most of us have experienced noisy 'first generation' fans that whine on for hours long after you've departed, like a particularly irritating swarm of bees. Not only are they annoying but they're largely ineffective unless you bathe exclusively after dark – no matter how steamy it is in the daytime, such fans don't work unless you put the light on. Thankfully, 'intelligent' extractor fans are now available which incorporate build-in 'humidistats'. Instead of being wired to

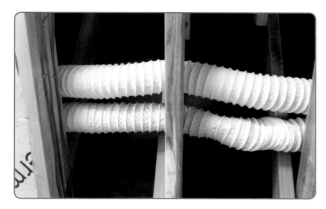

Flexible extractor fan ducting run through loft

the light switch, these relatively quiet, humidity-sensing fans activate automatically when the humidity in the room reaches a critical level (65% relative humidity) only coming on when needed regardless of whether the light is on or not.

They need to be set to operate at no higher than 70 per cent RH ('relative humidity') since once the humidity of the air in your house rises above this, black mould growth can form on your walls and ceilings.

One recent improvement is the requirement for isolator switches in bathrooms, so that defective fans can be worked on without having to disconnect the entire lighting circuit. These are usually located high up on the outer wall as you enter the bathroom.

Fans may be built into walls, with the moist air directly expelled to the outside, or they may be fitted to ceilings and linked to outdoors via a length of flexible 'concertina' ducting that runs up through the loft space to a roof or eaves vent. Try to avoid over-long ducts that reduce air flow rates and when run through cold lofts can cause steamy air to condense back into water before it is expelled. To prevent condensation dribbling back down, ducting can be insulated, or have 'condensation traps' fitted near the fan to divert moisture to an overflow pipe. The longer the duct, the weaker the fan's performance gets. Flat ducting such as the type used for kitchen chimney hoods running along the top of the wall units will reduce airflow even more than the rounded type, so a beefier fan unit may be needed.

But before you rush to install the biggest air-sucker you can get your hands on as a final solution to airborne dampness, first take a look around the room. There may be competition for valuable air, notably in the form of open-flued appliances. Whilst modern 'room-sealed' boilers aren't a problem, open fires need to take their combustion air directly from inside the room. If this air supply is stolen by your new turbocharged extractor fan, the consequential air starvation can leave the occupants gasping.

This is why open-flued solid fuel appliances like AGAs and wood burning stoves (unless externally vented) aren't necessarily compatible with extractor fans. Over-powerful extract fans can rob combustion air from the appliance

Room ventilation

BACKGROUND VENTILATION

Habitable rooms require a free airflow of 10,000mm² (4,000mm² to kitchens, bathrooms, utilities, and WCs). This is normally provided by trickle vents in the form of slots at the heads of windows, or airbricks sleeved through the cavity wall to an internal grille. Additional permanent ventilation is required for rooms containing heat-producing appliances, such as open-flued gas fires of rated input over 7kW and most 'living flame' effect fires.

RAPID/PURGE VENTILATION

Rapid ventilation (aka 'purge' ventilation) is provided by openable windows that allow the occupants to rapidly clear the air of paint fumes, foul toilet stenches, cooking smells etc. So the windows in all habitable rooms must be openable with a clear opening area equivalent to 1/20th of the floor area unless an approved mechanical ventilation system is installed.

EXTRACT VENTILATION

The Building Regs require extractor fans fitted in kitchens to be capable of shifting 60 litres of air per second, and those in bathrooms and utility rooms 15 and 30 litres per second respectively. The best type to fit are the relatively quiet humidity-sensing fans that only come on when humidity rises to a preset level, or heat-recovery fans that recycle heat from extracted air.

Alternatively, PSV or continuous mechanical systems are an acceptable form of extract ventilation where certified by an approved body.

As noted earlier, solid-fuel appliances aren't necessarily compatible with extractor fans. Open fires need to take their combustion air directly from inside the room. If this air supply is stolen by extractor fans, the consequential air starvation can leave occupants gasping. Hence the requirement for additional wall vents.

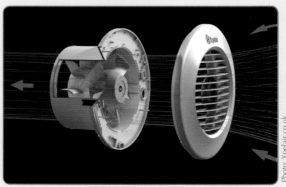

Photo: Xpelair.co.uk

causing them to leak deadly carbon monoxide (CO), so a CO detector must be fitted. You may also be required to insert air vents in the walls to introduce sufficient fresh air changes per hour and prevent any risk of you and the family suffocating. Building Control may require a 'spillage test' to check that the cooker burns correctly when the fan is running at full tilt. One possible solution is to fit fans with reduced output ratings.

For a more hi-tech solution, mechanical ventilation (MV) systems with heat exchangers can recover heat from the outgoing stale air and use it to warm the fresh air entering the house.

Smoke alarms

It's well known that the biggest killer in most house fires is not incineration by flames, but being overcome by smoke. Yet in many homes the smoke alarms have been incapacitated by having their batteries violently torn out. Distraught homeowners deafened by the wretched things bursting to life in error have been driven to take desperate measures to silence the uncontrollable 110 decibel shrieking. Somehow, there never seems to be a simple silence button that can stop the ear-piercing racket in the event of a toast-burning false alarm. But the fact is, all new extensions with bedrooms need smoke alarms which must be wired to the mains (via the lighting circuit or its own dedicated circuit) with battery back-up. Where there's more than one they must be interlinked to one another, so they all sound off together (so it's even harder to shut the things up!).

The solution of course to false alarms is to position them correctly in the first place. Where you've got 2 or more storeys at least one alarm should be positioned on each level. Outside bedrooms the alarm should be positioned on the landing or hallway within 7.5m of the bedroom door.

Don't fit them in kitchens, because steam and fumes from cooking areas can set them off. Boiler rooms and garages are also unsuitable locations, and to avoid

false alarms they shouldn't be sited near heaters or in bathrooms. However, because nearly half of all domestic fires start in kitchens, one should be sited nearby. Building Control normally like to see them positioned on ceilings, at least 300mm away from light fittings (which can obstruct them) and the same distance from corners of rooms (which smoke tends to avoid). Where wall-mounting is the only option, detectors should be fixed between 150mm and 300mm below the ceiling and above the level of doorways. And so they can be easily maintained and tested, it's best to avoid placing them above stairwells. If running cables is difficult you may be able to fit wireless-linked alarms instead.

Where you've got an open-plan kitchen layout it should be protected by a heat detector that only activates when temperature of 57 degrees C is reached. The same applies to integral garages.

Talking of gruesome deaths from smoke and fire, what could be more ironic than cheating the Grim Reaper by taking all the correct fire precautions only to be overcome in your sleep by carbon monoxide poisoning? More than 50 deaths a year in homes are due to inhaling invisible odourless CO. So if you find yourself nodding off in your armchair in front of a cosy fire in a draught-sealed room, it might later turn out to be a matter of some regret that a CO alarm wasn't fitted. As noted earlier, any appliances that take their combustion air direct from within the room, such as gas fires and solid fuel fireplaces, are a potential risk. So while you're at it why not fit combined smoke/CO alarms for peace of mind?

Gas

Modern mains supplies are run in yellow polyethylene plastic underground pipes, which have long superseded metal. The incoming mains gas pipe should be buried at least 375mm below ground, terminating at a stop valve by the gas meter. To extend the existing supply, perhaps to a new boiler or gas fire in your new extension, 22mm copper gas pipes are normally run externally along the outer

Photo: acanthalifestyle.com

Photo: shower-guide.com

walls near ground level. As a safety precaution, gas pipework inside the house should be kept at least 25mm away from electric cables, and no gas pipes may be run in unventilated voids to floors etc. Gas plumbing must always be done in copper pipe, not plastic.

Natural gas is not poisonous; the main risk is that of explosions. Hence work on gas appliances and pipework must by law only be carried out by qualified GAS SAFE-registered engineers. For oil-fired heating systems the equivalent body is OFTEC (Oil Firing Technical Association).

you feel confident, there's no reason why you shouldn't carry out some of the work yourself. Even installing new bathroom fittings shouldn't be too difficult. The fact that all the pipes and fittings are brand new makes it a lot easier than trying to connect a stunning new suite to decrepit old imperial-sized pipes. But if you feel the urge to tackle some jobs yourself, it's essential to first tell the main contractor – you can't suddenly announce your new-found interest in plumbing when they've already scheduled a plumber to do the work. Which just leaves one final thing to achieve perfect results - The Haynes *Home Plumbing Manual*!

Plumbing

If your home extension includes a new bathroom, WC, kitchen or utility room, the existing cold water supply will need to be extended. You're also likely to need some new CH pipes to serve additional radiators. All pipework should be properly secured with clips so as to discourage leaks and banging noises developing later in life.

But before the first monkey wrench is taken out of the toolbag it's always a good idea to discuss the desired layout of new pipes and appliances with your plumber. There will, of course, be physical limitations as to where pipework can be run, but with a little thought you can normally agree simple solutions, perhaps saving a lot of unnecessary expense.

Unlike doing work to electrics and gas appliances, the only restriction on DIY plumbing is competency. If

Traditional 15mm copper pipe with solder joints for visible radiator tails. Flow and return pipe runs under floor are in plastic.

Cold water supply

Cold water is supplied to your home below-ground from the mains in the street, via a stopcock in the pavement or front garden. On older houses it may be a shared supply, perhaps even crossing through back gardens. Underground water pipes should be buried at least 750mm deep to protect them from frost. Where run any higher or above ground they must be lagged to protect them.

Pressurised cold water supplies were originally run in pipework of cast iron or lead. If you still have original supply pipes contact your water company, as replacement with modern heavy-duty blue plastic (alkathene) pipework is often advisable.

The incoming mains supply normally runs

Photo: roycebathrooms.co.uk

New cold water supply pipe. Most extensions connect to existing unless incoming supply needs re-routing

Above and below: Plastic pipes being flexible can be run through holes drilled in joists – rather than cutting notches. Softwood joists (above) and I-joists (below)

direct to the kitchen sink (suitable for drinking water). There should be a stopcock inside the house, typically in the kitchen or cloakroom, that can be shut off in an emergency. Traditionally, the 'rising main' would then continue all the way up to a cold-water storage tank in the roof space, which in turn supplied water for bathrooms and WCs. But today most homes have mains supplied pressurised unvented hot water cylinders (e.g. 'Megaflo') or combination boilers with no need for storage tanks in the loft.

The average four-person home will typically use about 185m³ of water a year, the equivalent of over 2,000 baths, and in order to provide adequate flows of water to the taps, pipework must be correctly sized. Baths are generally supplied with 22mm pipes (hot and cold) and washbasins and WCs with 15mm pipes. Shower mixers may require either 15 or 22mm supplies so check with the manufacturer, as some mixers only work well via a pump. Plumbing is rapidly going plastic, although some plumbers remain loyal to copper. The Building Regs require new water supply pipes to taps and cisterns etc to be fitted with simple isolation valves to provide a handy on/off control to allow maintenance work.

Whilst you're in plumbing mode, you might want to take the opportunity to run a small branch pipe through the new wall for a handy garden tap, making sure, of course, that the pipes are insulated against frost and fitted with an internal stop valve.

DIY Plumbing – good advice
- Tell the contractor before doing any work.
- Allow plenty of time – don't hurry the job.
- Check all supplies are fully turned off, or drained down, before starting.
- Isolate the new work from the main house so that it's business as usual for the family.
- Don't get in the way of other trades.
- When finished, double-check that the system is fully watertight under pressure.

Cutting joists
Water pipes may be concealed in suspended floors, or else buried in solid floors within ducts. Keep a record of the location of any hidden pipe runs in case access is required in future. Where pipework is surface-mounted along walls, some of the pipe-fitting work can be left until after the walls have been plastered, or else boxed in before plastering.

The rules for cutting notches into joists without inviting disaster are similar to those for electric cables (see page 211). One advantage of using modern plastic pipes is they can be threaded through narrow holes drilled in joist centres, whereas more rigid copper pipes often need to be notched from the top. As noted earlier, the critical points structurally in joists are the centres and the ends:

- Don't cut too near the joist ends – not within the first quarter of the joist's span out from the wall.
- Don't cut notches closer than 100mm to holes drilled for cables.
- Cut no deeper into a joist than an eighth of its total depth.
- Joists should always be notched from the top.

It's a good idea to fit small steel shields over the top of cut notches to protect pipes from subsequent puncturing should anyone carelessly hammer nails into floorboards.

Cover openings to new waste pipes.

Maximum pipe lengths			
	Max length	Pipe diameter (internal	Fall (per metre run)
Basins	1.7m	32mm	18–90mm
Baths and showers	3m	40mm	18–90mm
Toilets	6m	110mm	18–30mm

Waste pipes

To some folk, what happens to the bathwater after they pull out the plug is a complete mystery. But taking a quick look down below reveals the hidden truth. The waste water discharges via one of the great inventions of modern civilisation – the U-shaped trap under the plughole. Traps cleverly prevent nasty sewer odours coming back up the pipes, since smells can't get past the water trapped in the bottom of the U, which forms a seal. The waste water then usually discharges into the soil stack (SVP) and away through the underground drainage system to the sewers, as described in Chapter 9.

Waste pipes can tell you a few things about the person who fitted them. A couple of good signs to look for are sufficient rodding eyes or access points provided on pipe bends, and sufficient support clips fitted to prevent pipes sagging (one at least every 500mm).

Whilst on the subject of picking a good plumber, it's worth taking the trouble to inspect some of their previous jobs before letting them loose on your designer bathroom. The airing cupboard is a good place to check the quality of their work, since if the pipework is neat and tidy in a place that's hidden from view it has to be an encouraging sign.

Modern plastic waste pipes should be relatively trouble-free if properly installed with sufficient support-clips and suitable falls – DIY plumbers sometimes forget that water runs downhill. Internal white plastic waste pipes and fittings are push-fit, usually either 32mm for basins, or 40mm for baths, showers and sinks. External pipes are usually run in UV-resistant grey plastic.

Your design must take account of the fact that waste pipes are only effective up to certain lengths before there's a risk of siphonage occurring. As noted in Chapter 9, this is a peculiar phenomenon which can allow foul odours to enter your house, accompanied by a cacophony of rude gurgling noises. It is caused when the protective seal of water in traps (to baths, basins, toilets etc) is literally sucked out by a deluge of outgoing waste water creating a build up of pressure in its slipstream. To avoid such

horrors, there's a maximum permitted length to which pipes of each diameter can be run before siphonage becomes a risk. Hence there's a maximum distance that you can safely locate your new sink, loo and bath from the waste stack. This constraint can profoundly influence the layout of new bathrooms. These distances are typically 3m for baths or showers, and less than 2m for most basins. For WCs you normally have 6m to play with.

If this restriction cripples your otherwise excellent bathroom layout, it may be possible to work around the problem by fitting special 'anti-siphonage' traps or bigger bore pipes. Or you can cheat by using self-sealing non-return valves that don't need a water sealed trap at all, such as 'HepVO' valves.

If you want to install a new bathroom or WC, fortunately you don't need to add another soil stack (SVP). Because your house will already have an SVP, you are allowed to use a short version known as a stub stack to serve extra bathrooms and loos, usually terminating with an 'air admittance valve' (AAV). Unlike SVPs these 'Durgo valves' are not permanently open. Instead, they're capped with a rubber diaphragm which opens automatically to relieve pressure and admits air into the system before sealing closed again, relieving excess pressure without emitting odours.

Because no unpleasant stench is emitted, they don't need to terminate way up above roof level, and instead can be neatly boxed in within bathrooms or placed unobtrusively in loft spaces. See Chapter 8.

WCs

At the design stage, one of the first questions you need to ask is where your drain runs are. This tells you where it would be realistic to fit new WCs and bathrooms without running into major plumbing problems, such as trying to fit a loo in the east wing of the house when your drains are perfectly happy over in the west wing. Indeed, such toilet exclusion zones were a hard fact of life until an anonymous genius came up with the concept of the 'macerator' one day whilst idly gazing at the food blender in the kitchen.

110mm foul waste underground pipe tail awaiting connection to WC (should be protected from debris with cover).

The famed Victorian toilet pioneer Thomas Crapper used to test the flushing power of his early WCs by simulating foul waste solids with apples bobbing about in the pan. Similarly, the macerator inventor realised that

if you can liquidise fruit in a smoothie-maker, why not apply the same technology to toilets? Mashed up liquid waste could then be pumped out through conventional narrow-bore 40mm pipes rather than requiring the normal cumbersome 110mm WC pipes. Quite ingenious – except for one tiny problem: macerators rely on electrical power to do the crucial pumping, which means they make a slightly alarming whirring noise when flushed. It also means that in the event of a power cut they're totally unserviceable. This means you're not allowed to rely exclusively on macerators. A home must have at least one conventional loo. But when building a new extension, the extra cost of excavating proper drains should in most cases be marginal, so macerators will not normally need to appear on your shopping list.

Showers

Baths and showers both now need to be thermostatically controlled. The water temperature is adjusted automatically, preventing unwitting shower-users suddenly getting scalded with super-hot water because someone else has just run a nearby cold tap and upset the hot/cold mix.

Showers also need a consistently powerful water supply for which modern mains pressure hot water systems are ideally suited. Otherwise flow rates may need to be beefed up by fitting powerful pumps. It's also often necessary to

install a separate cold supply direct to the shower from the cold water tank.

To surveyors, shower trays are rather like flat felted roofs – almost guaranteed to leak and cause problems at some point. If damp doesn't get down the seals at the edges of the tray sooner or later it'll probably infiltrate the tiling. Which is why it's advisable to tile onto a marine plywood or 'aquaboard' base rather than ordinary plasterboard. The worst offending trays are thin acrylic ones, which can be prone to flexing and distortion, especially when timber floor joists shrink. Ceramic or stonecast trays are preferable. Or take no chances and fit a modern all-in-one moulded cubicle. But whichever type you choose, it's advisable to build in an access point so the trap can be cleared, unless accessible from above. Alternatively, you could dispense with the tray altogether and build a 'wet room' with a drain fitted inside the floor void (which must be able to cope with a flow of 30 litres per minute). The floor needs to be waterproof and should slope towards the drain at 1:40 for a 1 metre zone around it. This is easier to achieve on a solid floor where you can build a 25mm depression into the screed; timber floors may need to be built up instead. If you'd rather keep life simple as well as conserve the budget, a standard shower-mixer over the bath should do nicely for the occasional shower. But bath seals and shower screens need to be very carefully fitted to remain leak-free.

Heating

Central heating

Your well-laid plans defining precisely where each piece of furniture is to be placed in your new rooms can be utterly ruined when you discover in horror that someone's stuck a radiator in the wrong place. So remember that unless you provide the plumber with a clear set of drawings showing exactly where you want your radiators positioned and pipes routed, it'll get done the way that suits them – probably with all the rads bunched back-to-back on internal walls, to save running much pipework.

Conventional CH systems pump hot water from the boiler to steel radiators in each room via pipework which comprises separate parallel 'flow and return' circuits, usually in 15mm or 8mm copper or equivalent plastic pipes (8mm 'microbore' piping is not ideal as it's more prone to blockage or damage). The 'flow' circuit feeds the hot water to each radiator and the 'return' circuit takes the old cooler water back to the boiler.

Below: Connecting woodburner stove pipe to main twinwall flue – needs careful planning!

For timber floors the pipework can be installed within the floor space. For concrete ground floors the pipework is normally surface-run along walls and boxed in, or sometimes run in special ducts embedded within the screed. To reduce heat loss and prevent freezing in winter pipework serving radiators should be lagged where run anywhere that's cold such as within suspended ground floor voids. Poorly supported pipes can be noisy and prone to damage, so 15mm pipework should be supported with a clip at least every 1.4m and at each change of direction. Larger sized pipes can have supports a little further apart.

Before installing radiators you need to calculate their required sizes to heat individual rooms. Radiator output is measured in BTUs (British Thermal Units) and is calculated according to the size of each room and its level of insulation (see website BTU calculator).

Gone are the days when you could have any radiator you wanted, as long as it was oblong and white-panelled. Today, adding a new rad means an opportunity to splash out on some seriously cool design. For the style conscious, the sky's the limit with all kinds of fun shapes to choose from.

For optimum room warmth, radiators are traditionally positioned under windows on outer walls since this is the point where the room is normally coldest (the rads counteract room air cooling where it meets a cold window and falls, becoming a draught). For bathrooms, a radiator towel rail is a useful addition.

Central heating systems need periodic maintenance including flushing-through to reduce limescale, and ideally should be checked annually under a service contract. Pressurised 'combi'-type systems require more frequent bleeding to release built-up air.

Electric heating is quite common in areas without a gas supply, typically comprising fixed storage heaters. These take down cheaper off-peak electricity at night, store it in special bricks and release the heat the next day. But electric heating is not only the most expensive system to run, but is also the most uncontrollable and the biggest CO_2 emitter. Popular alternative fuels in areas without a mains gas supply are oil, bottled LPG/Calor gas, and solid fuel (coal, coke, wood etc).

If you quite fancied the idea of having a living flame gas fire to add some glamour to your bedroom – tough. They're only permitted in reception rooms. Not only that, but all living flame gas fires, and most open-flued heating appliances (with a higher than 7kW input rating) require additional room ventilation usually in the form of a pair of 230 x 230mm airbricks in the wall.

Hot water

Deciding on the hot water system that's best for you isn't necessarily as straightforward as it sounds. A typical home of four people typically needs around 230 litres of hot water a day, heated to about 60°C. But the required volume of hot water is only one factor. Your choice of system

Photo: roycebathrooms.co.uk

will also depend on the required pressure of delivery (the flow rate), and how much space is available for boilers, hot water cylinders and tanks. But of course supplying a new extension normally involves extending the existing system where, typically, hot water is stored in a cylinder in the airing cupboard, which also usually incorporates an electric immersion heater. The water is heated by copper tubes inside the cylinder, which contain hot water from the boiler, transferring the heat to the water in the cylinder. The domestic hot water (DHW) doesn't pass through the boiler at all, so it's known as an 'indirect system'. An emergency

Unvented pressurised hot water cylinders supplied direct from mains with no need for loft tanks.

expansion pipe from the cylinder leads up to the 'feed and expansion' header tank above.

But things are changing. As noted earlier, with modern pressurised hot water systems (referred to as 'unvented') any emergency discharge is taken by a connected expansion vessel capable of storing hot water at mains pressure, rather than utilising loft tanks. In a typical system, incoming cold mains supply is heated either directly in the cylinder by an electric heater, or indirectly from your central heating boiler. When you open a tap, the hot water stored in the vessel is forced out by incoming mains cold water, hence you get hot water at mains pressure. This solves the problem of weedy flow rates to showers, but such systems need at least 2.5bar of mains water supply pressure to work well, and there is no back up storage tank in the event that your supply is cut off.

Boilers

Adding extra radiators to a creaky old existing system may be the straw that breaks the camel's back. The old boiler may not be of sufficient capacity to cope with heating the extra rooms. As a rough guide, depending on how they're maintained, boilers may last no more than around 15 years. So renewal may be overdue anyway.

Boilers are rated according to the power they produce, measured in BTUs. One kilowatt is equivalent to 3,410 BTUs. As a rule of thumb, a 40,000 BTU boiler should be capable of heating seven radiators, as well as producing hot water. But, as noted above, you need to carry out a heat calculation for each room to accurately determine how much boiler power is needed.

Boilers are awarded energy efficiency ratings, from A (90–94 per cent efficient) to G (50–70 per cent efficient). But as well as running costs, reliability is probably the single most important factor. The choice of available brands and models should be discussed with the contractor early on in the project, otherwise you may get lumbered with some obscure make for which spare parts are scarce.

Boilers are available that run on a wide variety of fuels as well as mains gas, such as oil, bottled gas (LPG/ propane), and even solid fuel. A useful website to compare boilers is www.seduk.com.

Every household in the UK creates around six tonnes of carbon dioxide emissions a year. Looked at another way, almost a third of the nation's CO2 emissions come from the energy used in our homes – which is why all new boilers are now of the 'condensing' type. The secret of modern boilers is their extra large heat exchangers, which make for a very efficient combustion process. Much of the waste heat pumped out in the exhaust gases is captured and recycled, so the exhaust temperatures can be as low as 50 degrees (compared to over 200 degrees on traditional boilers). This in turn means flues can be made of plastic, and accounts for the large, steamy clouds or 'plumes' of water vapour emitted from flue terminals. Another distinctive feature is their propensity to emit quantities of mildly acidic condensation, which needs to be piped to an outside gulley, or into the soil stack.

If you're installing a new boiler to serve your freshly extended home, you may want to consider fitting a combination boiler (which are also condensing boilers). Combis currently account for around 50% of UK boiler sales. The great thing about them is they are very efficient at providing endless hot water instantly, as well as taking care of your space heating requirements. They are bulkier than ordinary boilers since they contain a built-in hot-water vessel, but crucially the need for separate water tanks and cylinders is dispensed with, as well as all that costly associated plumbing. So although dearer to buy, they are actually cheaper and easier to install. Their limitations have traditionally been their low flow rates, so look for ones than can achieve more than 1.5 litres per minute. It's also worth noting that when hot water is simultaneously demanded at taps and for room heating the former takes priority. So for extended properties with multiple bathrooms a more powerful boiler and pressurised unvented cylinder system is likely to provide a better solution.

Modern wall-mounted boilers breathe through small circular balanced flues projecting through the wall. These are room-sealed, requiring no extra air vents to the room in which they're situated. They draw their air for combustion from outside (via the outer ring of the flue) and expel exhaust gases externally through the same flue (inner ring).

The rules governing location of balanced flue terminals are quite complex, but generally fan-assisted flues serving gas appliances should be at least 300mm away from opening windows, doors or vents and 150mm from window or door frames (ie the edge of an opening) For flues serving oil-fired appliances double these distances. Flues obviously shouldn't discharge into enclosed areas like side passages – they must have air passing freely over them. Internally, extendable flue ducts can provide greater flexibility for positioning of boilers.

The preferred location for boilers is within garages, kitchens, or utility rooms. Locating them in bedrooms or bathrooms is normally discouraged, although it should still be possible with a room-sealed appliance. But boilers in such locations should be boxed-in (eg enclosed within a cupboard) and may need external wall vents unless they're of a type that can work safely at higher temperatures. On a small extension there may be no spare wall space available, so vertical flues that pass through a roof can sometimes be fitted.

Until a few years ago, it was acceptable for boiler overflow pipes to be left poking crudely through outside walls. This of course meant that anyone hanging out down below would be in for a disagreeable surprise in the event of a faulty boiler suddenly squirting out a high pressure stream of boiling water. So the regulations now require pipes to be safely directed downward to ground level along the outer wall surface.

Controls

The task of wiring heating controls to boilers, programmers, pumps etc, is sometimes done by plumbers, although the electrician will need to position a fused spur socket nearby.

Extending your home's heating system means you have a perfect opportunity to fit better controls. This can have real benefits since central heating (CH) and hot water (HW) account for 75% of a home's typical energy bill (the rest being cooking, lighting, and plug-in appliances etc). There's a lot you can do to ensure you have effective controls to manage both hot water and room heating with aim of reducing energy use.

For room heating the best arrangement is to have a wall mounted master thermostat, in addition to adjustable thermostatic radiator valves (TRVs) fitted to each radiator,

Left: Boiler flues need to be positioned carefully.

Right: Chrome 15mm pipe tails are a nice touch.

allowing a custom temperature to be set for each room. Traditional room thermostats sense the air temperature in the room where they're installed. To work accurately they need to be positioned on a wall about 1.5m above floor level.

You need to be able to control heating and water separately and most makes of boiler now have the option of built-in clock programmers as well as a thermostat control that shuts off when the water gets to a certain temperature. Thermostats should also be fitted to hot water cylinders. Essentially, programmers are sophisticated on/off switches for the whole heating system, overriding other controls. Old systems relied on gravity and convection to move water around, but modern boilers use integral pumps. Extending your existing system may therefore require an additional electronic slave pump to improve flow.

However the limitation with these sort of conventional controls is they're inflexible. Standard time clocks are okay for people with predicable lifestyles, always knowing what time they'll be at home, go to bed and get up in the morning. For greater flexibility you can fit more sophisticated clock-programmers with three ON/OFF periods and weekend/holiday modes. But the trouble is, these tend to be fiddly to use, so most of us just stick to the factory settings.

This is where modern smart home technology can improve efficiency, by allowing us to control our heating on the go, from mobiles or tablets. The CH can be switched on or off automatically by linking to your mobile which knows where you are (known as 'occupancy detection'). You can even set the desired temperature for different rooms via an app (a Wi-Fi module is built into each rad). And if you're a bit of a geek it also lets you chart the energy consumption and cost of your heating. Some apps can additionally control lighting, audio-visual, security, and smoke alarms. You can even visually view your house remotely and control the sounds and lighting - perfect for foxing burglars!

There are 2 types of intelligent control systems (costing from around £200). Some use a device called a gateway which connects 'smart rads' to your Wi-Fi router. Other systems have built-in Wi-Fi which allows direct connection to your phone.

Boiler stoves

Woodburning stoves are a great way of giving your living space a massive heating boost in cold weather (see page 196). One major attraction is that you can harness 'free energy' whenever you feel like it by nipping down to the woods and shoving some of nature's offcuts into a sack. So it might be worth considering going one stage further by installing a woodburning boiler stove, combining the functions of a small boiler for hot water and conventional stove for space heating. Boiler stoves can churn out between 5 and 20 kW of water heating, plus an equivalent output to heat the room. Pellet stoves with back boilers

are larger than woodburners (around 1600mm tall) and have to be loaded from the top, usually via an automated hopper, and are often located in garages or outbuildings. Installation needs to be done by a HETAS registered engineer who can advise on connecting up an existing system with a hot water cylinder.

Underfloor heating (UFH)

After a slow start (it was invented by the Romans), underfloor heating is becoming increasingly popular in new properties, and is often installed in kitchens. Although costlier than just extending your central heating system, it does add a touch of luxury, plus there's the added benefit of freeing up wall space with no bulky radiators to get in the way of your furniture.

There are two main types:

- Wet piped systems: Warm water is pumped at low pressure via a manifold control centre through concealed pipework buried in the floor screed which acts as a heat reservoir, rather like a storage heater.
- Dry electric systems: Electric heating elements, in the form of ultra-thin flexible mats, can be laid directly under floor coverings. Especially popular with ceramic tiles. An easier choice for upgrading a small existing floor such as a cloakroom floor or for a very small extension. Installation costs are lower but long term running costs are expensive.

For new home extensions, wet systems are by far the best option. These employ a series of narrow plastic water pipes run in loops embedded within the floor covering.

UFH manifold 'control centre' takes hot water from boiler and directs it out to pipes embedded in screed

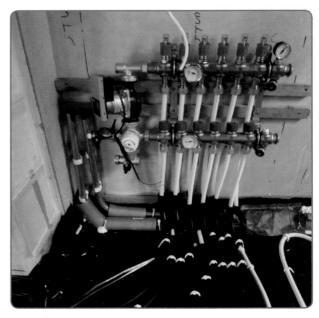

UFH pipes leading out from manifold to supply different floor zones

One dilemma when extending a kitchen, for example, is whether to dig up the old existing floor to get consistent heating across whole room, not just in the new extended part. But removing and reinstating an existing floor likely to be uneconomic, adding a four figure sum to build cost. However in some cases it may be possible to install a less expensive low-profile system designed to sit on top of existing floor.

Other design related issues to bear in mind:-

■ Flooring: Tiles, stone, and slate are ideal as they absorb heat along with the screed. Solid wood shouldn't be used as it insulates, but thinner profile engineered timber (less than 20mm) is compatible as there's little impact on heat output. Carpet and underlay is not ideal but can be acceptable if thermal resistance less than about 1.5 Togs.

■ Type of type and size of pipes: There are 2 types – standard single layer or multi-layer (can be mix of plastic and aluminium). Multi-layer is more efficient and durable, but dearer. You also need to decide where best to locate the manifold 'brain' that supplies the pipes.

■ Zone control: Larger extensions will need separate pipe runs to each room. Open plan layouts have several zones supplied direct from the manifold (so they heat up quicker).

■ Floor screeds: Traditional sand/cement screed is typically 60-75mm thick with a 2 or 3 hour reaction time. Modern liquid screeds have better thermal conductivity and need only be 40mm thick giving a reaction time of less than 1 hour.

UFH pipes buried in conventional sand/cement floor screed

Photos: Wavin Hepworth

They're normally laid above the insulation layer (obviously not below it) with the screed placed on top, so the heat is released slowly staying close to the floor. Most floor finishes are compatible, but they're especially effective when used with stone or tiled surfaces that would otherwise be cold. If you're worried about your dinner party guests complaining of scorched feet this shouldn't be a problem. Typical floor surface temperatures are a comfortable 26–29°C, and are temperature-controlled by room thermostats. Underfloor systems are actually highly energy efficient, since to heat an entire room they need only be set to relatively low room temperatures (10–15°) compared to radiator systems (18–30°). This suits modern condensing boilers, which are at their most efficient at lower temperatures, but can also work well with heat pumps.

UFH may be a little more expensive to install than standard rads, but is cheaper to run and can provide good background heat. Because it heats from the ground up, the area of the room we actually occupy gets warmed soonest, resulting in greater comfort and lower bills. By the windows, the rising warm air cancels out the cool air that's falling. In comparison, warmth from radiators rises up to heat the ceiling first and the floor last, so temperatures at ceiling level can reach 25 degrees before the floor reaches 20 degrees.

The only snag with UFH is the relatively slow response time. It's best to avoid switching it on and off in short cycles, so this may not be ideal for people who pop briefly in and out of their homes, only occupying them for a few hours a day. That said, modern liquid floor screeds can dramatically shorten response times. Also intelligent controls can be programmed to anticipate temperature changes, boosting warmth when needed. Many users find it best to leave them on 24/7 at a low level, just set at a lower temperature at night. The optimum arrangement is often to have UFH downstairs and radiators upstairs.

Main trades needed on site

■ **Electricians:** Running cables and boxes.
■ **Plumbers:** Running supply pipes, heating pipes and waste pipes. Fitting water tanks and CH systems.

www.home-extension.co.uk

15 PLASTERING, SCREED AND INTERNAL FINISHES

For many homeowners there's only one finish that looks right, and that's good honest plasterwork. Saving a few quid with a cheap and cheerful finish on your extension now could be a big mistake, and simply wouldn't do justice to all the hard work to date.

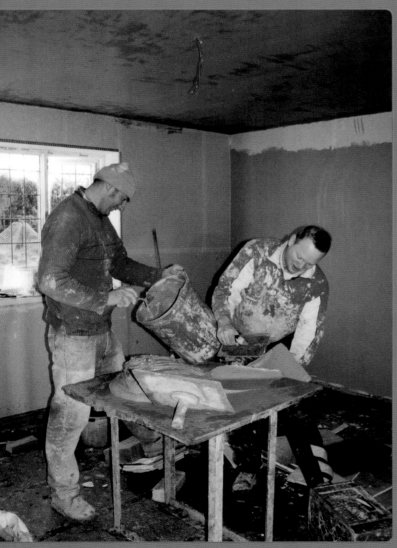

Photo: David Snell / Buildstore.co.uk

Steel angle corner beads create neat edges.

Psychologically, this is one of the big turning points in the entire project. A few days of 'bish, bash, bosh' and the resulting pinky-brown veneer on your walls creates a profound and pleasing transformation. Suddenly those unwelcoming expanses of mortar and masonry will become a recognisable living space and start to feel like part of your home, albeit one in need of decoration and fitting out.

But this brief description of plastering doesn't really do justice to the skills involved. Many of us who pride ourselves at being able to turn our hand to tackling most jobs have had a bash at plastering at one time or another, only to retreat chastened by the unfortunate experience to assess the saggy, uneven results from a safe distance.

So revered were plasterers during the late 1980s housing boom that the legendary 'Loadsamoney' TV character was cast as a high-earning member of this select band. But the expense of employing tax-exile plasterers resulted in a number of alternative finishes being introduced, such as

artex brush-on 'textured' paints designed to disguise rough surfaces (regarded by some as the height of naffness). Or the plastering process could be skipped altogether by 'tape and jointing', with emulsion applied directly to the plasterboard.

For most home extension projects the walls need to be dry-lined with plasterboard to help meet U-value insulation targets. This has largely superseded traditional hard plastered exterior masonry walls which require a base coat of bonding plaster (or sand/cement), plus a single smooth plaster finishing coat. The advantage of this method is that it's extremely durable. The disadvantages are colder wall surfaces, the risk of shrinkage cracking, and the fact that it puts enormous amounts of water into the structure, requiring long drying-out times. By way of contrast, plasterboard-lined walls can be skim-plastered to provide a surface finish. Once decorated, these should look indistinguishable from hard plaster.

There are some surfaces, however, that are better left naked. Where your extension joins the existing house there may be an old brick wall, the former outer wall surface. This can present an opportunity to create a stylish 'urban loft' look by leaving the brick or stonework exposed. Such 'feature brickwork' often looks the business, especially on older properties, and should be finished by applying a masonry sealer. You may even want to re-create the bare brick look on a fireplace chimney breast using reclaimed bricks. But be sure your intentions are clearly communicated to the plasterers or they'll automatically assume their mission is to obliterate every visible surface, and you'll get charged a second time for the extra labour involved in hacking it all off. Another alternative is Victorian pine matchboarding, fixed vertically between skirtings and dado rails, a useful device for hiding pipes and cable runs. But first, there are some key tasks that need to be done elsewhere.

What a smoothie! Multi-finish plaster skimmed plasterboard.

Below: The art of exposure - former Victorian external wall brickwork (left) and period stonework and timbers (right).

Window boards

Once the windows have been installed the inside ledges can be formed by fixing the window boards in place. Like skirting and architraves, window boards are sold in primed MDF or softwood, or dearer hardwood where you want to display their natural beauty. If your windows are of timber, and you're wondering what the horizontal grooves along the lower back are for, they're actually for the boards to be neatly rebated into. Some boards have a projecting thin rear lip designed to slot into these grooves, others have are flat at the back allowing more flexible positioning. The boards are fitted level and flat, with the curved 'nosing' edge projecting into the room. They usually extend about 20mm wider than the window itself, beyond the plastered wall reveals. So fitting the boards prior to lining the window opening reveals should save having to later cut slots in the plasterboard or rebate the window boards ends in an 'L' shape so the nosings extend either side.

Before the plastering work starts in earnest, to avoid getting mountainous blobs of indelible plaster all over your nice new window ledges it's advisable to cover them with protective sheets, thereby saving hours of laborious scraping and sanding.

Plasterboard

Plasterboard is an indispensable modern building material, providing a quick and easy way of covering large expanses of wall and ceiling. Essentially it comprises a thick layer of compressed rigid gypsum plaster sandwiched between heavy-duty sheets of lining paper. It has been universally used for many years for ceilings

Heavy ceiling boards fitted with aid of 'deadman' props (extension support rods) and a willing helper

and stud partition walls, having finally superseded traditional lath and plaster in the 1930s.

Whilst you might have justifiable misgivings about ever truly mastering the art of plastering, lining walls with plasterboard should be within the capabilities of most seasoned DIYers. Having said that, neat and accurate fixing is crucial to the finished appearance. It's also hard graft.

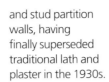

Above: Scrim tape seals joints.
Below: Stapling steel angle beads in place at corners.

Boards are commonly sold in thicknesses of 9.5mm and 12.5mm (some are also available in thicker 15mm sizes). They come in two main sheet sizes – giant economy size 2,400 x 1,200mm and the not quite so backbreaking 1,800 x 900mm size. These dimensions perfectly suit studs or joists spaced at 600, 450 or 400mm centres, so you could be in for a nasty surprise if you've spaced your studs any differently. In such a situation either the edges of boards will be left

Right and below: Taped and jointed – once neatly filled plasterboard can be decorated direct without plastering

unsupported (not a good idea) or the boards will have to be specially cut to fit.

Traditionally, boards had ivory-coloured paper on one side and a grey finish on the other. The ivory surface was for wallpapering onto directly, whereas the grey side would give a better bond when skimmed with a finishing plaster. Most plasterboard now comes with a grey surface suitable for either skimming or decorating. The main advantage to decorating direct to the plasterboard is that it's cheaper and a realistic DIY project, although taping and jointing needs to be done skillfully to look neat.

If you want to use something more exciting than standard off-the-shelf boards, you can pick from a variety of specialist products such as thick sheets of thermally insulated plasterboard, pink fire-resistant boards, the foil-backed type that blocks condensation, or moisture-resistant linings for use in steamy bathrooms. For beefed-up sound insulation try the special blue acoustic variety or gypsum fibre boards, which are not only more durable but are also strong enough to accept wall fixings directly.

Dry lining

It's standard practice for aerated blockwork inner leaf of main walls to be dry-lined and ceilings tacked before skim-coating the walls and ceilings. As well as providing a nice flat smooth surface, dry-lining cuts out the expense and hassle of wet plastering which would otherwise introduce damp into the building, whilst boosting the thermal insulation to help achieve good U-values. Although dry-lining is actually more expensive than traditional hard plastering, this is offset by savings from skimming (or decorating direct) with minimal delay before decorating. Skimmed plasterboard walls and ceilings of only 2mm thickness dry out very swiftly and can normally be decorated within a few days, using special 'fresh plaster' emulsion (the plaster visibly lightens colour as it dries out).

A useful tip for easier fixing of curtain rails and blinds later on is to fit plywood strips above each window prior to dry lining.

Plasterboard sheets can be fixed to the blockwork walls by squashing them on to blobs of plaster adhesive known as 'dabs', or tacked to a timber framework of battens fixed to the masonry, or to timber stud internal partition walls. In all cases the joints should be staggered, to reduce the risk of cracking. Where fixed to studwork, joists or rafters, plasterboard sheets are secured with dry wall screws using cordless screwdrivers (rather than hammering in old fashioned clout nails). Even so, with larger boards you'll need four hands rather than two. Having dabbed out the walls the boards can be stood up and pushed into place. A useful trick of the trade is to use a simple foot-lifter or 'seesaw' made from a spare offcut of wood, which can be wedged under the wall boards to lever them against the wall surface.

To conceal joints some boards have slightly thinner tapered edges, so that where they meet and are screwed in place the recess can be filled with scrim tape and jointing

compound. Some plasterers use superior quality 'silk' scrim for taping joints. Don't forget to tape junctions at corners between walls and also, if you're not using coving, at joints to ceilings using flexible metal corner tape. This binds the whole surface together to prevent subsequent shrinkage and cracking. At projecting wall corners, angle beads should be first fixed over them (e.g. using a staple gun) before being skimmed over for a neat finish.

Decorating directly onto plasterboard

- If you want to decorate direct to the surface without plastering it's best to use 'tapered-edge' boards rather than square-edged. These have thinner sides so that when they're butted together a very shallow recess is formed either side of a joint.
- The recess can be filled with jointing compound and then covered with joint tape (or a traditional cotton or hessian 'scrim').
- When dry, it is then filled with two more coats of jointing compound, each one sanded down when dry. Each coat has a setting time of roughly 90 minutes.
- Going over the edges with a damp sponge helps disguise the joint, leaving a smooth surface.
- Finally, the surface can be sealed before receiving two coats of emulsion.

Photos: Lafarge Plasterboard.

Rigid insulation boards cut and fitted between rafters and any gaps sealed with expanding foam.

Plastic sheet vapour barrier applied to stop moist air from room entering roof structure.

Ceilings

Exposed reclaimed timbers add instant character.

Your choice of plasterboard will depend on how the joists are spaced. The thicker 12.5mm type is needed where ceiling joists are at 600mm centres, since 9.5mm board can only realistically cope with spans of up to 400mm between joists.

Where you're boarding a ceiling which has a cold space on the other side, such as a typical bedroom ceiling (below the loft) it's recommended that special foil-backed plasterboard is used. The foil helps prevent warm moist air from the house getting through and condensing into damp in the roof. Alternatively, a large polythene sheet vapour barrier can be fixed to the joists or rafters before boarding. In some locations, such as when boarding direct onto the roof structure, you will first need to place insulation between joists or rafters before plasterboarding, usually with an additional layer of insulation, or under the rafters or joists (or use thick insulated plasterboard to combine both layers).

When it comes to boarding ceilings it helps if you have the physique of Iron Man. Failing that, see if you can

conjure up a willing (and preferably glamorous) assistant. It's not unknown for the professionals to accomplish the Herculean task of boarding ceilings single handed, holding full size plasterboard sheets above their heads before feeding them onto supporting props (known as 'dead men') and stepping onto a hop-up (folding aluminium step) to fix them using a dry wall screw gun. Not bad, bearing in mind thicker 15mm boards weigh 35kg each!

Once fully 'tacked out' ceilings are normally skim plastered. But first the joints between boards need to be scrim taped, similarly to the walls. The thin finishing coat of smooth plaster is applied by hand-held trowel, the plasterer standing on planks laid across small scaffold towers (or wearing special stilts!). Where you've got sloping bedroom ceilings, rolling the join between the sloped and horizontal planes of the ceilings will give the rooms a nice barn-like appearance. Any coving or decorative mouldings can be fitted afterwards.

Fire

There are about 60,000 house fires a year, with over 500 deaths – the vast majority of which are preventable with a few simple precautions. Fortunately, standard masonry and plasterboard are both naturally fire-resistant and should easily achieve the required surface spread fire rating ('Class 1'). Plasterboard ceilings can normally protect the floor structure above for at least 20 minutes. But despite being reassuringly non-combustible and inert, to be fully fireproof the surface needs to be skim plastered so that the paper lining doesn't get burnt and peel off. This is why ceilings and partition walls to integral garages must be plastered. In locations especially at risk from fire-

Far left and left: Insulated plasterboard fixed under rafters and skim plastered.

spread the best solution is to use special pink-coloured fire-rated type (either 12.5mm or 15mm).

In a typical house fire, flames will spread rapidly across the ceilings. It is at this juncture that some DIY enthusiasts have come to regret fitting highly combustible polystyrene foam tiles or timber cladding. It's a fact that in the space of just half an hour untreated softwood can burn through to a depth of at least 25mm, enough to weaken a timber structure

sufficiently to bring about collapse. So walls and ceilings cannot be lined with, say, untreated plywood, although paint-on coatings can be applied to protect timber surfaces if required.

Steels

The use of steel beams can permit designs that would otherwise be structurally impossible. Vast open roof spaces with cavernous ceilings, or sheet-glazed expanses of curtain walling are examples of the structural gymnastics afforded by monster UBs (Universal Beams). Tough though they undoubtedly are, as noted earlier, steels behave badly when confronted by fire, being prone to alarming degrees of buckling and twisting. This isn't what you want to see when your floors and walls are dependent on them for support. In short, they need protecting. Fortunately, the application of pink fire-rated board over a timber framework or 'cradle' (or double layers of conventional plasterboard) with a skim plaster finish should provide the required minimum 30 minutes fire resistance to keep Building Control happy. If, however, you favour the raw steel and bare brick 'warehouse look' in your extension, painting the exposed beams with special intumescent paint should do the trick (see Chapter 10). This is applied in 2 layers comprising an intumescent first coat and a flame-spread resistant top coat. When done it should look like any other painted finish.

Boarding internal walls

Back in Chapter 13 we left the freshly-built timber stud walls awaiting 'first fix'. This having now been done they are ready for tacking. This job is made more challenging by the profusion of cables and pipes sprouting out of the walls and it's advisable to protect such services with clingfilm or tape since plastering by its nature can be a messy business. Normally pipes and cables should be run centrally through studwork to keep them out of harm's way, beyond the reach of plasterboard dry-wall screws.

As noted earlier, for timber stud walls in locations that require better soundproofing or added resistance to the spread of fire, (such as those to integral garages), it's preferable to use the 12.5mm boards in double layers with staggered joints and a skim finish, or specially manufactured acoustic board or fire-board, with mineral wool stuffed between the studs.

Hard plastering

Modern gypsum plasters are far easier to use than traditional Victorian 'hair-lime' wall finishes (lime mixed with sand and a horsehair binder), being quicker to dry and less prone to cracking. However, that doesn't mean the finished job is guaranteed to be brilliant. The reality is that a lack of care on site means that a large percentage of the snagging issues that arise after completion often relate to plastering defects. Problems such as cracking or surface coats coming loose (due to shrinkage of backing coats) are not unusual. One particular weak point is where timber stud walls meet masonry brick or blockwork because of the risk of the plaster surfaces cracking at the join between the different materials, due to their different rates of expansion. Fixing metal lath over the join before plastering should hide any such movement. Likewise, where timber lintels or wallplates etc need to be plastered, metal lath

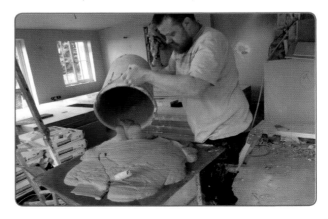

Plasters of the world

There are many brands and varieties of plaster on the market, including some special-purpose plasters such as those designed to give protection from X-rays! But whatever the brand name, they can generally be classified as:

- **Browning:** A lightweight gypsum plaster used for the base coat on normal surfaces such as blockwork. It's applied quite thickly to about 10mm to smooth any unevenness in the wall. Surfaces with high 'suction', such as aerated concrete blocks, may need a surface coat of PVA adhesive prior to plastering. Sets within about 2 hours.

- **Bonding:** An alternative lightweight gypsum plaster backing coat for surfaces that have poor 'suction', *ie* that don't readily absorb moisture, such as engineering bricks and some dense concrete blocks. Never use two layers of bonding plaster as it can cause shrivelling and crazing in the top coat – instead apply a layer of browning plaster over a layer of bonding. Sets within about 2 hours.

- **Sand/cement render:** So hard that it's normally used externally, render can also be used inside as a base coat. It's comparatively heavy and impact-resistant. Often used where there's some risk of damp, such as in basements or rooms prone to condensation. It needs to be 'scratched' and left to dry for a few days before the finish coat is applied.

- **Finishing:** A 'multi-finish' surface coat is applied as a 'skim' direct to plasterboard or on top of the base coat once it has hardened, to a depth of about 2mm (no more than 5mm). Can be trowelled off to produce a smooth 'polished' surface where walls are to be emulsioned. If you intend skimming over existing plaster or previously painted surfaces, rather than direct to plasterboard, then a coat of diluted PVA bonding should be applied, otherwise the surface may crack. Sets within about 1.5 hours.

- **One-coat:** Instead of requiring a day between coats of conventional plaster, one-coat plasters can allow the work to be carried out in one operation, but 'trowelling-off' takes more skill and patience.

Helpful tip: When mixing plaster, always add the plaster to the water, not the other way round.

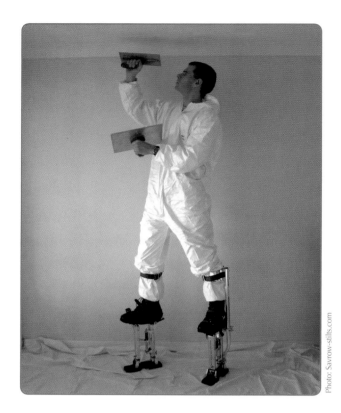

should be first put in place to carry the plaster surface over them and to protect the timber.

Some homeowners prefer the appeal of 'good solid' walls rather than conventional dry-lining which sounds disconcertingly hollow when you tap it, as well as being more difficult to hang things from. So if your internal walls are of blockwork, or your main walls are not dry-lined, they'll require the hard plaster treatment (not an option for timber-framers).

Here, two coats of plaster will be needed, a base coat to cover the rough blocks, and a lightweight gypsum plaster coat for a smooth finish. This, of course, assumes the walls have been reasonably well built – no amount of 'dubbing out' can easily overcome an out-of-plumb wall,

Skim plaster drying out from dark chocolate to pale pink, ready to decorate in a few days.

Nearly ready for second fix.

and no amount of paint or wallpapering will successfully cover bad plastering.

One of the secrets of successful plastering is to specify the right plaster for the job. The type of base coat to use will depend on the surface to be plastered. You may either choose a 'browning' or a 'bonding' plaster, or even a sand/cement render base coat. Porous masonry may first need to be brushed with diluted PVA to improve the bond. This 'floating coat', as it's known, is applied over the bare wall to a depth of about 8–16mm using a hawk and trowel. It is then 'scratched' to provide a key for the finish coat. The base coat is allowed to set for a few hours, but not to completely 'go off' and become too dry, otherwise it will need dampening before the smooth finishing coat can be applied. The skim coat is applied with a float, and a brush to flick water onto the surface to achieve a hard shiny finish (or a fine plant sprayer can come in useful). With modern plasters it should be possible to apply the base coat in the morning and the finish coat in the afternoon, or at least within 24 hours.

The drying-out process with traditional two-coat plasterwork can mean having to wait anything between two and six weeks before decorating. A 'breathable' water-based paint designed for fresh plaster should be used rather than vinyl emulsion, which can trap in any residual moisture. If your base coat is of sand/cement render, it may take even longer to fully dry out. The rule of thumb is to allow about one month per inch total thickness of plaster, but in reality the weather and localised conditions on site can significantly affect performance. Builders have been known

to assist nature's drying out process by installing battalions of industrial sized heaters, roaring away like jet engines. But overly-rapid drying can result in cracking and create moisture and condensation elsewhere, which doesn't do the timbers much good. Too much heat from air dryers will suck moisture off the face of the plaster, leading to a 'crazy-paving' effect. Just providing good ventilation to the room is normally the best approach.

Modern plaster contains a retardant to delay premature setting and to extend workability, but this becomes less efficient after a long storage period, so never use old plaster since it will dry too quickly. The shelf life for bags of new plaster may be no more than three to four months, and they should be stored on site within strong plastic bags to prevent damp finding its way in and making the material useless.

Many months later, when you've happily moved in and the building work is but a distant memory, it's not unknown for a strange phenomenon to occur. The plastered interiors of the main walls in some modern buildings have been known to develop a weird ghostly effect called 'pattern staining' where the shape of the concrete blocks can be made out, eerily appearing through coats of plaster and emulsion. This is normally down to the mortar joints becoming visible since they're less well insulated than the lightweight aerated blocks, and being colder they attract condensation from warm, humid indoor air. This in turn allows more dust to stick, creating the pattern. The solution is to wash the wall or redecorate, ideally with darker colours which will show it less. In severe cases, dry-lining over a problem wall with foil-backed plasterboard should help solve the problem.

Plastering a masonry wall

Plastering a wall requires considerable care and patience, as plaster is not the easiest of materials to work with. It may readily slip from the hawk or trowel, or may slump perilously down the wall.

Hard plaster applied to masonry in 2 coats takes longer to dry .

First, check that internal door linings are in place and positioned to suit the required depth of plaster (say about 12mm). Similarly, metal boxes for electric sockets and switches should have been set into the masonry but left projecting so that when the plastering is completed they'll be flush with the surface. Check that any conduits and pipes are securely fixed, with no pipes touching each other, and that there's sufficient space for them to be buried within the plaster covering.

Corner beading of galvanised metal or plastic should be fitted to any outer corners of walls, door openings, and window reveals. These are set in dabs of plaster and carefully aligned using a spirit level (or they can be anchored with galvanised masonry nails or a staple gun).

To ensure the correct depth of plaster across the entire wall it can be divided up into manageable sections, or bays, using vertical wooden battens temporarily nailed into place. These are known as 'grounds' and provide a useful guide to the plaster's depth. They should be set out using a spirit level so that they're truly vertical.

Working upwards from the bottom right corner of each bay, the plaster is applied in parallel vertical strips. Once each bay is plastered with its floating coat (base coat), its surface can be smoothed by running a wide horizontal batten up from ground level running along the 'grounds' on either side, like railway lines. This is performed with a sawing motion and then any low spots are filled with more plaster. As each bay is completed, the right hand 'ground' can be repositioned to form a new bay ready for plastering. Once the plaster surface has been keyed, the final thin layer of finishing plaster will later be applied.

Rigid floor insulation laid and joints sealed with expanding foam. Awaits plastic cover sheeting, UFH and screed.

Insulating the floor

Back in Chapter 8, when the ground floor was being constructed, it was suggested that the insulation layer was best left until later so it didn't get mashed up or buried under tonnes of muck and builders' junk food wrappers. So in most cases your concrete floor slab or beam and block structure will now need to be lined with a thick layer of insulation. The only time this wouldn't be needed is when solid concrete floors have already been insulated beneath the slab, at the foundation stage (or more rarely where you've opted for Victorian-style suspended timber floors with the insulation placed between the joists).

The first job is to seal around any pipes or service entry ducts sticking up through the floor structure or from the foundation walls to prevent air from entering the building by injecting expanding foam around them. The insulation around incoming water pipes and soil stacks should extend under the slab to protect against frost. As described earlier, a thick polythene DPM sheeting (1000 - 2000 gauge damp proof membrane) then needs to be laid over the clean surface of the grouted or blinded floor structure (see page 121). Adjoining DPM sheets need to be overlapped (minimum 100mm) and all the joints taped. Next, rigid sheets of special flooring-grade insulation materials (e.g. PUR, PIR or PF typically around 100mm thick) are cut and laid in place. Beam & block floors have a cambered surface so it's important to ensure the boards don't rock about when walked on, so it may help to use smaller sheets cut to size.

Floor screeding

Screed is a very effective way of levelling uneven ground floor structures. It is by far the most widely adopted type of surface upon which carpets, tiles or wood flooring etc can be laid. Conventionally, it takes the form of a traditional sand/cement mix and is usually carried out by the plasterers. However, there are alternatives to screeding, such as placing floorboarding over battens and a layer of polythene sheeting. And, as already noted, where solid concrete floors have already been insulated beneath the slab, together with the DPM, a sand/cement screed mix can now be applied directly over the slab to a relatively thin minimum depth of 40mm, the concrete having been dampened down with a bonding mixture. This 'grout' of water and cement is mixed to a creamy consistency with diluted PVA bonding and applied prior to laying the screed.

In most cases however at this stage your floor will be a sea of freshly laid thick insulation boards. The next step involves securely taping the joints between boards and at the edges. This is to prevent any liquid seeping between

Above and above right: Poured liquid screeds are self-levelling and thinner than sand/cement, ideal for UFH.

the boards when the screed is placed causing them to lift up and start floating, as well as preventing any reaction between the screed and insulation. There also needs to be an insulated upstand (25mm or thicker) placed around the perimeter walls. The 'floating screed' mix can now be poured. Traditional sand/cement screed needs to be laid to a minimum depth of 65mm. Modern liquid screeds however can be paid quicker and thinner - see boxout.

If you plan to run pipes or cables through the screed, purpose-made plastic ducts should be embedded within it, with access covers for maintenance (since unprotected copper pipes in concrete floors will corrode within a few years). Here it's advisable to add a minimum extra 10mm depth of screed to reduce the risk of cracking.

As a precaution, pipe ducts and conduits should be

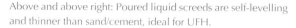

Below and below right: Traditional sand/cement screed trowelled and levelled by hand. External edges of floor must be protected with strips of insulation.

located away from the edges of the room to avoid any risk of puncture from overenthusiastic carpet fitters later banging in sharp carpet-gripper nails. Screeds usually don't need reinforcement, but where the floor loadings are likely to be unusually heavy, then reinforcement mesh can be placed within the mix to reduce the risk of cracking.

The screeding mix should be quite dry, without too much water, and can be mixed on site from cement and sharp sand. A mix of 1:3 cement/sand is better for flexible floor coverings like vinyl, and 1:4 for a rigid tile floor. To avoid sandy patches and hollow areas in the floor, the mortar must be well mixed. Or preferably have it delivered ready-mixed in truck-loads for guaranteed quality and consistency.

Achieving a nice, smooth, perfectly level surface is more difficult than it sounds – some builders have been known to produce floors you could ski down. Obtaining a level floor finish is made easier by dividing the slab into oblong strips or 'bays', using thin wooden planks known as 'screeding rails' to act as depth guides. These must be perfectly level and placed across the floor about every 450mm, parallel to each other. Once poured, the screed

Photo: Wavin Hepworth

Liquid screeds

Conventional sand/cement floor screeds mixed on site by labourers often suffer from patchy quality, uneven finish and surface cracking. Modern poured liquid screeds installed by specialist firms on the other hand produce a much higher quality floor. They are ideally suited to underfloor heating (UFH) being laid a lot thinner; some only need 20mm covering over the pipes (so about 35-40mm total thickness) making it far more efficient at conducting heat into the room with quicker response times to temperature changes. Also because the liquid fully envelopes the pipes eliminating voids, heat transfer between the pipes and the screed is further enhanced.

Most liquid screeds are made from gypsum (like wall plaster) but the terminology can be a little confusing because the terms 'anhydrite', 'calcium sulphate' and 'gypsum' are used interchangeably. The key ingredient is anhydrous (dry) calcium sulphate. Although the material itself costs about 50% more per cubic metre than ready mix sand/cement, being poured from a large hose makes it around 20 times quicker to lay with consequent savings on labour. Plus of course it's laid thinner.

One of the big advantages of pumped liquid screeds is that they're self-levelling and self-curing with an almost perfectly level finish. Anhydrite is far less prone to shrinkage than cement and for most extensions there's no need for expansion joints.

The downside is they are more expensive, require greater surface preparation before pouring, and need to be 100% dried and the surfaces-sanded before tiling. However some new cement-based liquid screeds claim to have overcome these drawbacks. But being self-levelling they can't be sculpted to form sloping floors in wet rooms like traditional sand/cement.

Preparation

With liquid screeds the floor surface needs to be prepared with a polythene sheet membrane (e.g. 500 gauge) overlapped and taped at joints, in effect forming a mini swimming pool so the liquid can't escape when poured. At the edges the membrane needs to be draped up the walls about 100mm. Where UFH is installed the pipes must be securely fixed over the polythene membrane/insulation and pressurised to prevent them lifting up as the screed is poured.

Placing

The installers usually arrive on site a couple of hours in advance to set up their pump and check floor measurements to ensure the amount of screed ordered will be sufficient. Working from a level datum point, such as the base of a doorway, a number of tripod levelling gauges are placed around the floor and adjusted to a consistent depth thereby ensuring the finished screed surface is level throughout. Once the mixer truck arrives the pre-mixed pumped screed is poured from a hefty looking hose until the surface level reaches the marker tripods which are then removed. An average extension takes about 30 minutes. To make sure the screed is smooth and level with no air bubbles the screed is then briefly manually agitated by hand using a 'dappling bar'. Any unused screed usually gets chucked in the client's skip.

Drying

Similarly to sand/cement, you can normally walk on the floor after about 48hours once it becomes solid. Normal site traffic can resume after about a week and partition walls etc can start to be erected. But floor coverings can't be laid until the screed is 100% dried out all the way through. The rule of thumb is to allow one day for every millimetre depth up to the first 40mm then 2 days per mm (so typically about a month and a half).

Tiling

With calcium sulphate screeds a fine surface coating of 'laitance' needs to be abraded by sanding after the first week or so, to prepare the surface for later tiling (not required for unbonded flooring such engineered timber boards). Prior to laying tiles porous surfaces also need to be sealed (using a gypsum-friendly sealant). You also need to use special anhydrite-compatible tile adhesives.

Nicely finished conventional sand/cement floor screed using ready mix.

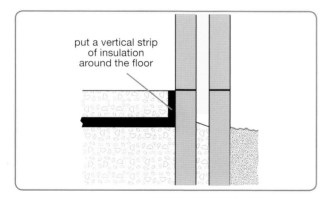

put a vertical strip of insulation around the floor

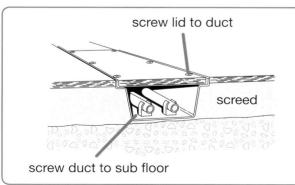

screw lid to duct

screed

screw duct to sub floor

can then easily be levelled by running a wide batten along the top of both rails. The final surface can be smoothed with a steel trowel, keeping the blade wet to lubricate it. Each batten can then be removed once the bays are filled, and each resulting narrow gap packed with screed and smoothed to match. Or the surface can be smoothed using a power float.

Once complete, the wet screed should be protected from over fast drying out in warm weather, and left to cure for at least three days before being walked on. Extra time must be allowed for the newly laid screed to thoroughly dry out before tiling or laying wood flooring etc. This normally means waiting at least another three or four weeks, which is why it makes sense to synchronise the job with the plaster drying-out period.

Main trades needed on site

■ **Carpenters:** Fitting timber window boards etc, fitting insulation
■ **Plasterers:** Dry-lining, plastering walls and ceilings, plasterboarding, fitting insulation, screeding concrete floors.
■ **Labourers:** Carrying materials, mixing plaster

www.home-extension.co.uk

Home Extension Manual

16 SECOND FIX

Once the walls are all nicely plastered, the electrician, plumber and joiner will need to return to complete their work. Whereas the first fix works are hidden away within the structure, the second fix items will be there for all to see. The bathroom sanitary fittings can now be installed, and the kitchen fittings connected up. But first, all the mess left behind by the 'wet trades' should be cleared and the site tidied.

Photo: InHouse kitchens

Although kitchens and bathrooms are one of the last areas to be completed, they depend on quite elaborate plumbing and electrical connections all being in the right place. It's therefore essential to carefully plan your requirements well in advance, to avoid the need for expensive alterations later.

Dream kitchens

During the 1990s, something happened to our relationships with kitchens. The old design template of a kitchenette stuck on the back of the house as something of an afterthought was no longer adequate. The traditional small kitchen and separate dining room layout was pronounced dead. Instead, new houses boasted generous open-plan kitchen/diners, some incorporating bright roof windows and super-wide bi-fold doors. This sudden desire for spacious family kitchens is probably the most significant change in interior layouts for 50 years, somewhat ironically coinciding with the nation's insatiable desire for takeaways and microwave meals. Today, the kitchen is very often the focal point of the home and one of the busiest rooms in the house. Hence the need for many of us to extend.

Designing your new kitchen sounds like fun, but it's fun with a potentially massive price tag attached. Getting carried away is easy, squandering a king's ransom on fabulous hand-crafted bespoke units. But unless you live in a very pukka residence indeed you probably don't need to part with huge piles of cash. The hard truth is, splashing out lavishly on custom fittings will probably make very little difference to the value of the average house when you finally come to sell. Obviously, if you insist on buying exclusive designer brand-name appliances your budget will evaporate more rapidly. But with a bit of thought it shouldn't be too hard to create an impression of opulence using relatively inexpensive units, perhaps set off with a good quality granite or hardwood worktop and some stylish fitted appliances.

Photo: Romanys, EBKE

Photo: Oakwrights.co.uk

Kitchen planning

There's considerably more to designing the layout of a kitchen than first meets the eye, and woe betide those who fail to first consult the ladies. Having to change the position of fittings at a later date is likely to mean re-routing the electrics, the gas pipes, and the plumbing, which will be neither cheap nor easy. So it pays to mull over the proposed kitchen layout at some length well in advance.

Kitchen suppliers are normally happy to create a detailed 3D image of the room so you can easily visualise the new units in place before placing your order. If, however, you don't want to rely entirely on the (not unbiased) opinion of an in-store salesperson, it's not too difficult to conceive your own 'virtual kitchen' before making that purchase commitment. If you're not overly confident with IT and, like most of us, not terribly CAD-literate, invest instead in a pad of graph paper. Carefully draw a scale plan of the kitchen, starting with the main walls, and then add all the window and door openings,

marking the positions of radiators and sockets. Then draw an elevation view looking at each wall in turn as if standing in the room. It may sound a little Blue Peter-ish, but cutting out scale shapes of units and appliances and sticking them on your grid-plan can prove extremely helpful, saving you from making grave errors later on site.

Fortunately, this is one part of the build where Lady Luck really is on your side. The great thing about building a purpose-made extension is that right from the start you can custom-design the room to suit the kitchen units and layout that you want. Need space for a king size wine rack? No problem, just make your extension 600mm bigger. It's far easier building it from scratch than trying to squeeze new kitchen units into an odd-shaped old room with bowed walls, minimal sockets and antique pipework.

Having said that, you still need to have your wits about you. It's scary how easily key design issues can get overlooked – for example, discovering at the last minute that there's a door to a wall or base unit that needs to open just where you wanted to put the fridge. So it's important to carefully plan the hot and cold water supply routes, the wastes for sinks, washing machines, and dishwashers, and vents for dryers. Check the position of all the new electric power point sockets and light switches in relation to the new units and appliances. Also bear in mind the positions for fused isolator switches, oven master controls, cooker hood fans and extractor vent ducting, as well as any under-unit lighting. Not forgetting to check available power supplies for waste disposal units or water softeners etc.

Work surfaces are normally 600mm deep and about 900mm above floor level. Base units are typically 720mm high (or super-tall 1965mm) with adjustable legs adding

Photo: Caple Kitchens

another 150mm or so. Wall units are a similar height but only about half as deep. If there is a standard width it's the 'appliance friendly' 600mm unit, although 300, 400, 450, 500, 1,000 and 1,200mm units are also available. Laminate worktops are usually sold in 38mm thicknesses, but dearer hardwood beech or oak ones can be 28mm or 38–42mm. Beech and birch are considerably cheaper than oak and walnut. Iroko is a popular mid priced alternative. Granite tends to be the most expensive choice but is extremely hard-wearing, along with marble, quartz, solid resin and laminated hardwood.

Builders can normally buy kitchen units at discounts of 20–50% off the list price (but kitchen list prices are generally pretty meaningless!). If your builder both supplies and fits the units, there should be no doubt about who's responsible for fixing any snags like gaps and loose fittings. If you supply your own units this may not be so straightforward.

Kitchen design

- ■ **Internal room measurements** must be accurate and in metric (usually mm). Ensure your kitchen supplier visits the site to take his own measurements, so that he can't blame you later if things don't fit!
- ■ **Check design restrictions** – *ie* the positions of boilers, doors, windows, supply pipes and waste pipes.
- ■ **Mark the position** of hot and cold supply pipes and waste pipes.
- ■ **Electric sockets and switches** must be well clear of hobs and sinks.
- ■ **Note the internal heights** of window sills, and the available ceiling space.
- ■ **Cookers** need a minimum 300mm of clear worktop space either side and should not be located next to a sink or beneath a window.
- ■ **Wall units** must not be fixed directly above a hob/oven or above a sink.
- ■ **Fridges or freezers** shouldn't be next to a cooker.
- ■ **Door swing openings** for all base and wall units should be marked on your plan.

There's a lot of detail to get right when installing new kitchens, so before parting with your next interim payment check that all the units are well fixed to the walls or floors, that the doors operate freely, and that the worktop is the correct thickness and is neatly joined with a decent seal or upstand where it meets the walls. Check also that the finishes have not been damaged or units weakened by holes cut for pipes and cables.

Designer bathrooms

The modern bathroom is much more than just somewhere to wash. If there's one room that can lend itself to a spot of soothing mood creation, this is probably it. Indeed, many sales brochures no longer even refer to '*bathrooms*' as such, instead promoting the virtues of '*aquatic rooms*' – '*havens of relaxation that will help you wash away your day leaving you peaceful and calm*'.

It's hard to argue with that, but what style of fittings would best suit your vibrant new 'aquatic room'? Choose from a mouth-watering selection of spa bath tubs, concealed and counter-sunk units, repro Victorian and Edwardian, corner baths, walk-ins, whirlpools and jacuzzis, massage and steam tubs and baths for aqua aerobics and yoga. Available in a choice of ceramic, marble, granite or glass. And that's before you encounter the wonders of themed panels and decorative toilet seats.

With such a bewildering choice it may help to focus on the original architecture of your house. For example, art deco style fittings should look good in 1920s and 1930s properties, whereas a post-modern glass and stainless steel bathroom won't do a lot to enhance the appeal of a Listed thatched cottage. Post-war houses generally allow more style-freedom and often suit the clean lines of modern designs.

Beyond the choice of sanitary fittings, there are other design issues to ponder, such as whether to install cupboards and bathroom furniture for storage space. If space permits, it's normally a good idea to have a separate

Photo: Heritage-Bathrooms.com

Photo: CPLraindance.com

shower cubicle within a bathroom rather than just a mixer over the bath. Or how about a Continental-style walk-in wet room, with fully-tiled waterproof floors and walls? Good tiling adds a vital water-resistant quality to walls and floors as well as perhaps creating a pleasant Mediterranean theme. Finally, you may wish to keep your towels dry with an ingeniously sculpted artistic heated towel rail for some added inspiration whilst 'washing away your day'.

On a more practical note, if the contractor is quoting to supply as well as to fit the bathroom, ask him to state the cost of the sanitary fittings separately. The contractor's price should be pretty close to the price you'd pay if buying them yourself. He'll get a trade discount

that will cover his 'margin' and so shouldn't need to bump up the price.

When the job is done pay careful attention to the detailing at the edges of baths and shower trays. Probably the most common cause of leaks in bathrooms comes from the joints where they abut walls, particularly if using plastic fittings. Never rely on grout, but rather use purpose-made sealing trim strips, or a suitable silicone mastic sealant. Many tell-tale brown stains on downstairs ceilings are due to such minor defects, or from ill-fitting shower screens on baths.

Baths

Chocolate advertisements and shampoo commercials have a lot to answer for. Some have achieved considerably more sales of exotic roll-top Victorian baths than crumbly chocolate treats. But bubbly notions of fabulous antique cast iron bath tubs gracing your dream bathroom may be swiftly discarded the moment you try to lift one. Even with the help of all your mates from the pub it may take the best part of an afternoon to install an original iron bath,

Photo: Romanys Architectural Ironmongers

before you notice it actually needs expensive re-enamelling. But the biggest problem is the miniscule claw feet, which transfer incredibly high loadings to the floor surface – as much in terms of pounds per square inch as a Challenger tank. A bit of chipboard floor panelling under the bath just isn't going to be up to the job, so if you don't want a moving experience when sitting in your bath be sure to first strengthen your floor.

Electrics

With all the plasterboarding and messy plastering out of the way, your chosen electrical surface fittings can now be connected to all the loose cables and back boxes that have lain dormant since first fix. The sudden appearance of socket covers, switches, ceiling roses, and light fittings throughout the extension lends it a homely aspect. This of course assumes that the electrician kept a clear record of the location of the now hidden cable runs and lighting points, and is still on speaking terms with the plasterers (who have an endearing tendency to leave pattress boxes caked in layers of pink gypsum).

As far as the lighting is concerned, it's no great surprise that Part L of the Building Regs is big on energy efficiency. Fortunately, to get your system to comply, all you should need to do in most cases is fit LED bulbs throughout (LEDs use around 90% less electricity than traditional incandescent lighting). In addition, any external lighting must have sensors so they only operate occasionally and switch off when daylight is sufficient. Also the bathroom light fittings must comply with IP safety ratings (see chapter 14) and need to be concealed to prevent any risk of direct contact with water (e.g. ceiling-recessed sealed shower downlighters). Because of the increased risk in wet rooms, supplementary cross bonding is required to any exposed metal work such as pipes, metal baths and showers (not normally required with plastic pipes and fibreglass baths etc). Green and yellow sleeved cables are attached to bare metal (not painted metal) with earthing clamps displaying safety labels saying '*Not to be removed*'.

Second fix electrics should be a fairly straightforward process, assuming there are no last minute changes of plan. So before the electricians start cutting holes into your neatly plastered ceilings for recessed lighting, make sure the positions have all been agreed! The electrician should also fit all the light bulbs, sometimes regarded as the client's job.

The various switches and socket covers are normally fitted before decoration, although any tiled wall surfaces should if possible be completed beforehand. It's not a bad idea to first paint the plastered zones around the still unconnected light fittings and pattresses so there's less fiddling about later. Otherwise the decorators will need to go round loosening the covers so as not to ruin their appearance by camouflaging them with artistic daubings

(they will then regard it as someone else's job to screw them all back again). Then once all the extractor fans, smoke alarms, and CO detectors etc are fixed in place you should be nearly done - it's worth noting that these are all things that Building Control are usually keen to check on their final inspection.

If the old consumer unit to the main house electrics needs to be upgraded (at extra cost), it's best to schedule this for a time when the family aren't all glued to their favourite TV soaps or computer games! Finally, an electrical test should be carried out and the system commissioned so the electrician can proceed to register their completed work at their trade body's online database. This will generates a paper safety certificate of Part P compliance that's posted to you, and an email notification to Building Control.

Plumbing

Second fix for heating and plumbing is a little more arduous than for the electrics. All the pipework tails will need connecting up to the various new kitchen and sanitary fittings. Dishwashers and washing machines should be connected with a cold supply and checked that they work properly – something often left for the client to struggle with. One other thing sometimes overlooked is the testing of new boilers, which should be jointly carried out by the electrician and plumber. In an ideal world the new plumbing system would be leak-free from the word go, but in reality a loose connection here or an unsoldered joint there isn't unusual. Just make sure the plumber hasn't disappeared without trace at the crucial moment. Small leaks usually manifest themselves within the first couple of days.

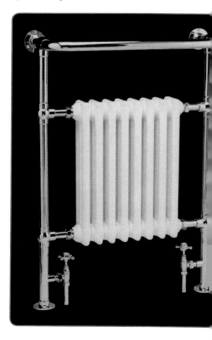

One job that you may prefer to leave until after the walls are decorated is the fixing in place of the radiators, because trying to paint behind them once fitted isn't much fun. When all the plumbing is complete and all the sinks, basins, baths, WCs and showers are fully connected up, Building Control may want to carry out checks, such as ensuring that foul waste from bathrooms etc isn't discharging into rainwater systems. They'll also want to be sure that all the above-ground pipework has been tested as fully watertight, which means the system being capable of holding water or air under pressure for at least three minutes.

Floor finishes

Beautiful flooring can give real character to even the plainest of rooms. But as anyone who's ever owned a plain beige carpet will tell you, floor coverings need above all to be practical. Where you've got underfloor heating (UFH) some floor coverings are not recommended (see page 223). Otherwise the choice of is very much down to personal taste. In recent years, the British love affair with wall-to-wall carpets has been on the wane, perhaps because laminate and wood flooring seems to make even the smallest rooms appear cavernous. Ceramic tiles and limestone floors need careful laying, but the results can be stunning, with the added benefits of easy cleaning and low maintenance. Traditionally found only in kitchens, bathrooms, and some hallways, their quality and durability means that they're now becoming popular in reception rooms and even bedrooms. Alternatively interlocking vinyl planks can be worth considering as they look similar to timber but are moisture-resistant. Note that where you want to tile over timber floor structures (typically in bathrooms) to prevent movement cracking the tiles need to be laid on a strong base of minimum 6mm cement board or marine plywood. Whatever flooring material you choose it's important to carefully check the description/packaging for its compatibility with moisture, UFH and how hard-wearing it is. Most products display ratings that tell you which rooms in the house they're suited to.

Internal joinery

The job isn't over until all your skirting boards, doors and architraves are in place. But this can't happen until your final floor levels are known and any floor tiles laid. Second fix carpentry is a bit of a mixed bag of different joinery jobs, and there may be other outstanding items, such as fitting staircase balustrades, boxing in pipes, fixing mouldings, dado and picture rails, and finishing off the kitchen units. The desired style of joinery, such as traditional Victorian ogee or modern plain chamfered, needs to be consistent throughout the new rooms, if possible matching the joinery in the main house.

The quality of finish is very important as it's the one thing most people notice above all. A lot of snagging items are concerned with getting the detail right – ensuring joinery is securely fixed with joins neatly mitred, and that any pipe ducts have screwed access panels.

Medium density fibreboard

There's not much in the way of internal joinery that you can't buy in MDF – picture rails, dado rails, architraves, skirting. Unlike real wood, it doesn't warp, split or shrink, nor does it suffer from the inconvenience of resinous knots that need additional knotting and sealing. But unlike timber its raw appearance isn't attractive and it needs to be painted, so it's best ordered ready-primed, ready for the topcoat, saving time and money. Once painted it's virtually impossible to tell apart visually from the real thing. A few years ago, a potential health issue linked to cutting and

Left: Traditional limestone flags help create 'farmhousey' feel.
Below: Spiral stairs available in kit form can be a good way to add style.

Photo: Oakwrights.co.uk

drilling large amounts of the stuff was flagged up. Ultra-fine dust particles emitted when cutting with electric saws can cause irritation to skin, eyes, and lungs, so it's essential to wear a suitable dust mask and protective head-gear.

Internal doors

As noted earlier, one of the joys of a newbuild project is that you don't have to muck about trying to squeeze standard-sized new doors into hideously warped old frames. Instead, your new doors should slide effortlessly into place. Most internal doors are hinged to a frame made of timber liners screwed to the studwork or blockwork wall. Only once the liners have been fitted, the plastering completed, and the final floor levels known should the internal doors be hung. Obviously a little consideration is first required as to whether the door is to open inwards or outwards, and which side of the frame you want the hinges to hang from, not forgetting to check how easy it is to find the light switch!

When it comes to selecting internal doors, the choice is essentially between hollow or solid. The majority of factory-made internal doors are of the hollow, lightweight, two skin variety. These are less robust than solid doors but cheaper, comprising a simple wooden frame with a honeycomb cardboard core containing lots of air spaces clad on both sides with moulded panelled covers. Before hanging hollow doors be aware that the timber frame on the side that is to be hinged is often slightly thicker to accommodate the screws, which is why it should be marked 'hinge side'. You also need to locate the solid wood block that will house the door latch (the metal tube that is embedded inside the door).

Solid doors are normally made of pine or similar softwood and have a more expensive feel, giving a more pleasing chunky sound when they shut. Being heavier they also have better soundproofing qualities, although some can weigh as much as 40 kg! Timber internal doors are either unfinished (for later staining, oiling or waxing) or primed ready for painting. Paint-only ones are often remarkably good value being made from cheaper timber, but this may contain dead knots, which can work loose. Stainable solid softwood doors can be twice as expensive, but don't cost anything like as much as solid hardwood oak or meranti doors. Hardwood veneer doors can be a less expensive compromise and can actually be a better option because their engineered timber core is less likely to twist than standard wood. Oak and walnut veneers cost about the same as a spray colour finish.

Fitting latches and locks in solid doors should be relatively straightforward. If your heart is set on having door knobs, rather than handles, they need to be set further in from the edge so that you don't scrape your knuckles on the frame every time you open the door. Because the hole in the latch determines how close the handle will be to the edge of the door, you need to use a longer 75mm latch rather than the standard 63mm size (or 95mm for external doors).

Fitting external doors inside the house is not a good idea, as their moisture content of around 18 per cent is way too high, so they tend to twist and warp. The moisture content of internal doors should ideally be about 10 per cent or lower.

It's unlikely that you will need fire doors in a typical home extension, unless it's three or more storeys high or you're building a self contained 'granny flat' dwelling or integral garage (the plans won't have been passed by Building Control without fire doors being specified where appropriate). That said, there's an increasing uptake from people converting standard doors, particularly to kitchens for peace of mind. They are specified normally as either FD30 or FD60 (minutes fire protection) and incorporate intumescent

243

strips which swell as a reaction to heat, forming a seal between the door and frame. Fire doors typically cost around 20% more than the standard equivalent.

Most internal doors can be supported by a pair of butt hinges – brass ones are preferable, especially in moist kitchens and bathrooms since they won't rust. As with exterior doors, upper hinges are positioned about 150mm from the top and lower ones 200–225mm from the bottom. For fire doors a third hinge is normally required on account of their weight, plus in some cases self-closers.

From a design viewpoint, part-glazed doors are a useful way to boost the amount of light in a room. You may want to create a sweeping entrance to a room with a pair of glazed double doors, but note that any glazed lower door panels need to be fitted with safety glass.

Your choice may be influenced by the doors in the rest of the house, unless you're replacing the whole lot. In terms of styles, there are plenty of options – such as smooth, modern flush doors, traditional four-panelled Victorian, six-panelled Georgian, 'one over three' panelled 1930s, or 'ledge and brace' cottage style.

Standard internal door sizes are 1981mm high by either 762 or 686mm wide and are normally 35mm thick. However in new homes wider 838mm internal doors are now often installed as they comply with the accessibility and mobility requirements of Building Regs Part M. Although this doesn't apply to extensions, fitting wider doors can create a pleasant feeling of space.

As noted earlier, the timber liners or casings from which the doors are hung are generally more reliable in terms of quality in MDF rather than softwood which can be prone to distortion (although some chippies reckon screws don't grip as well as in natural wood). Liners are sold in sizes designed to accept doors of standard heights and widths, although builders sometimes construct them from scratch. In which case, if you're feeling courageous, why not conjure up some quaint, curiously-dimensioned doors from the local salvage yard? As long as it's all planned in good time, well before the internal walls are built, this may not cost a great deal more than fitting ordinary doors, and is a great way to add some real style. Reclamation yards are great places to source all kinds of weird and wonderful objects – perhaps you'll unearth an intricately-carved *Grinling Gibbons* oak panelling. But before getting too carried away with bargain antique gems, bear in mind that warped doors can rarely be much improved, and most over-large doors can only be trimmed by a small amount before it affects their strength.

Door furniture should match the age and style of the property – for example, lever handles aren't architecturally suited to most pre-1950s houses, where knobs were often the order of the day. Salvage yards may once again stock some delightful and curiously shaped original handles.

Doorstops and architraves

Once the new door is swinging smoothly on its hinges and the catch clicks satisfyingly into place, the frame can be completed by fixing the doorstops in position. These are the long strips of typically 30 x 12mm softwood that are fitted up the middle of the liners, literally stopping the door from swinging through the frame. Each doorstop can be nailed into position on the liner using small 'lost-head' oval nails, their heads punched and buried below the surface ready for filling. Which just leaves one problem – what to do about the ugly joint between the door liner framework and the plaster.

Architraves are the time-honoured solution. These long strips of decorative moulded timber are fixed around the sides of the doorframe, neatly covering rough gaps. You can fix them in place using lost-head nails driven into the liner at an angle. Or if you believe the claims made by glue manufacturers, nails may not be required at all. The architraves are normally set back about 8mm from the inner edge of the door liner. At their top corners they're mitred and pinned together, and at their feet they may project out slightly, often being a little thicker than the adjoining skirting

boards. The architraves can then be skew-nailed into the skirting boards.

Skirting, dado and picture rails

The purpose of the humble skirting board is traditionally to disguise unseemly gaps where the plastering on the walls comes face-to-face with the floor. For the Victorians, the secondary purpose was to protect expensive wallpaper from damage, a task shared by the dado rails higher up the wall at waist level. Skirting is by no means essential, and is sometimes absent in properties where the detailing is neat enough to be left exposed, or in Mediterranean holiday homes with rendered walls that merge seamlessly with concrete floors.

However, skirting is an extremely handy device for covering the expansion gaps that must be left at the edges of various types of floor coverings, such as laminates and wood flooring. Skirting may be screwed, glued or nailed to the walls. The accuracy of mitring and fitting is more important when the wood is left exposed and varnished or stained, whereas a small amount of filler is permissible when it's to be painted.

Picture rails are slim horizontal moulded timber strips traditionally placed along walls about a foot below ceiling level. It's unlikely that you'd want to fit them other than where your new rooms need to match the style of a pre-war or period house. Dado rails situated roughly halfway up the wall have, on the other hand, made a bit of a comeback in recent years, allowing an appealing two-tone decorative regime to be applied to the walls.

Apples and pears

If, back in Chapter 13, your extension was one of the few requiring a new staircase to be installed, you'll now be glad that you took the precaution of protecting the staircase joinery. Dustsheets covering the treads, risers and strings will by now be hidden beneath a thick film of grime. Which all bears testimony to the good sense of waiting until now before fitting the handrail and balusters (spindles).

Finishing

Victory is now so close that you can almost touch the completion certificate shimmering tantalisingly on the horizon. But it's not over until the decorators have done their stuff.

This is when you may notice some rather ugly pieces of work left exposed, such as bathroom waste pipes, central

heating pipes and cables under boilers. Surely these should have all been neatly boxed in? Regrettably, unless clearly specified these are items commonly charged as 'extras'. And it's amazing how expensive a bit of 'two-by-one' covered with plywood can suddenly be.

Although your project may be getting very near its end, it's important to remember that a lot of trades will still need to come and go, ferrying tools and materials through the house. There remains real potential for your priceless Louis Vuitton cut-glass light shades to get accidentally smashed and for those beautifully mitred worktops and expensively veneered floors to get cracked, scratched, and sprayed with paint. If it can be damaged, it probably will be, so don't be too hasty whipping away those covers.

17 FINISHING THE JOB

Until now you may have been perfectly happy to stand back and let the professionals get on with the job of creating your new dream home. But if your budget is starting to wear a bit thin it might be worth considering tackling some of the finishing work yourself. Most of us are not averse to a spot of emulsioning, so perhaps doing a little decorating could help breathe some life back into the bank account.

New curved steps look good - but expect Building Control to ask about handrails!

Photo: Sadolin

Internal finishing

You may have been planning to get your hands dirty with a bit of DIY input right from the start, but if not, any such change of plan now could constitute a change in the contract and must be discussed. If your builder is willing to accept your proposal, he'll first need to formally agree to this in writing, with the contract sum reduced accordingly for savings in labour and materials.

But far from being crestfallen at the prospect of losing a profitable part of the job, it's not unusual for contractors to actually be quite happy to oblige. They'll know from bitter experience that it's now, at the decoration stage, that clients often feel confident enough to start changing their minds about colour schemes and generally interfering. This is also the phase where the contractor's sights are firmly set on the next job, and their prior enthusiasm for your project is rapidly wearing off. Seduced by the aroma of big bucks wafting over the fence, they might be only too keen to have everything wrapped up as swiftly as possible. So bringing forward the completion date and allowing them to get their hands on the final payment and some of the retention money could be a tempting proposition.

But taking such a shortcut could be counterproductive unless you're very confident in your own abilities. For many house buyers the quality of the finish is everything, and cutting corners with streaky, dripping and patchy decoration will spoil the job.

Decorating

People easily forget what a skilled job this is, because anyone can buy a can of emulsion and a roller and start slapping paint on a wall. But in reality achieving good results requires not just skill but a lot of hard graft. The old cliché is still very true – decoration can only be as good as the preparation. Which means plenty of perspiration. Laborious rubbing down, followed by filling and then rubbing down again, before going anywhere near a can of paint.

Bad paintwork will manifest itself in the form of runs, bubbles, streaks and gaps. There'll be rough lumpy surfaces and trapped dust. Poor varnishing will appear patchy and after the first few months may start to blister and peel off. Good decoration, on the other hand, can hide a multitude of sins, although obviously there are limits. Because this is the final finished surface that the client sees, decorators are sometimes unjustly put in the firing line for everybody else's rubbish work. Even the best spray paint job can't completely hide a rusty wreck underneath.

Within reason, it's the decorator's job to 'snag' the previous finishing trades – such as repairing around any holes cut by plumbers or electricians and filling edges of panelling and boxing that the carpenter has constructed. It's obviously important that no paint is applied until the dust in the air has settled and the immediate environment is clean, so a good decorator will avoid working where there are piles of rubbish or where other trades are still active.

The decorating trade is usually carried out on a labour only basis. Decorators normally supply their own brushes, filler and sandpaper etc, but the paint will be supplied by the main contractor, or by the client if the trades are being employed directly.

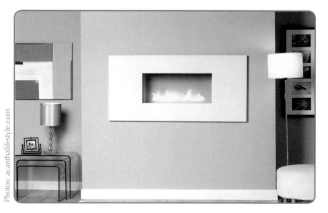

Photos: acanthalifestyle.com

Preparation

New timber surfaces should be rubbed down to a smooth finish before the first coat, using medium to fine paper of about 120 grit, and then rubbed down again between coats.

After initial sanding there may be small indentations, such as from nail heads, which need to be filled. It's a bit of a DIY myth that paint alone can fill holes; you really need to apply a suitable filler. For surfaces to be varnished, a wood filler should be used which matches the colour of the wood as closely as possible. There may be larger gaps where skirting and architraves meet the walls, which can be filled using flexible filler or decorators' caulking from a sealant gun.

Painting softwood

Time was when all the visually important internal joinery – the doors, skirting, architraves etc – was universally finished in good old gloss white. Today preserving the natural beauty of the wood using a stain, oil or wax finish is a popular alternative. A matt white or soft sheen cream finish can also add an element of charm to the interior design.

Where bare timber is to be painted it will typically require one or two coats of primer, after any knots have been treated. It should then be undercoated before the final coat of gloss, silk or matt paint is applied.

Knotting solution is used on resinous areas to prevent resin leaking and discolouring the subsequent layers of paint. Aggressive resins can even force the paint surface to separate entirely from the timber. Knotting solution takes approximately three hours to dry. Alternatively, a 'self-knotting' primer can be used.

Wood primer is a thin paint which soaks into the grain taking some of the porosity out of the new timber. This seals the surface to prevent further coats of paint soaking in. If you skip this and apply an undercoat or topcoat directly to bare wood the moisture is sucked out of it too quickly and the paint dries on the surface but is poorly bonded, and may quickly peel.

Varnish and wood stain

Applying drab, colourless gloss paint may not do justice to all that expensive new joinery. You may instead prefer

Photo: capitalfireplaces.co.uk

a transparent varnish or stain finish that displays the timber rather than hiding it. But this means any faults and blemishes in the joinery will stand out, so extra careful preparation is needed to achieve a good, natural finish. Varnish is popular for joinery and timber floors as it protects the wood and highlights the beauty of the grain. It is often applied before the walls are decorated, since careless emulsioning could leave visible marks showing through on the finished product. Varnish combines polyurethane with wood stain, so that the stain effectively sits on the surface of the timber rather than being absorbed into it. If you want to modify the colour of the joinery to blend in with other woods, coloured varnishes can be used, for example giving softwood the appearance of oak.

Preparation is similar to that for painting, but the sanding process needs to be more thorough, finishing off with a fine grade of paper. Note that sanding across the grain can leave scratches which may later become exaggerated. Varnish is applied in layers of two to four thin coats. To achieve a durable finish, the bare wood should first be sealed with a thinned coat of varnish diluted with about ten per cent solvent to key into the timber. Allow to dry and apply a further two coats of undiluted varnish. Remember that each coat applied will darken the wood, so once the desired shade has been achieved, subsequent coats of clear varnish can be applied. It's important to apply an even film to avoid patchy colours and brush marks, and to not double-coat the varnish (or wood stain) where it overlaps.

Wood stains are easy to use and resistant to fading. They consist of a colorant or dye suspended or dissolved in a spirit solvent, or may alternatively be water-based. The technique for applying wood stain is different from painting since the dye is much more fluid than paint and will dry very quickly into the wood. It can be applied quickly and evenly using a clean rag or paintbrush after the surfaces have first been sanded. Note that water-based dyes can cause the grain of the wood to temporarily swell when applied, so the wood should not be sanded directly after it's been dyed.

Painting new softwood

- Rub down with glasspaper to get a smooth finish over the entire surface.
- Apply knotting solution to any knots.
- Apply a coat of wood primer or universal primer.
- Fill any voids with a suitable filler and smooth using glasspaper.
- Brush off all dust.
- Touch up any exposed knots.
- Apply undercoat.
- Apply at least one top coat.

Oil and wax

Long before modern synthetic varnishes were devised, interior joinery was protected with beeswax dissolved in turpentine, boiled linseed oil, or natural resins dissolved in alcohol or turpentine. Unlike modern polyurethane-based finishes which don't penetrate the pores of the wood, natural oil and wax-based treatments soak into the grain, replenishing original plant oils and strengthening the wood from within. This means they don't rely on a surface coating like modern paints and varnishes which can be prone to cracking, peeling or blistering. The main attraction of using oils is the way they highlight the natural beauty, colour and grain of the wood. Clear or coloured, they are suitable for both hardwood and softwood and sold in a range of gloss, satin and matt sheens. Usually applied in 2 coats with no need for priming or sanding in between, most contain no biocides or artificial preservatives and provide a water-resistant protective finish. Some products combine natural oils and waxes to improve durability, although for very exposed, hard-wearing areas like floors, varnishes are a more resilient option.

Paint safety

Gloss paints, and spirit stains or varnishes contain chemical cocktails known as VOCs (volatile organic compounds). Research has shown that painters and decorators exposed to solvents in paint are likely to suffer from low-quality sperm – something that's not normally bragged about on site. Fortunately, the amount of these potentially harmful ingredients present in paint and varnishes has been legally restricted since 2010 prompting major changes to solvent-based coatings. But from a health risk point of view, as well as an ecological perspective, it's still advisable to specify low VOC paints, or water-based gloss paint. Water-based acrylics are more user-friendly and make washing out your brushes dead easy. Despite some trade prejudice against them, they perform as well as oil-based paints, but won't give a highly shiny gloss finish (but then silk or matt is often preferred).

When the job's done, flammable or polluting materials such as white spirit and paint should not be chucked away down drains, and skip-hire firms also bar them. So it's good news that local Council tips provide special waste disposal facilities.

Emulsioning

As noted earlier, you can't just slap ordinary emulsion onto a freshly plastered wall surface. If you do, it will shrink, crack and peel.

Once dried, newly plastered walls can be decorated with special vinyl-free 'paint for new plaster' available from DIY stores (principally in white and magnolia). These paints are specially formulated to allow the wall to continue drying after painting whereas ordinary vinyl emulsion prevents the substrate 'breathing', trapping any residual moisture. Alternatively, emulsion suitably diluted with water is sometimes used as a coat first to prime. Skimmed

Emulsioning plastered walls
- Rub down with fine glasspaper.
- Brush off to remove all dust and particles.
- Apply one coat of 'new plaster' paint or thinned emulsion (one part paint to three parts water) as primer.
- Apply two coats of non-vinyl emulsion.

plasterboard surfaces can normally be decorated within a week (once the moist dark chocolatey colour has turned light pink), but thicker two-coat 'hard plaster' finishes need to be left for a few weeks before painting, until dry to the touch. The best guide is to ask the plasterers about recommended drying-out times.

For wallpapering over hard plaster you may need to allow several months for the surface to completely dry out prior to wallpapering, so that any shrinkage cracks can be filled and sanded. Even then the surface must first be 'sized' with a coat of diluted wallpaper paste. Alternatively you can wallpaper directly over 'taped and jointed' smooth plasterboard but it's advisable to first seal the surface to make the paper less absorbent, otherwise if you want to strip the wallpaper in future it may prove impossible without tearing off chunks of plasterboard!

Tiling

Wall and floor tiles come in a bewildering variety of shapes, sizes, colours, textures and patterns. Yet nothing seems to date quicker than last year's tile styles. Indeed, you can often date the age of a house fairly accurately from its wall tiles alone. But don't let that put you off. Wall tiling should be well within most DIYers' capabilities. Fortunately, you'll be off to a flying start working with smooth newly

plastered surfaces rather then having to stick reluctant tiles to flaking plaster on old bowed walls - assuming of course that the plasterer maintained a consistently high standard throughout. To check how level the surface is, it's worth taking a moment to run a straight length of timber across the wall. Any apparent dips or bows can then be filled or sanded.

Wall tiling is normally carried out after the plastering is completed and fully dried out. It typically takes a tiler about an hour to fix a square metre of tiles plus another 10 minutes to grout them, although perfecting staggered bonding patterns and cutting tiles for shower cubicle corners etc may take a little longer. The use of the correct tile spacers is important to help even out any inconsistencies. Where timber-panelled surfaces or boxed-in pipes are to be tiled, the base is best made from water-resistant plywood or cement board.

When it comes to flooring, the choice of materials includes ceramic, porcelain, stone, slate or traditional square red quarry tiles. These are usually laid onto a screed base after priming to seal the surface (so the adhesive doesn't dry out too quickly and crack). Tiles can also be laid on timber floors but you need to first install a base of 6mm cement board so the surface is as rigid as possible and use a suitable adhesive. Note that when tiling onto gypsum-based liquid screeds, special adhesives and sealants must be used (as gypsum reacts with cement-based adhesives). Finally, it's a wise precaution to buy at least a half a dozen more tiles than you need – if breakages or cracks occur in future, the colour of new tiles from different batches may not match.

Insulating the roof space

What's the worst job you've ever had? Whatever the answer, it was probably a whole lot better than crawling around in hot cramped roof voids laying rolls of itchy

glassfibre or mineral wool insulation, a job traditionally given to the new boys on site. This job is often carried out soon after the roof has been constructed and the ceilings fitted, although the stage at which it's done isn't critical. But builders can sometimes be prone to overlooking this task, so it is always worth taking a quick glance up there prior to completion.

Insulation is not an optional extra. The Building Control Officer will not pass the project without the work having been done satisfactorily. Out of all the things you can do to insulate your home, laying loft insulation is one of the most cost-effective and efficient. Normally about 150mm depth of insulation is laid between the ceiling joists and another 150mm laid at right angles over the top (which will hide the joists from view, so watch where you tread). Fitting special plastic 'roof ventilator' trays at the eaves allows a clear passageway for air whilst letting you pack insulation into the eaves – a thermal weak point. Talking of which, don't forget to insulate the loft hatch and ensure it sits snugly at the edges, so that howling draughts don't make a mockery of all your careful insulation efforts.

Whilst there's no scientifically proven evidence to date of associated health risks from loft insulation, common sense would suggest that snorting in lots of fine, airborne fibres over time isn't likely to do your lungs a tremendous amount of good. So if you're going to lay your own loft insulation, be sure to wear eye protectors and a facemask, and when the job's done thoroughly hose yourself down and vacuum all the bits off your clothes. It's better to use 'clean' loft quilt that comes ready-encased in polythene sheeting. Sheep's wool is nicer to work with as it isn't itchy like synthetic fibreglass or mineral wool, but can be relatively expensive.

External finishing

Now for the finishing touches on the outside that will make your new home the envy of all who see it. Most extensions are finished in neat facing brick or rendered blockwork, but there's a wide range of exterior claddings worth considering if you want to spice things up a bit. Appearances can sometimes be transformed by applying contrasting finishes on small sections of the walls. The main function of cladding, apart from looking good and helping keep heat in, is to keep the weather out. Hence it's sometimes referred to as a 'rainscreen'. One popular material currently is unstained timber designed to weather naturally over time, lasting for decades without any applying surface coatings. Or there's Japanese-style 'charred timber' (just don't mention the Fire Regs!). Or you might prefer the look of traditional tile-hung walls, or the new trend for metal cladding in aluminium, zinc, copper, stainless steel, or even pre-weathered 'rusty' steel. But before getting too carried away, first we're going to look at how best to protect conventional external joinery – the eaves and bargeboards etc.

Painting

You need to be something of a natural optimist to be an outdoor painter in Britain, as well as being blessed with large reserves of patience and a generally philosophical attitude to life. If it's not raining, the weather is often too cold to achieve a sound finish. That's when it's not too windy, too humid, or even too hot. Damp or humid surfaces can prevent paint from sticking properly, leading to peeling. For a good result with external decoration, you ideally need weather that's calm, dry, and reasonably warm. A generous degree of flexibility needs to be built into your work programme so that you can wait for the right weather conditions to come along and then crack on with the job.

Fortunately, painters no longer need to be daredevils. Thanks to health and safety legislation the days of being sent on dangerous missions up impossibly high ladders are gone. Modern scaffold towers are easily erected and considerably safer.

External timbers

The traditional way of finishing external timbers is with oil-based gloss paint, applied in three coats – primer, undercoat and gloss. But today, new timber windows and doors should arrive on site ready-primed with a honey coloured stain basecoat, just awaiting their finish coats of stain or paint. If you want a painted finish it can save time and money to specify joinery ready primed with paint (rather than the standard stain basecoat). However, any bare timbers such as at roof level, will need the full treatment – which means knotting and priming (or a stain basecoat). Primer should be carefully brushed into all the corners and joints, working along the grain. Once dry, it can be rubbed down, and then the undercoat applied. This in turn is allowed to dry and is then sanded down. Finally, the surface coats of gloss paint are applied. The key to cutting decorating costs is reducing the number of coats needed to get a good quality finish, *eg* by using 'one coat' paints that let you dispense with the undercoat.

The main alternative to paint is wood stain – varnish is not now widely used externally as it can be prone to flaking

or blistering. Stains are dearer to buy than paint, but quicker to apply and modern stains should let you dispense with the traditional third coat. Because stain soaks into the timber it is far less prone to peeling than paint or varnish. The thicker stains are classed as 'medium build' and have a light treacly consistency. The thinner 'low-build' variety are used on sawn timber, which can guzzle a surprising amount of the stuff. Traditionally, stains have been spirit-based, but like paint they are now available as water-based acrylics and normally contain a fungicide to inhibit mould growth.

So far so good. The only snag with having immaculate, gleaming new paintwork tastefully adorning your extension is that it might make the old house look a bit shabby in comparison. Nowhere is this more obvious than at eaves level where the new fascia boards meet the flaking paintwork of the old ones. This is why many home extenders decide to grasp the nettle and give the old timbers a good rub down and a lick of paint whilst the scaffold towers (and decorators) are at hand. But apart from the well-known risks of working at height, there are other potential dangers lurking here. Using a flame gun or hot-air burner on old paintwork can release particles of poisonous lead from old lead paint, which was widely used up until the 1960s. Worse, it's not unknown for a momentary lapse of concentration to cause tinder-dry painted eaves and rafter feet to become badly scorched or even engulfed in flames.

Tile hanging

At the design stage you may have opted to partially clad the outside walls in a traditional architectural style that dates back centuries – vertically hung terracotta tiles or natural slates. The use of patterned ornamental tiles can create a decorative feature to spruce up an otherwise plain-looking wall. Tiles are not only

a good way of visually breaking up a large expanse of brickwork, but they're also extremely practical – they can help insulate an external wall whilst still allowing it to breathe. Tiling also requires very little maintenance, which may account for its enduring popularity.

Plain tiles are typically sized 265 x 165mm and each tile is hung on a batten and double nailed in place. A layer of 'breather-quality' (ie not polythene) underfelt is first laid below the preservative-treated battens, which are normally fixed to the blockwork. Above the tiles there should be a horizontal strip of lead apron (min. Code 4 lead) placed under windowsills and dressed over the tile course below by about 100mm, in order to make the joint watertight. Where walls need to be lightweight or particularly slim, 'brick slips' can be hung off a metal base fixed to the inner wall.

Weatherboarding

You don't have to live exclusively in East Anglia or Kent, the natural homes of 'clapboarding', to justify using traditional barn-style timber cladding on your house. This is a popular way of giving an instant character boost to otherwise conventional buildings. Currently, weatherboarding

Different types of boarding are available for cladding, and a good timber merchant should be able to supply a variety to choose from.

is rather in vogue, especially when painted pale colours rather than the traditional black.

It can also provide a handy method for disguising ugly old 1970s brick walls, whilst upping your insulation into the bargain. But this will have already been chewed over at some length, when your extension was a mere glint in the designer's eye.

From a pure design perspective, this is one of the few wall treatments that seems to produce harmonious results, almost regardless of the style of existing house that the extension is bolted on to. Its amazing versatility means you can mix and match, perhaps applying it on just one small part of the extension. It is often seen adding colour to upper walls, contrasting with brickwork or white render down below. Because it's fairly lightweight, particularly when combined with timber frame wall construction, it may provide a useful technical solution where loadings can't be too great, such as building over an existing single-storey extension with relatively shallow foundations.

However, there is a downside. It's not maintenance-free, so expect to spend a bit of time up your ladders wielding a brush every few years. It is good practice to apply at least one coat of stain or paint before fixing, to avoid the risk of bare strips peeping out at you between courses when the timber inevitably shrinks. Roughsawn timber drinks wood stain and needs a re-application about every seven years, but the amount of time required for keeping up appearances can be reduced by using special low maintenance wood stain or microporous paint or varnish. To protect against rot, all external timber should be pre-treated with preservative, ideally arriving on site already pressure-impregnated. Otherwise it will need liberal coats of preservative brushed well in, especially to the grain at cut ends.

If you prefer a maintenance-free lifestyle, some of the more expensive 'fit & forget' timbers such as western red cedar or heat treated redwood may be worth investigating. Cedar can cost five times the price of untreated softwood boarding, but it lasts for 60 years, although its original golden honey colour will, over time, become a silvery-grey. Oak, spruce and chestnut are less expensive 'maintenance-

TYPES OF WEATHERBOARDING

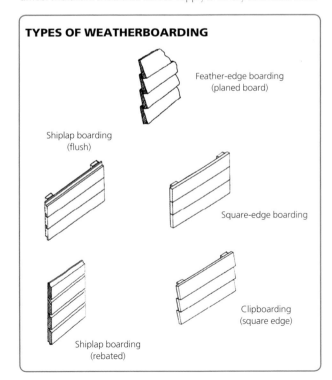

Feather-edge boarding (planed board)

Shiplap boarding (flush)

Square-edge boarding

Clipboarding (square edge)

Shiplap boarding (rebated)

free' alternatives, as is iroko. Native larch is also popular and is significantly cheaper than cedar or other hardwoods.

Alternatively, you may want to consider pre-coloured fibre-cement cladding boards that are manufactured to resemble timber but with none of the maintenance headaches. They are claimed to be 'durable to wind, rain, and sunlight', with minimal upkeep. Some are tongue & grooved and can be fitted flush or with a traditional clapboard effect with planks overlapping.

A recent development that arguably offers the best of both worlds is 'improved timber' boarding, such as Thermowood. UPVC cladding is available in a range of different colours, but whether this makes a suitable alternative to the real thing is really a matter of personal taste and depends on the type of house you're extending. It may be just the job for matching extensions to some 1960s or 1970s houses. Call us old-fashioned, but with traditional architecture you can't beat real wood for style and quality.

Timber cladding normally needs to be fixed to a timber sub-frame of battens, over the underlying blockwork. Laying the boards over a sheet of roofing felt will give greater weather protection. Special annular shank nails or purpose-made galvanised nails are recommended for fixing boards because they grip the wood very well, and the lost-head variety can be punched below the surface and concealed with filler.

There are different styles of timber cladding. Traditional overlapping 'barn style' cladding uses rough-sawn planks, fixed horizontally with a 30mm overlap. You can either use tapered 'feather-edge' boards or square-edged 'clapboarding'. Planed-timber rebated 'shiplap' cladding, on the other hand, uses interlocking boards that are laid completely flush. Similarly, square-edge boarding or tongued and grooved planed timber boards can be close-butted, and are sometimes fixed diagonally or vertically.

Starting at the bottom, boards can be nailed horizontally to 50 x 50mm battens over a breather membrane, usually to a blockwork wall surface. At least 150mm should be left between the bottom edge of the weatherboard and the ground. The corners can either be mitred or finished with a corner trim.

Rendering

In exposed locations where wild weather is no stranger, outer wall treatments often traditionally comprised of coatings of protective render. In order to enhance its weather-resistance, lumpy pebbledash or roughcast would commonly be applied, since these finishes are even better at deflecting rainwater than smooth sand/cement render – hence its popularity in stormy coastal areas such as parts of Scotland and Cornwall.

It's usually the plasterer's job to render the outside of the building. As with most cement-based materials, care should be taken to avoid applying render in frosty conditions or when temperatures, day or night, are likely to fall below 3°C, otherwise freezing will blow all your hard

Render can be left 'natural sandy colour' or lime rendered, contrasting nicely with larch or cedar cladding.

work. Render is normally applied directly to blockwork but can equally be spread on metal lathing nailed to battens or to insulation panels. It is applied in 2 layers, starting with a base 'scratch' coat, typically using a 4:1 mix of fine sharp plastering sand to cement, plus a waterproofer/plasticiser with polypropylene fibres sometimes also added to the mix to reinforce it. The blockwork substrate needs to be of a reasonably rough pattern to help provide 'grip', and may first need to be wetted, sometimes with PVA added to improve the bond. Thicknesses vary but scratch coats shouldn't normally exceed 15mm. At the corners and junctions, lengths of stainless steel beading are fixed into the render (avoid galvanised beading designed for internal use which will rust). There are 3 main types of beading: 'angle beads' used to form corners, 'stop ends' to create neat, crack-free joints with existing walls, and 'drip beads' placed horizontally above windows/doors. At the base, rendered wall surfaces should project outwards just above DPC level with a 'bellmouth drip' to disperse rainwater, also formed with drip beads. The surface of the base coat needs to be scratched while it's still wet to provide a key for the second 'floating' coat which can be applied once the scratch coat has set and cured (after a few days depending on the weather). This top coat should be thinner, typically around 5 - 7mm thick and uses a slightly weaker 5:1:1 mix of plastering sand, cement and lime or a waterproofer/plasticiser to give the finished render flexibility and help reduce cracking. In hot weather, or where the wind could dry out the render too quickly, it needs to be kept damp for the first 3 days with the use of protective sheeting, and will also need protection from driving rain.

Although there is no set overall thickness, the two coats combined would typically total around 20mm. For a smooth finish the top coat is levelled flat with a straight edge before being rubbed down using a plastic float or trowel to help 'close' the surface. It is then sponged over for a slightly sanded texture and to remove marks and small bumps.

If you want to match an existing pebbledash surface, this can be created by thickening the final coat and then throwing ('dashing') dry pea shingle against it so that the pebbles stick, and then pushing them home with a trowel. 'Roughcast'

Conventional sand/cement render needs periodic decorating with masonry paint, unlike dearer monocouche renders.

contains bigger lumps of shingle mixed into the final coat which is then thrown on and left rough. A modern variation on the theme is 'Tyrolean render', which is created by a hand-held 'snow machine' that sprays a mix of render and pebbles onto the render base coat. Or you might fancy a spot of traditional Olde-Worlde (or 1930s) 'half timbering' on your gables, comprising 50 x 125mm timbers fixed to the blockwork, infilled with render or herringbone pattern brickwork.

Plain render and roughcast are normally painted. White tends to be the colour of choice unless you happen to live in 'Balamory' or a quaint fishing village where rainbow colours make welcome relief from the constant drizzle. Render is therefore not maintenance free, requiring decoration every five years or so (although some paints claim up to 15 years before needing recoating). Masonry paint comprises special water-based emulsion with anti-bacterial properties, incorporating reinforcement for strength, and can be applied by roller, brush, or sometimes spray. However, before painting newly cement rendered walls, the underlying surface must first be allowed to fully dry out, which can take ages if the weather isn't clement. Once dry, the render should be sealed with a stabilising solution before painting, to bind the surface and make it less absorbent. But if you've already taken the scaffolding down, painting the walls will take twice as long.

MONOCOUCHE RENDERS

In recent years some interesting 'hi-tech' alternatives to conventional sand/cement have appeared on the scene. Pre-mixed through-coloured renders are increasingly popular and well known brands include *Weber*, *Parex*,

K-Rend and *Wetherby*. There are a number of different formulations, such as polymer and acrylic renders which include silicone or polymer additives and fibres to make them more flexible and help eliminate cracking, with a durable, long lasting finish. They are available in a wide variety of colours and textures, but the main attraction is that they're claimed to be maintenance-free, without all the hassle and expense of periodic painting. 'Monocouche' renders (French for 'single coat') are supplied in bag form ready for mixing with water, and can be applied by hand trowel or sprayed on by machine. These use white cement and are pre-coloured (any colour you want) and applied in one coat around 15mm thick. The main downside with using manufactured, through-coloured renders is the cost. But although they're considerably dearer in terms of materials than than plain old sand/cement, they're quicker to apply (assuming your trades have relevant experience) with consequent savings in labour. Plus of course there's the promise of substantial future savings in decoration and maintenance. One note of caution however, if you want your new extension to perfectly match existing sand/cement render on a house, you generally need to use the same materials. That said, you can request free made-up sample plates sent out to compare colours and textures.

Tidying up

Now that the building works are largely complete, it's tidy-up time. You may notice a marked lack of enthusiasm amongst site personnel by this stage, and if you want to know the true meaning of words like 'reluctant' or 'grudging', asking builders to clear up around the site at the end of the job is about as close as you're ever going to get. If you're employing trades directly, this will be pretty much down to you. But a good main contractor will see the job through to the bitter end, which not only means tidying up but also cleaning all the dust and debris both indoors and out, and generally leaving the place ready for occupation. Any brickwork that's been splashed with mortar should be cleaned and sticky labels removed from new glazing. Splashes of paint or plaster over indoor joinery and fittings must be cleaned off. Lastly that industrial-sized, muck-sucking vacuum must be put through its paces. Then, with hands all a-tremble, the protective covers can finally be whisked away, including those to smoke alarms and lights.

Landscaping

Landscaping works may be required as a condition of your planning consent. Or you might just have the urge to let rip and embark on some serious mulching. Either way, garden design has come a long way in recent years, with inspirational TV programmes spurring us into horticultural action. It's worth taking a bit of time to jazz up your own private slice of green belt, since creating the perfect garden terrace with some stylish lighting, exotic paving

Photo: acanthalifestyle.com

and a few gorgeous shrubs can transform your erstwhile building site into a mini paradise. But there are some practical considerations to consider.

If you recall all the trouble we took during the build to deter damp from the walls, it would be daft to now encourage damp problems by piling earth up against them, or to allow rain to splash so it continually dampens the brickwork. Patios are notorious for raising external ground levels excessively. The ground should be a minimum of 150mm below DPC level and if for any reason this can't be achieved, the next best option is to cut back the hard ground surface next to the walls of the house and create a shallow gravel-filled trench around them. This will allow any damp to evaporate and disperse safely. Paths and hard surfaces near the house should slope gently away to expel rainwater. If you prefer timber decking, select FSC-accredited timber bearing the mark of the Forestry Stewardship Council (so you can't be held personally responsible for destruction of the rainforests).

Access

The requirements for disabled access in Part M of the Building Regulations may have some influence on the design of your immediate garden area. Although they don't strictly apply to home extensions, it may be worth incorporating some of these features as they can make life easier for lots of people, including young children, pram pushers and wheely bin operatives. Or you may need to accommodate a family member with special needs. This means the pathways approaching the house should facilitate wheelchair access with shallow gradients leading up to external doors and ramps instead of steps where possible. On entering the house there should be level thresholds, especially to the main entrance door which should, if possible, have a minimum clear opening width of at least 800mm. Whilst there's no obligation to upgrade

your old house for disabled access and usability, your new extension must not adversely affect the existing building.

Planning your defences

There's always the risk that your stunning new extension might attract the wrong sort of attention – neighbourhood scumbags looking for rich pickings. It pays to think like a burglar in order to design-out opportunities for crime. Flat roofs and nearby trees can provide tempting pathways to upstairs windows. Easy ground cover from hedges and shrubs along with a swift escape route can also make your property an appealing target. All the evidence confirms that intruders are deterred by the sight of alarms and CCTV cameras, and good old-fashioned guard dogs are still a serious turn-off for opportunist thieves.

One thing to avoid, however, is indiscriminate use of PIR security lights, flooding the neighbourhood in dazzling white light every time a dog scratches its rear quarters, with the result that everyone ignores them, including the intruders. There should be an indoor override control switch for outdoor lighting. Similarly, oversensitive house alarms that sound-off routinely will inevitably be ignored the one time your home is in mortal danger.

Defensive planting

One well-kept secret that's not often mentioned by TV gardeners is the deterrent value of 'defensive shrubs' – a

little strategic planting of naturally sharp thorny species such as hawthorn, pyracantha ('firethorn'), blackberry, holly and rambling rose may be all you need to repel intruders.

Whilst on the subject of planting, if you want to live in peace with your neighbours it's best to avoid the notorious fast growing leylandii (cypresses), which can grow to an incredible three times the height of your house. Instead, try planting low water demand species such as holly, yews, silver birches, box, brooms, dwarf pines and privets.

Completion

The job is not officially sanctioned until you've notified Building Control and the final inspection has been carried out to their satisfaction. You'll then need to formally request that the all-important completion certificate is issued. The final inspection should always be arranged in good time before the contract with the builders has terminated and they've vanished off site. Failing this, any remedial work required will most likely end up being left unfinished. And without a sizeable carrot in the form of a final payment or large retention there's always the danger of the client getting lumbered.

NOTIFY BUILDING CONTROL 8
Final inspection – five days' notice

Unless already inspected at a previous stage, the Building Control Officer may want to check that the necessary thermal insulation has been installed, that the plumbing is all connected up and works satisfactorily, and that the necessary fire or sound protection is in place. Particular attention is often paid on the final inspection to anything where there's a risk of falling or personal injury, such as staircases and handrails, windows, balcony railings, escape from fire, woodburning stoves and flues, and that smoke/CO alarms are correctly positioned and working. If at the end of the inspection your lovingly created masterpiece doesn't immediately tick all the Building Regs compliance boxes don't worry. It's not unusual at this stage for a few

final tweaks to still be needed. But you need to clearly note down and agree the list of any outstanding items as this is often dependent on verbal communication as the Building Control Officer marches swiftly round the extension. Once these have been done, a follow-up visit can be booked a few days later to get it officially signed off.

It's very important to be aware that what Building Control consider complete, and what clients regard as complete, are usually two very different things. For example, they won't be terribly interested in all the cosmetic stuff, like whether the decorations and wall tiling have been done or the skirting boards and architraves are in place. Remember, the Building Regulations are only the minimum standard acceptable for safety and thermal efficiency etc. They aren't a guarantee that the builders have finished everything they were supposed to have done. That's where snagging comes in.

Snagging

The objective of the snagging inspection is to draw up a list of all remaining defects. These are normally very minor things, like paint blemishes, sticking doors and windows, loose joinery, missing mastic to joints, messy tile grouting and wonky wall sockets, sagging gutters or blown patches of render – in fact anything that doesn't look too clever. It's always best to go round the building unaccompanied as you write out your list, so you can concentrate and methodically inspect each room and component of the building in turn. Surveyors have a trained eye and are the best people to do this job, but if none are available ask a friend or colleague to take an independent look, in addition to making your own inspection.

You'll then need to provide the contractor with a copy and, together, take a long hard walk around the building to agree all the points. Later, when the work is done, check off all the snagging items that have been satisfactorily completed.

Practical completion and final payments

You may recall that useful 'builder-motivating device' known as a retention. If you don't, the builders certainly will, since you'll have kept back some of the money owed to them. But now is the day of reckoning. It's at this stage – known as 'Practical Completion' – that in accordance with the contract you'll be required to release half of the retained money. This can be paid together with the builder's final payment.

If you've employed an architect or surveyor to manage the project, they should be able to issue the certificate of practical completion once you're happy the snagging has been substantially completed. This will formally trigger the release of funds. If the contractor still needs to complete a few minor snagging items these can be listed along with the certificate.

However, the final totting up process can be quite complex, since any change instructions and extras will need to be taken into account. It's not unusual for there to be small differences of opinion, often due to fading memories, so some degree of compromise may be needed on both sides. After all, everyone now wants to get on with their lives rather than bickering over the last 99p.

There then follows a period known as the 'defects liability period', normally three or six months depending on the contract. It's during this period that any latent defects that appear (typically things like minor shrinkage cracks to plasterwork and small leaks) should be made good, with the help of a final snagging list. The architect or surveyor can then issue and sign the appropriate certificate triggering the release of the remaining retention money due to the contractor.

Insurance

Just to put a dampener on things, if your house suddenly burned down right now the insurance company could conceivably wriggle out of paying the full amount. Why? Because you've just massively added to the value of your home, and your house insurance may not have been increased to reflect it (assuming of course that anyone remembered to tell them in the first place). Calculating the rebuild insurance cost shouldn't be too hard, since it would normally equate approximately to the total amount you've paid for the build. Simply tot up all those sums of money you've generously gifted to the builders over these last few

About time the family lent a hand! Offcuts of wood can be burned to save on skip hire and landfill.

months and then add on the retention. Or if you prefer to use an online building cost calculator bear in mind that often they don't include things like VAT and professional fees.

Oh, and those nice people at the Council may have clocked your increased property value and are right now busy upping your council tax band.

House warming

You don't need a Haynes manual to tell you how to celebrate, but you deserve warm congratulations for seeing the job through. There's no such thing as a stress-free building project. There will always be challenging moments and potential for minor disputes. So if you've survived the job reasonably unscathed – well done! Hopefully, all the expense, hassle, noise, dust and dirt will have been worth it. Not just in terms of added property values and improved lifestyle but in terms of experience gained and one or two new friends made.

As we noted at the beginning, the skills required to do what you've just achieved are essentially no less than those needed for building your own house from scratch. Just be sure to give yourself a well-earned break before embarking on your next mammoth development project!

Main trades needed on site

- **Decorators:** Decorating walls and joinery, wall and floor tiling.
- **Labourers:** Tidying up, cleaning, insulating lofts, landscaping.
- **Carpenters:** Weatherboarding.
- **Tilers:** Tile hanging.
- **Plasterers:** Rendering.
www.home-extension.co.uk

Author	Ian Alistair Rock MRICS
Technical consultants	Colin K. Dale FRICS Michael Haslam MSc FRICS Basil Parylo, Building Control Leeds City Council
Photography	David Davies, Basil Parylo, Richard Woodroofe MRICS
Project Manager	Louise McIntyre
Copy Editor	Ian Heath
Page Build	James Robertson
Index	Dean Rockett